D1485090

Penguin Modern Psychology Readings

General Editor

B. M. Foss

PERSONALITY ASSESSMENT

Selected Readings

Edited by Boris Semeonoff

Penguin Books

Penguin Books Ltd, Harmondsworth,
Middlesex, England
Penguin Books Inc., 3300 Clipper Mill Road,
Baltimore 11, Md, U.S.A.
Penguin Books Australia Ltd, Ringwood,
Victoria, Australia

This selection first published by Penguin Books Ltd 1966
Copyright © Boris Semeonoff, 1966

Made and printed in Great Britain by
C. Nicholls & Company Ltd
Set in Monotype Times

Contents

Introduction

Crude misconceptions apart, Personality, like Intelligence, is a term which probably causes much less trouble to the informed – or even uninformed – layman than to the psychologist. Personality is commonly understood as what makes one man different from another. Taking this definition, if it can be regarded as such, one step further, it is recognized that although people are not always entirely consistent in their behaviour, one can predict, up to a point, how a given man or woman will react in a given situation, and that one bases one's predictions on one's knowledge of that individual's personality.

Everyone, then, who is at all interested in people has engaged in personality assessment, whether or not he is aware of having done so. Some people are more successful than others, perhaps because through experience they have become more adept at identifying relevant patterns of behaviour. Others work on the basis of preconceived notions, or of commonsense. Much of what we have been saying applies equally when personality assessment acquires sophistication and becomes a field of activity of the psychologist, whose approach may be either that of the 'pure' scientist, interested in general principles and theory, or that of the 'applied' scientist, whose main concern is with practical considerations, in relation to work, guidance, or therapy. The two orientations are not, of course, mutually antagonistic, and it goes – or at least should go – without saying that a system of personality assessment lacking any sort of theoretical foundation could not possibly be workable. Conversely, no theory of personality is valuable if it cannot be shown to work. By this I mean not so much that it should 'produce results' in an operational setting, but rather that it should be capable of accounting for variations in observed behaviour. All this perhaps amounts to little more than asseveration of the truism that theory and application are complementary, but perhaps it also helps towards defining the scope of the present book of Readings. Another volume in this series (*Personality*, Selected Readings: edited by R. S. Lazarus and E. M. Opton.) is primarily theoretical in orientation; in the present book the emphasis is more on techniques, detailed classificatory systems, and illustrative material.

Although interest in personality goes right back beyond the

beginnings of psychology as an independent discipline, the use of tests designed to yield what may be thought of as measurements, or to provide a basis for systematic description, is a rather recent development. Indeed, personality was not established as a main field within the general corpus of psychology until well into the thirties. Thus, the term 'personality' is absent from the index of MacDougall's *Outline of Psychology*, probably the most widely-used textbook of the twenties. When the term did appear in literature of the period it was mostly in relation to abnormal phenomena, such as dissociated or multiple personality. Interest in the abnormal has of course continued, although it may be said to have been diverted into different channels. Thus, a generalized instability factor is a key concept in one of the most widely known of the current systems of assessment, while other systems are explicitly designed to aid in the diagnosis of psychiatric syndromes.

Readings dealing with these topics are included in the present volume, but our main concern is rather with variations in 'normal' personality. In spite of what we have just said about the late emergence of personality study, as such, earlier psychological literature did recognize what it described as 'individual differences', frequently discussing these in relation to the 'nature-nurture controversy'. To demonstrate the role of heredity as a determinant of human variability was the aim underlying the pioneer researches of Francis Galton, researches which are recognized as having laid the foundations for the development of present-day statistical approaches to psychological measurement. Measurement was already being carried out in Wundt's psychological laboratory at Leipzig, but it was measurement of a different kind, and directed towards different ends. Sensory discrimination and human reaction time, two of Wundt's main preoccupations, readily lend themselves to quantitative treatment – at least on the side of the physical dimensions of the stimulus – and so open the way to the expression of human experience in terms of mathematical formulations. The importance Wundt attached to accurate introspection suggests that he was interested in individual experience, but his interest was fundamentally taxonomic, i.e., he collected and classified varieties of experience with a view to arriving at generalizations. Contrasting this standpoint with Galton's more explicit concern with individual differences as such, one might say that Wundt and Galton represent respectively, the nomothetic (legislative) and the idiographic (descriptive) approaches to the study of behaviour.

Personality study is, almost by definition, idiographic in character, and for this reason – as well as for others – it is appropriate that the opening extract in this book should be one from Galton.

I have been tempted to carry the Wundt-Galton opposition further, and attempt to trace contrasted threads of tradition running through the work of the other authors represented in this book of readings. While some degree of alignment is possible, no clearly discernible continuity can be demonstrated. Particularly is this so in relation to typologies, the invention of which, whether on *a priori* grounds or in an attempt to classify observed resemblances, is an activity that goes right back to earliest pre-psychology times. Two of our authors make explicit reference to Galen's theory of the four humours, for centuries believed to be the basis of varieties of human temperament, and even today occasionally invoked in ostensibly scientific writing.

Classification, whatever its level of scientific rigour, and by whatever method its data are collected, is undoubtedly the key concept in personality assessment. Hard and fast classification, however, seems almost inevitably to encounter hazards, and much the same is true of approaches to personality assessment and of the material I have chosen for inclusion in this book.

The individual contributions may, however, be thought of as falling into five main groups, although none of these groups represents an entirely homogeneous category, and there are certain overlaps between the groups as regards both orientation and method.

The first group, consisting of five papers, is the most miscellaneous. It opens with an example of Galton's work, to which reference has already been made. Allport's survey, which follows, may be said to build upon the foundation laid by Galton, in that it describes systematizations of the sort of *ad hoc* personality assessment we all carry out on the basis of everyday observation. Little in the way of specifically psychological techniques is involved, and the same is true of the typology of Sheldon, which is essentially somatic, and that of Jung which may perhaps best be described as philosophical. Hilgard's paper exemplifies the Freudian view of personality development, in many ways very different from Jung's, although it too embodies a very broadly conceived classification of personality or 'character' types.

The second group consists of what may be called 'operational' papers, mainly describing applications of principles set out or implied in the preceding group. The approach in all of these is sometimes described as 'global', in contrast to the 'dimensional' approach, to which a later group of papers is devoted. English and English in their *Comprehensive Dictionary of Psychological and Psychoanalytic Terms* define 'global' as 'taken as a whole without attempt to distinguish separate parts or functions'. That the orientation of the authors in the present section conforms precisely with this definition is of course untrue, but they are certainly concerned primarily with the man in action. Schafer's contribution stands a little apart: it shows that even testing as specific in its intention as intelligence assessment is complicated by 'personality factors'. In the language of the communication engineer they may be thought of as 'noise', but to the psychologist sympathetic to the approach under discussion they represent additional data, often transcending in value the purely quantitative 'measurements' which intelligence tests are designed to provide. It also acts as a bridge to the next group of papers, in that it shows how an individual may unwittingly 'project' elements of 'himself' into his reponse.

Projective techniques, already touched upon incidentally in Hilgard's paper, form the subject-matter of our third section. English and English define a projective technique as 'a procedure for discovering a person's characteristic modes of behaviour (his attitudes, motivations, or dynamic traits) by observing his behaviour in response to a situation that does not elicit or compel a particular response – i.e. to a relatively unstructured, ambiguous, or vague situation.' Superficially this would seem to imply a simple extension of the observational methods surveyed by Allport, but the operative word here is *procedure*. Whether the procedures which form the basis of projective techniques can be accorded scientific status is a question which has aroused much controversy – controversy possibly as acrimonious as any in the history of science. Some psychologists will have nothing to do with them; others form national and international associations for their study. Not all projective techniques are of equal value or respectability: some, indeed, even among those that are fairly well known, may be dismissed as spurious. In this book two articles are devoted to each of the two best established techniques, representing, respectively, the original formulations and the current position.

As already indicated, papers in the fourth group deal mostly with the dimensional approach to personality study. The term 'atomistic' has also been applied to this approach. Interest centres on the placement of individuals on continua measuring definable traits. Different writers show considerable divergence in respect of the nature and number of the traits or dimensions they distinguish, much in the way in which controversy used to proceed regarding the number of primary instincts. Conclusions have to a considerable extent been reached on the basis of factor analysis, and it is partly for this reason that I have included in this group a paper which stands apart from the rest, rather as Schafer's did in the second group. Osgood's 'semantic differential' is a device which seeks to analyse the dimensions not of personality but of concepts: personality is revealed in the individual's quantitative handling of concepts in terms of these dimensions. Thus the procedure has affinities with the projective approach. The paper by Osgood and Luria may again be compared to Schafer's in that it has a bridging function. This is why, although atypical, it precedes its companions in this section.

Dimensional studies in personality are usually based on questionnaires, 'inventories', or similar devices, and these of course depend for their validity on the *bona fides* of the subjects, or even on their understanding of what questions they are required to answer. These considerations also apply – possibly to a lesser extent, though some might say a greater – to projective or other global procedures. Consequently, general considerations regarding 'response style' may be said to apply to all techniques of personality assessment. Of the two papers forming the concluding section of this book, the first deals primarily with problems inherent in the use of inventories. The second, dealing with general problems of validity, has wider implications.

Such then are the plan and coverage of this book. Although I have referred to sections or groups of papers, the contents should be viewed rather as forming a sequence, with overlaps as indicated, and occasional discontinuities. Limitations of space have inevitably excluded many papers that might have found a place. Specific instances are noted, where relevant, in the introductions to individual papers, along with the appropriate references. Also absent are any papers dealing with certain wider topics, notably the use of the interview, as such, as an instrument of personality assessment; the sociometric approach originating in the work of J. L. Moreno (A.13) and used as an adjunct to many other procedures; direct 'trait-sampling', or the construction of miniature situations designed to measure specified traits in isolation, as distinct from 'global' situational testing. An outstanding example is the work of Hartshorne and May (A.11). Trait-sampling, however, has on the whole proved unfruitful, although it may be said to have cleared the way for the more sophisticated procedures discussed in our second group of papers, to which group all the approaches just mentioned would potentially belong.

Missing from the third group is any account of a projective technique of the 'construction' type, such as the Lowenfeld Mosaic Test (A.12) or the various 'World' or 'Village' techniques (e.g., Mucchieli's, A.14). All of these have a therapeutic as well as a diagnostic function, and as such shade over into play methods, and so to psychodrama. The relationship between personality and therapy is not a main concern of this book, but some reference to this topic will be found in Hilgard's article.

Passing from what has been omitted, some general remarks on what has been included would seem to be in order. The plan of this series of Penguin Modern Psychology Readings, calls for articles presenting 'essential reading, including both "classical" and recent contributions'. In the present volume distribution over the time-scale is as follows: one article from the nineteenth century; three from the nineteen-twenties or thirties; four each from the forties and fifties; seven from the sixties, culminating in two which were published after work on this book had actually begun. Thus the emphasis will be seen to be primarily on recent work. In a practical, 'assessment' field this is inevitable, since techniques become obsolete, and other significant advances are made.

Nevertheless, the value of original sources remains, and the reader is urged to go back to these whenever possible. Unfortunately, for purposes of inclusion in a book of readings this is a counsel of perfection often difficult or impossible to comply with. Understandably, the original statement of an author's position tends to be lengthy and unamenable to abridgement. And condensed statements, even an author's own, are not always suitable for the serious student for whom, rather than for the general public, this series is mainly intended.

These and other considerations have perhaps produced a collection of papers in which the level of scientific writing varies. It is hoped, however, that all will be found to have the quality of readability. I have almost entirely eschewed journal articles of a routine research report type. These tend to take too much previous knowledge for granted, and the presentation is often graceless and arid. Proliferation of references is another hazard that makes for uncomfortable reading, not only because it distracts, but also because it also affects the writer's style. References appearing in the original form of the article have almost invariably been retained, and it will be noticed that there is a remarkable difference in the number of references appended to the various articles: some indeed have none. When an article is of the survey type, numerous references are inevitable, but a well-written survey article, such as Allport's, can be read through without interruption, saving up the references *for reference*.

Suggestions for further reading are given in the introductions to individual papers. It may be taken for granted that books from which extracts have been reprinted come into this category. When such a book is itself a compilation, some indication of its other contents is given. Where the original form of publication was a journal article, it may, in most cases, be assumed that files of the journal, and future issues, are a potential source of other interesting material. In spite of the writer's seemingly low opinion of some journal articles, the habit of scanning 'the literature' is one which every student (using the word in its widest sense) should cultivate. A short bibliography of recommended reading of a more general kind will be found at the end of the book.

MENTAL IMAGERY

Considerable reference has been made in the general introduction to this book to Galton's place in the history of Psychology. To choose a representative passage from his *Inquiries into Human Faculty* was a difficult task. The discussion of visual imagery here reprinted is no more significant for personality study than some of the other topics he covered. Classification of people in terms of preferred mode of imagery has proved less fruitful than had at one time been hoped. Authors of current textbooks discuss the topic very briefly, if at all; an exception is McKellar (2) whose book, although not concerned with personality assessment as such, is in the Galton tradition – here very characteristically exemplified – by virtue of its careful sifting of available evidence.

The present extract from the *Inquiries* has been slightly abridged, the principal omissions being a short passage on blindfold chess, and a longer one about superior visualizing powers in 'uncivilized' races. The breadth of Galton's interest, and the range of information he had at his disposal are indeed astonishing, as is the number of key concepts in present-day psychology that owe their origin to Galton.

This is not the place to expand on this theme: excellent accounts have been given by Burt (1) and by Miller (3). Both writers call attention to the importance of Galton's ideas for other disciplines, notably sociology, anthropology and genetics. Less well known than the *Inquiries into Human Faculty*, Galton's *Hereditary Genius* (1869) is also a classic in its own field. It was the forerunner of the monumental work, starting in the twenties, of Terman and his co-writers (4), while the recent recrudescence of interest in 'creativity' (see **8**) and in gifted people generally may also be traced back to Galton.

References
1. Burt, C., Galton's Contributions to Psychology. *Bulletin of the British Psychological Society*. No. 45, 10–21, 1961.
2. McKellar, P., *Imagination and Thinking: a Psychological Analysis*. London; Cohen and West, 1957.

3. Miller, G. A. *Psychology: the Science of Mental Life*. London: Hutchinson. 1964, Chapter 9.
4. Terman, L. M. *et al.*, *Genetic studies of Genius*. 5 vols. Stanford: Stanford University Press. 1925–59, especially Vol. II: Cox, Catherine M., The Early Mental Traits of 300 Geniuses. 1926.

1 Francis Galton

Mental Imagery

F. Galton, *Inquiries into Human Faculty*, *E.M.L. 263*; J. M. Dent &
Sons, London; E. P. Dutton, New York.

Anecdotes find their way into print, from time to time, of persons
whose visual memory is so clear and sharp as to present mental
pictures that may be scrutinized with nearly as much ease and
prolonged attention as if they were real objects. I became interested in the subject and made a rather extensive inquiry into the
mode of visual presentation in different persons, so far as could
be gathered from their respective statements. It seemed to me
that the results might illustrate the essential differences between
the mental operations of different men, that they might give some
clue to the origin of visions, and that the course of the inquiry
might reveal some previously unnoticed facts. It has done all this
more or less, and I will explain the results in the present and in
the three following chapters.

It is not necessary to trouble the reader with my earlier tentative steps to find out what I desired to learn. After the inquiry had
been fairly started it took the form of submitting a certain number
of printed questions to a large number of persons. There is
hardly any more difficult task than that of framing questions
which are not likely to be misunderstood, which admit of easy
reply, and which cover the ground of inquiry. I did my best in
these respects, without forgetting the most important part of all –
namely, to tempt my correspondents to write freely in fuller explanation of their replies, and on cognate topics as well. These
separate letters have proved more instructive and interesting by
far than the replies to the set questions.

The first group of the rather long series of queries related to the
illumination, definition, and colouring of the mental image, and
were framed thus:

'Before addressing yourself to any of the Questions on the
opposite page, think of some definite object – suppose it is your
breakfast-table as you sat down to it this morning – and consider carefully the picture that rises before your mind's eye.

' 1. *Illumination.* – Is the image dim or fairly clear? Is its brightness comparable to that of the actual scene?

' 2. *Definition.* – Are all the objects pretty well defined at the

17

same time, or is the place of sharpest definition at any one moment more contracted than it is in a real scene?

' 3. *Colouring*. – Are the colours of the china, of the toast, bread-crust, mustard, meat, parsley, or whatever may have been on the table, quite distinct and natural?'

The earliest results of my inquiry amazed me. I had begun by questioning friends in the scientific world, as they were the most likely class of men to give accurate answers concerning this faculty of visualizing, to which novelists and poets continually allude, which has left an abiding mark on the vocabularies of every language, and which supplies the material out of which dreams and the well-known hallucinations of sick people are built.

To my astonishment, I found that the great majority of the men of science to whom I first applied protested that mental imagery was unknown to them, and they looked on me as fanciful and fantastic in supposing that the words 'mental imagery' really expressed what I believed everybody supposed them to mean. They had no more notion of its true nature than a colour-blind man, who has not discerned his defect, has of the nature of colour. They had a mental deficiency of which they were unaware, and naturally enough supposed that those who affirmed they possessed it, were romancing. To illustrate their mental attitude it will be sufficient to quote a few lines from the letter of one of my correspondents, who writes:

'These questions presuppose assent to some sort of a proposition regarding the "mind's eye", and the "images" which it sees ... This points to some initial fallacy ... It is only by a figure of speech that I can describe my recollection of a scene as a "mental image" which I can "see" with my "mind's eye" ... I do not see it ... any more than a man sees the thousand lines of Sophocles which under due pressure he is ready to repeat. The memory possesses it, etc.'

Much the same result followed inquiries made for me by a friend among members of the French Institute.

On the other hand, when I spoke to persons whom I met in general society, I found an entirely different disposition to prevail. Many men and a yet larger number of women, and many boys and girls, declared that they habitually see mental imagery, and that it was perfectly distinct to them and full of colour. The more I pressed and cross-questioned them, professing myself to be incredulous, the more obvious was the truth of their first assertions. They described their imagery in minute detail, and they spoke in a tone of surprise at my apparent hesitation in accepting what they said. I felt that I myself should have spoken exactly as they did if I had been describing a scene that lay before my eyes, in broad daylight, to a blind man who persisted in doubting the reality of vision. Reassured by this happier experience, I recommenced to inquire among scientific men, and soon found scattered instances of what I sought, though in by no means the same abundance as elsewhere. I then circulated my questions more generally among my friends and through their hands, and obtained the replies that are the main subject of this and of the three next chapters. They were from persons of both sexes, and of various ages, and in the end from occasional correspondents in nearly every civilized country.

I have also received batches of answers from various educational establishments both in England and America, which were made after the masters had fully explained the meaning of the questions, and interested the boys in them. These have the merit of returns derived from a general census, which my other data lack, because I cannot for a moment suppose that the writers of the latter are a haphazard proportion of those to whom they were sent. Indeed I know of some who, disavowing all possession of the power, and of many others who, possessing it in too faint a degree to enable them to express what their experiences really were, in a manner satisfactory to themselves, sent no returns at all. Considerable statistical similarity was, however, observed between the sets of returns furnished by the schoolboys and those sent by my separate correspondents, and I may add that they accord in this respect with the oral information I have elsewhere obtained. The conformity of replies from so many different sources which was clear from the first, the fact of their apparent trustworthiness being on the whole much increased by cross-examination (though I could give one or two amusing instances of break-down), and the evident effort made to give accurate answers, have convinced me that it is a much easier matter than I had anticipated to obtain trustworthy replies to psychological questions. Many persons, especially women and intelligent children, take pleasure in introspection, and strive their very best to explain their mental processes. I think that a delight in self-dissection must be a strong ingredient in the pleasure that many are said to take in confessing themselves to priests.

Here, then, are two rather notable results: the one is the proved facility of obtaining statistical insight into the processes of other persons' minds, whatever *a priori* objection may have been made as to its possibility; and the other is that scientific men, as a class, have feeble powers of visual representation. There is no doubt whatever on the latter point, however it may be accounted for. My own conclusion is, that an over-ready perception of sharp mental pictures is antagonistic to the acquirement of habits of highly generalized and abstract thought, especially when the steps of reasoning are carried on by words as symbols, and that if the faculty of seeing the pictures was ever possessed by men who think hard, it is very apt to be lost by disuse. The highest minds are probably those in which it is not lost, but subordinated, and is ready for use on suitable occasions. I am, however, bound to say, that the missing faculty seems to be replaced so serviceably by other modes of conception, chiefly, I believe, connected with the incipient motor sense, not of the eyeballs only but of the muscles generally, that men who declare themselves entirely deficient in the power of seeing mental pictures can nevertheless give life-like descriptions of what they have seen, and can otherwise express themselves as if they were gifted with a vivid visual imagination. They can also become painters of the rank of Royal Academicians.

The facts I am now about to relate are obtained from the returns of 100 adult men, of whom 19 are Fellows of the Royal Society, mostly of very high repute, and at least twice, and I think I may say three times, as many more are persons of distinction in various kinds of intellectual work. As already remarked, these returns taken by themselves do not profess to be of service in a general statistical sense, but they are of much importance in showing how men of exceptional accuracy express themselves when they are speaking of mental imagery. They also testify to the variety of experiences to be met with in a moderately large circle. I will begin by giving a few cases of the highest, of the medium, and of the lowest order of the faculty of visualizing. The hundred returns were classified according to the order of the faculty, as judged to the best of my ability from the whole of what was said in them, and of what I knew from other sources of the writers; and the number prefixed to each quotation shows its place in the class-list.

Vividness of Mental Imagery

(From returns, furnished by 100 men, at least half of whom are distinguished in science or in other fields of intellectual work.)

Cases Where the Faculty Is Very High

   1. Brilliant, distinct, never blotchy.

2. Quite comparable to the real object. I feel as though I was dazzled, e.g. when recalling the sun to my mental vision.

3. In some instances quite as bright as an actual scene.

4. Brightness as in the actual scene.

5. Thinking of the breakfast-table this morning, all the objects in my mental picture are as bright as the actual scene.

6. The image once seen is perfectly clear and bright.

7. Brightness at first quite comparable to actual scene.

8. The mental image appears to correspond in all respects with reality. I think it is as clear as the actual scene.

9. The brightness is perfectly comparable to that of the real scene.

10. I think the illumination of the imaginary image is nearly equal to that of the real one.

11. All clear and bright; all the objects seem to me well defined at the same time.

12. I can see my breakfast-table or any equally familiar thing with my mind's eye, quite as well in all particulars as I can do if the reality is before me. [. . . .]

Cases Where the Faculty Is Mediocre

46. Fairly clear and not incomparable in illumination with that of the real scene, especially when I first catch it. Apt to become fainter when more particularly attended to.

47. Fairly clear, not quite comparable to that of the actual scene. Some objects are more sharply defined than others, the more familiar objects coming more distinctly in my mind.

48. Fairly clear as a general image; details rather misty.

49. Fairly clear, but not equal to the scene. Defined, but not sharply; not all seen with equal clearness.

50. Fairly clear. Brightness probably at least one-half to two-thirds of original. (The writer is a physiologist.) Definition varies very much, one or two objects being much more distinct than the others, but the latter come out clearly if attention be paid to them.

51. Image of my breakfast-table fairly clear, but not quite so bright as the reality. Altogether it is pretty well defined; the part where I sit and its surroundings are pretty well so.

52. Fairly clear, but brightness not comparable to that of the actual scene. The objects are sharply defined; some of them are salient, and others insignificant and dim, but by separate efforts I can take a visualized inventory of the whole table.

53. Details of breakfast-table *when the scene is reflected on* are

fairly defined and complete, but I have had a familiarity of many years with my own breakfast-table, and the above would not be the case with a table seen casually unless there were some striking peculiarity in it.

54. I can recall any single object or group of objects, but not the whole table at once. The things recalled are generally clearly defined. Our table is a long one; I can in my mind pass my eyes all down the table and see the different things distinctly, but not the whole table at once. [. . . .]

Cases Where the Faculty Is At the Lowest

89. Dim and indistinct, yet I can give an account of this morning's breakfast-table; split herrings, broiled chickens, bacon, rolls, rather light-coloured marmalade, faint green plates with stiff pink flowers, the girls' dresses, etc., etc. I can also tell where all the dishes were, and where the people sat (I was on a visit). But my imagination is seldom pictorial except between sleeping and waking, when I sometimes see rather vivid forms.

90. Dim and not comparable in brightness to the real scene. Badly defined with blotches of light, very incomplete.

91. Dim, poor definition; could not sketch from it. I have a difficulty in seeing two images together.

92. Usually very dim. I cannot speak of its brightness, but only of its faintness. Not well defined and very incomplete.

93. Dim, imperfect.

94. I am very rarely able to recall any object whatever with any sort of distinctness. Very occasionally an object or image will recall itself, but even then it is more like a generalized image than an individual image. I seem to be almost destitute of visualizing power, as under control.

95. No power of visualizing. Between sleeping and waking, in illness and in health, with eyes closed, some remarkable scenes have occasionally presented themselves, but I cannot recall them when awake with eyes open, and by daylight, or under any circumstances whatever when a copy could be made of them on paper. I have drawn both men and places many days or weeks after seeing them, but it was by an effort of memory acting on study at the time, and assisted by trial and error on the paper or canvas, whether in black, yellow, or colour, afterwards.

96. It is only as a figure of speech that I can describe my recollection of a scene as a 'mental image' which I can 'see' with

my 'mind's eye'. . . The memory possesses it, and the mind can at will roam over the whole, or study minutely any part.

97. No individual objects, only a general idea of a very uncertain kind.

98. No. My memory is not of the nature of a spontaneous vision, though I remember well where a word occurs in a page, how furniture looks in a room, etc. The ideas not felt to be mental pictures, but rather the symbols of facts.

99. Extremely dim. The impressions are in all respects so dim, vague, and transient, that I doubt whether they can reasonably be called images. They are incomparably less than those of dreams.

100. My powers are zero. To my consciousness there is almost no association of memory with objective visual impressions. I recollect the breakfast-table, but do not see it.

These quotations clearly show the great variety of natural powers of visual representation, and though the returns from which they are taken have, as I said, no claim to be those of 100 Englishmen taken at haphazard, nevertheless, to the best of my judgement, they happen to differ among themselves in much the same way that such returns would have done. I cannot procure a strictly haphazard series for comparison, because in any group of persons whom I may question there are always many too indolent to reply, or incapable of expressing themselves, or who from some fancy of their own are unwilling to reply. Still, as already mentioned, I have got together several groups that approximate to what is wanted, usually from schools, and I have analysed them as well as I could, and the general result is that the above returns may be accepted as a fair representation of the visualizing powers of Englishmen. Treating these according to the method described in the chapter of statistics, we have the following results, in which, as a matter of interest, I have also recorded the highest and the lowest of the series:

Highest. – Brilliant, distinct, never blotchy.

First Suboctile. – The image once seen is perfectly clear and bright.
First Octile. – I can see my breakfast-table or any equally familiar thing with my mind's eye quite as well in all particulars as I can do if the reality is before me.
First Quartile. – Fairly clear; illumination of actual scene is fairly represented. Well defined. Parts do not obtrude themselves, but attention has to be directed to different points in succession to call up the whole

Middlemost. – Fairly clear. Brightness probably at least from one-half to two-thirds of the original. Definition varies very much, one or two objects being much more distinct than the others, but the latter come out clearly if attention be paid to them.

Last Quartile. – Dim, certainly not comparable to the actual scene. I have to think separately of the several things on the table to bring them clearly before the mind's eye, and when I think of some things the others fade away in confusion.

Last Octile. – Dim and not comparable in brightness to the real scene. Badly defined, with blotches of light; very incomplete; very little of one object is seen at one time.

Last Suboctile. – I am very rarely able to recall any object whatever with any sort of distinctness. Very occasionally an object or image will recall itself, but even then it is more like a generalized image than an individual one. I seem to be almost destitute of visualizing power as under control.

Lowest. – My powers are zero. To my consciousness there is almost no association of memory with objective visual impressions. I recollect the table, but do not see it.

I next proceed to colour, as specified in the third of my questions, and annex a selection from the returns classified on the same principle as in the preceding paragraph.

Colour Representation

Highest. – Perfectly distinct, bright, and natural.

First Suboctile. – White cloth, blue china, argand coffee-pot, buff stand with sienna drawing, toast – all clear.

First Octile. All details seen perfectly.

First Quartile. Colours distinct and natural till I begin to puzzle over them.

Middlemost. – Fairly distinct, though not certain that they are accurately recalled.

Last Quartile. – Natural, but very indistinct.

Last Octile. – Faint; can only recall colours by a special effort for each.

Last Suboctile. Power is nil.

Lowest. – Power is nil.

It may seem surprising that one out of every sixteen persons who are accustomed to use accurate expressions should speak of their mental imagery as perfectly clear and bright; but it is so, and many details are added in various returns emphasizing the assertion. One of the commonest of these is to the effect, 'If I could draw, I am sure I could draw perfectly from my mental image.' That some artists, such as Blake, have really done so is beyond dispute, but I have little doubt that there is an unconscious exaggeration in these returns. My reasons for saying so is that I have also returns from artists, who say as follows: 'My imagery is so clear, that if I had been unable to draw I should have unhesitatingly said that I could draw from it.' A foremost painter of the present day has used that expression. He finds deficiencies and gaps when he tries to draw from his mental vision. There is perhaps some analogy between these images and those of 'faces in the fire'. One may often fancy an exceedingly well-marked face or other object in the burning coals, but probably everyone will find, as I have done, that it is impossible to draw it, for as soon as its outlines are seriously studied, the fancy flies away.

Mr Flinders Petrie, a contributor of interesting experiments on kindred subjects to *Nature*, informs me that he habitually works out sums by aid of an imaginary sliding rule, which he sets in the desired way and reads off mentally. He does not usually visualize the whole rule, but only that part of it with which he is at the moment concerned. I think this is one of the most striking cases of accurate visualizing power it is possible to imagine.

I have many cases of persons mentally reading off scores when playing the pianoforte, or manuscript when they are making speeches. One statesman has assured me that a certain hesitation in utterance which he has at times, is due to his being plagued by the image of his manuscript speech with its original erasures and corrections. He cannot lay the ghost, and he puzzles in trying to decipher it.

Some few persons see mentally in print every word that is uttered; they attend to the visual equivalent and not to the sound of the words, and they read them off usually as from a long imaginary strip of paper, such as is unwound from telegraphic instruments. The experiences differ in detail as to size and kind of type, colour of paper, and so forth, but are always the same in the same person.

A well-known frequenter of the Royal Institution tells me that he often craves for an absence of visual perceptions, they are so brilliant and persistent. The Rev. George Henslow speaks of their extreme restlessness; 'they oscillate, rotate, and change.'

It is a mistake to suppose that sharp sight is accompanied by clear visual memory. I have not a few instances in which the independence of the two faculties is emphatically commented on; and I have at least one clear case where great interest in outlines and accurate appreciation of straightness, squareness, and the like, is unaccompanied by the power of visualizing. Neither does the faculty go with dreaming. I have cases where it is powerful, and at the same time where dreams are rare and faint or altogether absent. One friend tells me that his dreams have not the hundredth part of the vigour of his waking fancies.

The visualizing and the identifying powers are by no means necessarily combined. A distinguished writer on metaphysical topics assures me that he is exceptionally quick at recognizing a face that he has seen before, but that he cannot call up a mental image of any face with clearness.

Some persons have the power of combining in a single perception more than can be seen at any one moment by the two eyes. It is needless to insist on the fact that all who have two eyes see stereoscopically, and therefore somewhat round a corner. Children, who can focus their eyes on very near objects, must be able to comprise in a single mental image much more than a half of any small object they are examining. Animals such as hares, whose eyes are set more on the side of the head than ours, must be able to perceive at one and the same instant more of a panorama than we can. I find that a few persons can, by what they often describe as a kind of touch-sight, visualize at the same moment all round the image of a solid body. Many can do so nearly, but not altogether round that of a terrestrial globe. An eminent mineralogist assures me that he is able to imagine simultaneously all the sides of a crystal with which he is familiar. I may be allowed to quote a curious faculty of my own in respect to this. It is exercised only occasionally and in dreams, or rather in nightmares, but under those circumstances I am perfectly conscious of embracing an entire sphere in a single perception. It appears to lie within my mental eyeball, and to be viewed centripetally.

This power of comprehension is practically attained in many cases by indirect methods. It is a common feat to take in the whole surroundings of an imagined room with such a rapid mental sweep as to leave some doubt whether it has not been viewed simultaneously. Some persons have the habit of viewing objects as though they were partly transparent; thus, if they so dispose a globe in their imagination as to see both its north and south poles at the same time, they will not be able to see its equatorial parts. They can also perceive all the rooms of an imaginary house by a single mental glance, the walls and floors being as if made of glass. A fourth class of persons have the habit of recalling scenes, not from the point of view whence they were observed, but from a distance, and they visualize their own selves as actors on the mental stage. By one or other of these ways, the power of seeing the whole of an object, and not merely one aspect of it, is possessed by many persons.

The place where the image appears to lie differs much. Most persons see it in an indefinable sort of way, others see it in front of the eye, others at a distance corresponding to reality. There exists a power which is rare naturally, but can, I believe, be acquired without much difficulty, of projecting a mental picture upon a piece of paper, and of holding it fast there, so that it can be outlined with a pencil. To this I shall recur.

Images usually do not become stronger by dwelling on them; the first idea is commonly the most vigorous, but this is not always the case. Sometimes the mental view of a locality is inseparably connected with the sense of its position as regards the points of the compass, real or imaginary. I have received full and curious descriptions from very different sources of this strong geographical tendency, and in one or two cases I have reason to think it allied to a considerable faculty of geographical comprehension.

The power of visualizing is higher in the female sex than in the male, and is somewhat, but not much, higher in public schoolboys than in men. After maturity is reached, the further advance of age does not seem to dim the faculty, but rather the reverse, judging from numerous statements to that effect; but advancing years are sometimes accompanied by a growing habit of hard abstract thinking, and in these cases – not uncommon among those whom I have questioned – the faculty undoubtedly becomes impaired. There is reason to believe that it is very high in some young children, who seem to spend years of difficulty in distinguishing between the subjective and objective world. Language and book-learning certainly tend to dull it.

The visualizing faculty is a natural gift, and, like all natural gifts, has a tendency to be inherited. In this faculty the tendency to inheritance is exceptionally strong, as I have abundant evidence to prove, especially in respect to certain rather rare peculiarities, of which I shall speak in the next chapter, and which, when they exist at all, are usually found among two, three, or more brothers and sisters, parents, children, uncles and aunts, and cousins.

Since families differ so much in respect to this gift, we may suppose that races would also differ, and there can be no doubt that such is the case. I hardly like to refer to civilized nations, because their natural faculties are too much modified by education to allow of their being appraised in an off-hand fashion. I may, however, speak of the French, who appear to possess the visualizing faculty in a high degree. The peculiar ability they show in prearranging ceremonials and *fêtes* of all kinds, and their undoubted genius for tactics and strategy, show that they are able to foresee effects with unusual clearness. Their ingenuity in all technical contrivances is an additional testimony in the same direction, and so is their singular clearness of expression. Their phrase, 'figurez-vous', or 'picture to yourself', seems to express their dominant mode of perception. Our equivalent of 'imagine' is ambiguous.

There is abundant evidence that the visualizing faculty admits of being developed by education. The testimony on which I would lay especial stress is derived from the published experiences of M. Lecoq de Boisbaudran, late director of the École Nationale de Dessein, in Paris, which are related in his *Éducation de la Mémoire Pittoresque.** He trained his pupils with extraordinary success, beginning with the simplest figures. They were made to study the models thoroughly before they tried to draw them from memory. One favourite expedient was to associate the sight memory with the muscular memory, by making his pupils follow at a distance the outlines of the figures with a pencil held in their hands. After three or four months' practice, their visual memory became greatly strengthened. They had no difficulty in summoning images at will, in holding them steady, and in drawing them. Their copies were executed with marvellous fidelity, as attested by a commission of the Institute, appointed in 1852 to inquire into the matter, of which the eminent painter Horace Vernet was a member. The present Slade Professor of Fine Arts at University College, M. Légros, was a pupil of M. de Boisbaudran. He has expressed to me his indebtedness to the system, and he has assured me of his own success in teaching others in a somewhat similar way.

Colonel Moncrieff informs me that, when wintering in 1877 near Fort Garry in North America, young Indians occasionally came to his quarters, and that he found them much interested in any pictures or prints that were put before them. On one of these

*Republished in an 8vo, entitled *Enseignment Artistique*, Morel et Cie. Paris, 1879.

occasions he saw an Indian tracing the outline of a print from the *Illustrated News* very carefully with the point of his knife. The reason he gave for this odd manoeuvre was, that he would remember the better how to carve it when he returned home.

I could mention instances within my own experience in which the visualizing faculty has become strengthened by practice; notably one of an eminent electrical engineer, who had the power of recalling form with unusual precision, but not colour. A few weeks after he had replied to my questions, he told me that my inquiries had induced him to practise his colour memory, and that he had done so with such success that he was become quite an adept at it, and that the newly-acquired power was a source of much pleasure to him.

A useful faculty, easily developed by practice, is that of retaining a retinal picture. A scene is flashed upon the eye; the memory of it persists, and details, which escaped observation during the brief time when it was actually seen, may be analysed and studied at leisure in the subsequent vision.

The memories we should aim at acquiring are, however, such as are based on a thorough understanding of the objects observed. In no case is this more surely effected than in the processes of mechanical drawing, where the intended structure has to be portrayed so exactly in plan, elevation, side view, and sections, that the workman has simply to copy the drawing in metal, wood, or stone, as the case may be. It is undoubtedly the fact that mechanicians, engineers, and architects usually possess the faculty of seeing mental images with remarkable clearness and precision.

A few dots like those the Bushmen jot down, before running a free bold line from one to the other, give great assistance in creating an imaginary picture, as proved by our general habit of working out ideas by the help of marks and rude lines. The use of dolls by children also testifies to the value of an objective support in the construction of mental images. The doll serves as a kind of skeleton for the child to clothe with fantastic attributes, and the less individuality the doll has, the more it is appreciated by the child, who can the better utilize it as a lay figure in many different characters. The chief art of strengthening visual, as well as every other form of memory, lies in multiplying associations; the healthiest memory being that in which all the associations are logical, and toward which all the senses concur in their due proportions. It is wonderful how much the vividness of a recollection is increased when two or more lines of association are simultaneously excited. Thus the inside of a known house is much better visualized when we are looking at its outside than when we are away from it, and some chess-players have told me that it is easier for them to play a game from memory when they have a blank board before them than when they have not.

There is an absence of flexibility in the mental imagery of most persons. They find that the first image they have acquired of any scene is apt to hold its place tenaciously in spite of subsequent need of correction. They find a difficulty in shifting their mental view of an object, and examining it at pleasure in different positions. If they see an object equally often in many positions the memories combine and confuse one another, forming a 'composite' blur, which they cannot dissect into its components. They are less able to visualize the features of intimate friends than those of persons of whom they have caught only a single glance. Many such persons have expressed to me their grief at finding themselves powerless to recall the looks of dear relations whom they had lost, while they had no difficulty in recollecting faces that were uninteresting to them.

Others have a complete mastery over their mental images. They can call up the figure of a friend and make it sit on a chair or stand up at will; they can make it turn round and attitudinize in any way, as by mounting it on a bicycle or compelling it to perform gymnastic feats on a trapeze. They are able to build up elaborate geometric structures bit by bit in their mind's eye, and add, subtract, or alter at will and at leisure. This free action of a vivid visualizing faculty is of much importance in connexion with the higher processes of generalized thought, though it is commonly put to no such purpose, as may be easily explained by an example. Suppose a person suddenly to accost another with the following words: 'I want to tell you about a boat.' What is the idea that the word 'boat' would be likely to call up? I tried the experiment with this result. One person, a young lady, said that she immediately saw the image of a rather large boat pushing off from the shore, and that it was full of ladies and gentlemen, the ladies being dressed in white and blue. It is obvious that a tendency to give so specific an interpretation to a general word is absolutely opposed to philosophic thought. Another person, who was accustomed to philosophize, said that the word 'boat' had aroused no definite image, because he had purposely held his mind in suspense. He had exerted himself not to lapse into any one of the special ideas that he felt the word boat was ready to call up, such as a skiff, wherry, barge, launch, punt, or dinghy. Much more did he refuse to think of any one of these with any particular freight or from any particular point of view. A habit of suppressing mental imagery must therefore characterize men who deal much with abstract ideas; and as the power of dealing easily and firmly with these ideas is the surest criterion of a high order of intellect, we should expect that the visualizing faculty would be starved by disuse among philosophers, and this is precisely what I found on inquiry to be the case.

But there is no reason why it should be so, if the faculty is free in its action, and not tied to reproduce hard and persistent forms; it may then produce generalized pictures out of its past experiences quite automatically. It has no difficulty in reducing images to the same scale, owing to our constant practice in watching objects as they approach or recede, and consequently grow or diminish in apparent size. It readily shifts images to any desired point of the field of view, owing to our habit of looking at bodies in motion to the right or left, upward or downward. It selects images that present the same aspect, either by a simple act of memory or by a feat of imagination that forces them into the desired position, and it has little or no difficulty in reversing them from right to left, as if seen in a looking-glass. In illustration of these generalized mental images, let us recur to the boat, and suppose the speaker to continue as follows: 'The boat was a four-oared racing-boat, it was passing quickly to the left just in front of me, and the men were bending forward to take a fresh stroke.' Now at this point of the story the listener ought to have a picture well before his eye. It ought to have the distinctness of a real four-oar going to the left, at the moment when many of its details still remained unheeded, such as the dresses of the men and their individual features. It would be the generic image of a four-oar formed by the combination into a single picture of a great many sight memories of those boats.

In the highest minds a descriptive word is sufficient to evoke crowds of shadowy associations, each striving to manifest itself. When they differ so much from one another as to be unfitted for combination into a single idea, there will be a conflict, each being prevented by the rest from obtaining sole possession of the field of consciousness. There could, therefore, be no definite imagery so long as the aggregate of all the pictures that the word suggested of objects presenting similar aspects, reduced to the same size, and accurately superposed, resulted in a blur; but a picture would gradually evolve as qualifications were added to the word, and it would attain to the distinctness and vividness of a generic image long before the word had been so restricted as to be individualized.

31

If the intellect be slow, though correct in its operations, the associations will be few, and the generalized image based on insufficient data. If the visualizing power be faint, the generalized image will be indistinct.

I cannot discover any closer relation between high visualizing power and the intellectual faculties than between verbal memory and those same faculties. That it must afford immense help in some professions stands to reason, but in ordinary social life the possession of a high visualizing power, as of a high verbal memory, may pass quite unobserved. I have to the last failed in anticipating the character of the answers that my friends would give to my inquiries, judging from my previous knowledge of them; though I am bound to say that, having received their answers, I could usually persuade myself that they were justified by my recollections of their previous sayings and conduct generally.

The faculty is undoubtedly useful in a high degree to inventive mechanicians, and the great majority of those whom I have questioned have spoken of their powers as very considerable. They invent their machines as they walk, and see them in height, breadth, and depth as real objects, and they can also see them in action. In fact, a periodic action of any kind appears to be easily recalled. But the powers of other men are considerably less; thus an engineer officer who has himself great power of visual memory, and who has superintended the mathematical education of cadets, doubts if one in ten can visualize an object in three dimensions. I should have thought the faculty would be common among geometricians, but many of the highest seem able somehow to get on without much of it. There is a curious dictum of Napoleon I quoted in Hume's *Précis of Modern Tactics*, p. 15, of which I can neither find the original authority nor do I fully understand the meaning. He is reported to have said that 'there are some who, from some physical or moral peculiarity of character, form a picture (*tableau*) of everything. No matter what knowledge, intellect, courage, or good qualities they may have, these men are unfit to command.' It is possible that 'tableau' should be construed rather in the sense of a pictorial composition, which, like an epigrammatic sentence, may be very complete and effective, but not altogether true.

There can, however, be no doubt as to the utility of the visualizing faculty when it is duly subordinated to the higher intellectual operations. A visual image is the most perfect form of mental representation wherever the shape, position, and relations of objects in space are concerned. It is of importance in every handicraft and profession where design is required. The best workmen are those who visualize the whole of what they propose to do, before they take a tool in their hands. The village smith and the carpenter who are employed on odd jobs employ it no less for their work than the mechanician, the engineer, and the architect. The lady's maid who arranges a new dress requires it for the same reason as the decorator employed on a palace, or the agent who lays out great estates. Strategists, artists of all denominations, physicists who contrive new experiments, and in short all who do not follow routine, have need of it. The pleasure its use can afford is immense. I have many correspondents who say that the delight of recalling beautiful scenery and great works of art is the highest that they know; they carry whole picture galleries in their minds. Our bookish and wordy education tends to repress this valuable gift of nature. A faculty that is of importance in all technical and artistic occupations, that gives accuracy to our perceptions, and justness to our generalizations, is starved by lazy disuse, instead of being cultivated judiciously in such a way as will on the whole bring the best return. I believe that a serious study of the best method of developing and utilizing this faculty, without prejudice to the practice of abstract thought in symbols, is one of the many pressing desiderata in the yet unformed science of education.

EXPRESSIVE BEHAVIOUR

Little introduction is needed for this article, which appears, in slightly fuller form, as Chapter 19 of Allport's *Pattern and Growth in Personality*. The main omissions here are short passages on recognition of one's own expressive records, and on style; also some illustrations, and a proportion of the very full references given by the author. However, enough remain to make specific recommendations of other work in the same field unnecessary.

The parent volume is described by its author as 'in one sense ... a revision of my earlier book, *Personality: a Psychological Interpretation* ...' (1). The earlier book assumes more background in psychology, but is equally readable. One or other of the books seems destined to become a psychological classic – time will tell which. One advantage of the newer book is that it gives a much fuller account of what may be regarded as the central concept in Allport's writing – that of functional autonomy. This is defined by English and English as 'the tendency of a developed motive system to become independent of the primary drive from which it originated'. Identification and analysis of these systems, and their transformations, provide an attractively comprehensive framework for the understanding of the individual personality.

References
1. Allport, G. W., *Personality: a psychological interpretation*, New York: Holt, 1937.

2 G. W. Allport

Expressive Behavior

G. W. Allport, *Pattern and Growth in Personality*.
Holt, Rinehart and Winston, New York, 1961.

The term 'expression' is used in psychology with at least three different meanings. First is the common-sense use. We say that a man expresses an opinion, or a preference, or a point of view. That is, he tells us directly and deliberately something about his ideas or himself. We also say that an artist, a musician, or a dancer is expressing his feelings as well as some symbolized meaning in his production. Whether intellectual or artistic, this type of expression is deliberate and conscious. It normally is our chief channel for understanding other personalities.

The term has a more limited meaning when it refers to such bodily changes as blushing, laughing, dilation of the pupil, quaking of the knees. Darwin's *The Expression of Emotions in Men and Animals*, first published in 1872, established this meaning firmly. In this sense expression signifies involuntary response to emtional stimuli.

The third use of the term is subtler, but most appropriate to the present chapter. It refers to one's manner or style of behaving. Unlike the first meaning, it has nothing to do with the 'what' of an act, but only with the 'how'. Unlike the second meaning, it has nothing to do with the release of emotional tension; instead, it deals with the oblique mirroring of personal traits. Of course, all three types of expression tell us something about a person, but for analytic clarity it is important to make the distinction.

We can define expressive movement simply as 'one's manner of performing adaptive acts'. From our point of view, every single act a person performs has both its expressive and its adaptive (coping) aspects, sometimes more of one, sometimes more of the other. Let us examine this proposition more closely.

Expressive versus Coping Behavior

Every act that we perform copes with our environment. Even rest and sleep and play are no exceptions. There is a 'task' in hand (the 'what' of behavior). We must repair a lock, seek relaxation, summon a doctor, answer a question, or blink a speck of dust from our eyes. To cope with the task we employ our reflexes and habits or call upon our skills, our judgment and knowledge. But into this stream of activity there enter deeper trends in our nature. There are 'styles' of repairing locks, calling a doctor, relaxing, answering a question, or blinking the eye. Every action betrays 'both' a coping and an expressive aspect. One may think of coping as the 'predicate' of action (what we are doing); expression as the 'adverb' of action (how we are doing it).

Take the simple case of blinking the eye. The blink is provoked by irritation of the cornea. We cope with the irritation by closing the eyelid momentarily. But even this simple reflex activity shows the influence of other integrated neural centers. Some people blink with regularity, others in uneven rhythm, some close their eyes completely, others do not (33). Those who have seen cinema films of Mussolini may have noticed that his eyeblinks were infrequent but also astonishingly deliberate in appearance, as though his self-styled 'indomitable will' exerted itself in even this remote corner of his coping conduct. Similarly, sighs, coughs, sneezes, knee jerks are marked by individual differences.

Some of the differences between coping and expressive behavior may be summarized as follows:*

a. Coping is purposive and specifically motivated; expressive behavior is not.

b. Coping is determined by the needs of the moment and by the situation; expressive movement reflects deeper personal structure.

c. Coping is formally elicited; expressive behavior spontaneously 'emitted'.

d. Coping can be more readily controlled (inhibited, modified, conventionalized); expressive behavior is harder to alter and often uncontrollable. (Changing our style of handwriting, e.g., can be kept up for only a short time.)

e. Coping usually aims to change the environment; expressive behavior aims at nothing, though it may incidentally have effects (as when our manner of answering questions in an interview creates a good impression and lands us the job).

f. Typically coping is conscious, even though it may employ automatic skills; expressive behavior generally lies below the threshold of our awareness.

Figure 1 represents the essential situation schematically. (We shall soon discuss the factor of cultural and situational determinants.)

Although both coping and expression are present in every act (even the eyeblink), their proportion varies widely. The man on

*A similar but not identical list is given by A. H. Maslow (28).

DETERMINANTS

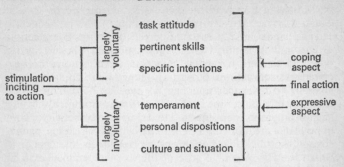

Figure 1   Behavior as Convergence of Coping and Expression.

the assembly line is held rigidly to his task. He must turn the wrench precisely so many millimetres, so many times a minute. Such behavior is frustrating to him, for it suppresses and holds in check all impulses arising from temperament and personality. It is no wonder that job dissatisfaction is greatest when the mechanical prescription of movement is highest. In a technological society more and more occupations require precision in coping and a suppression of individual styles. In former days there was more pride of authorship among artisans, cabinetmakers, illuminators of manuscripts, and makers of doughnuts.

Effort to do a task in a prescribed manner destroys the impulse to do it stylistically. There is less individuality in the handwriting of a bookkeeper or librarian than in most people's scripts. A radio announcer must use his voice as an instrument of coping; the result is less expressive individuality. An actor who plays many roles must squeeze out so far as he can all his personal mannerisms.

Theory of Expression

A 'stratification theory' is a metaphorical way of viewing the organization of personality in terms of layers. The method is favored by many German psychologists. A relatively early example comes from the work of Ludwig Klages (22), who made a sharp distinction between the upper overlaid layer, 'Geist' (mind, intellect, adaptive performance) and 'Seele' (soul, the diffuse elemental surge of life). Coping activity is a product of 'Geist'; expressive activity, of 'Seele'. The former acts as a restrainer, sometimes even as a destroyer of the basic rhythms that are carriers of vital expression. If we are to perceive the individuality of expressive behavior we must look beyond the specific intent of an act, beyond the conscious control, and beyond the conventions and skills employed in coping.

Take handwriting, a special interest of Klages. It is clearly a product of both coping ('Geist') and expression ('Seele'). On the one hand, the person is deliberately conveying his thoughts; he is employing conventions of writing taught him in school; he is adapting to the paper and pen he must use. All these reflect coping. At the same time his whole nature is, as it were, rebelling against prescribed convention. He departs from the school copy in ways that are individual to him; he betrays his energy, aggressiveness, hostility, fear, ambitions or rigidity in his manner of departure. His own vital style of life (his temperament and his personal characteristics) surges into his performance. It takes little skill to understand the coping aspect of the performance; it takes much skill to read the underlying surge of expression.

American psychology has developed no such comprehensive theory of expression. The reason is interesting. American psychology is, by and large, a psychology of 'reaction'. A specific stimulus demands a specific response. We are set in motion only when a coping action is required. We overlook the vital surge of life with its spontaneous contributions to every act.

It is only fair to mention voices of dissent. John Dewey often criticized the stimulus-response view as a 'monstrous assumption' of American psychology. People, he insisted, do not act only when compelled to act by some external goad or internal need. They act anyway; they can't help acting. A similar view is held by Woodworth (45); Maslow's is another voice of dissent (29).

Those who agree with this dissenting position will more easily turn their attention to the pervasive style of movement that enters spontaneously into the flow of conduct. As soon as we become interested in total 'activity', not merely in 'reactivity', we then appreciate the importance of expression as a complement to coping.

It is well, however, not to go to the opposite extreme. Every activity, even if loaded heavily with expressivity, has an origin somewhere. That is to say, some stimulus lies behind the scenes. Even a 'spontaneous' act follows some sequence of instigation. The play of a child, the painting of a picture, dancing, laughing are heavily laden with expressivity, but something somewhere started off the playing, painting, dancing, laughing. As Figure 1 shows, coping and expression are both present in every act, however unequal their ratios may be. We are not making the 'monstrous assumption' that the stimulus pulls the trigger and the act is a specific response. We are saying that spontaneity exists, though it should be defined simply as the contribution that the total organism makes to a coping performance. There seems to be no act that we can call purely and solely expressive, just as there is no act that is purely and solely coping.

At this point we need neurological theory to help us, but as yet it is lacking. It is, however, consistent with what is known to view any act as a 'final common path' representing the integration of many layers and levels of traces and impulses with the intention of the moment. Thus if I start to paint a picture there will necessarily be dominant coping movements (handling canvas and paints), but into the final product will flow concurrent impulses, traces, styles of expression – all that Klages would call my 'Seele'.

Finally, the problem of expression raises questions of social value. It is said that the tragedy of our culture is that coping is in the ascendancy, and that creative expression is suppressed. A technological civilization necessarily brings this imbalance. Workmen are rigidly held to the precision of coping; their efforts to repress individuality of expression cause frustration and dissatisfaction on the job. True, they have more leisure, but the leisure is for many a matter of consuming prefabricated TV sports, TV shows, TV dinners. An age of mechanical conformity threatens us. When expression is starved, our personalities shrivel, falling far below our human potentiality.

Additional Determinants

Our two-part analysis of the determinants of behavior is sound so far as it goes, but it is oversimplified. What shall we say about the following additional convergent factors that often help to shape the quality of an act?

a. cultural tradition
b. regional convention
c. passing emotional moods
d. conditions of strain and fatigue
e. age
f. sex
g. native muscular structure and bodily build
h. conditions of health and disease
i. accidental deformations of the body
j. special training (e.g., dramatics, military drill)
k. conditions of physical environment (e.g., pen, ink, paper in writing; he ground and climatic factors in walking)

All these determinants are important, and although they complicate our two-part analysis they do not destroy it.

The first two factors, cultural tradition and regional convention, provide a kind of basic ground for the expressive component. A young child takes into himself the prevailing cultural habits of gesticulation, the general norm for handwriting, or the common intonations of voice. Insofar as he is socialized (or acculturated), these ground norms become a part of his own nature. (Hence these factors are included in Figure 1 as truly expressive factors.) He will, of course, vary his individual style around these traditional norms, but underlying them he will, if he is Chinese, display the Chinese mode. Schopenhauer wrote: 'The English have a peculiar scorn of gesticulation and hold it to be something unworthy and common.' By contrast, most Jews from Eastern Europe gesticulate dramatically, and even their gait has a cultural distinctiveness (25).

Factors c and d, dealing with the temporary conditions of mood and fatigue, are often decisive. They, too, must be classed as expressive determinants, though in this case the expression is of transitory personal states, and not of enduring dispositions.

Factors e to i represent certain structural influences. A woman, light in weight, cannot have as heavy a tread, as strong a grip, as the average male. A hand crippled by arthritis will affect gesture and script. A heavy physique cannot poise itself lightly on the edge of a chair. Infirm age does tremulously what youth does with vigor. It is difficult to classify such influences as applying only to the coping or expressive determinants. In part they affect movement via skill; in part they are related to change in personality and therefore are expressive.

The final factors, j and k, are properly regarded as special cases of coping determinants. Especially is this true of conditions in the physical environment. On a hot day or on uneven ground anyone is likely to slacken pace or shorten stride; with a scratchy pen anyone is likely to write with uneven pressure. As for special habits of skill (the trained voice, the military manner), to some extent such training directly fashions personality, and therefore becomes incorporated into the expressive phase. Often, however, such conventions of movement are masklike and tend to conceal personal qualities.

Genesis of Expressive Behavior

If a young child is irritable he shows it openly in almost every movement he makes: he cries, fusses, whines, slaps. His expressiveness is diffuse and massive. An adult, by contrast, may show his irritable nature only by his restless fingers or shifting eyes. The growing differentiation and localizing of movement as a person matures is true not only of skilled coping but also of expression.

The fact that expression tends with growing maturity to become confined to limited regions of the body has important consequences for personality assessment. For one thing, it means that various features of expression are of unequal significance in different people. Some faces are open books; some are 'poker faces'. For some people gestures are merely conventional; for others, highly individual. Sometimes the style of clothing or the handwriting seems 'just like' the person; in other cases, entirely nonexpressive. One person reveals himself primarily in his speech; another, in his posture and gait; a third, in his style of clothing or ornamentation. As a promising hypothesis we suggest that every person has one or two leading expressive features which reveal his true nature. If this is so, it is somewhat futile to study all people by the same cues, e.g., voice, eyes, or handwriting. The cue that is revealing for one person is not necessarily revealing for another.

Every child is exposed to standard forms of expression which tend to limit his individual impulses in movement. He learns to write from a standard model, to play the piano or to dance according to rules. As Klages says, he tends to break away in part (but only in part), from the models. His handwriting acquires 'graphic maturity', his musical interpretation and his dancing steps are his own. Even the stenographer in time modifies her system of shorthand, and the physician, when no longer an intern, comes to practise his art in his own manner. But all people remain conventional to some degree. What is important is the extent to which they break through the prescriptions of training and convention, and develop their own stamp of individuality. And, as we have said, the stamp may be more apparent in some expressive features than in others.

The child, and especially the adolescent, is likely to adopt expressive styles by imitation. The small boy who envies the worldliness of the street-corner gang imitates their carefree manner of tilting the cap and spitting. The adolescent girl wears her hair as her favorite actress does. The college student apes the mannerisms of some coach or professor. Such superficial imitation is of psychological interest. At heart the youth wants the basic skills or attributes of his model. He is too young to attain them, and so he settles for the external expression of these attributes – for the kind of necktie or the haircut worn by the boss, for the swagger or stance of the athletic hero.

With maturity many of these imitative mannerisms are dropped. The office boy grown up to worldly wisdom can wear whatever necktie he likes; he no longer needs to ape the boss. And yet occasionally mannerisms in adulthood may be vestigial, indicating more the past history of one's development than its present state. Perhaps an expressive habit has become fixed by a kind of perseverative functional autonomy. In such a case we are dealing with a residue of earlier life, and should evaluate it as such. Thus if an adult has a habit of averting his eyes, biting his nails, or picking his nose, he *may* be evincing present conflict and present trends, or he *may* be carrying out a dissociated perseverative mannerism from childhood. Only close study will tell.

Autistic Gestures

Let us look more closely at the part played by internal conflict in the creation of certain expressive mannerisms.

A fastidious house-painter, who feels that his occupation is far beneath him, betrays his conflict through scrupulous care of his fingernails, which during work he polishes and inspects at frequent intervals.

A young man has a peculiar habit of jerking his arms whenever he thinks of embarrassing things. This habit goes back to a time when he had unpleasant compulsive thoughts of striking people on the street. At such times he would jerk his arms to throw off the impulse. But now he uses the mannerism whenever freedom from unpleasant thoughts is desired.

To such movements Krout (23) gives the name 'autistic gestures'. They have only unconscious meaning for the subject, and no meaning at all (unless carefully studied) for the observer. The theory holds that if a direct response is inhibited or tabooed it will be reduced to a mere vestigial state – to an autistic gesture.

Krout has ingeniously submitted the theory to experimental testing (24). In the subject he arouses a conflict. For example, he secures the subject's agreement to the proposition that people keep their crushes secret; but then asks the subject to think silently for half a minute and admit to the experimenter his (her) own crushes. Or again, the experimenter says, 'Now, no really normal person ever wishes his friends, especially his relatives, dead. Does he?' After the subject agrees, the experimenter says, 'I want you to think now. Did *you* ever wish that one of your relatives was dead? I want you to think.' During the interval of conflict thus induced – before the subject gives his answer – a record is taken of the movements of his hands. After the experiment the subject is asked what attitudinal state of mind he felt during the conflict.

By this procedure Krout reaches the conclusion that there are statistically significant equivalences between certain gestures and certain attitudes. The open hand dangling between the legs, he says, characteristically accompanies frustration; fingers folded at tips, suspicion or resignation; hand to nose, fear; finger to lips, shame; fist gestures, aggression; one finger enveloped by other hand, ego-inflation or encouragement.

These expressive signs Krout finds to be fairly general. The experiment is ingenious and may lead us eventually toward a general language of gesture. On the other hand, individuals also evolve their own personal patterns, and we cannot always read these from a standard lexicon of gestures. Cultural norms, too, may differ, and the two sexes, as Krout shows, seem to favor different gestural patterns. We may suspect that some high-strung temperaments make many movements lacking deeper significance, and that some who suffer from conflict may remain outwardly placid. If we keep such cautions in mind we can still learn much from this pioneer research.

We do not imply that all expressive movements have their origin in conflict, though undoubtedly some do. From our point of view expression reveals the conflict-free as well as the conflicted aspects of personality.

Are Expressive Movements Consistent?

Let us try a short and easy experiment.

On a sheet of paper letter label four lines a, b, c, d. Write on lines a, b, c your own name just as you usually sign it. But on line d make deliberately an exact copy of what you wrote on line c.

Now compare lines a and b; also c and d. You will undoubtedly find that the first two are much more similar than the last two.

Why are lines a and b so similar? The reason is that the instructions for coping ('write your name') were identical, and maximum freedom was allowed for expressive consistency. Line d, on the other hand, was written under very different conditions. The coping aspect was heavily loaded. It became a conscious task to 'make an exact copy'. Every movement was deliberate. Expressive consistency was suppressed. In the terms of Klages, the 'Geist' took command and stifled the harmonious flow of the individual 'Seele'.

45

This is a demonstration of expressive consistency. People develop highly characteristic styles of writing, talking, walking, sitting, gesturing, laughing, and shaking hands. At a distance we recognize a friend from his gait. Over the phone we know who greets us, not so much from what he says as from his voice and manner of speaking. Expression is perhaps the most stubborn part of our natures. Our coping is variable, depending on *what* we have to do. But *how* we do it carries an almost infallible signature.

For a given person patterns of expression are highly consistent over time. Mood does, of course, make some difference. If a person feels depressed his movements are relatively constricted; if he feels elated they are more expansive. His flow of speech is freer in elation than in depression (21). But differences in mood seem to change chiefly the energy that goes into an expression. The pattern (e.g., handwriting) remains about the same in form.

To what extent do various expressive features of the body agree with one another? Is it true, as Lavater asserted of old, 'one and the same spirit is manifest in all'? If Mr X has an emphatic voice, are his gestures emphatic, is his stride, his handshake, his pressure in writing?

To some extent laboratory measurements help us to answer this question. In one study subjects were asked to perform many tasks: writing on paper, on the blackboard, with the foot (in sand); reading aloud, walking, drawing, making check marks, estimating distances, and so on. It turned out that the subjects were notably consistent. For example, they showed throughout the experiment a characteristic level of emphaticness, also of expansive or constricted movement, also of outgoing (centrifugal) or inward (centripetal) movement.*

Besides laboratory measurement there is another way of demonstrating consistency: the method of 'matching'. I might show you the photograph of a stranger, and with it three samples of handwriting. I then ask you to tell which sample of handwriting was written by the stranger in the photograph. Of course by chance you would be right one time in three. But if your success is consistently greater we have evidence that there is some perceptible consistency between facial and graphic expression. The method can be elaborated in many ways. Thus records of voice can be matched with occupations; written themes, with drawings; or all these, with all the others (39).

The method of matching helps us demonstrate to what extent

*These experiments are described more fully by G. W. Allport and P. E. Vernon (2).

we can *perceive* the same expressive quality in different expressive records. It does not, however, tell us on what basis we reach our decision. The cues are often so subtle that they elude us and we do not know why we make the matching we do. Matching demonstrates that congruence exists but tells us nothing more.

The evidence we have reviewed justifies three conclusions:

1. Expressive features of the body are not independently activated. Any one of them may be affected in much the same way as any other.

2. The congruence, however, is never perfect. One feature is not an exact replica of another. If it were we would be justified in diagnosing the personality from any one feature – from handwriting or from the eyes, hands, or limbs. As matters stand, however, we cannot safely do so.

3. The unity of expression turns out, as we would expect, to be a question of degree, just as the unity of personality is a matter of degree.

Psychodiagnosis

Everyone 'reads character' from expressive movement. We cannot help doing so. Literary authors use it as a major device, as a few examples show:

'Hands in repose reflect breeding, sensibility, and regard for others.'

'Democritus knew Protagoras to be a scholar from seeing him bind up a faggot, and thrusting, as he did, the small twigs inward.'

'A man does not lay down his hat in coming into a room, or take it up in going out, but something escapes that reveals his nature.'

Statements of this order are often charming and plausible but they leave us wondering as to their trustworthiness.

In a nutshell, expressive behavior is without doubt a potential guide to the assessment of personality; but unfortunately psychologists have given it very little study. Krout's painstaking experiment [above, p. 44] may eventually lead to a correct reading of significance of certain gestures. Soon we shall turn to a few other facts that have come to light in studying other expressive features. But on the whole the realm of expression has not been deeply studied as an aid to diagnosis.

Up to now psychologists have given attention almost exclusively to the 'coping' aspect of personality. Most personality tests (including the so-called projective test) are coping tests. They instruct the subject to perform a task. The experimenter then measures the 'what' of the product, not the 'how'. The subject fills out a questionnaire, invents a 'projective' story, or tells what he sees on a Rorschach card. What is measured is the content of the response. The content is, of course, revealing, but so, too, are the expressive movements that go to waste. Emphasizing the 'Geist', psychologists are blind to the 'Seele' as reflected in postures, handwriting, eye movements, voice, and even doodles.

It will not be easy to bring the area of expression under scientific control to the point where we can be certain what the expressive aspect of an act signifies. As we have seen, many are the determinants that converge upon the 'final common path'. There are few simple one-to-one correspondences. We may say, for example, that a 'social introvert' would 'logically' make small and tight scribbles or doodles. Let us see what an experiment tells us:

The investigators asked subjects to draw doodles, and measured their area (constrictedness versus expansiveness). It is true that on the average the socially introverted subjects did tend to draw small and tight doodles, but there were marked exceptions. Some drew exaggeratedly large ones. Similarly, social extraverts did tend to draw large doodles, but again some of them scribbled in a markedly tiny and tight manner. What accounts for this confusing result? It turns out that the deviants were, by other measurements, highly *anxious* people. The anxious social introvert *compensated* for his anxiety by expansive drawing; the anxious social extravert *compensated* in the opposite way (40).

This finding should not surprise us. We all know of cases where an insecure adolescent develops a powerful and exaggerated handshake, or other hearty mannerisms with which he hopes to conceal his feelings of inferiority. His act of deception may be deliberate, or it may have become habitual. In any case, we conclude that to read aright any expressive act we need to know whether it contains in itself some compensatory deception. In other words, it is not enough to rely on the obvious interpretation (the face-validity) of an expressive movement. Ego-defensiveness and other countercurrents may be affecting the production.

Judging One's Own Expressions

Perhaps you have had the following experience. You once wrote a theme, drew a picture, or gave a gift to a friend, but have forgotten the fact. Now, years later, you encounter this object but still do not recognize it as your own production. Yet you *feel* very favorable toward it; it seems *good* to you. You think it is smart, intelligent, in good taste.

This somewhat rare but significant experience has been produced in the laboratory with important results. The technique was invented by W. Wolff and improved by Huntley (19).

The latter investigator succeeded in taking records of expressive behavior without his subjects knowing that he did so: photographs of hands and profile, recordings of voice, samples of handwriting and of style of retelling a story. Six months later each subject was asked to rate and characterize such expressive records, his own being mixed in with many others. In only one quarter of the cases did a subject recognize his own expressive record. (Voice is seldom recognized; handwriting was presented in a mirror image and this device reduces the chances of recognition.) When the subject did recognize his expression, his judgments turned out to be guarded, i.e., both moderate and modest. The important finding, however, is that for the three quarters of the judgments (unrecognized) the evaluations were usually extremely favorable, or occasionally extremely unfavorable. The judges were not neutral or moderate about their own unrecognized products.

Expressive Features

Any mobile region of the body in rest or in motion is expressive – eyes, mouth, head, trunk, shoulders, hands, fingers, legs. And any of their motions may be analyzed for their expressive significance: jumping, standing, walking, running, strolling, dancing, sitting, lying down, positions in sleeping, gesticulating, talking, laughing, weeping, shaking hands, smoking, handwriting, painting, musical performance, scientific work, play, dress, ornamentation. All these activities and more besides can be studied, separately or in combination.

To consider all these channels of expression, or even to consider any one completely, would be impossible. A few, however, will be singled out to show how constructive research can be done.

The Face

By far the most expressive region of the body is the face. Nature has provided it most lavishly with nerves and subtle muscles; it is unclothed and therefore the most visible region; the seat of the distance receptors, it is the region where the person meets the world head-on. As we have seen, most people locate the 'self' in close relation to the face. Our voice emanates from the face. And so, all in all, it is the region to which we give chief attention when we are observing others.

Psychologists have given much study to the facial expression of *emotion*, but this subject is not our present interest. From antiquity the art of physiognomy has persisted, but the insights of

Aristotle, Lavater, and all other historical figures have never been scientifically proved.

Most modern research has been devoted not to what the face reveals, but to what people *think* it reveals. It is wise to start with this more modest problem. Some of the generalizations coming from experimental studies follow.* In general (at least among American judges) there is a tendency –

1. to ascribe to dark-skinned people attributes of unfriendliness hostility, lack of humor.

2. to ascribe to blonds various favorable qualities. One study shows that fiction tends to make its heroes blond, its villains swarthy and dark (3).

3. to see faces with wrinkles at eye corners as friendly, humorous, easygoing.

4. to see older males as more distinguished, responsible, and refined than younger males.

5. to see older women as motherly.

6. to perceive people wearing eyeglasses or with high foreheads as more intelligent, dependable, industrious.

7. to perceive smiling faces as more intelligent. (The moral here is that if you are applying for a job submit a smiling photograph; if you are an employer pay no attention to it!)

8. to perceive women with thicker than average lips as sexy, and those with thin lips as asexual.

9. to consider bowed lips as indicating conceit, demandingness, even immorality.

10. to attribute to any Negro face the stereotypes of superstition, religiosity, easygoingness.

11. to see faces that are average in size of nose, hair grooming, set of jaw, and so on, as having more favorable traits than faces that deviate, e.g., by having prominent or receding features. Apparently we feel safer with someone who does not depart far from the cultural norm.

Although such judgmental tendencies seem to be fairly uniform, are they accurate? Probably only to a slight degree, if at all. They seem for the most part to be a product of an easy association of ideas. Most older women are mothers; a person wearing eyeglasses may have strained his eyes through study; people with high brows may have more room for brains – and so it goes. It seems that our experimental methods up to now succeed chiefly in uncovering what is stereotyped in our judgments of faces, not what is true.

A closer look at the relation between individual facial features

*Some of these findings are drawn from P. F. Secord (36).

and the impressions they create is achieved by a method invented by Brunswik and Reiter (4). The six schematic faces in Figure 2 are selected from a larger series of similar drawings. There are quantitative differences in respect to (1) the distance between the eyes, (2) height of the brow above the eyes, (3) position of the nose, (4) length of the nose, (5) position of the mouth. The judges are asked to rate each face according to such characteristics as intelligence, mood, age, occupation, energy. Figure 2 indicates the modal judgments for the six faces.

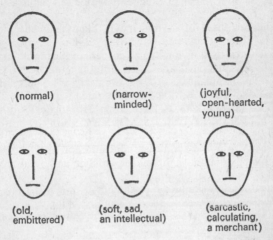

(normal)

(narrow-minded)

(joyful, open-hearted, young)

(old, embittered)

(soft, sad, an intellectual)

(sarcastic, calculating, a merchant)

Figure 2 Brunswik-Reiter Schematic Faces. Employed for the quantitative determination of the influence of various features, separately and in combination, upon physiognomic judgments (courtesy Frank Denticke, Vienna).

This method permits us to come closer to a precise analysis of elemental facial patterns in their relation to judgments of personality, but whether the findings from schematized faces carry over to real faces seems doubtful (34).

One finding from this experiment, and from others, is that in general the mouth is the most decisive facial feature in shaping our judgments.* The mouth is the most mobile region. And yet most people vote for the eyes as the most expressive feature. Eyes seem to us to be the visible center of another man's personality But actually the eye is relatively inexpressive; it can't 'do' as much

*N. G. Hanawalt, (17) however, suggests that the mouth region is superior only for happy emotions and not for surprise and fear.

51

as the mouth. Could it be that we *think* we learn most from another's eyes because we gain our impression through our *own* eyes? If so, there is a curious kind of projection under way.

It often happens that faces are asymmetrical. The right half does not exactly match the left. There are indications that when the asymmetry is marked we are more likely to be dealing with a neurotic personality (26). And one investigator suggests that the right half of the face ordinarily indicates the more public and conscious side of personality, while the left betrays the unconscious life (44). These are suggestive leads but require confirmation.

Another study of asymmetry is likewise challenging. The Lynns (27) find that a person who is right-handed and right-faced (as indicated by drawing up the corners of the mouth in smiling) is a better integrated and more outgoing individual than one where the dominance is crossed. Similarly, a left-left dominance (of hand and face) betokens an integrated personality. The neurological theory here is interesting. Homolateral dominance, where either the left or the right hemisphere of the brain is consistently in control, leads to a conflict-free, and therefore assertive, personality. By contrast, contra-lateral dominance throws the individual into slight motor conflict and retards activity, making him hesitant and unsure.

These are only samples of researches dealing with the face as an expressive agent. We are still far from reaching valid generalizations and laws, but the various lines of investigation hold promise.

Voice and Speech

Voice is only in part a coping instrument. To be sure, a person's enunciation must have a minimum of clarity; and for a professional singer, speaker, or radio or TV announcer, the proper adaptive use of the voice is of high importance. But untrained voices vary widely in pitch, timbre, and mannerism. Voice, therefore, especially if it is untrained, is a highly expressive instrument. *Speech*, by contrast, is concerned largely with coping (though, as we shall see, it, too, has marked expressive components). Our speech is composed of conventional words, put together according to rules of syntax, and directed toward purposive communication.

Although voice is highly expressive, psychologists have tended to neglect it in favor of speech. Vocal features are fugitive and hard to analyze. They include the dynamics of intonation, rhythm, brokenness or continuity, accent, pitch, richness, roughness, musical handling. Individual peculiarities of pronunciation should be included.

By the matching method, where the unanalyzed voice is compared with other products of expression or with facts concerning the speaker, we discover the following tendencies (5):

1. Untrained voices are more expressive (more often correctly matched than trained voices).

2. Age can usually be told within ten years.

3. Other physical features, such as height or complexion or physical appearance, are matched hardly above chance.

4. Deeper traits – whether the speaker is dominant, extraverted, esthetic, or religious in his interests, and so on, are judged with fair success.

5. *Complete* sketches of personality are matched with voice with still greater success. (This finding is important. It means that voice-as-a pattern is highly congruent with personality-as-a-whole, and therefore suggests that too fine an analysis may lose the diagnostic revelation of expressive features.)

Research on voice requires that all the subjects read aloud the same written passage. Otherwise the individuality of speech styles would enter to confuse judgments based on voice alone.

Speech may be oral or written. In either case we can count individual peculiarities in a large number of dimensions. Sanford lists over a hundred such dimensions (35). These include speed of speaking or writing; the characteristic length of an utterance or a sentence; repetitiveness; tendencies to rephrase or rewrite; clause construction; use of adverbs; the tense, voice, mood of verbs; conjunctions; slang; metaphors; grammatical errors. Furthermore, complex indexes can be constructed. What is the verb-adjective ratio for the speaker, his demonstrative-descriptive ratio for adjectives, his definite-indefinite ratio for articles, and so on? One useful index is called the 'type-token ratio', which in effect measures a person's vocabulary. If a person uses 100 words in a speech sample, and if 50 of them are different words, the TTR is ·50. The ratio can be determined for the total sample of speech or for any given part of speech (e.g., nouns or verbs) (8).

Perhaps the most striking finding from analytic research of this sort is the marked *consistency* of a person's speech. It is safe to say that every reported investigation proves that the speech style of a person is remarkably consistent from one occasion to another.

Relying on this fact, Yule applied the principle to determining the authorship of the famous book *Of the Imitation of Christ* (46). Was it written by the German theologian Thomas à Kempis, as commonly believed, or by a contemporary fifteenth-century French theologian, Jean de Gerson, who also wrote in Latin?

Yule counted the frequency with which certain nouns appeared in the 'Imitations' and in *other writings* of each author. Correlating the frequency of the use of these nouns in both sets of writings, he finds that the 'r' for Thomas à Kempis is ·91; for Gerson, ·81. On this basis Yule concludes that à Kempis is the true author. The high correlation for both authors is due, of course, to the fact that both were writing on the same religious subject. Both must have used 'Deus' an enormous number of times!

There is a special reason for citing this study. The fact that Yule finds a characteristic difference in the use of *nouns* is surprising, for of all the dimensions of speech, nouns would seem to be the least promising. Why is this? Because nouns are rigidly prescribed by our coping (by what we are doing). We have little expressive choice in the matter. Sanford's work, previously cited, suggests that the most individual and, therefore, the most expressive speech forms are verbs, adjectival and adverbial modifiers, and clause constructions. A person who uses active verbs, few modifiers, and simple declarative sentences is surely different from one who employs passive verbs, many modifiers, and many involved dependent clauses.

As for adjectival and adverbial modifiers, Doob discovers that people who use many of them also use active verbs. Furthermore, they give 'field-independent' judgments; for example, they are able to pick out hidden figures in a complex visual field (10). This little study shows well the whole logic of expression. People who are active, analytic, and discriminating in handling their environment show this same tendency in their stream of speech. They are not passive in accepting the outer environment – neither in their perception nor in their use of language.

We shall gradually learn just what aspects of speech are most useful for expressive diagnosis. Chapple (7) has invented an apparatus, the 'interaction chronograph', to tap important dimensions concerned with the length of speech samples and with the subject's tendency to interrupt or monopolize the conversation. Thorndike (37) tells us that in written speech punctuation is a consistent and revealing feature. All these and other leads merit further exploration.

Posture, Gesture, Gait

The position and movements of the limbs reflect the influence of *coping*, *cultural convention* and *personality*. The traffic policeman

stops the flow of vehicles with his left arm and motions to pedes-
trians with his right. In this case the nature of the task and cultural convention are largely responsible for the pattern of motion.
But even in this highly prescribed sequence we may detect subtle
individuality of expression, sometimes suggesting friendliness,
boredom, or arrogance.

Take posture. Man differs from the apes by his standing posture, a fact that has enormous consequences for his mobility and
intelligence. An anthropological investigation indicates that the
human body is capable of assuming about one thousand different
steady postures. 'Steady' means a static position that one can
maintain comfortably for some time (18). To some extent these
preferred positions depend on cultural habits (e.g., whether or not
chairs are used), but still to a large extent the posture one finds
congenial is a matter of his own choosing. Posture during sleep is
also a highly stable personal characteristic (17). Adler (1) boldly
suggests that 'pessimists' curl themselves into the smallest possible space and draw the covers over their heads. Psychodiagnosis
has not yet tested this claim. Psychoanalysts tell us that the postures of patients upon the couch are revealing and merit study
(9).

Limbs in action are still more revealing, although here too we
must read through the coping and cultural components. Culture,
we know, has a marked influence on hand gesticulation. Some
movements, on the other hand, are more culture-free, and therefore potentially more revealing of personality; a good example is
jumping (16).

Psychologists, of course, would like to bring the problem under
experimental control for closer study. Two attempts are described
below.

Giese (15) gave his subjects batons and asked them to beat time to
various musical recordings. The room was dark and a bulb at the end
of the baton permitted photographing the movements on a cinema
film. From these records it was possible to identify the effects of sheer
convention (beating time in the usual style of orchestra leaders), also a
style of motion to accord with the composition (Beethoven versus
jazz), and finally a definite individuality in movement (expressive only
of the subject himself).

Mira (31) has developed a major method called 'myokinetic diagnosis'. The subject starts to copy a simple design, e.g., a staircase. As soon
as he gets under way a shield is placed in front of his eyes so that he
can no longer see what he is doing, but he continues the drawing. In
this way the cues for coping are reduced and the expressive component
becomes prominent. Does the subject continue accurately, does he

wobble, does his hand start making exaggerated outward or inward errors? Does he become more expansive or more constricted? Mira claims that from these styles of deviation one can validly infer certain personal traits.

Such methods are admittedly artificial, a long way from the fleeting gestures of daily life, but they may be the best way to bring the problem under control.

Gait is a topic of special fascination. In the Apocrypha (*Ecclesiasticus;* 19, 27) we read: 'The attire of the body, and the laughter of the teeth, and the gait of the man, shew what he is.' But here again controlled analysis is just beginning. Wilsmann (41) suggests that there are seven measurable attributes in gait: regularity, speed, pressure, length of stride, elasticity, definiteness of direction, and variability. To this list he adds an attribute pertaining to the total swing which he calls rhythm.

Over and over again in all the channels of expression the problem of rhythm recurs. It is a poorly defined concept. Sometimes it refers to the periodicity of some aspect of the movement pattern. But usually the term points to an unanalyzed (and perhaps unanalyzable) effect created by the whole pattern of movement. 'Rhythm', like 'style', is as yet a vague and nonoperational concept.

Since gait is an important topic for medical practice, considerable progress has been made in inventing instruments for the precise study of leg motions in walking, and in establishing norms for cadence, stride length, and speed (11). Such basic research will serve as a springboard for psychologists who, we hope, will soon concern themselves with the characterological significance of gait.

A particularly interesting discovery was made by Wolff (42), who found that subjects always recognized their own gait, far better in fact than they recognized that of their friends.

The experiment was conducted by dressing subjects in loose fitting garments to conceal the head and all additional cues of identification. Cinema records were made, and subjects asked to identify the walker.

We recall from our earlier discussion [page 48] that self-recognition from expressive features is not accurate. A person rarely recognizes his own voice, hands, or mirrored handwriting. But gait is another matter. It would seem that we identify the movement of our trunk and limbs unerringly by a kind of *empathy*. The perception of the total swing immediately arouses like muscular impulses which we promptly recognize as our own.

As with all other channels of expressive movement, the preliminary work in analyzing gait has gone further than the study of its diagnostic significance. There is one study, however, that suggests that the trait of dominance in personality can be read from gait 'a little better than chance' (13).

Handwriting

Handwriting is, of all the forms of expression, by far the most popular. Graphologists may make a living by 'reading character from handwriting'. Psychologists increasingly, if somewhat reluctantly, are turning their attention to this field of investigation. For one thing, they have invented clever instruments for measuring the three dimensions of script – its vertical length, its width, and its pressure (38).

There is a strong case to be made for handwriting analysis. It is, as proponents argue, not merely handwriting, but also 'brain writing', influenced by all manner of expressive neural impulses giving individual flavor to the coping movements of the hand. As 'crystallized gesture', it is by all odds the most accessible of expressive movements for study; all other movements are fugitive and more difficult to measure. Part, but not all, of the popularity of studying handwriting is due to its easy availability.

Critics who say flatly that there is 'nothing in graphology' are simply wrong. Many studies show that graphologists are in fact able to diagnose some characteristics above chance.* And it is not only professionals who have skill; probably all of us have to some extent. For example, it is commonly found that a random sample of people can tell the sex of writers correctly from script alone in about 70 per cent of the cases. Though far from perfect, this degree of success is above chance (12).

If some critics claim too little for graphology, enthusiasts certainly claim too much. Sometimes charlatanry is involved, as when a graphologist gives us a 'reading' of a well-known political figure or actress. The characteristics reported are probably not discovered from the script at all but merely repeat common knowledge about the personage in question.

Charlatans aside, many workers in the field make serious attempts to discover the most appropriate dimensions of handwriting for use. Broadly speaking, there is a quarrel between those who favor specific graphic signs and those who look only at molar features of script. The former group might claim, e.g., that

*Studies on this point are numerous. Examples are H. J. Eysenck, (14) H. Cantril, G. W. Allport and H. A. Rand (6), G. R. Pascal (32).

a forward slant indicates 'sympathy', or that writing uphill signifies 'optimism', or that a person who writes 'o' open at the top is 'open' and 'generous'. This is the graphic-sign approach, and probably is less valid.

Others prefer to study global features. We have seen that Klages's theory [page 40] requires that one start one's analysis by estimating the departure of a script from school copy, in order to determine the general level of expressivity that a person shows. Klages would also study such broad syndromes as 'bonds and release', i.e., the constriction or expansion of writing. A person overwhelmed by the external world tends to write in a constricted fashion, as shown by such graphic bonds as smallness of script, heavy pressure, verticality, regularity, narrowness, long lower and short upper strokes, decreasing left margins, and so on. A person who masters his world would show the opposite graphic syndrome.

Some investigators claim that handwriting has not only expressive but also 'projective' significance. Like autistic gestures, it may tell much about specific unconscious conflicts in the personality (43, 30).

One problem that urgently needs exploration is this: What aspects of personality can be validly determined from script and what aspects cannot be? One study shows, for example, that a person's outstanding values can be fairly well identified (e.g., whether he is a markedly religious person), but we certainly cannot decide from handwriting alone whether the writer is a Catholic, Baptist, or Jew (6). And also, in line with our argument on page 40, we must expect some people to reveal more of their personal traits in handwriting than others. A librarian, for example, might have an inexpressive script, but a revealing voice or gait.

These limitations lead us to our main conclusion: All avenues of expression deserve study. We dare not rest our practice of psychodiagnosis on any one 'monosymptomatic' feature. To study expression adequately we should explore all channels.

References
1. Adler, A. *Understanding human nature* (New York: Greenberg, 1927) p. 176.
2. Allport, G. W. and P. E. Vernon, *Studies in expressive movement* (New York: Macmillan, 1933).
3. Berelson, B. and Salter, P. J., Majority and minority Americans: an analysis of magazine fiction, *Publ. Opin. Quart.*, 1946, *10*, 168–90.
4. Brunswik, E. and Reiter, Lotte, Eindruckscharaktere schematisierter Gesichter, *Z. f. Psychol.*, 1937, *142*, 67–134.

5. Cantril, H. and Allport, G. W., *The psychology of radio* (New York: Harper, 1935).
6. Cantril, H., Allport, G. W., and Rand, H. A., The determination of personal interests by psychological and graphological methods, *Charact. & Pers.*, 1943, *12*, 123–44.
7. Chapple, E. D., The measurement of interpersonal behavior, *Trans. N.Y. Acad. Sci.*, 1942, *4*, 222–33.
8. Chotlos, J. W., A statistical and comparative analysis of individual written language samples, *Psychol. Monogr.*, 1944, *56*, No. 2.
9. Deutsch, F., Analysis of postural behavior, *Psychoanal. Quart.*, 1947, *16*, 195–213.
10. Doob, L. W., Behavior and grammatical style, *J. abnorm. soc. Psychol.*, 1958, *56*, 398–401.
11. Drillis, R., Objective recording and biomechanics of pathological gait, *Ann. N.Y. Acad. Sci.*, 1958, *74*, 86–109.
12. Eisenberg, P., Judging expressive movement: I. Judgments of sex and dominance-feeling from handwriting samples of dominant and non-dominant men and women, *J. appl. Psychol.*, 1938, *22*, 480–86.
13. Eisenberg, P. and Reichline, P. B., Judging expressive movement: II. Judgments of dominance-feeling from motion pictures of gait, *J. soc. Psychol.*, 1939, *10*, 345–57.
14. Eysenck, H. J., Graphological analysis and psychiatry: an experimental study, *Brit. J. Psychol.*, 1945, *35*, 70–81.
15. Giese, F., Individuum und Epoche in Taktierbewegung bei verschiedenen Komponisten, *Arch. f. d. Ges. Psychol.*, 1934, *90*, 380–426.
16. Halsman, P., *Jump Book* (New York: Simon & Schuster, 1959).
17. Hanawalt, N. G., The role of the upper and lower parts of the face as a basis for judging facial expressions: II. In posed expressions and 'candid camera' pictures. *J. gen. Psychol.*, 1944, *31*, 23–36.
18. Hewes, G. W., World distribution of certain postural habits, *Amer. Anthrop.*, 1955, *57*, 231–44.
19. Huntley, C. W., Judgments of self based upon records of expressive behavior, *J. abnorm. soc. Psychol.*, 1940, *35*, 398–427.
20. Johnson, H. M., Swan, T. H., and Wiegard, G. E., In what positions do healthy people sleep? *J. Amer. med. Assn.*, 1930, *94*, 2058–62.
21. Johnson, Winifred B., Euphoric and depressed moods in normal subjects, *Charact. & Pers.*, 1937–38, *6*, 79–98 and 188–202. *J. abnorm. soc. Psychol.*, 1960, *60*, 117–26.
22. Klages, L., *Der Geist als Widersacher der Seele* (3 vols.; Leipzig: Barth, 1929–32).
23. Krout, M. H., Autistic gestures: an experimental study in symbolic movement, *Psychol. Monogr.*, 1935, No. 208.
24. Krout, M. H., An experimental attempt to produce unconscious manual symbolic movements, *J. gen. Psychol.*, 1954, *51*, 93–152.
25. La Barre, W., The cultural basis of emotion and gestures, *J. Person.*, 1947, *16*, 49–68.
26. Lindzey, G., Prince, Blanche, and Wright, H. K., A study of facial asymmetry, *J. Person.*, 1952–53, *21*, 68–84.
27. Lynn, J. G. and Lynn, D. R., Face-hand laterality in relation to personality, *J. abnorm. soc. Psychol.*, 1938, *33*, 291–322.
28. Maslow, A. H., The expressive component of behavior, *Psychol. Rev.*, 1949, *56*, 261–72.

29. Maslow, A. H. *Motivation and personality* (New York: Harper, 1954).
30. McNeil, E. B. and Blum, G. S., Handwriting and psychosexual dimensions of personality, *J. proj. Techniques*, 1952, *16*, 476–84.
31. Mira, E., *M.K.P.-Myokinetic diagnosis* (New York: Logos, 1958).
32. Pascal, G. R., The analysis of handwriting: a test of significance, *Charact. & Pers.*, 1943, *12*, 123–44.
33. Ponder, E. and Kennedy, W. P., On the act of blinking, *Quart. J. exper. Physiol.*, 1927, *18*, 89–110.
34. Samuels, Myra R., Judgment of faces, *Charact. & Pers.*, 1939, *8*, 18–27.
35. Sanford, F. H., Speech and personality: a comparative case study, *Charact. & Pers.*, 1942, *10*, 169–98.
36. Secord, P. F., Facial features and inference processes in inter-personal perception. In Tagiuri, R., and Petrullo, L., (Eds.) *Person perception and interpersonal behavior*, Stanford: University Press, 1958
37. Thorndike, E. L., Psychology of punctuation, *Amer. J. Psychol.*, 1948, *61*, 222–8.
38. Tripp, C. A., Fluckiger, F. A., and Weinberg, G. H., Measurement of handwriting variables, *Percept. & Motor Skills*, 1957, *7*, 279–94.
39. Vernon, P. E., The matching method applied to investigations of personality, *Psychol. Bull.*, 1936, *33*, 149–77.
40. Wallach, M. A. and Gahm, Ruthellen C., Personality functions of graphic constriction and expansiveness, *J. Person.*, 1960, *28*, 73–88.
41. Wilsmann, A. C., Charakterologische Bedeutung von Einzelmerkmalen. In H. Bogen and O. Lipmann (Eds.), Gang und Charakter, *Beihefte zur Z. f. angew. Psychol.*, 1931, No. 6.
42. Wolff, W., Zuordnung individueller Gangmerkmale zur Individualcharakteristik. In Bogen, H., and Lipmann, O., (Eds.) Gang und Charakter. *Beihefte zur Z. f. angew. Psychol*, 1931, No. 6.
43. Wolff, W., *Diagrams of the unconscious* (New York: Grune & Stratton, 1948).
44. Wolff, W., *The expression of personality* (New York: Harper, 1943).
45. Woodworth, R. S., *Dynamics of behavior* (New York: Holt, Rinehart and Winston, 1958).
46. Yule, G. U., *The statistical study of literary vocabulary* (Cambridge, England: Cambridge Univ. Press, 1944).

THE VARIETIES OF TEMPERAMENT

The present text is reprinted from the book of the same name, where it appears as Chapter 1. 'Introduction and Summary'.

That there is a relationship between physical and mental or moral characteristics is one of the most deeply-rooted of human beliefs. It pervades literature of all ages, whether imaginative or philosophical-scientific. Many of the correspondences can be attributed to *a priori* expectations, but some stand up, at least in general terms, to empirical verification.

In modern times, two systems have each contributed to the generally accepted language of science. Kretschmer (2), working from the standpoint of psychiatry, invented the terms 'asthenic' and 'pyknic', applying these to the varieties of body-build believed to be associated, respectively, with schizophrenia and manic-depressive psychosis. The names have become firmly established, but with a few exceptions (notably Professor Eysenck) psychologists now pay more attention to Sheldon's system, here summarized.

Sheldon's approach is essentially that of the anthropometrician, and a criticism frequently expressed is that while the system of measurement is valid enough, nutrition and other extraneous factors may obscure the subject's 'real' somatotype. There has been little independent verification of the basic hypotheses, but discrimination in terms of somatotypes has been reported by the Gluecks (1) and others.

References
1. Glueck, S. and E., *Unravelling Juvenile Delinquency.* Cambridge, Mass.: Harvard University Press, 1950.
2. Kretschmer, E., *Körperbau and Charakter.* Berlin: Springer, 1921. Transl. by W. J. H. Sprott as *Physique and Character.* New York: Harcourt and Brace, 1926.

3 W. H. Sheldon and S. S. Stevens

The Varieties of Temperament

W. H. Sheldon and S. S. Stevens,
The Varieties of Temperament, 1942, Chapter 1, 'Introduction and Summary', 1–11.

Tradition has it that fat men are jolly and generous, that lean men are dour, that short men are aggressive, and that strong men are silent and confident. But tradition is sometimes wise and sometimes stupid, for seldom does it distinguish between the accumulated wisdom of the ages and the superstitions of ignorance. Especially as regards physique and temperament have the conclusions of careful students been contaminated by the stereotypes of the street and by the dogmatism of the side-show phrenologist. But if we ignore these last and ask only about the opinions of the scholars, the writers, and the artists we find a persistent tradition that the shape of a man promises certain traits in his temperament.

Scholars have sometimes set off physiques and temperaments into *types*. Hippocrates may not have been the first to systematize his observations regarding the dependence of personality on morphology, but he long ago set forth a scheme that has reappeared under various forms in repeated generations. The writers and the artists establish their typologies more by implication than by argument and statistics. They cast their characters by rules mostly unexpressed, but seldom if ever do they put the temperament of a Falstaff into a lean and wiry body, or paint the face of a Scrooge as apple-cheeked and rolypoly.

Now our present concern is not with the traditions of history, except in so far as they suggest that those who have scrutinized people have seen certain resemblances and certain differences, and that various traits of character sometimes pair off with aspects of bodily structure in a way that holds out a hope against chaos and a promise of scientific order. But, since a hope and a promise do not make a science, our present concern is with techniques of inquiry. How shall we observe men, classify them, and measure them? How shall we learn to tell them apart, not as Jim and Joe but as kinds and types of animals? In short, how shall we proceed if we are to ignore superficialities and fasten attention on the basic, first-order variables of a science of individual differences?

Why Individual Differences?

It does not take a science to tell that no two human beings are identically alike, but it does require the discipline of systematic inquiry to give, in terms of scales and categories, a useful description of individual differences. The basic dimensions of human variation are not always obvious. But, granted that there are such things as first-order factors affecting human differences, why should we bother ourselves to discover them? Why, when our usually acknowledged scientific aim is to seek out the generalities contained in the laws of nature, should we be diverted toward the problem of exceptions and differences?

The answer is simple enough. The statement of a scientific law is complete only to the extent that it can account for individual differences. To illustrate, let us consider a simple law of physics. The falling apple gathers speed as it descends. In fact its velocity is very nearly proportional to the time during which it has fallen. The observation that this is true of many different objects leads to a simple generalization relating velocity and time – Galileo's law of falling bodies. But suppose we drop a feather instead of an apple. The feather drifting lazily to earth suggests at least that individual differences among falling bodies are not to be ignored, and we begin to suspect a certain incompleteness in our previous generalization. We have neglected to state for what conditions – for what parameters – the law is true. Here the study of individual differences leads us to correct the equation for falling bodies by a term relating to the size and shape and weight of the object.

We learn from this simple example the importance of parameters – the conditions attached to the operation of a law. In 'human engineering', where we can seldom write simple equations for any part of behavior, the importance of parameters is quite as crucial. We learn the laws of a certain disease: bacteria enter the body and multiply at the expense of the host. But in some bodies they do not multiply. Obviously a full understanding of the disease demands an explanation of such individual differences. Emotional upsets, we discover, lead to personality difficulties. But equivalent upsets leave some persons quite as happy and stable as before. How shall we understand the effects of traumatic experiences if we ignore this variability? And so with almost everything from physiological functions to human learning – the *kind* of individual involved enters as a parameter in our laws.

A plea for the study of individual differences, then, becomes a plea for the recognition of parameters. Our aim is to present a system for treating the problem of individual differences in terms of what appear to be basic components of temperament. These components in turn are tied back to and interpreted in terms of basic components of morphology. The emphasis is upon constitutional factors, upon the relatively stable qualities of a man which give him his basic individuality. In such an emphasis there is always a danger of creating a wrong impression regarding the relative importance to personality of nature and nurture, or of heredity and environment, those two concepts that have so often split scholars into factions. The study of constitutional differences need in no wise depreciate the effects of environmental influences – nor ought the study of environmental factors to neglect the parameters of individuality. The matter may be resolved· by a proper phrasing of the problem. We may ask, 'What are the effects of culture (or environment or learning) upon temperament (or personality or attitudes)?' Or we may ask, 'What are the effects of different types of "nurture" upon various aspects of behavior *for persons of differing constitutional endowment*?' The importance of putting the question in this latter form is expressed by the old saying, 'What is one man's meat is another man's poison.'

Statics and Dynamics in Psychology

Constitutional psychology seeks a basic taxonomy of human beings. It asks for a frame of reference against which individuality may be set off and classified and scaled – a frame of reference simple enough to be comprehensible, yet full enough to account for most of the variety of human differences. Since the complexity of human beings makes it advisable to subdivide the problem in such a way that separate attacks can be made at different levels, we have attempted to devise both a taxonomy of structure and a taxonomy of function.

But function itself can be regarded as divisible into levels extending all the way from physiological functions and locomotion to such things as the expression of political beliefs, and it is hopeless to probe all these levels at once. Consequently we have limited the present study to the level called temperament. The level of temperament, like any level of investigation, has no sharp boundaries to mark it off unequivocally from its neighboring regions, but by temperament we shall mean, roughly, the level of personality just above physiological function and below acquired attitudes and beliefs. It is the level where basic patterns of motivation manifest themselves. But for an adequate operational definition of temperament we must refer the reader to the scale of temperament presented below (Chapter III). This scale is the best ostensive definition of what we mean by temperament.

A taxonomy of structure was developed in a previous volume, *The Varieties of Human Physique* (Harper & Brothers, 1940). That study of the size and shape of human beings, expressed in terms of three basic morphological components, constitutes the *statics* of constitutional psychology. Pursuing the analogy further, we may regard the study of temperament as *dynamics*. The study of statics in the field of psychology is the study of the balance among the components comprising the morphology of man at rest. Dynamic psychology, then, is the science of man in motion. When structure takes on function, when man gets up and moves around, expressing his desires and motivations and interacting with his fellows, then he becomes a dynamic organism. And the study of his behavior in its more elemental manifestations is the part of dynamics called the science of temperament.

Viewed in this fashion, physique and temperament are clearly two aspects of the same thing, and we are not surprised if we are led to expect that the dynamics of an individual should be related to the static picture he presents. It is the old notion that structure must somehow determine function. In the face of this expectation it is rather astonishing that in the past so little relation has been discovered between the shape of a man and the way he behaves. Of course it is possible that there is no such relation. But it is also possible that the relation is definite, although concealed in complexity, and that it is only to be disclosed when we shall have learned to choose the proper variables for our studies. As later chapters will show, there are dynamic and static variables which correlate sufficiently highly to reaffirm our faith in the possibility of a useful science of constitutional differences.

The problem of this volume, and of the earlier work on human physique, is mainly the problem of variables – the search for basic factors. The outcome of the search for basic dynamic components of temperament is told in later chapters, but before proceeding to them let us first indulge in a bird's-eye view of the constitutional project as a whole.

A Summary

Chronologically the studies of temperament, which are here for the first time published, were begun before our morphological investigations were undertaken. The reversal of this order in publication is merely for logical reasons: it has seemed wise to follow the medical precedent of beginning with anatomy, and since the reader may not be familiar with the earlier work (*The Varieties of Human Physique*) we shall first outline the morphological studies.

The Primary Components of Morphology

Having failed in several efforts to arrive at a useful morphological taxonomy through anthropometric techniques alone, we very early came to the conclusion that in order to set up the framework of such a taxonomy *ab initio* it would be desirable to scrutinize a large number of physiques all at one time. Photography not only would make this possible, but also would permit us to see each physique from as many directions at once as might be desirable. Accordingly a procedure was adopted in which the individual is photographed in a standardized posture from the frontal, lateral, and dorsal positions on a single film.

When four thousand photographs were assembled in one place, so that they could be arranged experimentally in series, it was found that a certain orderliness of nature could be made out by the unaided eye. Certainly there were no 'types', but there were obvious dimensions of variation.

The first problem, then, was to determine how many dimensions or components of structural variation could be recognized. The criteria we employed in seeking 'primary structural components' were two: (1) Could the entire collection of photographs be arranged in an ascending (or a descending) progression of strength in the characteristic under consideration, with agreement between experimenters working independently? (2) In the case of a suspected new component of structural variation, is it, upon examination of the photographs, found to be impossible to define this apparently new component in terms of mixtures, regular or dysplastic, of the other components already accepted? Application of these two criteria revealed the presence of three primary components of structural variation, and we were unable to find a fourth structural variant that was not obviously the result of a mixture of the three.

To arrange the entire series of four thousand along each of the three accepted axes of variation was relatively easy, not only for the body as a whole but also for different regions of the body separately (thus providing a method for the ultimate measurement of dysplasia). The distributions for the body as a whole were then scaled tentatively by the method of equal-appearing intervals, and we had at hand a rough approximation to the general pattern-ing of a continuous tridimensional distribution that was true to life. This was not yet an objectively defined distribution, but the first step toward meaningful objectification had been taken. We now had a fairly good idea of what could most profitably be meas-ured, and were ready to make use of anthropometry.

The second problem was to find such anthropometric measure-ments as would, (1) most reliably reflect those obvious differences in physique that anthroposcopic inspection had already shown to be present, and (2) refine and objectify these differences so that precise allocations of physiques on the tridimensional distribution could be made. Such measurements were selected by trial and error. It was found that the measurements most valuable for the purpose were certain diameters expressed as ratios to stature, and that most of these diameters could be taken with needle-point dividers from the film more accurately (more reliably) than from the living subjects, provided the photographs were posed in a standardized manner.

The question of how many such diameters to use is simply the question of how precisely accurate an allocation is desired. In dealing with groups statistically, we scale the strength of each of the primary components on a 7-point scale. For this purpose a minimum of seventeen diameter measurements is adequate for determining what is called the *somatotype*. In the detailed analysis of an individual, more precise differentiation may be made by using a greater number of measurements.

In order more readily to determine the somatotype from a series of measurements, a machine was constructed into which the measurements may be entered. The manipulation of switches then discloses the correct somatotype. This machine, as at present constructed, may be used for the somatotyping of any male in-dividual in the age range of 16 to 21.

The somatotype is a series of three numerals, each expressing the approximate strength of one of the primary components in a physique. The first numeral always refers to *endomorphy* (see below), the second to *mesomorphy*, and the third to *ectomorphy*. Thus, when a 7-point scale is used, a 7–1–1 is the most extreme endomorph, a 1–7–1 is the most extreme mesomorph, and a 1–1–7 the most extreme ectomorph. The 4–4–4 falls at the mid point (of the scale, not of the frequency distribution) with respect to all three components.

As these components occur in nature they are single, continuous variables. The designation of the somatotype merely serves the purpose of bracketing a physique within certain defined boundaries. When the somatotype is determined, analysis of the physique is only begun, but the somatotype provides the basis for a morphological taxonomy that is both comprehensive and statistically manipulable. The bugaboo of types disappears in a continuous distribution in which every physique has a place, and the establishment of norms becomes a routine.

Now for a description of the static components:

When *endomorphy* predominates, the digestive viscera are massive and highly developed, while the somatic structures are relatively weak and undeveloped. Endomorphs are of low specific gravity. They float high in the water. Nutrition may vary to some degree independently of the primary components. Endomorphs are usually fat but they are sometimes seen emaciated. In the latter event they do not change into mesomorphs or ectomorphs any more than a starved mastiff will change into a spaniel or a collie. They become simply emaciated endomorphs.

When *mesomorphy* predominates, the somatic structures (bone, muscle, and connective tissue) are in the ascendancy. The mesomorphic physique is high in specific gravity and is hard, firm, upright, and relatively strong and tough. Blood vessels are large, especially the arteries. The skin is relatively thick, with large pores, and it is heavily reinforced with underlying connective tissue. The hallmark of mesomorphy is uprightness and sturdiness of structure, as the hallmark of endomorphy is softness and sphericity.

Ectomorphy means fragility, linearity, flatness of the chest, and delicacy throughout the body. There is relatively slight development of both the visceral and somatic structures. The ectomorph has long, slender, poorly muscled extremities with delicate, pipe-stem bones, and he has, relative to his mass, the greatest surface area and hence the greatest sensory exposure to the outside world. He is thus in one sense overly exposed and naked to his world. His nervous system and sensory tissue have relatively poor protection. It might be said that the ectomorph is biologically 'extraverted', as the endomorph is biologically 'introverted'. Psychologically, as we shall see later, these characteristics are usually reversed – the ectomorph is the introvert, the endomorph is *one type* of extravert.

The digestive viscera (dominant in endomorphy) are derived principally from the endodermal embryonic layer. The somatic tissues (dominant in mesomorphy) are derived from the mesodermal layer, while the skin and nervous system, which are relatively predominant in ectomorphy, come from the ectodermal embryonic layer.

The anthropometric measurements used to determine the somatotype are standardized for normal or average nutrition within a particular age range. Therefore those measurements which change with nutritional changes readily detect the under- or over-nourished individual. But apparently no nutritional change can cause the measurements of a person of one somatotype exactly to simulate those of another somatotype. Nutritional changes are recognized as such by the somatotyping process. When an individual's measurements are posted in the somatotyping machine, the machine indicates where the somatotype lies. If a severe nutritional disturbance is present, the machine does not indicate a false somatotype but indicates only an unusual aberration from a normal pattern. We have as yet seen no case in which metabolic or nutritional changes led us to the assignment of two different somatotypes for the same individual, although we have somatotyped people from photographs taken at different periods in their (adult) lives when a weight change of as much as one hundred pounds had taken place.

When the relative strength of the three primary components of morphology has been determined, the physical analysis may be said to be anchored. But identification of the somatotype is only a beginning. So many secondary variables still remain to be described that the horizon of individuality seems only to broaden and to recede to greater distance as the techniques of physical description mature to usefulness.

Some of the important secondary variables are dysplasia (different mixtures of the primary components in differing regions of the body), gynandromorphy (physical bisexuality), texture (fineness or coarseness of tissue, aesthetic harmony of structure), secondary local dysplasias or hereditary local patternings of the primary components often called racial characteristics, pigmentation, distribution of secondary sexual characteristics (gynandromorphic dysplasias and characteristic patterns), hirsutism and hair distribution, and so on. We have tried to standardize the scaling of most of these characteristics just mentioned, but many other important physical variables lie on beyond these. Furthermore the work on secondary factors is for the most part new and incomplete, since none of this work could be done in a meaningful frame of reference until the somatotyping techniques and the norms for the primary components were well established. [. . . .]

The Dynamic Components of Temperament

As in the studies of morphology, the first problem at this more complex level of personality was to discover and define criteria for a useful basic taxonomy. It was necessary at the beginning to determine what first-order components are present in temperament. The method which has finally yielded fruitful results is a variation on the technique of factor analysis applied to quantitative ratings on a group of traits.

We have been able to standardize the descriptions of sixty traits – twenty in each of three correlated clusters – which collectively make up a scale for measuring what appear to be three primary components of temperament. Within each of the clusters the traits are positively correlated, while all of the intercorrelations between traits not of the same cluster are negative. [. . . .]

Names have been given to the three correlated groups of traits. *Viscerotonia*, the first component, in its extreme manifestation is characterized by general relaxation, love of comfort, sociability, conviviality, gluttony for food, for people, and for affection. The viscerotonic extremes are people who 'suck hard at the breast of mother earth' and love physical proximity with others. The motivational organization is dominated by the gut and by the function of anabolism. The personality seems to center around the viscera. The digestive tract is king, and its welfare appears to define the primary purpose of life.

Somatotonia, the second component, is roughly a predominance of muscular activity and of vigorous bodily assertiveness. The motivational organization seems dominated by the soma. These people have vigor and push. The executive department of their internal economy is strongly vested in their somatic muscular systems. Action and power define life's primary purpose.

Cerebrotonia, the third component, is roughly a predominance of the element of restraint, inhibition, and of the desire for concealment. Cerebrotonic people shrink away from sociality as from too strong a light. They 'repress' somatic and visceral expression, are hyperattentional, and sedulously avoid attracting attention to themselves. Their behavior seems dominated by the inhibitory and attentional functions of the cerebrum, and their motivational hierarchy appears to define an antithesis to both of the other extremes.

Physique and Temperament

In a study extending through a period of five years we have been

71

able to analyze 200 young men both morphologically and temperamentally, measuring in addition to the primary components a number of apparently secondary temperamental characteristics. Correlations of the order of about $+\cdot80$ between the two levels of personality (morphological and temperamental) indicate that temperament may be much more closely related to the physical constitution than has usually been supposed.

However, the correlation between the two levels is by no means perfect, and from the point of view of individual analysis it seems to be the disagreements or inconsistencies between the physical and temperamental pattern that throw the most light on behavior. We find, roughly, at least four general factors at work in the development of a personality: (1) the total strength of endowment in each of the three primary components, (2) the quality of such endowment, (3) the mixture of the components, or their order of relative strength, and (4) the incompatibilities between morphology and manifest temperament. Of the latter, several subvarieties can be made out and are often encountered in the analysis of personalities having a history of severe internal conflict. [. . . .]

PSYCHOLOGICAL TYPES

Although historically Jung comes after Freud, this paper has been given precedence over Hilgard's account of Freud's treatment of personality development because of the central position in contemporary (and earlier) personality theory of the concept of introversion-extraversion. This opposition has provided the basis for a universally recognized dimension of personality, and reference to its measurement will be found elsewhere in this book.

The present text, originally delivered as a lecture, gives only a brief statement of Jung's system: a much fuller account is given in his book of the same name (2). In particular, the lecture deals rather perfunctorily with Jung's notion of 'psychic functions', which he usually groups in pairs: two 'modes of apprehension' (sensation and intuition) and two 'modes of judgement' (feeling and thinking). This part of Jung's analysis of personality is less well known, and on the whole less well accepted (see, e.g., Munroe, 4). Many psychologists are still less favourably inclined to other aspects of Jung's psychology, such as his teaching on symbols, archetypes, and the racial unconscious.

Different in kind, and more relevant to the subject matter of this book, although to a different section of it, is Jung's work on *Word Association* (1). The original publication, in the form of a journal article, was in 1910, the same year as the work of Kent and Rosanoff (3). Based on an experimental technique developed in Wundt's laboratory, *Word Association* provides a link between classical experimental psychology and personality study.

References
1. Jung, C. G., Studies in *Word Association*. Transl. by M. D. Eder. London: Heinemann, 1918.
2. Jung, C. G., *Psychological Types*. Transl. by H. G. Baynes. London: Routledge and Kegan Paul, 1923.
3. Kent, G. H., and Rosanoff, A. J. *A Study of Association in Insanity American J. of Insanity*, 67, 37–96; 317–90. 1910.
4. Munroe, Ruth L., *Schools of Psychoanalytic Thought*. London: Hutchinson, 1957, Chapter 13.

4 C. G. Jung

Psychological Types

From *Contributions to Analytical Psychology;* Routledge & Kegan Paul, London; Bollingen Foundation, New York, 1928, 295–312.

Of ancient origin indeed are the attempts to solve the problem of types. Some thinkers have tried to establish definite categories in which to catch the manifold differences of human individuals, while others have tried to break down the apparent uniformity of mankind by a sharper characterization of certain typical differences. Without caring to go too deeply into the history and development of such attempts, I would like to call attention to the fact that the oldest categories known originated with physicians. Among the latter, Claudius Galen deserves especial notice, the Greek physician who lived in the second century after Christ. He distinguished four fundamental temperaments, the sanguine, the phlegmatic, the choleric, and the melancholic. But the idea at the root of this differentiation goes back to the fifth century before Christ, to the teachings of Hippocrates who described the human body as composed of the four elements, air, water, fire, and earth. Corresponding to these elements, four substances were to be found in the living body: blood, phlegm, yellow and black bile; and it was Galen's idea that, by virtue of the varying admixture of these four substances, men could be separated into four different classes. When blood predominated the sanguine type resulted; a preponderance of phlegm produced the phlegmatic; yellow bile produced the choleric, and black bile the melancholic. As our modern speech testifies these differentiations of temperament have become immortal, but their naïveté from the standpoint of psychological theory has long since been apparent.

Galen undoubtedly deserves the credit of having created a psychological classification of human individuals which has endured for two thousand years, a classification which rests upon perceptible differences of emotional or affective constitution. It is interesting to note that the first attempt at classification of types is concerned with the emotional behaviour of men; manifestly because the play of emotion forms the most frequent and obviously striking feature of any behaviour.

But affect is by no means the only thing that is characteristic of mankind; characteristic data can be expected from other functions as well, the only requirement being that we perceive and observe the other functions with the same distinctness that we naturally give to affect. In the earlier centuries, when the concept 'psychology' as we know it today was almost entirely lacking, the other psychological functions were veiled in obscurity; as indeed to the great majority of people today they seem to be scarcely discernible subtleties. Affects are revealed at once, even to superficial observation, and the unpsychological man, that is, the man to whom his neighbour's mind presents no problem, contents himself with this kind of observation. The perception of affect in his fellow-man is enough for him; if he sees none then the other person is psychologically invisible to him, because apart from affects, nothing is discernible in another's consciousness. He is, in fact, blind to the other functions.

The primary condition, whereby we can discover functions in our fellow-men other than affects, is secured when we ourselves pass from an 'unproblematical' to a problematical condition of consciousness. By 'unproblematical' I mean the instinctive attitude toward life as exemplified by the primitive, whereas 'problematical' denotes the state of mind in which the easy attitude that takes things for granted has changed into one in which a certain amount of psychological tension exists. In this latter state our fellow-man emerges from invisibility and becomes a factor with which we have to grapple consciously. Resuming the thread of the argument: in so far as we judge others only by affects, we show that our chief, and perhaps only, criterion is affect. This means that this criterion is also valid for our own psychology, which is equivalent to saying that our psychological judgement in general has neither objectivity nor independence, but is a slave to affect. This is, in fact, a truth which holds good for the majority of people, and upon this fact rests the psychological possibility of a murderous war and its ever probable recurrence, notwithstanding the blind optimism that clings to the opposite view. This must always be so long as a man judges those on the 'other side' by his own affect or emotion. I call such a state of consciousness unproblematical, because manifestly it has never been regarded itself as a problem; there is no sense of inadequacy or maladaptation to the facts involved. It only becomes a problem when a doubt arises as to whether the affect, that is one's own affect, offers a satisfactory basis for forming psychological judgements. We cannot deny the fact that we are always inclined to justify ourselves to anyone who holds us responsible for an emotional act, by saying that we acted only on impulse, and that we are not usually in that condition. When it concerns ourselves we are glad to explain affect as an exceptional condition of lessened accountability, but we are loath to make the same allowance for others. Even if this be regarded as an attempt, not altogether admirable perhaps, to exonerate the beloved ego, still in the feeling of justification fostered by this excuse there lies a positive element; namely, the attempt to distinguish oneself from one's own affect, which distinction must also eventually include one's fellow-man. And even if my excuse is only a subterfuge, it is nevertheless an effort to cast a doubt on the validity of affect as the sole index of personality, an effort, furthermore, to make myself aware of other psychological functions that are just as characteristic of the self as the affect, if not more so. If a man judges us by our affect, we readily accuse him of lack of understanding, or even injustice. But this puts us under the obligation of refraining from affect-judgement ourselves.

The primitive, unpsychological man, who regards affect in himself and others as the only essential criterion, must if he means to cure himself of his affect-judgement, develop in himself a problematical condition of consciousness; that is to say, he must reach a condition in which other factors are appreciated as valid besides affect. In this problematical condition a paradoxical judgement takes place, namely, 'I am this affect', and 'I am not this affect'. This antithesis forces a splitting of the ego, or rather, a splitting of the psychological material which constitutes the ego. By recognizing myself in my affect as well as in something that is not my affect, I differentiate an affective from other psychological factors, and in so doing, I bring the affect from its original heights of unlimited power into its proper place in the hierarchy of psychological functions.

Only when a man has performed this operation on himself, and has thereby produced a discrimination between various psychological factors in himself, is he in a position to summon criteria other than affect in his psychological judgement of others. Only in this way is the development of a really objective psychological critique possible.

What we call 'psychology' today is a science that is possible only on the basis of certain historical and moral presuppositions which have been produced by Christian education during nearly two thousand years. Such a saying for example as 'Judge not that ye be not judged' has, through its religious connotation, created the possibility of a will which, in the last resort, strives towards a simple objectivity of judgement. And this objectivity, being not merely an attitude of disinterestedness towards others, but resting, as it does, on the fact that we wish others to benefit by the fundamental principles by which we excuse ourselves, this objectivity is the fundamental presupposition by which a just evaluation of our fellow-men can be achieved. You wonder perhaps why I dwell so emphatically on the question of objectivity, but you would cease to wonder if you should ever try to classify people in practice. A man of pronounced sanguine temperament will tell you that fundamentally he is deeply melancholic; a 'choleric', that his only fault consists in his having been always too phlegmatic. But a human classification, in the validity of which I alone believe, is about as helpful as a universal church of which I am the sole member. We have therefore to find criteria which can be fully accepted not only by the judging subject, but also by the judged object.

In complete contrast to the old system of classification according to temperaments, the problem of a new division of types begins with the express convention, neither to allow oneself to be judged by affect, nor so to judge others, since, as a final statement, no one will admit himself to be identical with his affect. If, therefore, affect is used as the criterion, the general agreement which science demands can never be reached. Hence we must cast around for those factors which we call to our aid when we wish to excuse ourselves for an emotional act. We might say, 'Granted that I have said this or that in a state of affect, it was of course an exaggeration and no harm was meant. As a matter of fact, what I really mean is thus and so, etc.' A very naughty child who has caused his mother a lot of trouble might say, 'I didn't mean to do it. I didn't mean to hurt you. I love you very much.'

Such explanations refer to the existence of a different kind of personality than the one that appeared in the affect. In both cases the affect-personality appears as something inferior that seized upon and obscured the real ego. But it may be that the personality revealed in such an affect is a higher and a better one, whose heights unfortunately cannot be sustained. There are well-known instances of generosity, altruism, sacrifice, and similar 'beautiful gestures', for which, as an ironical observer might spitefully remark, one does not care to be held responsible – perhaps a reason why many people do so little good.

But in both cases the affect obtains as an exceptional condition the character of which is represented either as a falsification of the 'real' personality, or as not belonging to it as an authentic attribute. What then is this 'real' personality? Manifestly it is partly that which every man distinguishes in himself as distinct from affect, and partly that in everyone which is regarded as inessential in the judgement of others. Since it is impossible to deny that the condition of affect pertains to the ego, it follows that the ego remains the same in the affect as in the so-called 'real' condition, although in a different attitude toward the existing psychological facts. In the affective state the ego is unfree, driven, in a state of compulsion. In contrast to this the normal state is understood as a condition of free-choice, of disposability of one's mental powers; in other words, the affective state is unproblematical, while the normal state is problematical, that is, it comprises both the problem and the possibility of choice. In the latter state an understanding becomes possible, because only in this state does the possibility of the recognition of motives and self-knowledge exist. Discrimination is indispensable to knowledge. But discrimination means the splitting up of the content of consciousness into distinguishable factors. Therefore, if we wish to define the individuality of a man in terms that will satisfy not our judgement alone, but also that of the man judged, we must take as our criterion that condition or attitude, which is felt by the object to be a conscious, normal state of mind. Accordingly, we must make the conscious motives our chief concern, while abstracting from the situation our own arbitrary interpretations.

Proceeding thus we shall discover, after a time, that in spite of a great variety of motives and tendencies, certain groups of individuals, characterized by an obvious conformity in their manner of motivation, can be differentiated. For example, we shall come upon individuals who in all their conclusions, apperceptions, feeling-valuations, affects and actions, feel a predominating motive-power in external factors, or, at least, weight is given to these in their conception of the situation, whether causal or final motives are in question. I will give some illustrations of what I mean. St Augustine says, 'I would not believe in the Evangels if the authority of the Church did not compel it.' A daughter says, 'I could not think something that would be displeasing to my father.' A certain person finds a work of modern music beautiful because everybody acclaims it is. Or there is the case of the man who has married in a way pleasing to his parents, but very much against his own interest. There are those people who make themselves absurd in order to amuse others; they may even prefer to make butts of themselves rather than remain unnoticed. There are, in fact, not a few who in all their reactions, have but one consideration in mind; namely, what do others think of them?

Someone has said, 'One need not be ashamed of a thing if nobody knows about it.' There are those who can realize happiness only when it excites the envy of others; there are also individuals who wish for troubles, and even create them for themselves, in order to enjoy the sympathy of their fellow-men.

Such examples could be multiplied indefinitely. They point to a psychological peculiarity that can be sharply distinguished from another attitude which, in contradistinction to the former, is conditioned chiefly by inner or subjective factors. A man of this type might say, 'I know I could give my father the greatest pleasure if I did thus and so, but nevertheless I have a different idea about it'; or, 'I see that the weather is vile, but in spite of it I shall carry out the plan I made yesterday.' Such a man does not travel for pleasure, but in order to carry out a plan. A man may say, 'Apparently my book is incomprehensible, but it is perfectly clear to me.' Another typical example is as follows, taken from an actual case, 'Everybody believes I could do something, but nothing is more certain to me than the fact that I can do nothing.' Such a man can be so ashamed of himself as literally to isolate himself. Among this group are to be found those individuals who can experience happiness only when they are sure that no one knows about it, and to these people a thing is disagreeable just because it is pleasing to everybody else. Value is sought, as far as possible, where no one would think of finding it. At every step the sanction of the subject must be obtained, and without it nothing can be undertaken or carried out. Such a one would say to St Augustine, 'I would believe in the Evangels if the authority of the Church did not coerce me to do it.' Constantly he has to prove that everything he does rests entirely upon his own decision and conviction, and never because he is influenced by anyone, or desires to please and conciliate some person or opinion. This attitude characterizes a second group of individuals whose motivations are derived chiefly from the subject, i.e., from inner necessities.

Finally there is a third group, in which it is hard to say whether the motivation is derived mainly from within or without. This group is the most numerous, and includes the less differentiated normal man, who is normal partly because nothing excessive is allowed, and partly because he is exempt from the need to exceed. According to definition, the normal man is influenced in equal measure from within as from without. He makes up, as has been said, the extensive middle group. On one side of this group are those individuals whose motivations are mainly conditioned by the outer object, and on the other are those who allow themselves to be determined principally by the subject. I have designated the first group as extraverted, the latter as introverted. These terms scarcely need special elucidation, since from what has been said they explain themselves.

Although doubtless there are certain individuals in whom one can recognize the type at a first glance, this is by no means always the case. As a rule, only careful observation and weighing of the evidence permits a sure classification. However clear and simple the fundamental principle of the opposing attitudes may be, their concrete reality is none the less complicated and obscure, for every individual is an exception to the rule. Therefore one can never give a description of a type, no matter how complete, which absolutely applies to one individual, despite the fact that thousands might, in a certain sense, be strikingly characterized by it. Conformity is one side of a man, uniqueness is the other. The individual soul is not explained by classification, yet at the same time, through the understanding of the psychological types, a way is opened to a better understanding of human psychology in general.

The differentiation of type begins often very early, so early that in certain cases one must speak of it as being innate. The earliest mark of extraversion in a child is his quick adaptation to the environment, and the extraordinary attention he gives to objects, especially to his effect upon them. Shyness in regard to objects is very slight; the child moves and lives among them with trust. He makes quick perceptions, but in a haphazard way. Apparently he develops more quickly than an introverted child, since he is less cautious, and as a rule, has no fear. Apparently, too, he feels no barrier between himself and objects, and hence he can play with them freely and learn through them. He gladly pushes his undertakings to an extreme, and risks himself in the attempt. Everything unknown seems alluring.

Reversing the picture, one of the earliest marks of introversion in a child is a reflective, thoughtful manner, a pronounced shyness, even a certain fear concerning unknown objects. Very early a tendency appears towards a certain self-assertion in relation to the object, with definite attempts to master it. Everything unknown is regarded with mistrust. Outside influence is, in the main, met with emphatic resistance. The child wants his own way, and under no circumstances will he submit to a strange rule that he does not understand. When he questions, it is not from curiosity or desire for sensation, but because he wants names, meanings, and explanations which could provide him with a subjective security over against the object. I have seen an introverted child who made her first efforts to walk, only after she had learnt the names of all the things in the room with which she might come in contact. Thus very early in an introverted child the characteristic defensive attitude can be noted which the adult introvert shows towards the object; just as, in the case of the extraverted child, one can very early observe a marked assurance and enterprise, and a happy trustfulness in his relations with objects. This then is the basic characteristic of the extraverted attitude; the psychic life is as it were displayed outside the individual in objects and in relationships to objects. In especially marked cases there occurs a sort of blindness for his own individuality. The introvert, on the contrary, always behaves towards the object as though the latter possessed a superior power over him, against which he has to defend himself. But his real world is the inner one, his subject.

It is a sad, but none the less frequent occurrence that the two types are inclined to depreciate each other. This will certainly strike anyone who investigates the problem. It depends upon the fact that the psychic values have a completely opposite disposition in the two types. The introvert sees all that holds value for him in the subject, while the extravert sees it in the object. But this dependence upon the object appears to the introvert as a great inferiority, while to the extravert the inferior condition lies in an unmitigated subjectivity. He can see nothing in such an attitude but infantile auto-erotism.

It is not surprising, then, that the two types are often in conflict. But this fact does not, in the majority of cases, prevent a man from marrying a woman of the opposite type. Such marriages are very valuable as psychological symbioses, so long as the partners do not attempt a mutual 'psychological' understanding. But such a phase belongs to the normal development of every marriage in which the couple has either the necessary leisure, or the necessary urge to development. Though even if both these requirements are present, a certain real courage is needed to risk the rupture of marital peace. If, however, circumstances favour it, this phase enters automatically into the lives of both types, and for the following reasons: each type is a one-sided development. The one develops only his outer relations, and neglects the inner; while the other develops inwardly, while remaining externally at a standstill. But in time a necessity arises for the individual to develop what has been previously neglected. This development takes the form of a differentiation of certain functions and, because of their importance for the type-problem, I must now take up the question of these functions.

The conscious psyche is an apparatus for adaptation or orientation, and it consists of a number of psychic functions. Of these we can distinguish four fundamental functions, namely, sensation, thinking, feeling, and intuition. Under the heading sensation I include all perception by means of the sense organs; by thinking I understand the function of intellectual cognition, and the forming of logical conclusions; feeling is a function of subjective evaluation, and intuition I hold to be perception by way of the unconscious, or the perception of an unconscious content. As far as my experience goes, these four fundamental functions appear to me to be sufficient to express and represent the ways and means of conscious orientation. For a complete orientation of consciousness all the functions should cooperate equally; thinking should make cognition and the forming of judgements possible; feeling should say to us how and in what way a thing is important or unimportant for us; sensation by means of sight, hearing, taste, etc., should enable us to perceive and grip on to concrete reality; and finally intuition should permit us to divine the more or less hidden possibilities and backgrounds of a situation, since these hidden factors also belong to a complete picture of a given moment. But in reality it is seldom or never that these fundamental functions are uniformly developed and correspondingly disposable by the will. As a rule one or another function is in the foreground, while the rest remain in the background, relatively or quite undifferentiated. Thus there are many people who restrict themselves to a simple perception of concrete reality, without reflecting much about it, or taking into account the feeling values involved. They bother themselves little about the possibilities which lie hidden in a situation. Such people I describe as sensation types. Others are exclusively influenced by what they think, and simply cannot adapt themselves to a situation which they cannot comprehend intellectually. I term such people thinking types. Again there are others who are guided in everything wholly by their feelings. They merely ask themselves if something is pleasant or the reverse, and orientate themselves by their feeling impressions. These are the feeling types. Finally, intuitives concern themselves neither with ideas nor with feeling reactions, nor yet with the reality of things, but give themselves up wholly to the lure of possibilities, and abandon every situation in which no further possibilities are scented.

Each one of these types presents a different kind of one-sidedness, but one which is complicated in a peculiar way with the generally extraverted and introverted attitudes. Just because of this complication I was forced to mention the existence of these function-types, and, bearing it in mind, let us now return to the question outlined above, that is, the one-sidedness of the extraverted and introverted attitudes. This one-sidedness would indeed lead to a complete loss of balance if it were not psychically compensated by an unconscious counter-position. The investigation of the unconscious has revealed the fact, that in the case of an introvert, for example, there exists alongside, or rather behind his conscious attitude, an unconscious extraverted attitude which automatically compensates his conscious one-sidedness.

Naturally, in practice, one can surmise intuitively the existence of an introverted or extraverted attitude in general, but an exact scientific investigation cannot content itself with an intuition, but must concern itself with the actual material presented. We then discover that no person is simply extraverted or introverted, but that he is so in the form of certain functions. Let us take for example an intellectual type; most of the conscious material which he presents to observation consists of thoughts, conclu, sions, deliberations, as well as actions, affects, feeling valuations- and perceptions of an intellectual nature, or at least directly dependent on intellectual premises. We must interpret the essence of his general attitude from the peculiarity of this material. The material presented by a feeling type will be of a different kind, that is, feelings and emotional contents of all sorts, thoughts, deliberations, and perceptions dependent upon emotional premises. Therefore, only by reason of the peculiar nature of his feelings shall we be in a position to say whether this individual belongs to this or that general type. For this reason I must again mention the function-types, because in individual cases the extraverted and introverted attitudes can never be demonstrated as existing *per se*; they appear rather as the characteristics of the dominating conscious functions. Similarly, there is no general attitude of the unconscious, but only typically modified forms of unconscious functions, and only through the investigation of the unconscious functions and their peculiarities can the unconscious attitude be scientifically determined.

It is hardly possible to speak of typical unconscious functions, although in the economics of the psyche we must attribute a function to the unconscious. It is best, I think, to express oneself rather cautiously in this respect, and therefore I would rather not go beyond the statement that the unconscious, so far as we can now see, has a compensatory function in respect to consciousness. What the unconscious is in itself, it is idle to speculate. By its very nature it is beyond our cognition. We can merely postulate its existence from its so-called products, as, for instance, dreams and phantasies. It is an assured finding of scientific experience that dreams, for example, almost invariably have a content which can act as an essential corrective to the conscious attitude. Hence our justification for speaking of a compensatory function of the unconscious.

Besides this general function in relation to the conscious, the unconscious also contains functions which under other circumstances can become conscious. The thinking type, for example, must necessarily always suppress and exclude feeling, since nothing disturbs thinking so much as feeling, and conversely, the feeling type must avoid thinking as far as possible, since nothing is more disastrous to feeling than thinking. Repressed functions lapse into the unconscious. Just as, of the four sons to Horus, only one had a human head, so with the four basic functions, only one as a rule is fully conscious and differentiated, so that it is free and subject to the direction of the will, the other three functions remaining partly or wholly unconscious. By this 'unconsciousness' I do not of course mean that an intellectual, for example, would be unconscious of feeling. He knows his feelings very well, in so far as he has any power of introspection, but he gives them no value and allows them no influence. They happen to him, as it were, against his intention; being spontaneous and autonomous, they finally possess themselves of the validity which consciousness denies. They are activated by unconscious stimulation, forming indeed something like a counter-personality whose existence can only be divined through the analysis of the unconscious products.

When a function has not the character of disposability, when it is felt as a disturbance of the conscious function, when it is moody, now appearing and now vanishing, when it has an obsessive character, or remains obstinately in hiding when most needed – these qualities are characteristic of a function existing mainly in the unconscious. Such a function has further qualities that are worthy of note; there is something unindividual about it, that is, it contains elements which do not necessarily belong to it. Thus, for example, the unconscious feeling of the intellectual is peculiarly phantastic, often in grotesque contrast to the exaggerated, rationalistic intellectualism of the conscious. In contrast to the purposeful and controlled character of the conscious thinking, his feeling is impulsive, uncontrolled, moody, irrational, primitive, archaic; in fact, very like the feeling of a savage.

The same thing is true of every function that is repressed into the unconscious. It remains there undeveloped, fused with other elements not proper to it. It remains in a certain primordial condition, since the unconscious is the psychic residue of un-domesticated nature in us, just as it is also the matrix of our uncreated future. Thus the undeveloped functions are always the fruitful ones, and it is no wonder that in the course of life the necessity increases for a completion and transformation of the conscious attitude.

Besides these qualities I have mentioned, the undeveloped functions possess the further peculiarity, that when the conscious attitude is introverted they are extraverted in character, and vice versa. In other words, they compensate the conscious attitude. One could expect therefore to discover extraverted feelings in an introverted intellectual, and the idea was wittily expressed by just such a type when he said, 'Before dinner I am a Kantian, but after dinner a Nietzschean.' In his habitual attitude, that is to say, he is intellectual, but under the stimulus of a good meal a Diony-sian wave breaks through his conscious attitude.

Just here we meet a great difficulty in the diagnosis of the types. The outside observer sees the manifestations of the conscious attitude, as well as the autonomous phenomena of the uncon-scious, and he will be uncertain as to what he should ascribe to the conscious and what to the unconscious. Under such circumstances the differential diagnosis can only be founded on a careful study of the material. We must try to discover which phenomena proceed from consciously chosen motives and which are spon-taneous; we must also determine which manifestations possess an adapted, and which an unadapted, archaic character.

It will be now sufficiently clear that the qualities of the main conscious function, that is, the qualities of the general conscious attitude, are in strict contrast to the qualities of the unconscious attitude. Expressed in other words, we can say that between the conscious and the unconscious there is normally an opposition. This contrast is not perceived as a conflict, however, so long as the conscious is not too remote from the unconscious attitude. But if the latter should be the case, then the Kantian is unpleasantly surprised by his Dionysian antithesis, since it begins to develop impulses that are highly unsuitable. The conscious attitude then sees itself called upon to suppress the autonomous manifestations of the unconscious, and therewith the conflict is staged. The unconscious, in fact, when once it is brought into active opposition to the conscious simply will not permit itself to be repressed. It is true that the particular manifestations against which the conscious especially directs itself, are not especially difficult to repress, but then the unconscious impulses simply seek other less easily recognizable exits.

When once such indirect safety-valves are opened, the way of the neurosis has already been entered upon. It is indeed possible through analysis to make each of these false ways again accessible to the reason, and thus to submit it to conscious repression, but its determining power is not thereby eradicated; it is merely pushed back further into a corner, unless, together with the understanding of the indirect way taken by the suppression, there comes an equally clear realization of the one-sidedness of the attitude. In other words, along with the understanding of the unconscious impulses there must also come a change of the conscious attitude; because the activation of the unconscious opposition has grown out of this one-sidedness and the recognition of the unconscious impulses is fruitful, only when it can also effect a real compensation of the conscious one-sidedness.

But the transformation of the conscious attitude is no small matter, for the sum total of a general attitude is always more or less of a conscious ideal, sanctified by custom and historical tradition, solidly founded on the rockbottom of innate temperament. The conscious attitude is always in the nature of a philosophy of life, when it is not definitely a religion. It is this fact which makes the problem of the types so important. The opposition between the types is not only an external conflict between men, but also the source of endless inner conflicts; not only the cause of external disagreements and antagonism, but also the inner occasion of nervous illness and psychic disorders. It is this fact also that forces us as physicians to extend the limits of what was originally a purely medico-psychological horizon so as to include within its range not only general psychological viewpoints, but also the problem of a conceptually formulated view of life (*Weltanschauung*).

Within the limits of a lecture, I am unable, of course, to give you any idea of the depth and extent of these problems. I must needs content myself with a rather formal outline of the main facts, and of the general implications of the problems involved. For the fuller elaboration of the problem I must refer you to its detailed presentation in my book *Psychological Types*.

Recapitulating, I would like to stress certain points: Each of the two attitudes introversion and extraversion appears in the individual through a special kind of predominance of one of the four basic functions. Strictly speaking, there are in reality no unqualified extraverts or introverts, but extraverted and introverted function-types, such as thinking types, sensation types, etc. Thus there arise a minimum of eight clearly distinguishable types. Obviously one could increase this number at will if each of the function-types were split into three sub-groups, which, empirically speaking, would be far from impossible. One could, for example, easily divide the intellect into its three well-known forms: first, the intuitive-speculative; second, the logical-mathematical; third, the empirical form which rests chiefly on sense perception. Similar divisions could be carried out with the other functions, as, for instance, in the case of intuition, which has an intellectual as well as a feeling aspect. With such a splitting up into component parts a large number of types could be laid down, each new division becoming increasingly subtle.

For the sake of completeness, I must also observe that the classification of types according to extraversion and introversion is by no means to be regarded as the only possible method. Any other psychological criterion could be equally well employed, although, in my view, no other possesses so great a practical significance.

EXPERIMENTAL APPROACHES TO PSYCHOANALYSIS

The text here reprinted represents an abridgement of the first two of a series of five lectures delivered at the California Institute of Technology. The main omissions are sections on 'The Theory of Dreams' and 'The Production and Cure of Neurotic Disturbances in Animals', and a short summing-up.

Less widely known to the layman, and of less direct relevance to actual techniques of personality assessment, Freud's teaching on the psychosexual stages of development has been very influential, particularly in the field of child psychology. In relation to the adult, fixation at or regression to an earlier stage may be a factor in maladjustment or neurosis. In addition to the references quoted by Hilgard, a very brief and succinct summary was given by Freud himself in the posthumously published *Outline of Psychoanalysis* (1). Munroe (2) gives a full discussion, with critical comment.

Much of the teaching of psychoanalysis seems implausible – even ridiculous – to the lay reader, and, in fact, to many psychologists. The psychoanalyst would say that this rejection is inherent in the very nature of the phenomena with which psychoanalysis largely deals – i.e., material that is the subject of taboo. Nevertheless, it is possible to approach the subject dispassionately, in the context of scientific inquiry, as Professor Hilgard has done.

References
1. Freud, S. *An Outline of Psychoanalysis.* Transl. by James Strachey. London: Hogarth. 1949.
2. Munroe, Ruth L. *Schools of Psychoanalytic Thought.* London: Hutchinson. 1957. Chapter 5.

5 E. R. Hilgard

Experimental Approaches to Psychoanalysis

From *Psychoanalysis as Science*, by Ernest R. Hilgard, Ph.D., Lawrence
S. Kubie, M.D., E. Pumpian-Mindlin, M.D., copyright, © 1952, by
California Institute of Technology, Basic Books Inc., Publishers.

[. . . .]

I. Psychodynamics

In these two lectures, I am to deal with efforts to test some of the
teachings of psychoanalysis, and not with an appraisal of the
results of full-fledged psychoanalytic treatment. This obviously
has its limitations, for the complete story of psychoanalysis can
be told only in the reconstruction of individual biographies, pain-
stakingly (and somewhat painfully) revealed in hour after hour on
the psychoanalytic couch. Much that I report may seem trivial
compared with the richness of such individual biographies, but it
is always one of the tasks of science to make its problems bite-
size, so that they can be worked upon with the instruments that
the scientist has at his disposal. In this lecture I propose to discuss
what have come to be called 'psychodynamics', that is, some of
the principles of development, motivation, and conduct that are
part of the fabric of psychoanalytic theory. In the second lecture I
shall discuss principles of psychotherapy — not the appraisal of
full-scale analysis, but the conjectures about the turning points in
a patient's progress that can be selected for separate study.

The Consequences of Infantile Frustration

The importance of early childhood is one of the most familiar
teachings of psychoanalysis. We hear a great deal about sucking
and toilet-training as important background factors in the formation of later personality or character structure. These early
experiences of the child are said to result in a secure individual,
provided the needs they represent are appropriately gratified.
Such a child will take the hurdles of growing up in stride. If,
however, the needs are met in such a way as to induce frustration,
the consequent insecurity and anxiety will hound the individual
throughout his life.

Here, then, are some generalizations that can be restated more
precisely and subjected to investigation. I shall delve into the
growing literature only at one or two points, in order to show what
is involved in trying to experiment in these fields.

The Need to Suck, and Consequences of its Frustration

One generalization that takes shape is that the infant has a *need to suck*, as well as to receive nourishment. If this is true, it may be inferred that if the infant is fed too rapidly it will have to fulfill its quota of sucking by sucking its thumb, or the bedclothes, or some convenient nipple substitute.

David Levy studied this problem by selecting a litter of six puppies, and dividing them into three pairs (20). One pair remained at the mother's breast. The two other pairs were fed by bottle. The 'long-feeders' had a small hole in the bottle's nipple, and after feeding sucked as long as they wished on a nipple-covered finger. The 'short-feeders' received their milk through a large-holed bottle and did not have the nipple-covered finger to suck upon. The results agreed in general with the theory. That is, the short-feeders as compared with the long-feeders did much more sucking between meals on each others' bodies, on rubber balls, and other objects, and were more responsive to sucking tests with the experimenter's finger between meals. The breast-fed dogs did the least body- and finger-sucking. These results with dogs were in line with results Levy had earlier reported for human infants (21). More recently, a group of workers including pediatricians and psychologists have studied the consequences of feeding human infants from a cup, beginning at birth. Only preliminary reports are available, but the suggestion comes out that the need to suck may be an acquired one (5). For infants who have not learned to suck it appears that not to suck is not frustrating. If these results are confirmed, the generalizations about the need to suck will have to be somewhat modified. It might then be stated that the sucking experience is one in which a need to suck may be learned, and, when the need has been acquired, unless appropriately gratified, it may produce the behavior characteristic of frustration. Perhaps this points out what I mean when I say that the final generalization need not be the original psychoanalytic one in order for psychoanalysis to have been of service. It is useful if it provides a first approximation to the generalization, and thus defines the field of inquiry.

In addition to the immediate consequences of frustration, resulting, in the case of frustrated sucking, in such substitutive behavior as thumb-sucking, the theory goes on to assume that there are more remote consequences. Even though there is a period that is symptom-free, perhaps when a new crisis develops, say at adolescence, the consequences of infantile insecurity may again manifest themselves.

Hoarding as a Consequence of Infantile Frustration

We may try to state a more precise theorem about this. If through frustration in infancy food has been the occasion for anxiety, there will be a tendency to overanxiety about food in adulthood, manifested, for example, in a tendency to hoard excessive amounts of food. This is perhaps illustrated by the American housewife who felt so threatened by the shortages during the war. According to this theory, her anxiety would be explained by feeding difficulties associated with the child-rearing practices of the last generation.

An experiment was performed with that favorite animal of the psychological laboratory – the white rat (16). Litter mates provided control groups. One group of young rats was fed consistently, after weaning always having enough food and water present to satisfy hunger and thirst. The second group suffered feeding frustration and deprivation through irregular feeding. While fed enough to maintain growth, there was great inconsistency in feeding, so that the animals were occasionally without food for long stretches. It is presumed that we here have an analogue of infantile frustration. After this differential treatment, the groups were again fed alike for some weeks and appeared to behave alike. The test of the remote consequences of infantile frustration came when, in late adolescence or early maturity, both groups of rats were subjected to irregular feeding, the one group for the first time, the other reinstating a childhood experience. Following this period of frustration, both groups were tested in an apparatus permitting food hoarding. An alleyway from the living cage led to a food supply at its end. The rats that had been frustrated in infancy hoarded over twice as many food pellets as the rats that in infancy had developed a secure feeling about food. The experiment has since been repeated several times with modifications. The later results are, in general, consonant with the earlier ones (23).

We are primarily interested in man, and when we make use of studies with animals we are seeking to exhibit in comparative fashion some of the principles believed to apply to human behavior. In the end, however, it will always be necessary to validate the principles through observations of man himself. The principle that early food frustration may lead to later hoarding behavior, as shown in the animal studies, has been interpreted as applying to some primitive human societies. Some of the observations have been summarized as follows by Hunt (16).

Tribes using relatively similar practices in nursing, weaning, toilet training, etc., appear to have similar typical personalities even though the geographical circumstances in which they live might appear to dictate different types of personalities. The Arapesh of New Guinea are generous, co-operative, and peaceful, in spite of the fact that they live on unfertile mountainous land and seldom have ample food. The Pitchentera of Central Australia are generous, often fatally optimistic, and do not hoard food, even though they live in a land of frequent famine. From the anthropological reports, it appears that both of these tribes are accustomed to provide infants with frequent and affectionate nursing. Crying is answered with immediate suckling. Weaning is late; and, among the Pitchentera at least, little attention is paid to toilet habits, and children are not expected to be clean. On the other hand, the Normanby Islanders, although they live where food is abundant, are dominated by a desire to collect large stores of food. They are competitive, and frequently quarrelsome. Their children, however, are nursed briefly, and without affection. The Mundugumor, a people of the same race as the Arapesh, who live on the fertile lowlands of New Guinea, are arrogant, aggressive, impatient, and quarrelsome in the extreme. These Mundugumor nurse their children standing up for very brief periods, treat crying with slaps, and not infrequently permit their children to die from neglect.

Interesting as such parallel histories of development are, two important precautions need to be stated. First, there are many cultures in which the relationship between infant handling and adult behavior does not conform at all neatly to the hypothesis (24). Second, children are influenced throughout life by the adults with whom they live, so that adult behavior cannot be attributed solely to training in infancy. Children who grow up in a friendly culture (or in a quarrelsome one) continue to learn what is expected of them as they grow up. It would be instructive to see what would happen to an Arapesh child adopted into a Mundugumor household beyond the age of infancy. Would the child grow up aggressive like the Mundugumor or peace loving like the Arapesh? His adult personality would provide a better test of the influence of the early years than it would were he to grow up among the same people who provided his environment in infancy.

Our own society shows reflections of food anxiety, typified by the hoarding behavior during the war, or by the carrying over of home-canned fruit from one season to the next by a thrifty housewife. If our infant handling is now becoming more permissive and less frustrating to the child, we would have to predict, according to the hypothesis under discussion, that the next generation would be less threatened were it again necessary to institute rationing of food.

Defense Mechanisms

Let us turn now to defense mechanisms. The defense mechanisms were those features of psychoanalytic theory first domesticated by academic psychology, so that now every student of elementary psychology knows about rationalization and projection and compensation and sublimation. How long a list of mechanisms he knows depends upon who his teacher is and which textbook he reads. He may know a great many of them, however, without knowing anything about their origin in psychoanalytic theory.

The specific mechanisms lend themselves readily to experimental study. The studies have been ably reviewed by Sears (27) and the mechanisms given extended treatment in recent books by Symonds (30). These treatments are by academic psychologists. Among the psychoanalytic discussions, that by Anna Freud (9), *The Ego and the Mechanisms of Defense*, is perhaps the best single source. I shall characterize a few studies briefly, chiefly to give an over-all picture of the kind of thing being done in the laboratory.

1. *Repression.* There is abundant clinical evidence for repression as a mechanism of defense. Perhaps the most convincing evidence to the outsider is that from amnesia, when a person loses his personal memories, often to recover them later without relearning. Amnesias show that memories may be unavailable even though they are not really lost.

Experimental studies of repression have been directed very largely to one problem: the selective forgetting of the unpleasant as compared with the pleasant. Most of these studies have made the mistake of confusing the pleasantness or unpleasantness of *subject matter* with the pleasantness or unpleasantness of *recalling* it. In a list of words containing the words quinine and sugar, for example, the mere fact that quinine is bitter and sugar sweet has little relevance to Freud's theory. Yet many experiments have been done to determine whether the word quinine would be forgotten more readily than the word sugar. More sophisticated experiments seek to find items out of the personal biography that arouse anxiety when they are recalled. It is such items that should undergo repression, according to the theory.

Despite the crudity of the experiments, nearly all of them have shown that pleasant items or experiences are more readily recalled than unpleasant ones, and that memories that reduce self-esteem are recalled with greater difficulty than those that enhance self-esteem. Thus the experimental results in general agree with psychoanalytic theory, though few of the experiments have been very helpful in moving us forward in our understanding of the phenomena. In the next lecture I shall describe one somewhat more satisfactory experiment in which repression is produced and then relieved. The study of repression remains a promising field of experimentation.

2. *Projection.* One form of the mechanism of projection is that of attributing to others unpleasant traits in ourselves that we would prefer to deny. Sears (28) had a group of college fraternity men rate each other on several traits. By comparing self-ratings with the ratings of others, projection could be ascertained. Those who lacked insight into their own traits, for such an undesirable trait as stinginess, tended to assign higher stinginess scores to other students than those students assigned to each other. This accords with the theory of seeing our weaknesses in others. Frenkel-Brunswik (8) in a somewhat related study found a tendency to convert our own traits to the opposite; that is, a subject might say, 'Above all else, I am kind', when others are likely to rate him as unkind.

3. *Regression.* The tendency, under frustrating circumstances, to return to an earlier or more primitive mode of behavior is known as regression. The question arises whether or not this is an actual age regression, that is, a return to one's own earlier years, or merely a primitivization, that is, a turning to less mature ways of responding, though not necessarily ways closely related to his own personal biography. An adult, in anger, might engage in a fist fight even though he had not engaged in such fights as a child. That would be primitivization without age regression.

Following frustration, children often act like children a year or two younger than they, whether judged by the kind of play they engage in or by their scores on intelligence tests. Results such as these are best interpreted as primitivization.

In one such experiment (3) children of kindergarten age were permitted to play first in a room of part-toys. They filled in the gaps imaginatively, drawing tracks for the train to run on, or using paper as the water in which to sail a boat. Then they were shown into a larger playroom, where richer material could be found. There was a real track for the train, a real pond for the boat. The frustrating experience was provided by withdrawing the child from the larger room to the original one, though the larger one now remained visible through a wire screen. Under these circumstances the constructiveness of play deteriorated. Drawings became scribbles. Toys previously acceptable now were rejected, sometimes thrown or jumped on. Quantitative treatment of the observations showed that the children who experienced frustration acted, on the average, more than a year younger after the frustration than before.

In another experiment (19) a prize was offered to the child who succeeded in solving a problem that looked easy but was actually baffling. The problem was to remove a ball from a wastebasket that was out of reach. Few properties were provided. A toy dog on a leash had to be used as a tool to bounce the ball out of the basket. Even when the appropriate method was chosen, the success was partly a matter of good fortune. Half the boys who participated in the experiment left gleefully with their prizes, half left disappointed. The boys were tested with intelligence test items from the Stanford-Binet both before and after the experimental success or failure. Those who experienced failure showed a significant drop in tested mental age following the frustrating episode.

The regression in both of these experiments suggests behavior of younger children, but not necessarily behavior dating back to an earlier period in the individual biography of the frustrated child.

There have been a number of experiments on regression under hypnosis in which the individual is told to act as he did at a given age. Here the second conception of regression, as a real return to early life, is under investigation. True (32) used as the test of the success of true age regression the ability to recall the day of the week on which the child's birthday occurred at ages ten, seven, and four. In the waking state, the subjects are quite unable to recall childhood birthdays, but under hypnotic regression the reported success is remarkable. Of fifty subjects aged twenty to twenty-four, forty-one were able to give entirely accurate statements of their birthdays and the day of the week on which Christmas fell for the three years in which they were four, seven, and ten years old. The hypnotist, of course, is able to check the calendar to verify the true birthday and Christmas Day.

Hypnosis is a very promising method for the study of psychodynamics, but its results have to be interpreted with extreme caution. This is not a matter of questioning the reality of hypnosis, for the phenomena are now quite generally accepted by psychologists. The problems are those of experimental control. Hypnotic subjects are unusually cooperative, and they may even practice outside the laboratory what they expect the hypnotist to demand of them. One striking case was provided by a subject who showed monocular blindness under hypnotic suggestion. The usual methods of showing the presence of vision in the blind eye by the use of misleading lens systems failed to break through the monocular blindness. The experimenter was even able to plot the blind spot of the seeing eye while both eyes were open, a feat quite impossible for those who see normally with both eyes. Only the persistent skepticism of the experimenter led finally, under deep hypnosis, to the patient's admission that she had practised plotting her blind spot at home so that she knew its outline and could simulate one-eyed plotting while both eyes were open. Her monocular blindness, that stood up test after test, was an unconscious expression of her desire to do what the experimenter wanted her to do (25).

In experiments on hypnosis it is always necessary to select those subjects who are hypnotizable, and then they are usually brought back for successive sessions. Because there is incomplete control of what goes on between sessions, every precaution has to be taken lest the subjects' cooperation be mistaken for unusual ability under hypnosis. With proper precautions, hypnosis offers an unusually favorable method for the study of the mechanisms, of which regression is but one.

4. *Aggression.* In the foregoing discussion, illustrations have been given of approaches to repression, projection, and regression. One final illustration will suffice to complete these examples of avenues of approach to the study of the mechanisms. This final line of investigation is that concerned with aggression as a consequence of frustration. The hypothesis that aggression is a typical consequence of frustration was brought strongly to psychologists' attention by a book from the Yale Institute of Human Relations entitled *Frustration and Aggression* (6). In this, many instances were collected from the laboratory and from social and political behavior, giving support to the hypothesis.

The problems of *displaced* aggression are particularly pertinent because they illustrate the nature of the irrational derivatives of our impulses. When it is impossible to locate the source of frustration, or when the source is not vulnerable to our attack, then aggression is directed to some convenient substitute, some innocent bystander, some scapegoat. This is known as displaced aggression. Some of the studies from the University of California at Berkeley have been pointing out the extent to which anti-Semitism among college students represents such displaced hostility (2).

As a laboratory illustration of the mechanism of displacement I wish to call attention to some experiments by Neal Miller (22) with white rats. Rats were taught to fight each other in order to obtain release from electric shock. Two rats were placed in a small compartment with a floor consisting of a grid that could be electrified. The current was turned off if they struck each other. By the ordinary methods of trial and error they soon learned this, and so began to strike each other when placed in the compartment.

A rubber doll standing in the corner of the apparatus – the innocent bystander – was ignored so long as the other rat (the direct object of learned aggression) was present. When a rat found himself alone in the apparatus, however, and the mounting current began to make him uneasy, he turned his attack upon the available scapegoat – the rubber doll. Miller goes on in the experiment to determine the nature of the object towards which aggression is likely to be displaced. Thus his experiment goes beyond a mere demonstration of displaced aggression to some clarification of its operation. The purpose of experimentation is to extend knowledge, not merely to illustrate what we already know. [. . . .]

Psychosexual Development

Inherent in the importance attributed by psychoanalysis to early childhood is the notion of the continuity of development. Let me illustrate. We have already seen how frustrated sucking may give rise to thumb-sucking. Perhaps thumb-sucking may later turn into cigarette smoking. Some smokers may be classified as suckers, some as biters. Pipe smokers are more apt to be biters, although they may be either suckers or biters. The point is that what smoking means to the individual could be traced back, if we were able to untangle the threads, to something beginning in infancy.

This general principle of continuity has, however, some more universal characteristics attributed to it, so that all individuals are said to progress through several stages in the course of normal development. There may be arrested development at one or another of these stages, in which case we find some sort of personality distortion. The classical formulation of the stages of psychosexual or libidinal development is that of Abraham (1). The six stages are, in order: (1) Early oral (sucking) stage, (2) late oral-sadistic (cannibalistic) stage, (3) early anal-sadistic stage, (4) late anal-sadistic stage, (5) early genital (phallic) stage, and (6) final genital stage. Corresponding to each of these stages there are corresponding developments of object love, and the various types of neurotic or psychotic disease are said to be related to dominant points of fixation when the normal transition from one stage to the next has failed to occur.

An experimental approach to this theory is a large order. I am going to refer to three experiments, merely to point out that we are not completely helpless when it comes to trying to get data that are relevant.

The Anal Character

One kind of personality syndrome recognized by Freud (10) was the so-called anal character. This term characterizes the individual who carries into adult life some of the problems of anal stages earlier referred to. The traits that are said to represent such a character are those of *stinginess*, *obstinacy*, and *orderliness*. A remote, but nevertheless legitimate, test of the theory is provided by a determination whether or not these three traits do, in fact, go together as a cluster. Such a test was made by Sears (28) as part of the experiment cited earlier. Ratings were made of each other by thirty-seven men living together in college fraternities. Ratings were made on a seven-point scale, so that it was possible to obtain an average rating for each of the men on each of the traits of stinginess, obstinacy, and orderliness. The reliabilities of the pooled ratings were found to be statistically satisfactory by correlating the ratings made by half of the raters with those made by the other half, the reliabilities being represented by coefficients of correlation of ·85 for stinginess, ·93 for obstinacy, and ·96 for orderliness. What this means is that there was substantial agreement by the raters as to the position of each of the men on each of the traits. Now the test of the theory comes in finding a correspondence among the traits. The correlations between the pairs of traits were found to be as follows:

Stinginess and orderliness	+ ·39
Stinginess and obstinacy	+ ·37
Obstinacy and orderliness	+ ·36

The correlations, while low, are all positive and in the expected direction. The results are all the more convincing when it is pointed out that orderliness is considered a desirable trait and stinginess and obstinacy undesirable traits. This was demonstrated within the experiment by a popularity rating. Popularity correlated *negatively* with stinginess and obstinacy, but slightly *positively* with orderliness. Despite this attenuating factor in ratings, the three traits hang together. As Sears has pointed out, the mere fact of this trait cluster would not necessarily make it dependent upon anal eroticism, although earlier data by Hamilton (15) make it plausible that there is such a connexion. Out of a group of a hundred married men and women, Hamilton found that thirty-five men and twenty-four women recalled some form of anal eroticism in childhood. These men and women, as adults, showed a higher frequency of reported stinginess or extravagance than the non-anal ones, showed more frequently reported fetishism, more concern for clothes, more sadism and masochism. These differences are all in line with the theory of the anal character.

The Oral Character

In the discussion of the need to suck, it was suggested that adult personality might be influenced by food frustration in infancy. Such frustration is a result not only of the prevailing practices within a culture but of the specific handling of the individual child. It has been conjectured that there is an oral character, which, like the anal character, reflects residues from early experiences. A test of the oral character, somewhat along the lines of Scars's test of the anal character, has been made by Goldman (14). On the basis of self-ratings of one hundred and fifteen young adults, she selected twenty extreme cases representing the orally satisfied and orally unsatisfied. The trait clusters of these extreme groups corresponded roughly to the theoretical expectations from the theory of oral character formation. [. . . .]

The Blacky Test

The third experiment bearing upon the theory of libidinal stages provides another illustration as to how we may find ways of putting psychoanalytic conjectures to a test. I refer to a monograph by Blum (4), entitled 'A Study of the Psychoanalytic Theory of Psychosexual Development'. This was a Ph.D. dissertation in clinical psychology done at Stanford.

The task that Blum set himself was to find an experiment conceived within the framework of psychoanalytic theory, and yet designed so that it would not bias the results in such a manner as to enforce confirmation of the theory. He hit upon a projective test, whereby, through processes of thinly veiled identification, adult individuals might reveal their own psychosexual histories as represented in their present attitudes.

The test consists of twelve cartoon drawings or caricatures depicting the adventures of a dog named Blacky. The cast of characters includes Blacky, Mama, Papa, and Tippy (a sibling figure of unspecified age and sex). The first cartoon introduces the characters, and the rest portray either stages in libidinal development or object relationships characteristic of the stages. When the test is presented to a male, Blacky is described as the 'son'; when

101

presented to a female, Blacky is described as the 'daughter'. The author of the test defends his choice of dog characters because of the greater freedom of personal expression as contrasted with human figures which would be 'too close to home'. He points out that the canine medium, thanks to Walt Disney cartoons and comic strips, still preserves sufficient reality so that subjects can identify themselves quite fully with the cartoon figures and project their innermost feelings.

The rather playful way in which Blacky's problems are depicted can be told best by describing a few of the pictures.

After the introductory cartoon that gives the cast of characters, the next is designed to exhibit oral eroticism. Blacky, who is almost too big, is shown nursing his (or her) mother.

Here is a response to this picture that would be scored as showing strong oral eroticism in the adult subject whose statement this is:

Blacky has just discovered the delightful nectar that Mama can supply – it is an endless supply and she is enjoying it. She doesn't know where it is coming from, but she doesn't care. Mama is pacific throughout it all – she doesn't particularly like this business of supplying milk, but she is resigned to it. It is a pretty day and they are both calm and happy.

A later cartoon depicts the problem of castration anxiety in males and penis envy in females by displacing the problem to that of the sibling Tippy standing blindfolded before a chopping block, with a knife threatening his (or her) tail. Blacky is shown watching this threatening attack on his sibling's tail.

That the intended effect is produced in the responses of at least some of the subjects is shown in this spontaneous account by one of the young women given the test.

Blacky's curiosity has been aroused about the opposite sex and she decides to look closely at Tippy's sex organs when he is not aware that she is looking at him. Tippy's tail is going to be cut off and Blacky watches interestedly.

In this particular case, the subject went back and revised the story, striking out the material on the curiosity about sex organs. The full story is, of course, more revealing than the expurgated version, that now became simply: 'Tippy's tail is going to be cut off and Blacky watches interestedly.'

The cartoon showing positive identification is of Blacky making an assertive gesture towards a toy dog. Here is a representative protocol:

'Now listen you, you little pooch, when I bark, you jump, do you get that?' Blacky feels very superior to this little dog. He is making believe that he is the boss, or maybe pretending to be his father talking to him in a superior tone.

Although in clinical practice the test is administered individually, a group form worked satisfactorily for experimental purposes. The subjects were given the following instructions:

What we have here is a bunch of cartoons, like you see in the funny papers, except that there are no words. We'll show them to you one cartoon at a time and the idea is for you to make up a little story about each one – just tell what is happening in the picture, why it's happening, and so on. Since this is a sort of test of how good your imagination can be, try to write vividly about how the characters feel. You will have two minutes for each story, which means about one or two paragraphs on each cartoon. It is desirable to write as much as possible within the time limit.

Following the spontaneous account, the subject was asked a few questions, chiefly of the multiple-choice type. Because in a projective test of this sort, it is possible to go off in several directions, the fixed-alternative questions assure that each subject gives some replies in a common context. This corrupts the replies to some extent through restricting spontaneity, but makes the statistical handling of the data much easier. It is an inevitable paradox of quantitative methods in science that some of the richness of the original experience has to be lost in order to improve the precision of the findings.

Before turning to some of the data obtained through the use of the Blacky test, we may well ask to what extent we are here dealing with a scientific experiment. If all we come out with are some data illustrative of psychoanalytic ways of thinking, that is not enough. Other criteria of science must be met. Let me suggest two ways in which this investigation justifies its classification as an experiment.

1. One feature of an experiment is that observations are made under conditions specified by the experimenter and, to some extent, controlled by him. In this experiment those to participate were selected from a general college population, so that the results are applicable to such a population, and not merely to those who for whatever reason seek psychoanalytic treatment. Furthermore, their responses were obtained under the standard conditions of the Blacky test. The element of control is present.

2. A second feature of an experiment is that there is in it some design, so that the data obtained can be made to bear crucially

upon some hypothesis. Such design involves both theory about the events under study and an understanding of the logic of proof. The theory about the events under study in this experiment is classical psychoanalytic theory, especially as developed by Abraham (1) and later by Fenichel (7). The logic of proof in this case requires a little further discussion.

Because the projective test was designed to draw out information based on the theory of libidinal stages, it introduced a bias in favor of finding such stages. Thus the evidence from the study is not much good for showing that adults sometimes talk about the satisfactions of the nursing experience, or that they talk about mutilation threats, or that they identify with parents. The pictures themselves give such strong suggestions that the data are corrupted by the theory. I am not here denying the validity of the experiment. I merely point out that we have to be careful about noting what it *can* and what it *cannot* prove. These limitations are present in all experiments. I may point out, as an aside, that these limitations are much more difficult to surmount when clinical case studies are interpreted. In the Blacky test we know the extent of the suggestions given by the pictures; in the psychoanalytic interview we seldom know the extent of the suggestions given by the analyst's interpretations.

The design of the experiment allowed for independent study of two sets of hypotheses arising from the theory of libidinal development. That is, evidence bearing upon these hypotheses was not biased by the experimental arrangements; evidence could either agree with or refute the predictions from the hypotheses.

We may turn now to some of the data. The first hypothesis to be tested has to do with the differences in libidinal development of men and of women. The matter is too complex to go into here in any detail, but the main point is that boys and girls are said to differ in the ways in which they progress through the stages of libidinal development, and in the residues that remain from each of the stages as they grow older. As one illustration, Fenichel says that, in normal development, the relationship of women to their mothers is more frequently ambivalent than is that of most men to their fathers (7). This assertion can be tested within the Blacky test by studying the identification of men and women with parental figures. If the assertion is correct, the ambivalence represented in women's replies to the cards should exceed that represented by men's replies to the cards. The usual statistical tests can be applied to ascertain whether or not the differences found are in excess of differences that might arise by chance.

Behind the ambivalence toward the mother is said to lie disappointment in the mother because of experiences associated with weaning, toilet-training, and the birth of siblings, as well as the disappointment over the lack of a penis, for which the mother is held responsible. Freud links the girl's hostility directly to oral frustration (11):

The [girl's] complaint against the mother that harks back furthest is that she has given the child too little milk, which is taken as indicating lack of love.

One of the pictures of the Blacky test that tests oral sadism, a consequence of oral frustration, is that in which Blacky is shown chewing Mama's collar.

One of the questions asked following the spontaneous account of this picture was as follows:

What will Blacky do next with Mama's collar?
1. Get tired of it and leave it on the ground.
2. Return it to Mama.
3. Angrily chew it to shreds.

Confronted with these alternatives, more females than males chose the sadistic alternative (Angrily chew it to shreds). This finding is then in agreement with the theoretical expectation that more females than males will retain oral-sadistic tendencies.

Perhaps this is enough to show how the test is used in the study of sex differences. Even though the dog chewing Mama's collar strongly suggests oral sadism, there is no bias in favor of more replies in the sadistic direction by women than by men. The presence of oral sadism is suggested, but its *relative intensity* in men and in women is a matter of *data*. Following this general pattern of analysis, it was found possible to select from theoretical sources seven areas in which specific sex differences ought to be found. For two additional areas, reasonably good conjectures could be made as to what psychoanalytic theory would predict.

A number of additional areas could have been studied with the aid of the test, but psychoanalytic theory is itself too unclear in the treatment of sex differences for any firm predictions to be stated and then tested. Of the nine areas in which conjectures could be made, results from the test were consonant with the theory in eight. That is, in each of these eight areas replies by men differed from replies by women in a statistically satisfactory manner in the direction predicted from theory.

The one area of disagreement is a matter of some interest. The superego figure, represented as a personified conscience in the Blacky test, is more often seen as a mother figure by the women, and as a father figure by the men. According to Fenichel, the male superego should have been decisive for both sexes. The author of the monograph under discussion says that this departure from Fenichel's stated opinion may very possibly be a reflection of the increasing influence of the mother in American life, in contrast to the patriarchal European society in which psychoanalysis grew up. On the whole, the agreement between the test results and the theory is rather striking. A score of eight hits out of nine tries is a very good one.

The second set of hypotheses put to test in this experiment was concerned with the interrelationships between stages of development. Thus those who show developmental disturbances at one level should show them at others. Such interrelationships can be demonstrated by correlation coefficients. For example, Fenichel says: 'Guilt feeling not only has an oral character in general but an oral-sadistic character in particular'. We can infer, then, that there will be some correspondence between *oral-sadistic* responses to the dog chewing the collar and recognized *guilt feelings* in relation to the superego figure of the later cartoon. The inference can be tested by correlating the scores of the responses to the two pictures.

How successful was the test in detecting interrelationships predicted by the theory? Fourteen significant correlations were obtained related to intercorrelational statements or inferences from the writings of Freud and Fenichel. In *every case* these correlations were in the direction predicted from theory; that is, they showed significant positive correspondence when the theory demanded that, and significant negative relationship when the theory demanded that.

The real productiveness of an experimental approach of this kind rests not only in its support (or refutation) of previously stated psychoanalytic principles, but in its discovery of correlations not anticipated by earlier theory. Because it was Blum's purpose to test classical theory, he did not elaborate the additional possibilities within his data. Those possibilities exist, however, so that contribution in line with the fundamental purpose of science, to discover new truth, is not excluded.

I have devoted so much time to this one experiment because I believe it illustrates the possibility of experimentation closely related to psychoanalytic concepts kept in their context. In some respects it is more satisfactory than the earlier experiments with animals and human subjects that isolate one generalization at a time. The experiment has a number of difficulties inherent in such experimentation, difficulties that its author is the first to acknowledge. One source of awkwardness so far as interpretation is concerned is the large number of nonsignificant correlations that were discarded. For the purposes of preliminary experimentation, the author used as tests of theory only correlations that were significantly negative or significantly positive. A tighter experiment has to interpret its nonsignificant correlations as well as its significant ones. Let us not rush off, then, believing that this experiment has proved the psychoanalytic theory of libidinal development beyond all doubt. I believe that it has demonstrated the plausibility of many relationships stressed by classical psychoanalysts. It has not, of course, shown how these relationships are caused, and it has nothing to say about the relative influences of biology and of culture. Hence many of the controversies among contemporary psychoanalysts cannot be resolved by an appeal to these data. At the same time, the 'caustic critic' of psychoanalysis is here confronted by many correspondences between data and theory, which at least invite his inspection.

Experimental Psychodynamics

We have made a fairly hasty acquaintance with what is by now a substantial literature in a field that may be described as experimental psychodynamics. I prefer to call it that rather than experimental psychoanalysis because it is not necessary to confine the experiments to the confirmation or disproof of psychoanalytic concepts. The basic problem is to make good science in the field opened up by psychoanalysis.

The possiblities before us are numerous. I wish, by way of summary, to call attention to a few of them.

I wish to note first of all that the experiments reported in this lecture were all concerned with normal individuals, whether animals, children, or adults. It is not necessary to confine the study of psychoanalytic concepts to the neurotic people who present themselves for treatment. Freud, of course, set the stage for the study of normal people in his observations on the psychopathology of everyday life (12).

A second observation is that all of the studies reported were carried out without the use of the psychoanalytic method, as defined by what goes on within psychoanalytic therapy. Of the methods used, two, however, are analogous to psychoanalysis.

One of these is hypnosis. While hypnosis was rejected as a method by Freud early in his career, the state of *rapport* in hypnosis has affiliations with *transference* in psychoanalysis. A sophisticated use of hypnosis is likely to prove one of the most revealing methods for testing psychoanalytic principles. The second method is that of the projective test, illustrated by the Blacky experiment. The associations with such pictures have much in common with free associations within the analytic hour. The relationships established within short experimental periods may be superficial, but their careful study may tell us a good deal about the more penetrating consequences of a long-continued psychoanalysis. [....]

II. Psychotherapy

I do not intend to enter here into the professional problems of conducting a psychoanalysis, or into controversy as to just where psychotherapy ends and psychoanalysis begins. I am using the word psychotherapy as a classificatory word for the process of achieving changes in emotional adjustment by psychological means. I am interested in what we have found out, and what we can find out, about how the changes in the patient take place, so that these changes, and the control of them, may become part of established psychological science.

The general conduct of a psychoanalysis has become familiar to the public through the motion picture, through cartoons in the weekly magazines, and even in the comic strip of the daily newspaper, with the usual distortions that these media produce. Let me describe what psychoanalysis is actually like. The analyst usually begins by getting something of the personal biography of the patient, after the manner of a social worker's case history. The patient sits up and talks as he would to any physician. The analyst may have better interviewing methods, but there is little that is distinctive about the early sessions. There may be several sessions before the patient takes to the couch, before the typical free association method is used. Then the patient is taught to follow, as well as he is able, *the basic rule:* to say everything that enters his mind, without selection. This is much harder than it sounds, even for patients who are eager to cooperate with the analyst. As Fenichel puts it, 'Even the patient who tries to adhere to the basic rule fails to tell many things because he considers them too unimportant, too stupid, too indiscreet, and so on. There are many who never learn to apply the basic rule because their fear of losing control is too great, and before they can give expression to anything they must examine it to see exactly what it is' (7). In fact, the whole lifetime has been spent learning to be tactful, to achieve self-control, to avoid outbursts of emotion, to do what is proper rather than what is impulsive. This all has to be unlearned for successful free association.

What free association aims at is the bringing to awareness of impulses and thoughts of which the person is not aware. Because these impulses are active, but out of awareness, they are called unconscious. It is necessary to break through resistances in order to bring them to awareness. The role of the psychoanalyst is, essentially, to help the patient break down these resistances, so that he may face his disguised motives and hidden thoughts frankly, and then come to grips in realistic manner with whatever problems or conflicts are then brought into view.

The activity of the analyst is directed skillfully at this task of helping the patient eliminate resistances. He does this in part by pointing out to the patient the consequences of his resistances: the times of silence when his mind seems to go blank, forgetting what he intended to say, perhaps forgetting to show up at an appointment, drifting into superficial associations, or giving glib interpretations of his own. The analyst not only calls attention to signs of resistance, but he also interprets the patient's associations in such a way as to facilitate further associations.

Fenichel defines interpretation as 'helping something unconscious to become conscious by naming it at the moment it is striving to break through'. If this is accepted, then the first interpretations are necessarily fairly 'shallow' ones, the 'deeper' interpretations waiting until the patient is ready for them.

The deeper interpretations are the ones we often think of in characterizing psychoanalysis, but very much of the time in an actual psychoanalysis is spent in rather matter-of-fact discussion of attitudes toward other people and toward oneself as they show themselves in daily life, without recourse to universal symbols, references to libidinal stages, and so on. Not all psychoanalysts agree on just how interpretations should be made, or when they should be made, and it is my guess that those who think they do agree may actually behave quite differently when conducting analyses of their patients. This is one reason why it is difficult to study psychoanalytic therapy, and a reason, also, why there are so many schisms within psychoanalytic societies.

Another aspect of the psychoanalytic therapy goes by the name of 'transference'. Transference refers to the tendency for the patient to make of the analyst an object of his motivational or emotional attachments. It is too simple to say that the patient

109

falls in love with the analyst. Sometimes he makes of the analyst a loved parent, sometimes a hated parent; sometimes the analyst substitutes for a brother or sister, or for the boss at the office. The patient unconsciously assigns roles to the analyst of the important people in the patient's own life. Part of the task of the analyst is to handle the transference. The word 'handle' is easily spoken, but this handling of the transference is said to be the most difficult part of the analyst's art.

The psychoanalytic interview is a social one, an interpersonal one, with two people involved. The analyst is a person, too, and he reacts to the adoration and abuse of the patient he is analyzing. He is a good analyst to the extent that he understands himself well enough so that he preserves his role in the analytic situation, and does not himself become involved, as his patient is, in what is called countertransference, that is, using the patient as an outlet for his own emotions. If the patient's exploits become the occasion for the analyst's fantasy life, then the analyst gets preoccupied with his own free associations and cannot listen attentively to his patient. The discipline of learning to listen, and only to listen, is considered by Frieda Fromm-Reichmann (13) to be the essence of the analyst's problem.

I have gone this much into detail here because the public does not always understand why psychoanalysts insist that they must themselves be analyzed. The reason is that they could not otherwise handle the problems of transference with the kind of detachment that is necessary if the patient is to be helped. The reason is not that they must have a laying on of hands or special indoctrination in order to transmit the faith held by their therapist. If it works that way, as it occasionally does, then the training analysis has been unsuccessful in achieving its aim (as it undoubtedly is in some instances). To make the blanket charge that psychoanalysis is unscientific because the method requires that the analyst himself be analyzed is unwarranted, although this charge is commonly made. There is a danger that analysts become too doctrinaire. If you ask an analyst about his theoretical position, he may reply by telling you under whom he had his analysis. There are parallels in other sciences as well. A biologist's or a physicist's work often reflects the master under whom the scientist studied. There is need for caution in both instances. To cite but one example from the field of physiology: the word 'inhibition' suggests an entirely different set of pheneomena to those who studied under Sherrington from what it suggests to those who studied under Pavlov. Because there is danger of indoctrination does not mean that there are not ways of avoiding that danger. For example, psychoanalysts profit greatly from doing control analyses under more than one training analyst, representing somewhat divergent viewpoints. Postdoctoral fellows in the natural sciences often prefer to work in laboratories at a different place from the one in which they received their training, in order to break their provincialism. It may be that a personal analysis is as essential to conducting a psychoanalysis as learning calculus is to becoming an engineer. The problem then becomes how to achieve the gains and avoid the pitfalls.

Very often there is within the midst of psychoanalysis a state in which the patient is more disturbed than he was before entering treatment. Those unfriendly to psychoanalysis occasionally use this as an indication of its therapeutic ineffectiveness (18). Two comments can be made here. First, what appears to others to be disturbance may not be 'neurotic' at all. Some individuals are excessively kind to other people, at great cost to themselves. If they suddenly express their feelings more openly, they may become less pleasant to live with or to work with, because they can no longer be exploited. The troublesome child may be a healthier child than the child who is too 'good'. If a person changes, new social adjustments are required, and some that were in equilibrium now get out of focus. This is the first observation regarding apparent disturbance in the midst of analysis. The second comment is that the disturbance in the midst of analysis may be a genuinely neurotic one, an aggravation of the typical transference. That is, the substitution of the analyst for other figures emotionally important to the patient may produce an emotional crisis, in which the patient actually acts more irrationally than before treatment. If this crisis is well handled, the patient emerges the better for it. Although some analysts believe that such crises are inevitable in an analysis, other analysts attempt to ward them off by such devices as less frequent therapeutic sessions when transference problems become too hard to handle. In any case, the fact that an aggravated transference neurosis may occur does not invalidate the therapeutic usefulness of psychoanalytic technique.

Three words often crop up in discussion of what is taking place as the patient improves. These are 'abreaction', 'insight', and 'working through'. 'Abreaction' refers to a living again of an earlier emotion, in a kind of emotional catharsis – literally getting some of the dammed-up emotion out of the system. The therapeutic need is that described by the poet:

> Home they brought her warrior dead.
> She nor swooned nor uttered cry.
> All her maidens watching said:
> 'She must weep or she will die.'

Tennyson, *The Princess*

'Insight' refers to seeing clearly what motives are at work, what the nature of the problem is, so that instinctual conflicts, as psychoanalysts call them, are recognized for what they are. Insight is not limited to the recovery of dramatic incidents in early childhood that were later repressed. Sometimes such insights do occur, and sometimes they are associated with relief of symptoms. But neither a single flood of emotion in abreaction nor a single occasion of surprised insight relieves the patient of his symptoms. He requires, instead, the process of 'working through', that is, facing again and again the same old conflicts and finding himself reacting in the same old ways to them, until eventually the slow processes of re-education manifest themselves and he reacts more nearly in accordance with the objective demands of the situation and less in accordance with distortions that his private needs create.

It is chiefly because the process of working through takes so long that psychoanalysis takes so long. The psychoanalyst often has the basic insights into the patient's problems quite early in treatment, but the patient is unready for them and could not understand the analyst if he were to insist upon confronting him with these interpretations. I have sometimes likened an analysis to the process of learning to play the piano. It is not enough to know what a good performance is and to wish to give one. The process has to be learned. The learner may know all about musical notation and may have manual skill and musical appreciation. But there is no short cut. Even with a good teacher the lessons must continue week after week before the player can achieve the kind of spontaneous performance he wishes to achieve. We do not begrudge this time, because we believe that the end is worth it. What the analyst is attempting to do is far more complex than what the piano teacher is attempting to do. The skilled management of a life is more difficult than the skilled management of a keyboard.

It must be clear by this time that laboratory experimentation that preserves anything like the richness of a psychoanalysis will be very difficult indeed, if not, perhaps, impossible. [. . . .]

Experimental Studies of Psychotherapy
with Human Subjects

One kind of venture is that which seeks to evaluate the relative success of different kinds of therapy without any experimental control of the therapy itself. Such investigations are important, but the scientific generalizations from them are bound to be meager. They may tell what kind of patient ought to go to what kind of physician, but then we would still have to ask why one is more successful than the other. We might find, for example, that Alcoholics Anonymous did more than psychoanalysts for alcoholics. But this would be only a start in further inquiry. Today we are concerned with what goes on within psychotherapy, not with what kind of therapeutic arrangements are to be recommended in the community.

I wish to give one illustration of the kind of data that can be obtained from therapeutic sessions that deal with the course of treatments of real people who come to a psychotherapist for help. Sometimes scientists use data that they create for experimental purposes; sometimes they turn available data to scientific use. This first illustration is the kind of situation in which available data are turned to scientific account. I refer to some studies of short psychotherapy made by Carl Rogers and his students in the counseling center at the University of Chicago (26, 29). To those of us oriented in the field of contemporary clinical psychology, it may seem somewhat surprising that I bring Rogers into a discussion of psychoanalysis, for he is, in some sense, an enemy, or at least a competitor. But a person in trouble who is being counseled is not concerned about the theory that is being used on him. He is burdened by his troubles, and if he finds relief and we discover how, the principles are important ones, no matter who his therapist is. In some sense, Rogers' antagonism to psychoanalysis produces interviews that reveal better than psychoanalysis itself some of the principles about which analysts speak.

Rogers' method, known as nondirective therapy, consists in a supportive therapy based primarily upon the permissiveness of the therapist. An effort is made to avoid getting embroiled in transference, and interpretations are at a minimum. The therapist listens attentively and reflects the feeling in the assertions of the patient, avoiding evaluations or judgments of his own. What then happens during successive sessions?

Rogers and his students have systematically recorded what is said in their interviews, using the modern electromagnetic records. Secretaries are taught to transcribe the 'mm's' and 'ah's' and to note the lengths of rest pauses. Hence it is possible to make detailed content analyses of the interviews to give quantitative answers to some questions about what goes on. It is said, for example, that in the early interviews the patient commonly restates his problem, returning over and over again to the same point of difficulty, but after he has been in the situation awhile he gradually achieves insight, and these occasions of insight are signs of therapeutic progress. By carefully coding what is happening in the interviews we may ascertain whether or not this march of events does in fact go forward. In Figure 1 are plotted the average results of ten cases for whom there were from three to nine interviews each. When the records are divided into fifths, we see that the statement and restatement of the problem decreases relative to the increase in statements revealing insight and understanding.

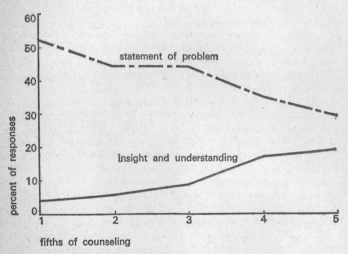

Figure 1 Changes taking place during brief psychotherapy. Statements by the patient during the psychotherapeutic sessions are recorded electromagnetically, transcribed, and coded. Restatements of the problem occur with less relative frequency, while statements of insight and understanding increase. Replotted from data presented by Seeman (29).

One can imagine a real experimental design superimposed upon a process of this sort. For example, at some stage the therapist might deliberately introduce interpretations of the kind carefully avoided in the nondirective method. If the height of the line showing statements of insight and understanding increased, by this criterion the interpretation would be shown to be helpful; if the line were to taper off, it would show that the interpretations slowed up the progress.

One of the chief advantages of Rogers' method for purposes of research on psychotherapy is that it provides a highly disciplined interview technique, with minimum active participation by the therapist. Hence other methods might well use it as a control method, noting how the other methods accelerate or slow up progress. Fortunately, the consequences of Rogers' nondirective method are generally benign, so that no harm would be done in using it as a reference method.

A start has been made in the direction of comparing two methods in a very ingenious experiment by Keet (17). I wish to describe his experiment in some detail because it serves as a useful model of experimental design in this difficult field. If its results are substantiated by others, I believe that the experiment will prove to be something of a landmark.

Thirty normal subjects participated in this experiment designed to compare the effectiveness of two counseling techniques in overcoming a conflict symptomatized by the inability to recall a word just memorized. Through a cleverly devised method, the subject learned a list of six words, including a critical word to which he had shown emotional responses in a word association test.

The word association test was the one made familiar by Jung. A list of one hundred words is read off to the subject, one word at a time. The subject is instructed to reply as promptly as possible with the first word that he thinks of. The experimenter notes the word, and records the time of response with a stop watch. The list is gone through a second time. Emotional conflict is shown in a number of ways, according to what have come to be known as 'complex indicators'. These include far-fetched responses, failure to respond, repeating back the stimulus word, repeating an earlier response, and so on. In this experiment two complex-indicators were chosen. First, those words were selected for which responses were changed from the first to the second reading. Second, among these words, that one was chosen for the purpose of the experiment that had the longest reaction time. By this strictly objective method, a critical family of three words was selected, one stimulus word and the two words given as responses to it on the two trials. In the example to which we are about to turn the set of key words was 'nasty – messy – mean'. That is, to the word 'nasty' the subject had replied 'messy' after a delay on the first trial, and then on the second trial had replied 'mean', but also after a delay.

The critical stimulus word was then imbedded in a list including five neutral words. Subjects experienced no difficulty in learning and remembering this list of six words. But now a new list of six words was memorized, producing some interference with recall of the first list. We experimental psychologists have a fancy expression for this interference. We call it retroactive inhibition. When the effort was made to recall the first list, twenty-five of the thirty subjects forgot the critical word but remembered the remaining five neutral words. We here see the activity of a moderate repression. The emotionally loaded word is forgotten when conditions for recall are made slightly more difficult, even though the word was freely recalled in the process of memorizing the list of six words. Subjects felt very annoyed that they could not recall this word that was 'right on the tip of the tongue'.

This 'microneurosis' provided an opportunity for short therapy, the success of the therapy to be judged, first of all, by the recovery of the forgotten word. Two therapeutic techniques were compared. One of these, called the 'expressive technique', was permissive, and allowed expression of feeling. It was very close to Rogers' nondirective technique. As used in this experiment it was unsuccessful. It failed in all thirteen of the cases with whom it was used. That is, none of the thirteen recovered the forgotten word during the therapeutic session. The second technique, called the 'interpretive technique', had all the features of the first, but added the more active interpretive comments of the therapist at appropriate times. Thus to the insights of the client were added those of the therapist, at, of course, a 'shallow' level from the point of view of psychoanalysis. But the method deviates from the Rogers method in the direction of the psychoanalytic method. The method was highly successful. Eleven of twelve subjects met the first criterion of therapeutic success: that is, they recalled the forgotten word within the therapeutic session.

The question we wish to ask is this: Just how did interpretation help to bring about the recall of the forgotten word? The author Keet suggests that through interpretation his subjects were freer to use normal associative processes. Then the affective experience that determined the failure to recall came into awareness. Once the affective experience was in awareness, the conflict over recall could be resolved, because the subject was able to recall the circumstances under which the critical word was forgotten.

I wish to present a verbatim account of one of Keet's interpretive therapeutic sessions, to illustrate the nature of his interpretations and provide evidence that will permit us to judge whether or not the consequences are as he describes them.

The subject, a young married woman, replied to the word 'nasty' first with the word 'messy', then with the word 'mean'. Because both of the replies were long delayed, the word 'nasty' was chosen as the critical word in the memory experiment. She first memorized the following list of six words: green, make, ask, nasty, paper, sad. This she did without difficulty. Then she learned another list of six words. The memory method used was somewhat unusual, but I am not going to take the time to give the details. After the memorization of the second list she was asked to recall the first. It is at this point that the therapeutic interview took place.

EXPERIMENTER: Now please repeat the first set of key words.

SUBJECT (*confidently*): Green, make, ask, paper, sad. (*A pause followed with the experimenter looking inquiringly at the subject.*) Wait a minute, there were six and I have only five. That's silly. Of course there were six. I should be able to remember the sixth one. Let me see. Green, make, ask, sad, paper. No, that's wrong. Paper comes before sad. That's right, isn't it?

E: You want me to help you. [This is a characteristic Rogers nondirective response.]

S: If you would only tell me that, then I would perhaps remember the missing word. (*Pause.*) It's annoying. . . . It's funny. . . . I know it was in the fourth place, wasn't it?

E: Try to work it out by yourself, by . . .

S: I see you want me to recall the word by myself.

E: That would be more satisfying, wouldn't it?

S: Sure. I mean it is always nice to solve a little problem. It's quite an easy job remembering six words after you've said them several times. (*She moves in the chair and gives vent to little sounds of annoyance . . . a considerable pause.*)

E: You are quite annoyed with yourself.

S: Yes, I am, why should I be so stupid. . . . Green, make, ask, blank, paper, sad . . . sad, paper, blank, ask. Oh, that will be no use. (*She tries again, counting on fingers and apparently saying the words silently. Makes exclamations of annoyance.*) Is it bread? No, it isn't. That's in the second lot. . . . *Is* it bread?

E: We agreed that it would perhaps be better if you tried to remember it yourself.

S: I am too annoyed to think clearly. All sorts of words pop into my mind. Is it all right if I say them?

E: You are free to go about it any way you please.

S: Well, the last set was water, long, try, bread ... er ... er ... bird, wasn't it?

E: You do want help, don't you?

S (*laughs heartily*): Yes, I'm all mixed up. If I could get certainty on the last list it might help me to remember.

E: You feel confused.

S (*laughs*): Yes, all mixed up and disturbed. It's funny that I can remember the last list and not the first one. One word in the first one: blank, blank, blank. That's no good. I shall have to give up.

E: You are quite free to do that, you know.

Up to this point the interview has followed the general pattern of the expressive technique. The experimenter has been permissive, has recognized the subject's feeling, but has not interpreted. The permissiveness of the experimenter's last response ('You are quite free ...') releases a good deal of expressed emotion in the next response. This is the kind of therapeutic consequence claimed for the nondirective method. The first response classified as an interpretation follows this release of feeling by the subject.

S: That's a relief. You think me very stupid, don't you? (*Laughs.*) I suppose I am, really. I should be able to recall the word. It is most exasperating. I feel quite angry with you, sitting there smug and self-satisfied. Could you do it? I mean have you tried it on yourself? (*She laughs when she sees the experimenter smiling.*) Oh, is the word 'green'? That doesn't seem to ring quite true. I am sure it is not 'green'. I went overseas once and got quite seasick ... turned green ... (*pause*).

[Now note that the experimenter departs from the nondirective method to offer a simple interpretation.]

E: Perhaps there is something about the word itself.... You may have had some experience, or something like that....

S: I often used to feel sick when I got angry. I did a moment ago. Just the faintest feeling in my stomach when I felt a bit angry with you. I was very seasick when I went to Europe. Turned pasty and green.... I was all alone ... the youngest in a swimming team. Pasty. (*Pause.*)

[You will notice the similarity between the word 'pasty' and the word she is trying to recall which is 'nasty'. The experimenter stays with the problem of her feelings, however.]

E: You say you feel a little nauseated when you are angry.

S: Yes, whenever my sister and I quarreled and I got very angry I was nauseated. Once I even got sick and vomited. I didn't like the mess. This is not so bad nowadays. Only when I try to hold my irritation back, then I get it. I always thought my sister was stronger than I am. We used to have real fights sometimes. (*Laughs.*) I don't feel so confused any more. Do you think the blank, blank word ... (*laughs*). I can't remember it yet. Can it have something to do with my quarreling with my sister? My father liked her very much more than he did me. (*Pause.*)

E: Maybe. And perhaps it is connected with some more recent experience.

[These interpretations by the experimenter may seem to be very trivial, but their importance lies in their timing. He had noted in the subject's hesitation at this point something that might be interpreted as a thought near to expression. Her response proves the correctness of his hunch.]

S: You mean with my husband.... Oh, that just slipped out. (*Laughs.*) Now I have said it, I might as well tell you we had a quarrel the other day – a rather bitter one. (*Pause.*) I still think he was very mean. (*With some vindictiveness.*) When people get nasty like that I get very angry. I mean nasty. Of course, that is the word. 'Nasty'. Well, I never. How do you like that! Do you really think this has something to do with my quarrel with my husband? It is very funny.

The success of the cases in which there were these rather simple interpretative intrusions as contrasted with those in which interpretations were avoided gives clarity to the manner in which such interpretations help penetrate a thin veil of resistance. The element of surprise at what she discovers is, by the way, characteristic of the insights that come in psychotherapy.

But I am not yet through talking about this experiment. So far we have seen one therapeutic result: the recall of a word that had undergone repression within the experiment.

The experimenter was not satisfied with this, for that would be mere symptom alleviation. Therapy must go deeper than that. Now, he asked, did the therapy here go any deeper, or, to put it another way, can any generalization or spread of its results be detected?

The second cycle of the experiment was almost a repeat of the first, by again introducing the learning of a list, the learning of a second list, and then the attempted recall of the first. But this time one of the response words in the critical set was used. The subject who said to 'nasty' first 'messy' and then 'mean' is now asked to learn a list in which the first response word ('messy') is included. The conjecture is as follows. If the therapy really released some of the emotion or produced some insight connected with the disturbing set of key words, then the repressive tendencies should have been weakened. Hence those whose therapy was unsuccessful should repress the new word, while those whose therapy was successful should be able to recall the word without trouble. The conjecture was completely substantiated. Those who forgot and never recovered the original stimulus word in the first part of the experiment *also* forgot the response word in the second part of the experiment; those who forgot, but later recovered the stimulus word, had no trouble in recalling the response word in the second cycle of the experiment.

If we take the experiment at its face value it is a beautiful epitome of much that is said to go on within psychoanalysis. I have no reason to doubt the experimental findings, except that psychologists are brought up to be skeptics, and I shall not rest happy until someone repeats and confirms the experiment. Whether or not the results in a repetition turn out as decisive as Keet's results, I believe he has set a very useful pattern for further work.

There are several very good features to Keet's experimental design. (1) In the first place, the subjects are selected from the general population for the purposes of the experiment. They are not people who come to a physician because they believe themselves to be sick. (2) In the second place, a symptom is produced under laboratory conditions, so that an element of control is introduced. (3) In the third place, the methods of therapy used are clearly delineated, and criteria of therapeutic success operationally defined. (4) Fourth, all of this is superimposed upon a recognition that a laboratory neurosis is necessarily connected with the biography of the individual. The word association test in this experiment provides a bridge to the real person, so that the experiment does not take place in a psychological vacuum. The importance of this is readily recognized when you recall the highly personal and individual material that comes out even in this very brief psychotherapeutic session. [. . . .]

References
 1. Abraham, K. *Selected Papers on Psychoanalysis*. London: Hogarth Press, 1927.
 2. Adorno, T. W., Frenkel-Brunswik, Else, Levinson, D. J., and Sanford, R. N. *The Authoritarian Personality*. New York: Harper & Brothers, 1950.
 3. Barker, R., Dembo, T., and Lewin, K. 'Frustration and Regression: An Experiment with Young Children', *Univ. Iowa Studies Child Welf.*, 1941, *18*, No. 1.
 4. Blum, G. S. 'A Study of the Psychoanalytic Theory of Psychosexual Development', *Genet. Psych. Monogr.*, 1949, *39*, 3–99.
 5. Davis, H. V., Sears, R. R., Miller, H. C., and Brodbeck, A. J. 'Effects of Cup, Bottle, and Breast Feeding on Oral Activities of Newborn Infants', *Pediatrics*, 1948, *2*, 549–58.
 6. Dollard, J., Doob, L. W., Miller, N. E., Mowrer, O. H., and Sears, R. R. *Frustration and Aggression*. New Haven: Yale University Press, 1939.
 7. Fenichel, Otto. *The Psychoanalytic Theory of Neurosis*. New York: W. W. Norton & Company, Inc., 1945.

8. Frenkel-Brunswik, Else, 'Mechanisms of Self-Deception', *J. Soc. Psych.*, 1939, *10*, 409–20.

9. Freud, Anna. *The Ego and the Mechanisms of Defence.* London, Hogarth Press, 1937.

10. Freud, S. *Character and Anal Erotism.* Coll. Papers, 1908, *2*, 45–50.

11. —. *New Introductory Lectures on Psychoanalysis.* New York: W. W. Norton & Company, Inc., 1933.

12. —. *The Psychopathology of Everyday Life* (1904), in *Basic Writings of Sigmund Freud.* New York: Modern Library, 1938.

13. Fromm-Reichmann, Frieda. 'Notes on the Personal and Professional Requirements of a Psychotherapist', *Psychiatry*, 1949, *12*, 361–78.

14. Goldman, Frieda. 'Breast-feeding and Character-Formation', *J. Personality*, 1948, *17*, 83–103.

15. Hamilton, G. V. *A Research in Marriage.* New York: Boni, 1929.

16. Hunt, J. McV. 'The Effects of Infant Feeding-Frustration upon Adult Hoarding in the Albino Rat', *J. Abnorm. Soc. Psych.*, 1941, *36*, 338–60.

17. Keet, C. D. 'Two Verbal Techniques in a Miniature Counselling Situation', *Psych. Monogr.*, 1948, *62*, No. 294.

18. Landis, C. 'Psychoanalytic Phenomena', *J. Abnorm. Soc. Psych.*, 1940, *35*, 17–28.

19. Lantz, Beatrice. 'Some Dynamic Aspects of Success and Failure', *Psych. Monogr.*, 1945, *59*, No. 271.

20. Levy, D. M. 'Experiments on the Sucking Reflex and Social Behavior of Dogs', *Am. J. Orthopsychiat.*, 1934, *4*, 203–24.

21. —. 'Fingersucking and Accessory Movements in Early Infancy', *Am. J. Psychiat.*, 1928, *7*, 881–918.

22. Miller, N. E. 'Theory and Experiment Relating Psychoanalytic Displacement to Stimulus-Response Generalization', *J. Abnorm. Soc., Psych.*, 1948, *43*, 155–78.

23. Morgan, C. T. 'The Hoarding Instinct', *Psych. Rev.*, 1947, *54*, 335–41.

24. Orlansky, H. 'Infant Care and Personality', *Psych. Bull.*, 1949, *46*, 1–48.

25. Pattie, F. A. Jr. 'A Report of Attempts to Produce Uniocular Blindness by Hypnotic Suggestion', *Brit. J. Med. Psych.*, 1935, *15*, 230–41.

26. Rogers, C. R. 'A Coordinated Research in Psychotherapy', *J. Consulting Psych.*, 1949, *13*, 149–220.

27. Sears, R. R. 'Experimental Analysis of Psychoanalytic Phenomena', in Hunt, J. McV. (ed.), *Personality and the Behavior Disorders.* New York: The Ronald Press Company, 1944, 306–22.

28. —. 'Experimental Studies of Projection: I. Attribution of Traits', *J. Soc. Psych.*, 1936, *7*, 151–63.

29. Seeman, J. 'The Process of Nondirective Therapy', *J. Consulting Psych.*, 1949.

30. Symonds, P. M. *Dynamic Psychology.* New York: Appleton-Century Crofts, Inc., 1949.

31. —. *The Dynamics of Human Adjustment.* New York: D. Appleton-Century Company, Inc., 1946.

32. True, R. M. 'Experimental Control in Hypnotic Age Regression States', *Science*, 1949, *110*, 583–4.

PRINCIPLES OF ASSESSMENT IN SITUATIONAL TESTING

Although this article precedes Professor Morris's in the context of this book, it was the work of the British War Office Selection Boards that provided the model for the American Office of Strategic Services, rather than vice versa. This order has been chosen because the present article describes principles – which were largely common to both projects – while its successor deals mostly with results.

A non-technical account of procedure at a British equivalent of the OSS boards has been given by Morgan (1). One of the lessons learned was that irrespective of the overall validity of situational testing, in this or any other context, attempts to devise real-life situations to measure separate traits were doomed to failure. Thus, a proposed test of 'observation' seemed rather to measure attitudes, while tests of 'ingenuity', of 'Morse aptitude' and others functioned mainly as 'g' tests of low validity. Conversely, tests intended for strictly psychometric purposes were much affected by personality variables. (See also the introduction to 11, below).

A further point worth stressing is that while all situations at these Boards (and at WOSBs) were made as realistic as possible, fantasy, as such, was discouraged. Thus a candidate was not allowed to 'give up his life' in the interests of the group. Nevertheless, a factor analysis of individual situational tests at 'Pemberley' (see 1) suggested that ability to enter into fantasy activity accounted for a proportion of the variance of these tests. Such an ability is clearly irrelevant – if not worse – to the purpose of this sort of procedure.

The symbols 'S' and 'W' in the present text refer to the 'stations' at which the work was carried out. 'Station S' was the original and principal unit, operating a three-day procedure; 'Station W', inaugurated later, worked on a one-day basis.

References
1. Morgan, W. J., *Spies and Saboteurs*. London. Gollancz, 1955.

6 The O.S.S. Assessment Staff

Principles of Assessment in Situational Testing

Assessment of Men; Rinehart, New York, 1948, pp. 26–57.

[. . . .]

In presenting a conceptual framework for the OSS system of assessment we did not suppose that it would be possible to include the whole range of theories and hypotheses entertained by the men and women who, at one time or another, had taken part in the undertaking. Their views were never expressed except incidentally and 'off the cuff' in a fragmentary manner. But we did expect that we could arrive at a number of generalizations to which most members of the staff would give assent. Together we had garnered an abundant harvest of experiences; would it be right to leave the sheaves standing, the grain unthreshed? Preferable to this, in our judgment, was to allow three or four members of the staff, unrepresentative as they might be, to work the material and extract what scientific nourishment they could from it.

This decision gave rise to several months' labor on the conceptual level which resulted in a brood of theoretical propositions. But when these were finally examined with a cool, impartial eye, the impression was inescapable that they were not of the sort that would be accepted readily by a majority of the staff members. Regretfully we concluded that any serious attempt to define basic concepts and postulates underlying assessment practices would lead almost inevitably to new conceptions, very possibly requiring new terminology, which, at best, could scarcely invite immediate and unanimous approval.

There was no possibility of testing this suspicion by assembling our collaborators, most of whom, at that date, were scattered far and wide, some in the Far East. A symposium was out of the question. And so it was decided that, rather than run the risk of publishing theories to which many of the staff could not subscribe, it would be better to curb ambition, scrap our speculations, and resign ourselves to the more modest task of explaining the OSS system of assessment on a relatively concrete level and then, possibly, of setting down a few of the assumptions about personality on the basis of which our procedures could be rationalized. [. . . .]

The scheme employed by us might be called the multiform organismic system of assessment: 'multiform' because it consists of a rather large number of procedures based on different principles, and 'organismic' (or 'Gestalt', or 'holistic') because it utilized the data obtained through these procedures for attempting to arrive at a picture of personality as a whole; i.e., at the organization of the essential dynamic features of the individual. The knowledge of this organization serves as a basis both for understanding and for predicting the subject's specific behavior.

The system may be set forth most simply as a series of steps each of which is based on one or more psychological principles.

Every step described below is either one which was taken by us or one which would have been taken by us if conditions had permitted it.

At the end of the undertaking, a rigorous analysis of our results disclosed errors which could be attributed to methodological defects, for each of which reflection yielded remedies. [. . . .]

Step 1
Make a preparatory analysis of all the jobs for which candidates are to be assessed. This step, of course, is fundamental, since it is impossible to predict whether a given person, no matter how accurately his skills are estimated, is suitable for a job of an unknown nature. To state this more generally, it is impossible to predict whether one thing, A, which is present and open to measurement, will fit another thing, B, which is absent, if the dimensions of B are not known.

As explained in Chapter I, this most important first step in an assessment program could not be achieved, except to a slight extent, in setting up the OSS screening process. Furthermore, we were unable to recruit, as members of the assessment staff, men who had had military experience overseas of such a nature as would equip them to judge, without the benefit of job analyses, the suitability of candidates for OSS assignments. Therefore, as already described, our conceptions of the various jobs were products of our imaginations working with the few facts that were supplied by branch chiefs, their administrative officers, and other administrators in Washington.

Inasmuch as the duties of the OSS assessment staff did not include the measurement of a hundred and one highly technical skills, analyses of the latter were not required. Hence, in this respect, our task was less inclusive and exacting than that of other selection agencies.

At the time of the initiation of the program the members of the staff did not realize how thoroughly this first step, or principle, should be applied in order to justify a scientific system of assessment. They did not realize that besides obtaining (1) a functional analysis of each role and (2) an analysis of each of the physical and social environments in which these roles would have to be performed, it was necessary to design, at the very start, a satisfactory system of appraisal (validation), which would include (3) a scale for theater ratings of effectiveness in the performance of each function. The members of the staff, at this early date, did not distinctly see that the actual target of their undertaking, the standard against which their efforts would eventually be evaluated, was the worth of each man as rated, not by an ideal omniscient judge, but by his all too human associates. For scientific assessments it is necessary to determine, first of all, the range of functional effectiveness and of general conduct that is acceptable to the administrators of the organization to be served, and, also, an account of all the factors which may operate to put a man outside the range of acceptability. [. . . .]

The psychological principle underlying Step 1 may be stated as follows: a large proportion of the determinants of the direction and efficiency of a person's behavior consists of components of the environmental situation; therefore, the more precise and complete the definition of the environment, the more accurate will be the predictions of behavior. Among the chief components of the environment are the institutional expectations in respect to the role-functions which the individual has had assigned to him.

Step 2

On the basis of the preparatory analysis of jobs, list all the personality determinants of success or failure in the performance of each job; and from this list select the variables to be measured by the assessment process. The OSS staff was unable to follow this directive in any thoroughgoing fashion. In the first place it was agreed that it was not possible for the assessment staff at any one station to test suitability for the great variety of highly technical functions embraced by the OSS (e.g. piloting an airplane, parachuting, translating Albanian, drawing posters to influence Germans, setting Japanese type, and so on); hence the measurement of such very specific factors was not included among the responsibilities of our staff. In the second place, we did not obtain sufficient information about the less special functions and about the conditions in the different theaters to enable us to discover most of the nontechnical determinants of success or failure. Finally, even if we had secured the required information, passing judgment on a candidate according to his apparent suitability for a specific assignment turned out, in a large proportion of cases, to be more or less irrelevant, since the job that was assigned to him in the theater was different from the one proposed for him in Washington.

For these and other reasons it was decided at the start that we should assess each man not primarily in relation to our conception, such as it was, of a special designated assignment, but in relation to a cluster of general qualifications (dispositions, abilities, traits) which were essential to the effective performance of almost every OSS job overseas. Before Station S was opened, in fact, one of the members of the staff (Lieutenant Gardner), by interviewing various branch chiefs and their administrative officers, obtained what seemed the next best thing to job descriptions – a list of abilities and qualities which these officers considered necessary for the accomplishment of the projects planned by their section. At the end of this inquiry we had a sizable array of requirements which could be abbreviated without much distortion by resolving differences in terminology and by combining related factors under a single term. For the first five months we worked with a list of about twenty variables, some of which, as time passed, had their hair trimmed, their beards shaved, and their names changed. At the end of this period we succeeded in combining these into the following seven major variables (basic to the needs of OSS):

1. *Motivation for Assignment*: war morale, interest in proposed job.

2. *Energy and Initiative*: activity level, zest, effort, initiative.

3. *Effective Intelligence*: ability to select strategic goals and the most efficient means of attaining them; quick practical thought – resourcefulness, originality, good judgment – in dealing with things, people, or ideas.

4. *Emotional Stability*: ability to govern disturbing emotions, steadiness and endurance under pressure, snafu tolerance, freedom from neurotic tendencies.

5. *Social Relations*: ability to get along well with other people, good will, team play, tact, freedom from disturbing prejudices, freedom from annoying traits.

6. *Leadership*: social initiative, ability to evoke cooperation, organizing and administering ability, acceptance of responsibility.

7. *Security*: ability to keep secrets; caution, discretion, ability to bluff and to mislead.

Such were the *general qualifications* for all O S S men and women (leadership excepted in some cases). Distinguished from these were the *special qualifications* applicable for the most part to the undertakings of one or two branches only. Of these, three were added to the list of general qualifications printed on the formal report sheet:

8. *Physical Ability*: agility, daring, ruggedness, stamina.

9. *Observing and Reporting*: ability to observe and to remember accurately significant facts and their relations, to evaluate information, to report succinctly.

10. *Propaganda Skills:* ability to apperceive the psychological vulnerabilities of the enemy; to devise subversive techniques of one sort or another; to speak, write, or draw persuasively.

Besides these there were a few abilities (Teaching Ability, Recruiting Ability, for instance) which were measured in special cases and an indefinite number of variables used in writing sketches of the candidates' personalities, which were not included in the formal list, either because they were too specific (pertinent to a few jobs only), or because they were not readily measurable in all candidates under the conditions set up at S and at W.

For the last three months of its twenty months' service, the assessment staff, besides rating the seven general variables mentioned above, assessed the suitability of every candidate for each of three locations in the theater (relative to the front), for each of three levels of authority, and for each of ten job categories. This seemed to be the only way of partially solving two of our most vexing problems: how to record (for later evaluation) our estimates of a candidate's fitness for jobs other than the one proposed for him in Washington, and how to transmit judgments that would help in the reassignment of a candidate in the theater.

One might almost say, exaggerating a little, that in the O S S the conventional role of the administrator and the role of the technical expert were reversed. Commonly it is an administrator who passes on the general suitability of a candidate in respect to personal appearance, energy, temperament, interest in the job, likability, tact, cooperativeness, leadership qualities, and so forth; and it is the personnel psychologist who classifies him according to his special talents. In the O S S, on the other hand, it was the recruiting officers and the administrative officers who decided (on the basis of work history and other data) whether a candidate had the required technical proficiency and it was the professional assessment staff that passed on his general social qualifications, his mental health, and his power to abstain from actions which might bring discredit to the organization.

Step 3

Define (in words that are intelligible to the personnel officers and administrators of the organization) a rating scale for each of the personality variables on the selected list as well as for the one overall variable Job Fitness. The members of the OSS staff found a six-point rating scale well suited to their purpose:

0	1	2	3	4	5
Very Inferior	Inferior	Low Average	High Average	Superior	Very Superior
7%	18%	25%	25%	18%	7%

The percentages indicate the proportion of men that would fall in each category if the variable in question happened to be normally distributed in the candidate population. One of the advantages of this scale is that it can easily be converted into a two-point, three-point, or four-point scale, or, by using pluses and minuses in marking, into an eighteen-point scale (in practice a sixteen-point scale, since the extreme ratings 0— and 5+ are rarely used). By combining the lower two categories and the upper two categories, the six-point scale becomes a four-point scale, which, according to our experience, is the most useful one in obtaining ratings from nonprofessionals (other members of the organization):

1	2	3	4
Inferior	Low Average	High Average	Superior
Unsatisfactory	Satisfactory	Very Satisfactory	Outstanding

[. . . .]

Rating variables is an exceedingly crude and abstract mode of representing certain realities of personality; but it is a useful and defensible procedure notwithstanding. It serves to focus the attention of the assessors on the most crucial components and to force them to make repeated attempts to justify their ratings by recalling concrete samples of behavior. It provides a rough summary of a large number of judgments which assists the staff in arriving at a final assessment. It transmutes clinical observations into the only form which can be handled statistically. Finally, it constitutes a brief and intelligible mode of communicating estimates and predictions to the officers of the institution. The errors to which abstract symbols of this sort are liable to give rise may be corrected to some extent by combining them with a more concrete personality sketch which describes the interactions of the rated variables and their characteristic manifestations under varying conditions.

The unsatisfactoriness of variables that are as general and ambiguous as those used by OSS assessment units can be reduced to some extent by listing under each heading, as we did, several more specific modes of behavior which may be regarded either as components or as criteria of the variable. Thus under Emotional Stability we included adaptability, maturity, steadiness under pressure, snafu tolerance, freedom from neurotic symptoms. We made a practice of underlining on the final report sheet the subvariables which were considered strong and crossing out those which were considered weak. [. . . .]

Step 4
Design a program of assessment procedures which will reveal the strength of the selected variables.

Substep 4.1
Plant the assessment procedures within a social matrix composed of staff and candidates. Our experience shows that it is not difficult to create an informal, sincerely genial atmosphere at the assessment station and that under these conditions most of the assessees will enjoy themselves and be more inclined to tolerate an exacting and stressful schedule of procedures than they would be in a less agreeable social climate; and also under these conditions they will be disposed to relax during the times when they are not engaged in assigned tasks and conduct themselves somewhat as they would in everyday life. Further, our experience shows that the staff can acquire invaluable impressions of the candidates during these hours of relaxation: from a wisecrack overheard in the hall, from a heated conversation at dinner, from the way a clique forms in the living room, from the gesture with which a man reacts to defeat in a game of bridge, from a breakfast-table report of the sleeping behavior of one of the candidates, from frank comments on the testing procedures elicited during a casual conversation after supper, from sentiments privately expressed while taking a snack in the kitchen before going to bed, and so forth. When the candidates live and eat with the staff members for two or three days, the situation has some of the flavor of a house party, and

consequently the offering of liquor on the last evening comes within the range of habitual expectations and is not often interpreted as a stratagem to entangle the unwary.

It is hard to get to know a man merely by observing him behave in a controlled situation. Impressions obtained at such times require complementation and reinforcement by others gained from numerous casual contacts at moments when the candidate is less guardedly aware that his actions are under scrutiny. Also, in the process of developing a conception of the man's character it is advantageous to have him under the same roof so that he will be repeatedly seen in the ordinary course of events, and can, when necessary, be engaged, as if off-handedly, in conversation.

Furthermore, if the candidates live for several days together and suffer the same trials and frustrations, and together laugh at the same humorous incidents, the majority become welded, even in this short space of time, into a mutually sympathetic whole, and on leaving, each man – with some exceptions, naturally – carries with him a favorable opinion of the assessment process which has become solidified in his mind by the consensus of the group. It was found, for example, that the 'graduates' of the three-day system at S were decidedly more enthusiastic about the merits of assessment than were the 'graduates' of the one-day system at W, who had little chance to develop mutuality of feeling. Thus if it happens to be necessary to convince the members of an organization of the value of assessment procedures, the living-together system as practiced at Station S can be highly recommended. Finally, under 'house party' conditions the candidates have numerous opportunities to size each other up, and, therefore, more reliance can be placed on the returns of a sociometric test which may advisedly be scheduled as the last procedure on the program.

Substep 4.2
Select several different types of procedures and several procedures of the same type for estimating the strength of each variable. In the *ideal* assessment program there will be *numerous* procedures for predicting the strength of *each* variable, since experience has shown that no single test has a very high degree of validity. These procedures will be of different types (e.g., interview method, questionnaire method, situational method) because each type (method) has certain specific advantages as well as specific disadvantages. Some subjects are better revealed by one method, others by another. Finally, each method will be represented by

several different procedures (varieties of the same method), since no one operation of personality can be taken as a valid index of what an individual will or can do in dealing with situations of a certain type. It is necessary to know the degree of consistency of a personality.

At Station S, for example, the variable Social Relations (disposition and ability to get along with others) was revealed by six different methods:

1. Interview.
2. Informal observations through three-day period.
3. Individual task situations, where the single candidate was faced by the necessity of dealing with one or more persons (sometimes stooges) in achieving his end.
4. Group task situations, where a team of candidates was instructed to cooperate in performing a prescribed task.
5. Projection tests which revealed some of the inhibited or unconscious social tendencies of the candidates.
6. Sociometric questionnaire in which the candidate's acceptance or rejection by his fellow candidates was estimated.

Furthermore, several of these methods were represented by two or three different procedures. For instance, there were three individual task situations:

3a. *Construction Test*, in which the candidate had to direct two recalcitrant 'assistants' (stooges) in helping him to erect a wooden structure within a given length of time.

3b. *Recruiting Test*, in which the candidate had to interview a person (stooge) applying for a position in a secret organization.

3c. *Improvisations*, where two candidates had to deal with each other in a face-to-face situation of a prescribed character.

The multiform method of examination does not require ten or twelve times as many procedures as there are variables, because many procedures yield ratings on several different factors. Almost every factor, for instance, can be roughly estimated on the basis of an interview. Or, to take another example, one questionnaire can be constructed which lists every condition that is likely to be encountered in the field and which asks the subject to estimate the positive or negative appeal of each of these for him.

Underlying our recommendation for the inclusion of *many varied* procedures is the well-accepted fact that in order to formulate a personality one must know many of its components, and therefore, since in a single event only a relatively few components are exhibited, the more events of which we have accurate reports the better. Also, since a man reacts differently to different

133

situations, we need reports of a wide variety of events in which the subject has participated. As a rule, the more varied the situations, the more varied will be the components of personality which are evoked. The conclusion is obvious: to arrive at a conception of the different systems and different resources of a man's personality, one must discover his emotional responses to, and his effectiveness in dealing with, *different kinds* of situations.

Finally, it is necessary to ascertain how the subject reacts to various situations of the *same kind*, since no man is entirely consistent. As a rule, each need or system of a personality is characterized by an area of generality (a large number of situations which evoke similar patterns of response) and a few foci of specificity (a small number of situations which evoke contrasting patterns). There are some people, for example, who are generally timid – that is, they have a high degree of sensitivity to most of the different varieties of danger – and yet they are fearless in certain situations which frighten many of their associates. Contrariwise, there are other people who are not sensitive to most dangers but suffer from a single intense phobia. Thus we require several procedures to discover the consistencies and inconsistencies of each reaction system of the personality. The same applies in the sphere of abilities.

In an ideal assessment program the candidate's ability to perform (or to learn to perform) each of the several functions of a given role would be estimated separately, since it cannot be assumed that excellence in one function is highly correlated, in a given individual, with excellence in another. Furthermore, since no function (disposition and ability) can be accurately measured by a single test, a battery of tests is required to provide a sound basis for predictions.

In obtaining records of *many varied* proceedings of a personality, members of an assessment staff have three sources available: (1) the subject himself, who can be encouraged to talk or to write about his past experiences; (2) acquaintances of the subject; (3) the assessors, who create many varied situations the responses to which can be observed directly. No explanation of all this is required; it is clear that the more one knows about a man the more comprehensive will be one's understanding of his unique nature.

If it is discovered that an increase in the number of procedures (length of the assessment period) is not accompanied by an increase in the amount of pertinent data obtained, or that an increase in the amount of pertinent data is not accompanied by greater accuracy and completeness of the personality formulations, then one should suspect the intrusion of errors in theory or in practice. [. . . .]

We are recommending a variety of methods, not only because each method, by confronting the subject with a somewhat different situation, is likely to evoke different components of personality, but because each method which merits consideration has certain unique advantages and disadvantages, and the disadvantages of one method may be overcome by the advantages of another. For instance, a method may be very economical – it can be administered by one man to a large group of subjects at once – but the whole situation may be artificial, unlike anything which the subjects are apt to meet in everyday life, and their actions may be artificially constrained to a few preselected categories which allow no place for typical individual patterns of response. Other contrasting methods present the subject with a lifelike situation permissive of spontaneity, but are very expensive in man-hours – subjects must be taken one at a time or in small groups requiring two or three observers. Some methods yield objective, mechanically obtained quantitative scores, but the relation between the segmental processes so measured and the functioning of the total personality is dubious, if not definitely insignificant. Other methods bring important components of personality into operation, but estimates of the intensity of these components are matters of unreliable subjective judgments. And so it goes.

A brief list of some of the ways in which techniques may vary should be helpful at this point:

1. *The kinds of components of personality that are revealed,* such as energy level, temperament, sentiments, knowledge, theories, needs, concrete goals, degree of integration, ability to deal with things, with people, with ideas, and so forth.

2. *The components and structure of the situation confronting the subject.*

a. *Physical setting:* outdoor or indoor; open or confined space; degree of temperature and light; and so on.

b. *Nature of objects to which subject must relate his efforts:* physical obstacles to be overcome; physical objects (materials, tools, gadgets) to be manipulated; human objects (interviewer, stooges, co-actors) to govern or adjust to; symbols (oral or written words or concepts, pictures, ink blots, or other representations) and areas of symbolic reference (topics of discourse and knowledge) to be dealt with.

135

c. *Social structure:* number, roles, types, and attitudes of persons engaged in the situation.

i. *Number, roles, types, and attitudes of assessors:* physical presence or absence of official observer (if absent, whether a recording device or system of mirrors which permits overhearing or overseeing is suspected); number of assessors (e.g., interpersonal interview or board of judges); physique, age, sex, rank, race, type of assessor(s) (e.g., conspicuous or inconspicuous, detached or participating, formal or informal, strict or lenient, friendly or unfriendly).

ii. *Number, roles, types, and attitudes of other subjects:* presence or absence of other subjects; an interpersonal or group situation; a mere aggregate (e.g., sitting at separate desks) or a reciprocating or collaborating group; physique, age, sex, rank, race, type of other subjects; attitude of others (e.g., friendly or not, helpful or not, critical or not).

d. *Expectations of assessor(s) as understood by subject:* number of directions (rules) or no directions; degree of constraint of directions (e.g., formal or informal, strict or lenient, definite or ambiguous). The assessor says or seems to say (according as subject interprets his aim) one, two, or all of three things: 'Show me how much you know or how well you can do this' (performance test), or 'Let me see how you react (emotionally or directionally) to this situation' (reaction study), or 'Tell me all (or all I want to know) about yourself' (self-communicative situation).

e. *Degree of situational control exercised by assessor(s):* extent to which the situation is made to conform to an inflexible, uniform, prearranged pattern (e.g., an entirely uncontrolled natural situation at one extreme and, at the other, a situation in which all variables are kept constant).

3. *The method of recording subject's behavior.* Reliance may be placed on the assessor's unaided observation and memory, or recording aids (e.g., motion-picture camera with sound track) may be employed. In a great many procedures the subject records his responses on a paper form; in others his responses are recorded mechanically (e.g., psychogalvanometer).

Clinical psychology and psychiatry have yet to reach their full growth. No methods are entirely satisfactory. There must be constant experimentation. Since it is too early to limit a program of assessment to a fixed number of procedures, space should be left open for new techniques.

For a short over-all assessment the interview is probably the best and only indispensable method we have, but many others are very useful: intelligence tests (Bellevue-Wechsler, Mechanical Comprehension, and others), projective tests (Rorschach, TAT, Sentence Completion, for example), questionnaires (e.g., psycho-somatic inventory, attitude scales, Study of Values, Minnesota Multiphasic), autobiography (or filling out a personal history form), informal observations of behavior, and situational tests. Since the last are not well known and need to have attention called to them, we are making a separate recommendation in their behalf.

Substep 4·3

Include in the program a number of situational tests in which the candidate is required to function at the same level of integration and under somewhat similar conditions as he will be expected to function under in the field. This is based on the principle of consistency (the most fundamental of scientific assumptions), which states that the interactions that occur in two identical situations will be identical, or more specifically, that a given subject will respond to similar environmental situations in a similar manner. Of course we know that the personality of one man at two different times is never the same, and that one can rarely say that two situations are identical, and finally that there seems to be a force (which might be called the need for novelty) in some people that prompts them to act differently from the way they did before 'just for a change'. And then, as far as assessment is concerned, it is not possible to predict the forms of the scores of situations a candidate will encounter in the future; consequently strict conformity to the scientific ideal is out of the question. The best that can be done – and this is a good deal – is to expose a man to a *variety of situations of the same type as those he will meet in the field*, and, allowing for certain expected developments in his personality during the coming months, predict future performance level on the assumption of consistency.

All we are affirming here is that the 'real' test of a football player is playing in a real football game, or, if you choose, in a season of football games; and therefore the best way to assess a football player is to confront him with the necessity of playing in a simulated football game which includes as many components of a real game as possible. This assumption, a commonplace to lay-men, is not without novelty in the field of psychological testing. It is fundamental, however, to the organismic method as distin-guished from the widely accepted elementalistic method of assess-ment – a statement which calls for an explanation.

The organismic method of assessment is based on the fact that behavior of the highest order of effectiveness depends on (1) the individual's ability to perceive and interpret properly the whole situation that confronts him (e.g., to distinguish the major and minor determinants, to omit nothing that is critically important, to predict the probable course of events if he does not intervene) and (2) his ability to coordinate his acts and direct them in proper sequence toward the proper objects (to visualize the end that will appease his needs, to see the shortest pathways to this end and the agencies that are available to him, and to order the spatio-temporal sequence of his actions, and so on) in such a way that a satisfying effect will be produced. Ordinarily the majority of these processes occur automatically, many of them unconsciously, but, in any event, they all require *organization*: the organization of successive perceptions into a rough schema of the developing event; the organization of images, words, and concepts in relation to this schema to constitute its diagnosis and prognosis; the organization of this prognosis in relation to a visualized purpose (images of a desired modification); the organization of actones (muscles and words) and of agencies (instruments and fellow workers); the organization of these means in relation to the environmental objects that must be adjusted to, interested, or controlled; and then, finally, the organization of these partial or subordinate aims in relation to the visualized purpose. The effectiveness of the whole action depends on the integration (internal coherence) of the constituent operations in the brain and on the adjustment (congruent application) of these operations to successive parts of the environment. Consequently, in devising tests of effectiveness the organismic psychologist will choose tasks and situations which cannot be properly solved without organization, since it is the power to organize, as much as any other power, that he wishes to measure.

The elementalistic approach, on the other hand, calls for an analysis of a proposed function into its component operations and then the invention and standardization of one or more tests for each operation. Some of these tests can be administered to many subjects at once, others must be administered individually.

The elementalistic method is abstract and unrealistic, since no attempt is made to reproduce the conditions under which the man will eventually perform. It is scientific, however, in the sense that each test measures the goodness and speed of a well-defined process in objective quantitative terms, thus eliminating from the scoring the all too frequent errors inherent in subjective judgments. In adopting this method, however, the psychologist makes a radical subjective judgment at the very start by electing to abstract from a complex configurated process a few elementary constituent processes, testing for these separately, and then *adding* the scores to arrive at a final rating. He does this even though he knows that in actual life the mind does not *add* sequences of elementary processes to produce results, but *organizes* them into effective forms.

The organismic method depends for its success upon the ability of the psychologist to observe the pattern and effectiveness of the candidate's behavior and to identify the factors which promote and the factors which impede the forward course of the action. And so it could be said that this method calls for the improvement of the psychologist as observer and interpreter rather than the improvement of mechanical instruments and test materials. Because of the well-known unreliability of individual judgments, the organismic method as it stands today requires two or three competent observers for each event. Thus it is much more expensive in respect to time and personnel than elementalistic tests, many of which are suitable for large groups.

Leaving aside the great factor of motivation and considering only the nature of good thinking – the over-all importance of organization and of imagination – and the conditions under which it must ordinarily proceed, in contact with men and under stress, it must be clear that an elementalistic intelligence test could not possibly be an adequate measure of effective intellection, even of abstract intellection, in an adult member of society. What the intelligence test certainly can do is to distinguish those who lack the pieces with which to build the whole, who are incapable of the partial comprehensions that are necessary for a total act of comprehension. In doing this efficiently, the classic intelligence test has proved itself a useful instrument and deserves to be retained. But it is necessary to recognize its limitations since great injustice can be done to individuals if the test is used as a criterion of thinking capacity among those whose scores range above a certain level.

The striking and impressive feature of all elementalistic methods is that they provide quantitative objective measures of relatively simple processes, and thus seem to conform to the great tradition of science. An elementalistic testing program can be made into a series of almost mechanical procedures which can be conducted for the most part by technicians pure and simple, and the psychologist as observer, interpreter, diagnostician, and valuator is all but eliminated. Everyone who scores the tests gets precisely the same result and this gives rise to a general feeling of satisfaction, a feeling of 'truth', since consensus among experts is the nearest we can ever get to justified certainty. But suppose a biologist comes along and says: 'Gentlemen, I am impressed by the unanimity of your judgments. I can see no evidence of subjective bias in your readings, scorings, and computations. But on the other hand, it seems to me that subjective bias figured prominently in your decision to separate out one fraction of the concrete complex event and accept the measurement of this as a proper index of the total process. There, at the very start, is where the personal element – the feeling and the sentiment – entered into your procedure. As I see it, this focalization is an example of what Whitehead calls "misplaced concreteness". Actually the score that you have obtained on this test is not a representation of reality – any more than the measurement of one muscle contraction is an adequate representation of the form and effectiveness of a complete bodily movement, the act, let us say, of driving a golf ball.' This judgment, it seems to us, cannot be gainsaid. The subjectivity of the elementalist comes in at the beginning when he plans his procedure, and at the very end when, despite protestations to the contrary, he is inclined to rely on his test as a valid measure of over-all ability.

The elementalistic approach calls for accurate quantitative measurements of partial, isolated processes, whereas the organismic approach comes down to inaccurate estimations of total integrated processes. From a practical standpoint the question is, Which method has a higher predictive validity? At the moment this question cannot be answered, no adequate researches bearing on this point having been reported. The result of an investigation along these lines will depend in large measure on which areas of personality are chosen for study, on the suitability of the elementalistic tests that are selected, and on the ability of the organismic psychologists who act as observers. At present the great advantages of elementalistic methods are (1) that they can be administered by almost anyone after a short training period; (2) that many of them can be presented to a large group at one time or to individuals in rapid succession, and hence are suitable for mass testing; (3) that they are generally successful in picking out those who are entirely unqualified for a certain task, or those who have some definite defect; and (4) that subjective bias does not enter into the scoring of the results. Furthermore, elementalists can point to positive correlations in a large number of studies to prove the effectiveness of their methods, whereas organicists have as yet nothing definite to show for their theories.

The differences between elementalistic and organismic methodology have been magnified in this section in order to clarify the theoretical ground on which situational tests are founded. The OSS assessment staffs were faced by the problem of discriminating between candidates who fell, for the most part, in the upper half of the distribution curve of general competence or of some special skill, men who had been recruited because of demonstrated ability in some particular field of endeavor. Consequently, elementalistic tests which had proved valid in testing children and in distinguishing adults at the lower end of the distribution curve, but not in accurately predicting different degrees of excellence among adults in the upper brackets, could not be counted on to carry the whole burden of answering the questions that were asked of us. Therefore we added procedures of a different kind, tasks which required mental operations on a higher integrative level; and since there is a difference between 'know-how' and 'can-do' – the two are not always correlated – we made the candidates actually attempt the tasks with their muscles or spoken words, rather than merely indicate on paper how the tasks could be done. We were prompted to introduce realistic tests of ability by such findings as this: that men who earn a high score in Mechanical Comprehension, a paper-and-pencil test, may be below average when it comes to solving mechanical problems with their hands. Furthermore, because a great deal of the work of the world must be accomplished in a social context and also because the OSS staff was expected to estimate every candidate's disposition and aptitude for harmonious social relations, a good many of the tasks which we devised for the candidates had to be accomplished in collaboration with others. Finally, since most of the critical situations which were confronting the majority of OSS men in the field were both novel and stressful, we made our testing situations novel and stressful. Thus it may be said that the situational tests used at OSS assessment stations were as lifelike as circumstances permitted, incorporating some of the major components of situations that would naturally arise in the course of operations in the field. In other words, we tried to design assessment situations that would be somewhat similar to the situations in the management of which candidates would be judged by their superior officers and associates in the theater.

In retrospect it seems a little peculiar that for thirty years we psychologists should have devoted so much time to improving the reliability of our tests and so little time to improving their validity. Even more peculiar is the almost exclusive attention to paper-and-pencil tests when the results of studies of the reliability of these tests were all pointing to the importance of the principle of similarity – similar situation, similar response. Time and time again test constructors have found that to obtain a high correlation between two tests of the same function, the forms of the tests must be very similar. For some reason, however, the principle of similarity has rarely been applied to the primary task of test invention. Few people seem to have been at all disquieted by the fact that taking a conventional paper-and-pencil test is very different from solving a problem in everyday life. Finally, as previously stated, all of us have been lax in bringing our critical reflections and techniques to bear on the crucial task of validation. Surely, the essential criterion of a good test is its congruence with reality; its coherence with other tests is a matter of secondary concern. At this stage, in fact, the problem of validity is so important that we would suggest a reversal of the usual procedure: that tests which are being developed should be administered only to persons who have been thoroughly studied, persons about whose activities sufficient data have already been collected.

Situational tests have a long and honorable pedigree that reaches back into Biblical times, and if American psychologists were as pious as the early settlers of their country they would undoubtedly have come upon the records of these ancient experiments and recast them into modern forms. It was none other than Jehovah who improvised the first large-scale situational test, the object being to provide Gideon with a reliable basis for picking the best warriors from among ten thousand volunteers.

And the Lord said unto Gideon, The people are yet too many; bring them down unto the water, and I will try them for thee there: and it shall be, that of whom I say unto thee, This shall go with thee, the same shall go with thee; and of whomsoever I say unto thee, This shall not go with thee, the same shall not go. So he brought down the people unto the water: and the Lord said unto Gideon, Everyone that lappeth of the water with his tongue, as a dog lappeth, him shalt thou set by himself; likewise every one that boweth down upon his knees to drink. And the number of them that lapped, putting their hand to their mouth, were three hundred men; but all the rest of the people bowed down upon their knees to drink water. And the Lord said unto Gideon, By the three hundred men that lapped will I save you, and deliver the Midianites into thine hand: and let all the other people go every man unto his place. (*Judges* 7: 4–7)

As proof of the efficacy of this test is the recorded fact that the three hundred put to rout the host of Midian, drove them across the Jordan and out of the land of Israel. There was no mention of cowards among the three hundred, who even while drinking had remained alertly aware of the possibility of being attacked by the enemy.

Step 5

Construct a sufficient formulation of the personality of each assessee before making specific ratings, predictions, and recommendations. This is the second of the two major technical principles of the organismic system of assessment. Like the first major principle (Substep 4.3), it is derived from the general proposition that the whole and its parts are mutually dependent. If this is true – and, today, who doubts it? – it follows that to explain or to predict the manifested parts of a personality in a specified situation one must discover the nature of the personality as a whole. Although the expression 'personality as a whole' has become fashionable in certain professional circles, it has never been precisely defined and the best we can do, as we proceed, is to explain what we mean by it in the context of this section.

Let us start by placing personality in space. Where is it? The processes and integrations of processes which constitute personality *occur in the brain*. This is the seat of the government of the organism, since it is the only place where sensory processes from the entire body terminate and motor processes to the entire body originate. It is the locus of the feelings which evaluate events as they occur and discriminate goals for action. It is the seat of consciousness, of thought, of conflict, and of decision. It is also the repository of all traces of past experiences, of percepts, symbols, concepts, values, emotional attachments, commitments, plans, resolutions, and anticipations. Thus the enduring latent establishments as well as the kinetic processes of personality are in the head.

Next, let us place personality in time. What is the duration of personality? Personality is a developing 'institution' which functions from birth to death. During sleep, unconscious anabolic processes regenerate the sources of the energies that are expended in the ceaseless activities which constitute its waking life. The history of a personality might be represented as a long sequence of *proceedings*. Some of these are *internal proceedings* during which the personality, abstracted from its environment, is daydreaming, or attempting to understand and evaluate past events, or to predict the future, or to assess its own capacities, or to settle

143

some conflict, or to solve some intellectual problem, or to lay out a course of action, or to decide what to say on an anticipated occasion. Others are *external proceedings* during which the personality is overtly engaged in dealing with its environment, in observing, enjoying, manipulating, complying with, defending itself against, or avoiding, other personalities or physical objects. Every proceeding leaves behind it some traces of its occurrence, traces of its novel elements especially. In this manner the more or less enduring *establishments* of personality – its supplies of facts, concepts, values, action-patterns – are extended and modified from day to day by the results of its functional operations. Most personalities are developing along certain lines – by assimilations, differentiations, and integrations – throughout life, although in other respects they may be merely conserving what they have acquired, or perhaps losing it regressively. Anyhow, the establishments of personality, cross-sectionally considered at different points in its life history, are different.

Since we cannot observe the establishments of personality in the brain, and we have no instruments capable of directly recording its functional processes, and, since it has been shown that not all these processes have the property of consciousness, it is evident that the components and structures of personality *must be inferred* from their manifestations in the stream of consciousness and from their manifestations in the flow of overt speech and action. The data consist of *subjective facts* reported by the individual and of *objective facts* observed by the psychologist or by others. With these in mind the psychologist attempts to arrive at a conception of the forms of the determining variables. Thus the personality is not a series of perceptible facts, but, in actual practice, a *hypothetical formulation*, the aim of which is to *explain* and to *predict* the perceptible facts.

Another point which must be held firmly in mind is that in analysing and reconstructing each of the significant external proceedings of personality, it is as necessary to define the structure of the environmental situation, the attitudes and actions of the object, as it is to define the attitudes and actions of the subject. One must not represent a personality as if it existed in a vacuum. Its establishments must be connected with the objects and situations which evoke them. This is particularly true in formulating the developing series of proceedings, or the *serial*, which constitutes the history of an interpersonal relationship, a friendship, or marriage: the representation of the personality of the object is essential to an understanding of the subject. In other words, although the processes of personality occur in the brain, they cannot be described or explained without reference to external objects and settings. Consequently, *the environment is included in every adequate formulation of personality.*

Now, perhaps, we are in a position to consider the meaning of 'whole' as applied to personality. Some people use 'whole personality' comprehensively to denote the total or entire personality. Here there are two possibilities: the whole longitudinal, or temporal, personality, and the whole cross-sectional personality. The former is relatively concrete and referential: personality is the entire sequence of organized psychological processes in the brain from birth to death. The cross-sectional definition, on the other hand, is very abstract and hypothetical: personality is the entire constitution of *potential* psychological processes and structures in the brain at a given moment. This latter definition depends on a morphological supposition inasmuch as it assumes the existence or some more or less enduring physicochemical structures, or establishments of personality, which remain dormant except when activated by certain stimuli. The establishments, however, are never described in morphological terms, but rather as they are objectified in temporal patterns of activity. These two conceptions of the 'whole personality' might be combined into an all-inclusive notion which embraces not only the history of the proceedings of personality (longitudinal view), but the history of its developing establishments as portrayed by a series of cross-sectional formulations.

The next point to be noted is that a *complete* formulation of the *whole* personality, longitudinal or cross-sectional, is not only far beyond the powers of any group of psychologists today, but, if achievable, would be much too long and complicated for ordinary use. Consequently, we speak of a *sufficient* formulation, meaning sufficient for a designated purpose, which, in the present case, is the assessment of men and women. Inasmuch as a complete formulation is both impossible and undesirable, the term 'formulation' can be used to denote a 'sufficient formulation'. Since a formulation that is sufficient for one purpose – say, assessment – will not usually be sufficient for another – say, psychotherapy – there may be several different formulations of the same personality, all of which are correct. But, as we see it, every formulation should give an outline, not of the 'whole personality', but of the 'personality as a whole'.

'Personality as a whole' does not mean the whole, entire personality; it means the over-all unity and organization of parts that is attained during a designated period of the subject's life. It refers to the degree of unity and coordination (wholeness) that the personality exhibits during one short functional operation, or in a long series of progressions, day after day, towards a distal goal, or in the establishment, over a lifetime, of a harmonious way of life which allows for the successive satisfaction of its major needs. Whatever the degree of unity that is achieved, it comes out of conflicts and resolutions of conflicts; and these should be included in the formulation. This conception of the 'personality as a whole' points to a goal-directed force, or conation, as the chief unifying and integrating factor in personality. Psychologists are not yet agreed as to the proper representation of the basic determinants of effective action, but universal human experience teaches us that it is emotional, intellectual, and conative energy directed towards a defined *purpose* which organizes the psychological processes into a temporal whole. This is the outstanding *conscious* fact, regardless of the number and nature of the underlying needs or drives which will be appeased by the action. An extreme case of wholeness would be a personality that is completely controlled by one persisting, superordinate, long-range purpose. The definition of this purpose would be enough to explain most of the functional operations. Since in actual life one never finds a personality so unified, the representation of 'wholeness' is more complicated. It usually comes down to a formulation of the relations between the major dynamic systems, each of which consists of a combination of needs directed towards a combination of goals, and, integrated with these, one or more valued goal objects and goal places, and a large number of action patterns and agencies. The degree of effectiveness of each dynamic system should be included in the account.

Beside vectorial forces there are a number of other variables which have a broadly determining, and so, in a sense, unifying, influence on the personality. Among these are energy level, temperament, subjectivity-objectivity, introversion-extraversion, egocentricity-sociocentricity, conformity-nonconformity, and so forth. But we are not going to discuss the problem of what variables are required for a sufficient formulation of personality, first, because there is no possibility of doing justice to the subject in the space allotted, and, second, because we abandoned the plan of attempting to set forth the products of our theoretical reflections, fearing, as explained in the first part of this chapter, that no statement would conform to the views of the majority of the members of our staff.

Up to now no proposed definition of personality has proved satisfactory to all schools of psychology, and there has been no unanimity as to how one should go about formulating the events of a person's life for purposes of explanation, prediction, and control. There are no available holistic conceptions for representing *normal* personalities. But the psychologist is not without instruments of thought. He possesses, in fact, a large number of fairly well-defined concepts which stand for (1) certain hypothetical structures of the personality (e.g., ego, superego, ideal ego); (2) certain hypothetical components (e.g., inferiority complex, sentiment *pro* underprivileged, agoraphobia, need for support, political orientation); (3) certain modes of feeling, thought and action (e.g., cycloid temperament, objectivity, flight of ideas, impulsivity); (4) certain kinds of effectiveness (e.g., general intelligence, mechanical ability); and also (5) certain disease entities (e.g., compulsion neurosis, schizophrenia). The latter might be considered holistic formulations in so far as each of them defines a rather large number of intercorrelated variables and (for each disease) the general structure of their interactions. But the compound concept of each disease reconstructs a certain variety of disturbance (conflict, dissociation, and so on) which occurs *within* a total personality. The effective health-producing processes of the personality, which vary from case to case, are not included in the formulation.

Besides concepts of this sort, there are excellent descriptions in the literature of rudimentary typologies based on a few variables, usually a dichotomy (e.g., subjective-objective, introversive-extratensive) or a trichotomy (e.g., narcistic, obsessive, and erotic). But all of these require further analysis in conjunction with studies of other variables. To identify a man as an introvert, for example, gives us no information as to his energy level, his fluctuations of mood, his enduring emotional attachments, his membership systems, his political ideology, the pattern of his erotic fantasies, the strength of his conscience, his major dilemmas, his intelligence, his initiative and resourcefulness, the degree of his self-confidence, his dominant aims, the level of his aspiration, his chief abilities, and a great many other important components. Psychiatrists and psychologists are just now in the process of identifying and defining these separable variables. They have not reached the point of attempting to combine a sufficient number of them into tentative formulations susceptible of verification by detailed personality studies. It is worthy of note that very many of the concepts which are commonly used today in formulating personalities have been contributed by psycho-analysts and psychiatrists who are inclined, partly by the demands of their profession, to an organismic frame of reference.

We shall make no attempt to list the notions which were most commonly employed in attempting to represent the personalities of the candidates at assessment. Since there was no time to construct a common conceptual scheme, each senior staff member whose duty it was to write personality sketches used the concepts which he considered most adequate in portraying to himself and to his fellow workers the underlying dynamics. Since the sketches were composed for laymen (the administrative officers of the OSS), they were not written in abstract terms, but on the level of ordinary discourse. These sketches were the only records that were made of the results of holistic reflections, and so it is not possible now to state how far toward 'wholeness' the staff members carried their conceptualizations of the different personalities. The process which took place in their heads is not on paper. Certainly most of us never approximated the ideal: a formulation of the 'personality as a whole'. This expression, consequently, must be understood as a somewhat pretentious overstatement. But current usage provides no other term to distinguish our *attempt* from the elementalistic mode of procedure.

Here it is perhaps worth pointing out that the task of a present-day clinical student of psychology is that of an explorer and experimenter rather than that of a diagnostician. To make this plain we might consider a greatly oversimplified statement of the problem in the form of an analogy. Take the case of the organic chemist whose function is to predict the behavior of a sample of any compound that is handed to him. What will he do? He will note its physical properties and then observe its reactions to a number of known substances. The results of a few tests of this sort will usually enable him to name the substance and then to predict immediately the processes which will ensue when it is confronted by this and that compound under specified conditions. Now, one reason, among several, why the predictions of the chemist are highly valid is the fact that the properties of most of the objects with which he deals have been thoroughly studied, and so his routine task is that of distinguishing (naming) an entity about which there is a mass of ordered knowledge summarized in manuals and textbooks, rather than that of discovering the nature of an entity about which little or nothing is known. (The latter is the task of an experimental chemist.) Here it should be noted that knowledge about a compound is mostly contained in statements as to its chemical properties, that is, in representations of the nature and effect of its reactions with other *known* compounds under *known* conditions. In other words, to know (understand, formulate) a compound in 'functional' terms, one must possess an equal amount of knowledge about (1) each of the different entities with which it reacts, (2) the product of each reaction, and (3) the setting in which the reaction occurs. One thing is defined in relation to each of a number of other things. Since about three hundred thousand compounds have been defined, the population of entities within the modern chemist's empire includes a great many 'knowns'; and as soon as he has identified (named) one of them, he is prepared, with the manual at his side, to predict its behavior in the presence of each of a large number of others. The naturalist, with his definitions of thousands of different species, and the physician, with his integrated mental representations of scores of different ailments, are in a similar position, in so far as each is able to make a number of reasonably valid predictions (prognoses) as soon as he has correctly discriminated the entity before him. He can do this because, like the chemist, he has at his disposal a mass of scientific information – collected, sifted, correlated, and ordered by generations of workers – about most of the entities which belong within his province.

Now, for the moment, let us imagine a state of affairs which would enable a psychologist to function as does the chemist, the naturalist, and the physician. Let us suppose that the most fundamental and most crucial variables of personality have already been discovered, and, for simplicity's sake, say that these variables are dynamic systems, each of which involves a pattern of specified actions in relation to a pattern of specified situations. Let us suppose that millions of people have been thoroughly studied and it has been found that they fall into one thousand types, each of which has been properly defined and named. Let 'definition of a type' be equivalent to 'formulation of the personality as a whole'. Since in the process of arriving at the different types (the thousand different conceptions), minor variables (slight differences in form and numerous insignificant elements) were necessarily disregarded, a formulation will not represent the 'whole' (entire, complete) personality of a man, but his personality 'as a whole'; that is, the organization of the dominant action systems. Let us further suppose that the lives of one hundred individuals corresponding to each of the thousand types have been exhaustively studied and there is now available a great deal of ordered knowledge about the behavioral variations within each

149

type. According to this fantasy the psychologist is now in the position of a chemist, naturalist, or physician. His task is to make a diagnosis, to identify the type, to recognize an entity about which much is known. Since to accomplish this, a few tests will often be sufficient, it could be said that this fictitious professional, by discovering a little about a man, can suddenly know a lot – everything that has been written about the given type. With this knowledge he is able to predict with a reasonable degree of accuracy how he is likely to react and with what effect in this and that situation.

All this, of course, is a wish-fulfilling fairy tale. For no satisfactory formulation of a personality as a whole has ever been published. None of us knows exactly what elements should be included, or how the various inter-relationships, or patterns, of these elements should be represented. At present the psychologist is more in the position of a chemist who encounters an entirely new and different compound, except that he is not acquainted with all the elements that could possibly exist in the object of his interest, and he is not familiar with the consequences of different possible combinations of the elements with which he *is* acquainted. His task is not one of recognizing an old acquaintance (apperception), but of discovering the nature of a stranger (conceptualization).

We have violently oversimplified the contrasting situations of chemist and psychologist in the hope of clarifying the latter's job and of indicating a strategic course for research and reflection, namely, the development of a typology which incorporates a sufficient number of variables. Since the formulation of a type must be based on an understanding of the mode of *organization* of variables, the undertaking calls for an organismic, or holistic, approach. This is another reason why we are not enthusiastic about the elementalistic method of testing when dissociated from the study of each person functioning as a unit. The elementalistic statistical mode of advance may succeed in telling us what variables are commonly combined in one person, but, as yet, it cannot reveal the form in which they are combined.

At this stage in the development of our science, each conception of a personality is a compound of inferences, a product of the imagination, which must be verified by observations of behavior in the future. It is a conception which might be compared to a model of an extinct type of man constructed by a palaeontologist, except that the palaeontologist, having learned a good deal about the evolution of the human skeleton, is probably justified in making his rough reconstruction of the never observed whole body of a primitive man on the basis of one or two fragments – an unearthed jawbone, or even a single tooth. But if no entire human skeleton had ever been studied, the discovery of a few pieces of bone could hardly lead to a valid inference as to the total structure. One could not even 'understand' the pieces. It would be necessary to collect a great many more fragments in order to build a rough model of the whole, and only then would it be possible to perceive the relations, and hence the meaning and significance, of the initially discovered parts.

This illustrates in a crude way one of the chief purposes of a conception of the whole: it provides ground for a reinterpretation and re-evaluation of the manifested parts, the very parts which led to the conception. Another analogy, though static, might serve to clarify this point. Suppose you were given only twenty (out of a total of two hundred) pieces of a jigsaw picture puzzle. If you tried to guess the meaning of each of these pieces isolated from the others, you might conclude that a particular light blue piece, for example, was a fragment of sky because 80 per cent of all light blue pieces in one thousand puzzles studied represented sky. But, on the other hand, if you examined all twenty pieces in relation to each other, it might become apparent that the light blue piece was probably not sky at all, but part of a woman's dress, since there was another piece which showed a light blue sleeve reaching to the wrist of a delicate, bejewelled hand. Furthermore, several other pieces might clearly indicate that you were dealing with an indoor rather than an outdoor scene. Finally, if the twenty selected pieces came from critical areas of the picture, it might be possible for you to draw a rough hypothetical sketch of the whole design, many details being necessarily omitted. This hypothetical picture-as-a-whole would be analogous to one of the several meanings of the term 'personality-as-a-whole'.

The method we are supporting here is that of predicting the future by thinking inductively from an observed set of facts to a conception (a hypothetical formulation of the personality), and then by thinking deductively from this conception to the facts which should be expected. In contrast to this is the practice, common among those using testing techniques today, of predicting the future by proceeding mechanically from the observed facts to the expected facts. To make this clear we shall once more call to mind the elementalist, the fictional character portrayed in the previous section, and exaggerate the differences between his methodology and that of the organicist.

Let us assume that the task is to predict the rating of over-all effectiveness which will be given a man after one year of vocational performances in a specified environment. If the members of the assessment staff are elementalists, they will perform this task by administering a number of specific tests which can be scored objectively and mechanically, and then, by combining in a formula the scores obtained by the candidate on the different tests, calculate a quotient which will rigidly determine the prediction of the future rating. Thus from relatively precise measures of a few performances the elementalist will directly and mechanically arrive at his estimate, without the embarrassment of any intermediate process of thought. The advantages of this method are considerable: (1) it is relatively quick, because it eliminates interviewing as well as all reflection and discussion as to the character and merits of each candidate; (2) because it is quick, it permits the assessment of a relatively large number of candidates in a given unit of time; (3) it is relatively cheap, because it is quick and because suitable staff members can be engaged at a relatively low salary, since, once the separate tests have been constructed, they can be administered and scored by anyone capable of learning the simple technical rules; (4) it can be employed on a large scale, because it is quick and cheap, and because it is possible to find a relatively large number of technicians with sufficient ability to practise it; and, finally, (5) it eliminates the errors inherent in subjective judgments. If the elementalist is scrupulous about validating each test against adequate criteria, he will discover, by trying one test after another, which battery has the highest predictive value.

The organicist does, or should do, everything that the elementalist does; but he does something in addition which takes time and thought: he carries out a number of supplementary procedures (interviews, situational tests, and soon), makes tentative interpretations of the facts so gained, and attempts to arrive at a plausible representation of the personality as a whole. The efficacy of this process in sizing up some kinds of cases, such as neuropsychiatric disorders, is generally acknowledged, but its efficacy in assessing the run of normal persons is still to be determined.

Organismic assessment is based on the hypothesis that a trained psychologist or psychiatrist, with a fund of additional facts at his disposal, is, today, capable of improving to a significant degree the accuracy of mechanical predictions derived from test scores alone. The truth of this hypothesis depends on the definition of 'significant degree' as well as on (1) the competence of the psychiatrist or psychologist, (2) the number and kinds of procedures used for obtaining additional facts, (3) the time allowed for diagnosis and prognosis (the length of the assessment period), (4) the kinds of jobs which assessees will be expected to perform, (5) the adequacy of the psychologist's or psychiatrist's knowledge of these jobs; and so forth.

The second hypothesis made by the advocates of organismic assessment is that, whether the first hypothesis be true or false, the repeated practice of this system will result in developments of techniques and of the abilities involved in making dependable observations and judgments which together will eventually lead to a decided increase in the validity of predictions.

Finally, there is the supremely important point that the organismic system is an admirable way of studying personality and, if systematically pursued, should greatly advance the science of man, which, in turn will lead to practical knowledge, useful not only in the field of selection and placement, but in many other fields.

The organismic system is founded on several well-accepted facts, one of which is that the action patterns observed or the performances measured during the assessment period are not always representative of the candidate's usual behavior, because of the operation of transient factors or because some commonly recurrent variables of personality are either intentionally inhibited or not excited by any of the tests or situations constituting the program.

Among the transient factors which were often found to be operating at Station S are the following: (1) poor athletic condition (being out of training) as the result of months without exercise; (2) state of mental exhaustion when taking the tests on the first night as the result of a sleepless night on the train; (3) excessively high motivation because of the candidate's disposition to exert himself to the limit when competing in the presence of others (supervisors, critics, judges); (4) low motivation because of a candidate's transient underestimation of the proposed assignment or because of a doubt as to the suitableness of the job proposed for him. In addition to these are the disturbing preoccupations (overlapping situations) which the candidates bring with them – temporary worries about family and business affairs, and so forth.

Every assessee, on the other hand, will possess numerous established dispositions which will not be manifested during the assessment period, either because he is able to inhibit them over a period of a few days (e.g., neurotic tendencies, unacceptable sentiments, inclination to indolence, moodiness, or irritability), or because no situation excites them (e.g., fear of horseback riding, dislike of colored people, stubborn aversion to domineering leaders), or because there are no free time and no favorable conditions for their operation (e.g., alcoholism, pursuit of distracting and wholly personal aims).

These considerations have led organicists to the conclusion that additional procedures (e.g., autobiography, interviews, situational tests, psychodrama, projection tests) should be included in the assessment program in order to obtain the information necessary (1) for estimating the strength of other determining variables (besides those which are directly involved in vocational activities), and (2) for arriving at a sufficient formulation of the personality as a whole. These two aims are complementary, since the exposition and preliminary estimation of the additional variables (energy, motivation, emotional stability, social relations, and so on) are steps along the path to a formulation and a formulation provides the framework for a final re-evaluation of these variables.

It was one of the noteworthy features of the OSS assessment system that it recognized explicitly the necessity of relating all observations to each other, not in a mechanical way, but by an interpretive process aiming at the discovery of general patterns and action systems, and made this the guiding principle of all its operations. At times a thoroughgoing application of this policy was blocked by the pressure of work which reduced to a minimum the time available for discussions and reflections. The discontent of the staff members with the results of their work at such times indicates that this phase of assessment was felt to be indispensable.

Not less noteworthy is the way in which this basic principle was implemented and at the same time guarded against subjective distortion, through group participation in all phases of the work. The policy of group discussion and group decision as distinct from a mere mechanical process of averaging scores or counting votes presupposes the possibility of arriving, in a favorable case, at a common conception. Whenever this common conception succeeds in encompassing and integrating all the aspects of a personality noted by the different staff members it comes as near to the status of an objective judgment as it is possible to come under the given conditions.

Step 6

Write, in nontechnical language, a personality sketch of each assessee, which predictively describes him as a functioning member of the organization. A list of ratings is an exceedingly abstract mode of representing a personality. It conveys no impression of the man in action. It does not show how the different variables are integrated into a purposive whole. It obliterates subtle characteristics which may be crucially important. Therefore, a personality sketch which incorporates the information that is not conveyable through ratings is an essential supplement to the latter. It is our conclusion, indeed, after canvassing the opinions of OSS administrative officers, that the personality sketch is capable of communicating the more useful findings.

The personality sketch is a translation of the abstract formulation into everyday speech with the elimination of everything that is not relevant to the administrator's task of placement and management of personnel.

For the first few months the sketches written at Station S were very short – one or two paragraphs – but they increased in length as time went on, and for the last year of assessment averaged about eight hundred words each. Although the writers of these sketches were not bound to follow a rigid form, it became customary to start each sketch with an outline of the candidate's past history and record of achievement; to follow this with an account of his performances during the three-day period at Station S; and to end the sketch with a discussion of the interpretations and conclusions which led to the final recommendation.

A survey of these sketches has revealed two outstanding defects: space devoted to an array of uninterpreted facts and space devoted to the diagnosis of variables the relevance of which is not explained. In both cases the administrative officer is left to make up his own mind as to the meaning and significance of the findings.

To turn in a personality sketch composed entirely of accounts of the subject's behavior in a variety of situations is scientifically useless, if not harmful, unless it goes to an officer who is more talented and experienced than the assessor who made the observations. A fact is a fact, and as such provides no ground for a predictive judgment. In order to predict one must at least infer, implicitly or explicitly, that a persisting disposition or attribute of the personality lies behind the fact. It is the professional function of the psychologist to make inferences of this sort as well as to report the observations which justify them. In writing sketches for laymen, facts which do not justify inferences should be omitted, because the layman will certainly make his own inferences, automatically if not deliberately, and if these are unjustified, the decisions that flow from them may be unfortunate.

Most of the members of the staff were psychiatrists or clinical psychologists who had been trained to explore the minds of their subjects for memories of childhood events and to report their formulations of family structure, infantile dispositions and fantasies, unconscious complexes, and so forth. Naturally, they were inclined to proceed along the same lines in interviewing candidates at S and in writing their personality sketches. But in most instances we ourselves did not know to what extent, if any, these childhood situations and events were relevant to the administrator's task of placing and managing his men, and certainly the administrator himself could not be expected to make the legitimate deductions. Consequently, the inclusion of diagnoses of this order represented so much wasted time and space; and, by confusing the administrator, might occasionally have resulted in unwarranted decisions.

The ideal personality sketch is one which pictures the candidate in action, performing work similar to that which he will be expected to do in the future. It is, of course, the product of the assessor's subjective processes, of intuition and reason, but this is unavoidable at the present stage of psychology. So long as a subjective factor must operate in every decision that is made, it is better to bring it out into the open by making explicit predictions, each one of which is virtually a hypothesis which will be proved or disproved in the course of events.

At Station S the subjective factor was held in check by the collective effort of the staff. The sketch itself was the work of two assessors, who, though covering different phases of the personality, were obliged to arrive at conceptions acceptable to both. Then, the reading of the report in the staff conference, as we shall see, brought further checks. Each generalization had to be supported by sufficient evidence to make it plausible, and no generalization that seemed unwarranted or disregarded contradictory data was permitted to go unchallenged. Thus each personality sketch corresponded to the conclusions of several different minds.

Step 7
At the end of the assessment period hold a staff conference for the

purpose of reviewing and correcting the personality sketch and of deciding on the ratings and recommendations of each assessee. Our experience has shown that it is better to have the personality sketch written *before* the conference, so that it can be read at that time to the entire staff. One advantage of this practice is that the discussion of a case, instead of being random and diffuse, is focused on certain crucial points which have been highlighted, after some reflection, by the only assessor who is in possession of the intimate facts of the candidate's past history. Another and still greater advantage is that no personality sketch is incorporated in the official report and sent to the administrative officers which has not been approved by all the assessors.

According to this scheme, then, the personality sketch provides structure for the discussion, the purpose of which is to change or eliminate statements unjustified by the evidence, and, if necessary, to add other statements to cover manifestations of the personality which escaped the notice of the writer.

Our hypothesis is that individual judgments made *before* listening to a group discussion are generally less valid than individual judgments made *after* listening to a group discussion. The chief reason for this would seem to be that group discussion brings into each man's sphere of reflection more facts and more interpretations than were there before. Thus the errors that come from ignorance of all the available evidence and the errors that come from an inability to conceive of all plausible interpretations will be reduced. As a rule, those who abandon the decision they reached before discussion in favor of one proposed by another member of the group do so because the latter seems more valid to them. Certainly they are influenced, but they are influenced in the right direction more often than in the wrong direction, because, in general, those who are most competent in analyzing and reconstructing events, in distinguishing the chief determinants, are those whose presentations and arguments are most convincing.

There are a number of other factors, of course, besides sheer diagnostic ability, which play a part in determining to what extent a given assessor's judgments will be accepted or rejected: energy, desire to persuade, verbal facility, egocentricity, valuation of his own ideas, attitude toward the ideas of others, general social attitudes, reputation, role (in line of authority), popularity, and so forth. Also, a number of factors besides intelligence determine the extent to which a given assessor will accept the opinions of others: need for affiliation, dislike of controversy, suggestibility, negativisim, obstinacy. Variables of this class may operate powerfully in some cases, as when a modest, able man is overshadowed by an aggressive one with less ability; but in a group of five or more, which is controlled in a democratic fashion, these factors become less significant as time goes on. The insightfulness of the unobtrusive man becomes recognized, and the force of the more assertive person is corrected for. Anyhow, there is a tendency for these determinants to balance out, leaving diagnostic ability as the chief factor in deciding the course of group opinion.

The other hypothesis on which the staff conference is founded is that the judgments of the majority are, in the long run, more valid than the judgments of any one member of a group, assuming that the disparity in ability among the members is not great. One can, of course, imagine a group composed of one incomparable genius and several bumptious ignoramuses who do not recognize his superiority, in which the judgment of the majority would be regularly less valid than the judgment of the talented individual, but a group of this order is confined, as far as we know, to the world of fantasy. Under certain circumstances, however, it may be advisable to leave final decisions to a diagnostic council composed of the more talented and experienced members of the staff.

Step 8

Construct experimental designs as frames for assessment procedures so that all the data necessary for the solution of strategic problems will be systematically obtained and recorded. At this early stage in the development of psychology the evaluation of each technique, of the final ratings, and of the over-all conclusions should be considered an essential part of every assessment program. The efficacy of no psychological test is so well established that one can afford to continue using it without periodic checks. This means that a satisfactory *appraisal* system must be devised for estimating the effectiveness of every accepted assessee after he has worked for a number of months as a member of the organization. The appraisal system must be devised and tested at the very start, because it defines the target at which all assessment procedures should be directed. If the target is not precisely discriminated, there will be no definite criteria for deciding which tests should be included in the original schedule.

Besides the evaluation of the different technical procedures there are many important psychological problems which can be illumined, if not solved, by a multiform organismic assessment program. But to accomplish this in a scientific manner it is necessary to set up an experimental design suitable to each problem. Consequently, before selecting the techniques and arranging the schedule, the members of the staff should decide which problems they will attack first. Here again it is a matter of delineating goals, so that means can be improvised for obtaining the necessary data and provisions made for tabulating them in an orderly manner. Since the solution of many of the problems will involve hundreds of statistical computations, and since it is desirable to know as soon as possible which tests are of little value in predicting appraisals of job performances, the practice of transferring the data on to punch cards can be highly recommended. [. . . .]

OFFICER SELECTION IN THE BRITISH ARMY, 1942-5

War-time selection procedures are now, perhaps, ancient history, but even ancient history can be important, and in more than a narrowly historical sense. The work described in the present article set a pattern which has been followed in many spheres of vocational selection, including the now famous 'country-house' method adopted by the British Civil Service Commission (3). Furthermore, its principles are closely related to those of group therapy and group interaction generally. In this way it links up with current interest in community studies and in the study of inter-person relationships.

Validation of an operationally-based selection procedure presents almost insoluble problems, since it is impossible to follow up rejected candidates, and not even always practicable to discriminate adequately between degrees of acceptability. The present article gives some data on this point in relation to officer selection; as regards reliability the position will be seen to be much better. While considerable doubt has been expressed regarding the scientific value of the procedure, even the most cautious writers – at any rate among those who had direct contact with this work – concede its morale-building qualities. Thus, Vernon and Parry (4) sum up their discussion of Officer Selection in these words: '. . . it probably made numerous incorrect choices. But other selection techniques too are far from perfect, and . . . it was certainly an improvement on older methods.'

No very detailed 'official' description of the day-to-day procedure at a W.O.S.B. has appeared, but Harris (2) gives a stimulating if highly idiosyncratic account. Ahrenfeldt (1) covers much the same ground as the present article, but also places the work in its general context in Army psychiatry, a theme which carries implications far beyond its purely military aspects. He also carries the story beyond the end of the war.

References
1. Ahrenfeldt, R. H., *Psychiatry in the British Army in the Second World War*. London: Routledge and Kegan Paul, 1958.
2. Harris, H., *The Group Approach to Leadership Testing*. London: Routledge and Kegan Paul, 1949.
3. Vernon, P. E., The Validation of Civil Service Selection Board Procedures, *Occupational Psychology*, 24, 75–95, 1950.
4. Vernon, P. E. and Parry, J. B., *Personnel Selection in the British Forces*. London: London University Press, 1949.

7 B. S. Morris

Officer Selection in the British Army, 1942-5

B. S. Morris, *Occupational Psychology*, National Institute of Industrial
Psychology, 1949, Vol. 23, pp. 219–34.

The aim of this paper is to attempt, within a very small compass,
some evaluation of the work of War Office Selection Boards
(W.O.S.B.s) and of the principles they have employed. The work
to be reported is, of course, that of a very large number of
people. In effect, it is the result of large-scale cooperative research.
The views expressed are in no sense official and, while they would
probably be shared by the group who were the author's colleagues on the Research Staff during the war, he must take
personal responsibility for the form given to them in this paper.
It will be realized that only the briefest survey of an enormous
mass of data can be attempted in it. It is concerned with the period
from the formation of War Office Selection Boards till the end of
the war – a period of about three years. It will perforce assume
that the reader is generally acquainted with the structure and
working of these Boards. If this is an unwarrantable assumption
his indulgence must be asked since there is space here for only the
briefest description. A useful and non-technical outline of
W.O.S.B. procedures has already appeared in this journal (1).
Some accounts of their applications and developments have also
been published (2, 3, 4, 5, 6).

Before the war and during its early stages the Army had, by
and large, found its officers from among those men who had
taken a School Certificate or some equivalent examination, and
who had at the same time attended one of those schools which
provided an Officer Training Corps. At the end of 1941 selection
was being carried out by Interview Boards attached to Army
Commands, each Board consisting of three members. The
technique was that of the simple interview. Upon the candidate's
answers to questions, and such traits of character or deportment
as he betrayed during the twenty minutes or so that he was
before the Board, was based the assessment of his suitability.

In 1940–41 it became evident that this traditional method of
officer selection was breaking down. The failure rate at Officer
Cadet Training Units had risen to rather alarming proportions.
Besides its wastage, this state of affairs had a very bad effect on

the morale of the ranks, and as a consequence applications for commissions were not being received in anything like the numbers required. Moreover, psychiatric examination of officers who had suffered a breakdown on service showed that many of these men should never have held commissioned rank. By the middle of 1941, the number of parliamentary questions, sometimes as many as thirty a week, reflected a growing public concern inside and outside the Army.

Many reasons could be given for the failure of the traditional methods. First and perhaps most important of all, officers hitherto had come almost entirely from one section of society. Traditional methods of selection were based upon this fact, and upon one of its corollaries, namely the existence of a social background common to selectors and candidates. For this reason such methods could afford to rely largely on intuitive judgements. Selectors acquired an 'eye' for those candidates who most closely resembled themselves or their ideal of the 'good officer'. It is reasonable to assume that within such a situation, and with their task presented to them in this way, members of selection boards generally made shrewd judgements and thus performed their task satisfactorily. Moreover, the existence of this kind of procedure constitutes no kind of reflection on the Regular Army, nor was it by any means peculiar to the Army. In fact it represents what has been for a long period in the history of our society the accepted kind of procedure for recruitment to groups with specialized social functions and high social status.

But with the emergence of a new and urgent military need greatly to increase the size of the officer corps, and to ensure that methods of officer recruitment took account of the scope of the officer's job in a modern war involving a conscripted citizen Army, it was inevitable that the flow of candidates should begin to approximate to a complete cross-section of the populace. It is therefore scarcely surprising that, faced with candidates of unfamiliar personality and background, the traditional methods should have been found inadequate.

There were also a number of important contributory factors. The other Services had had first call on a considerable proportion of the cream of the country's man-power. Lack of actual fighting had resulted in a lack of military records on which any reliance could be placed. The methods used were not scientifically based, and therefore did not contain within them the seeds of their own improvement.

As regards the methods themselves, complaints began to

accumulate that sufficient time and trouble was not taken by the average Board in assessing the potentialities of each candidate, and that the qualities which the Board looked for and the principles on which it worked were not evident.

Finally there grew up among candidates, especially among those who did not come from that section of society from which officers traditionally had been recruited, a belief that differences in social background between them and the Board were unduly influencing the judgement of the latter. It should be clear that the question of the truth of such a belief does not necessarily involve the assumption of conscious prejudice on the part of Board members. While there is no doubt that cases of such prejudice did occur, it is also highly probable that their prevalence was exaggerated. The major point, however, is that the existence of such a belief, whether assuming conscious prejudice or not, and whether true or false, had an adverse effect on the morale of the ranks regarding applications for commissions.

W.O.S.B.s attempted to remedy these deficiencies. They came into general operation in the summer of 1942 after a pilot model had been tried out for a number of months. They were based first of all on an attempt to obtain a fairly comprehensive acquaintance with each candidate, as an individual, and as a member of a group, during the period of residence with the Board, usually of three days.

Secondly, and independently, the task was undertaken of analysing the variety of roles filled by an officer in modern warfare in order to provide criteria for selection. During residence at the Board, information was obtained by a number of observers having different functions, and basing their judgements on a variety of standardized quasi real-life situations; on interviews; and on standardized pencil-and-paper tests. A typical Board consisted of a President (a Regimental Officer with the rank of full Colonel) and his advisers. These advisers consisted of a number of officers with regimental experience, referred to as 'Military' Testing Officers, and a psychological staff consisting of a Psychiatrist, a number of Psychological Assistants (N.C.O.s) and latterly, an Officer Psychologist as well. Judgements were pooled, the President taking the final decision, and, in the name of the Army, responsibility for recommendation or rejection.

The Problem of Evaluation

In approaching the problem of evaluating the work of W.O.S.B.s, it is necessary to consider very carefully what kinds of questions arise, which of them are capable of being answered under the conditions which existed, and with what degree of certainty and precision such answers may be given. This is not so simple as it might appear. Questions which quickly spring to mind are, for example, 'What was all this effort worth?', 'What did it achieve?', 'How well did W.O.S.B. procedure work in practice and what is the nature and worth of the evidence of how well it worked?' Reflection on such questions should speedily banish any notion that they can all be adequately answered in terms of, for example, correlation coefficients alone, or any other simple and isolated propositions expressed in highly condensed mathematical form, necessary as is the information which such measurements may provide for complete and exact evaluation. In social science oriented to the solution of current practical problems, there are always important questions which, during developmental phases, are incapable of formulation in a way which permits of exact quantitative answers being given. This will always be so: it is inherent in the nature of social action. Indeed it must be admitted that 'there is a sense in which logical and mathematical proofs are what the psychology of advertising has called "rationalization copy". Scientific insight, as everyday perception, has ever run ahead of measurement and mathematical proof' (7). Realization of this is salutary and reassuring so long as it is not allowed to act as an excuse for failing to push quantitative investigation to the limit of its usefulness.

War Office Selection Boards were a type of institution new to the Army, and at the broadest level their performance has to be judged in relation to the character of the task which they were set. Such a judgement would have to consider, for example, the extent to which W.O.S.B.s achieved an adaptation of scientific methods to a military 'culture', or vice versa, and this would have to include an assessment of the success of educating the Army to make use of skills evolved in the first place for use by psychological technicians. Thus the work of W.O.S.B.s can only be fully evaluated in relation to the whole social process of which they were a part, and this evaluation itself has to take its place as an emergent function of the task which W.O.S.B.s were called upon to perform, with the limitations as well as the advantages which this fact entails. It may be noted that this emergence of research as a function of a social task is becoming increasingly common in modern work in social psychology (8).

Put succinctly, W.O.S.B.s were faced with a crisis situation, in which the traditional methods had broken down, and in this situation they were asked to do two things: (*a*) to raise the morale of the Army regarding applications for commissions; and (*b*) to provide the Army with a sufficient number of officers of 'satisfactory' quality – 'satisfactory', that is, in battle and in other 'operationally definable' military situations. They were thus faced primarily with an immense social task. The size of this task may be gauged from the fact that in the three years 1942 to 1945 W.O.S.B.s dealt with applications for commissions to the order of about one hundred thousand.

It seems appropriate, therefore, to consider first of all, if only very briefly, two broad questions:

1. How satisfactory, in general, was the performance in officer roles of candidates selected by W.O.S.B. methods?
2. How far did W.O.S.B.s satisfy the expectancies and needs of the Army and civilian communities, including the officer candidates themselves?

Thereafter, it will be fitting to deal at somewhat greater length with three questions of a kind rather more familiar to psychologists, questions dealing with the comparative merits of W.O.S.B.s and Old Procedure Boards (Simple Interview Boards), and with the validity and reliability of W.O.S.B. procedure itself.

3. How did officers selected by W.O.S.B. methods compare with those selected by the Old Procedure?
4. What was the relationship between W.O.S.B. assessments of officer candidates and the proficiency ratings they later received?
5. What was the reliability (in the usual technical sense of self-consistency) of W.O.S.B. assessments?

It will readily be conceded that the first two questions are considerably less precise than the last three. The former are not concerned with explicit and exact comparisons, nor with predictions. They are rather concerned with historical facts relating to a social process, in which comparisons are implicit and inexact, and the facts themselves, while sometimes capable of behavioural definition, and even of quantification, are often of a kind which are observable only to participants and hence are difficult to record, except in terms of actual experience. Matters of this order are none the less facts, unless one is willing to bear the strain of the logical dilemmas and inconsistencies which result from a definition of fact which expressly excludes the testimony of such experience. It is readily conceded, of course, that the evaluation of such experience cannot, for science, remain a private matter.

167

It could, however, equally well be said that, compared with the last three questions, the first two carry much wider implications regarding the social sanctioning necessary for the introduction and development of scientific methods for handling human problems within a large area of social life. Such questions do belong within psychology – social psychology – but they are 'synoptic' rather than 'precise' in the sense in which Karl Pearson used those terms to distinguish between the various sciences.*

To be concerned entirely with these first two questions would, of course, be to adopt a largely pre-scientific attitude, while refusal to consider them at all would be scientifically naïve as well as socially irresponsible. It may indeed be urged that the time has come for present-day psychologists, as a scientific group, to give, as their predecessors once gave, rather more attention to the status and developmental character of human knowledge and its relation to action, to the variety of methods through which knowledge is acquired, to the degree of certainty and precision which can be expected in a given area of knowledge at a particular historical moment, and to the relevance of such knowledge, certain and uncertain, precise and imprecise, to the solution of practical problems. It would be unnecessary to say this were there not noticeable a certain tendency to cavalier treatment of all questions not at present capable of being classified as 'precise' in Pearson's sense. A remark made in a rather different although related connexion, by an eminent modern logician and philosopher of science, is in its essential meaning very apposite here. 'It is only too tempting to push a very difficult problem aside, and by stigmatizing it as meaningless to discourage further investigation. If, for example, some of the extremely tough-minded psychologists relegate questions such as those concerning instincts, the unconscious, or the relative roles of constitution and environment, to the limbo of metaphysics, then they cut with Occam's razor far

*Thus, in his day, although much less so in ours, it was true to say as he did, 'The distinction between Astronomy and Meteorology is just the distinction between the Precise and the Synoptic Sciences.' And again, 'Science is not a mere catalogue of facts, but is the conceptual model by which we briefly resume our experiences of these facts. Hence we find that many branches of science, which call for admission into a practical classification, are in reality only sciences in the making and correspond to the "catalogue raisonné" rather than to the complete conceptual model' (9). It was Pearson's firm belief that such distinctions between the 'Sciences' were not inherent in the nature of their particular problems, but were functions of historical development. The progress of science since his day gives some solid reasons for supposing that this belief will ultimately be justified.

into the flesh of knowledge, instead of merely shaving away the metaphysical whiskers' (10, pp. 386–7).

The More General Questions

An adequate discussion of the two general questions which have been raised would go far beyond the scope of this paper. For present purposes it is a question primarily of perspective and a very brief treatment will have to suffice for this. In follow-up studies in the Mediterranean Campaign (1943–4) it was found that in the opinion of Commanding Officers 76 per cent of officers selected by W.O.S.B. methods were giving completely satisfactory service. The clearly unsatisfactory amounted to 12 per cent. In British Liberation Armies (1944-45) the proportion giving complete satisfaction was for Infantry 76 per cent, the proportion clearly unsatisfactory only 7 per cent. For Royal Artillery, in this investigation, the corresponding figures were 59 per cent, and 12 per cent. In this case 88 per cent were giving fair satisfaction. The percentage of unsatisfactory officers appeared therefore to be of the order of about 1 in 10.* It is also necessary to see these figures in relation to the whole selection and training process, in which over a two-year period (1943–5) the wastage rate at the training stage (rejection at O.C.T.U.) was only 8 per cent.

It may be asked 'What do these figures mean – what standards can be applied?' Since they represent the first recorded measurement of the satisfactoriness of the junior officer cadres of an Army in the field, there can, of course, at present be no exact standard with which to compare them. But this does not mean that 'no control exists' and therefore that they cannot be evaluated. If the figures had turned out to be, say, 25 per cent satisfactory and 75 per cent unsatisfactory, then there is no doubt at all that official reactions would have been very different from what they were.† In fact a control does operate, only it is implicit, inexact and largely unconscious, and this is shown by the fact that a selection procedure is only socially tolerated, if its efficiency rises above a

*As is pointed out later, no strict comparison can be made between officers selected by W.O.S.B.s and those selected by Old Procedure Boards (Simple Interview Boards). In the Mediterranean Campaign the 'Satisfaction Rate' for Old Procedure officers was of the same order – slightly but not significantly lower – as for W.O.S.B.s, but the majority of these officers were passed by Old Procedure Boards before W.O.S.B.s came into being. For the period of common operation of the two systems, the difference is statistically of borderline significance, in favour of W.O.S.B.s.

†Such a state of affairs would, of course, have been revealed long before any follow-up studies could have been undertaken.

certain limit, which, however difficult to specify, clearly does exist. It was ultimately, of course, because the efficiency of Old Procedure Boards fell below this limit that they were replaced by W.O.S.B.s. Comparisons in such cases are implicitly made with an existing social norm whose meaning is definable in terms of social necessity. It is in fact a matter for congratulation that it proved possible to make a numerical assessment of 'satisfactoriness' of junior officers in a campaign for the first time in history. A preliminary, but explicitly quantitative, basis of comparison was thereby established for all future work.

In a similar way it might be held that the question whether W.O.S.B.s satisfied the expectancies and needs of the military and civil communities was a matter of opinion. But, once again, there are facts which have to be taken into consideration and an attempt made to erect the most probable hypothesis which could account for them. There was the high degree of acceptability which W.O.S.B.s eventually achieved with all ranks. There was the rise in morale regarding applications for commissions, shown by the large increase in the flow of candidates which took place shortly after the general adoption of W.O.S.B. methods.* Lastly, there were the views of W.O.S.B. candidates themselves. The opinions of candidates were regularly sought by means of an anonymous questionnaire. Their verdict, without being uncritical, was overwhelmingly favourable to W.O.S.B.s, both in the case of rejected as well as of successful candidates. It is difficult to suggest any hypothesis which could account for all these facts, other than that W.O.S.B. methods, by and large, satisfied the felt needs, for a fair and scientifically based procedure of officer selection. It is to be noted that such an hypothesis makes no claims regarding the validity and reliability of W.O.S.B. methods, except in the sense that their general efficiency was felt to be above the socially permissible minimum.

Comparative Merits of W.O.S.B.s and Old Procedure Boards

Comparison of Candidates Chosen by W.O.S.B.s with Candidates Chosen by Old Procedure Boards, at Officer Cadet Training Units; and in Commissioned Rank

---

*It has sometimes been claimed that the large drop in rejections from O.C.T.U. which took place late in 1942 was also due to the introduction of W.O.S.B. methods. This claim cannot be substantiated. An upper limit for the rejection rate at O.C.T.U.s was, during this particular period, laid down by War Office Order.

(1) *At Officer Cadet Training Units (O.C.T.U.s)*

At the training stage a fairly clear and satisfactory answer was obtained in this comparison. Reports were obtained on over 1,200 candidates, 700 from W.O.S.B.s and 500 from Old Procedure Boards, all of whom had been selected during the same period, when W.O.S.B.s and Old Procedure Boards were working simultaneously. These reports were made by O.C.T.U. instructors by means of standard questionnaires, personally administered by field workers, within the framework of a controlled interview situation. This inquiry covered 10 O.C.T.U.s of different Arms. The results may conveniently be expressed by means of ratings on a three point scale. In rounded percentages they were as shown in the following table.

Overall comparison between W.O.S.B. and Old Procedure Cadets (all O.C.T.U.s combined)

| | Percentage Rated | | | |
	Above Average	Average	Below Average	Total Number
W.O.S.B.	35	40	25	721
Old Procedure	22	41	37	491

It will be seen that, whereas 35 per cent of W.O.S.B. cadets were rated *above average*, only 22 per cent of Old Procedure cadets were so rated, and that 25 per cent of W.O.S.B. cadets were rated *below average* as against 37 per cent Old Procedure cadets. Treated as a 3 by 2 table, the two distributions are significantly different at the 1 per cent level. Thus W.O.S.B.s not only significantly reduced the below average material but added significantly to the above average material.

When the results for the 10 different O.C.T.U.s were treated separately, it was found that at four of them differences in favour of W.O.S.B.s were significant between the 5 and 2 per cent levels; at three, the differences were of borderline significance; and at the remaining three there were no significant differences. At no single O.C.T.U. was a significant difference found in favour of the Old Procedure.

It was also shown that the difference in performance of W.O.S.B. and Old Procedure cadets held true, with one or two exceptions only, for each Selection Board taken separately. With one single exception, every W.O.S.B. had a better record than every Old Procedure Board, although all the differences did not reach statistical significance.

It remains to be asked whether any hypothesis other than the superiority of the W.O.S.B. procedure could be held responsible for the observed differences. Two inter-related hypotheses suggest themselves: (*i*) W.O.S.B.s may have accepted far fewer of the candidates available and thus sent on to O.C.T.U. only 'safe bets'; that is, the obtained difference might be a function of different acceptance rates at the two types of Board. But W.O.S.B.s in fact showed a slightly lower acceptance rate than Old Procedure Boards, 58·9 per cent as against 62·4 per cent, a difference which is not significant and which could not possibly account for the observed differences. (*ii*) W.O.S.B.s may have had more and better candidates to choose from; that is, the obtained difference might be a function of supply rate and/or quality of supply. But in fact it was shown that W.O.S.B.s had rather fewer candidates per Board to choose from, and examination of the sources of supply revealed no evidence which suggested that candidates going before the two types of Board were likely to differ in quality.

Finally, multiple reports were obtained from O.C.T.U.s; that is, as many instructors as possible reported on each cadet. By using an item analysis of questionnaires to reveal instructors' discriminating powers, and combining this with the field workers' independent rating of each instructor, it was possible to grade instructors for quality of reporting. In this way, a number of proficiency criteria were evolved differing in their stringency. It was found that, in general, the more stringent the criterion, the greater the difference between W.O.S.B. and Old Procedure Cadets, in favour of the former. The superiority of W.O.S.B.s so far as this training criterion is concerned, may, therefore, be safely inferred.

This investigation has been dealt with at some length, because it was the first major follow-up inquiry to be carried out, because it gives a fairly clear and unequivocal answer to the questions asked, and because it presents a fair example of the care taken in evaluating the data obtained.

(2) *In Commissioned Rank*

Here a rather different state of affairs is found. In all, three major investigations were undertaken in commissioned rank, one in Home Commands, one during the Mediterranean Campaign, and one in British Liberation Armies shortly before they crossed the Rhine. The samples investigated were the remnants of the sample described above, which could be traced into these theatres, and were accessible to investigation. In fact, it proved impossible to get really satisfactory samples. Moreover, in no case was any clear difference found between W.O.S.B. and Old Procedure officers in general, in either direction. A number of specific differences in favour of W.O.S.B.s were found, but on the whole the evidence was conflicting and exceedingly difficult to evaluate.

In the investigation in Home Commands, the following specific findings resulted. W.O.S.B. officers had a higher 'Satisfaction Rate' than Old Procedure officers in the cases of (i) officers in Infantry under 23 years old, and (ii) officers in Infantry with less than one year's service in the ranks. This gave some evidence to suggest that W.O.S.B.s were better at selecting from among young and inexperienced candidates, but the evidence at this stage could not be called conclusive.

Even using the more sensitive criterion which was later evolved – a combination of ranking and rating – it did not prove possible to show any significant difference between the two classes of officers. In view of the sampling problems and other difficulties to be mentioned later, the only legitimate inference is not that there was no difference, but that the case for or against any such difference is not proven. It should be remembered however, that Old Procedure Boards never really had to face the problems which confronted W.O.S.B.s; for example, the great influx of new types of candidates in the autumn of 1942, or the steady decline in candidate quality as the war went on. Any strict comparison is, in fact, out of the question.

Validity of W.O.S.B. Procedures

(1) *Conditions Affecting the Investigation of Relationships Between W.O.S.B. Assessments and Later Proficiency Ratings*

Investigation into the relationship between W.O.S.B. assessments and later proficiency ratings suffered gravely under three unfortunate circumstances:

1. A uniform system of grading was not introduced into W.O.S.B.s until early in 1943. It was thus not until the final Officer Follow-Up in B.L.A. in 1945 that a sample of officers was found for whom this data was available.

2. Even when it was introduced, W.O.S.B. staff never received any adequate common and systematic training in the use of this grading system; and, as we shall see, in spite of all that the Research Staff could do to mitigate the effects of this, different standards grew up at different Boards.

3. It was not found possible to introduce into common use any form of profile assessment of personality variables, until the war was over. Apart from data collected by the psychological department, on intelligence tests, and objective variables like educational standard, type of schooling, age, and length of service, the only other W.O.S.B. assessment available during the war period was the Final Grading.

(2) *W.O.S.B. Assessments and O.C.T.U. Grades*

As a result of a number of specific investigations at the O.C.T.U. stage, the correlation between W.O.S.B. Final Grades and O.C.T.U. grades was shown to be of the order of $0·3$ and just significant. The correlation between O.C.T.U. grade and intelligence was about $·35$, which is about what might be expected considering the degree of selection involved. Correlation with the other objective variables was of the same order. A multiple correlation using 6 variables, including Final Grade, gave a figure of $0·58$ with O.C.T.U. outcome. This is not of much use for predictive purposes, since it accounts for about only one third of the variance of the criterion. Obviously the most important factors determining O.C.T.U. outcome were not among the six variables considered; that is, W.O.S.B. Final Grade, intelligence, educational standard, type of school, age, and length of Other Rank service. Moreover, comparison between W.O.S.B. grades of cadets passed at O.C.T.U. and those failed showed very little difference. Yet, as has been mentioned, the overall rejection rate at O.C.T.U.s over a two-year period was only 8 per cent. It became clear that the very basis of the overall assessment of candidates differed, not only as among W.O.S.B.s, but as between W.O.S.B.s and O.C.T.U.s themselves. The difficulties of bringing these various assessments into line were, under the conditions obtaining, quite insuperable.

(3) *W.O.S.B. Assessments and Proficiency Ratings by Commanding Officers*

In the final Officer Follow-Up in B.L.A. it did prove possible to show that a small positive relationship existed between W.O.S.B. Grades and the opinions of Commanding Officers. The natures of the results are portrayed by the following table, which is meant as an example only, selected from among those available, but the trends shown also characterized most of the other samples. In obtaining the opinions of C.O.s a ranking method was used and ranks were converted into mean sigma scores.

Mean Sigma scores of Officers given Different W.O.S.B. Gradings

| | Sub-sample: Infantry | |
W.O.S.B. Grading	Opinion of Commanding Officer Mean Sigma Score	Number
Above Average	+ ·05	23
Average	— ·06	60
Below Average	— ·32	92

The difference in mean sigma score between Above Average and Below Average (·37) is significant at the 5 per cent level.

It has already been mentioned that some evidence was found earlier to support the view that W.O.S.B. selection procedure was more efficient for younger than for older candidates. This surmise was confirmed by the findings in B.L.A. where it was shown that the difference between mean sigma scores (opinions of C.O.s) of officers rated above and below average at W.O.S.B.s decreased with increasing age.

(4) *Reflections on the Interpretation of Follow-Up Data in this Field*

In evaluating the size of the relationship which has been shown to exist between W.O.S.B. assessments and later proficiency ratings, the difficulties produced by differing standards and criteria of judgement, and by the effect of purely statistical factors such as sampling and selection, will be readily granted. Similarly, the difficulties of the field problems encountered in follow-up are notorious. There are, however, difficulties of another kind which have not, it may be suggested, received the attention they deserve. If one takes seriously the notion which regards behaviour as a function of the complex of variables, 'personality in environment', one has to ask whether sufficient attention has yet been given to the question of the effect on behaviour of environmental variations, particularly variations in social structure, stress and relationships.

The answer given to this question should profoundly affect attitudes to the problems of predicting behaviour by means of selection tests. A strong case may be made out that knowledge of how different personality structures react to variations in environmental pressures is as yet inadequate to allow any reasonable expectation to be entertained of obtaining high predictive efficiency in work like officer selection. The follow-up in the Mediterranean Campaign gave qualitative evidence of the effect on assessments of such factors as unit morale and mode of introduction into battle. It may therefore be suggested that social psychology has a profound contribution to make to selection and guidance studies. It might be argued that to say this is only to demand a better job analysis. Rather it means carrying out job analysis of a kind radically different from those usually attempted.

There will be those who will conclude from the figures reported in this section, that the results of follow-up studies of the work of W.O.S.B.s are disappointing. Any such conclusion, whether favourable or unfavourable, is a function of expectancy and of the level of social and scientific realism brought to bear on these questions. The difficulties encountered are by no means unique, but they are not necessarily discouraging. Those interested will find a most illuminating account of somewhat similar work and very similar problems and difficulties in the work done in the selection of personnel for the Office of Strategic Services (O.S.S.) of the American Forces (11, p. 392).

Reliability of W.O.S.B. Procedures

It soon became evident that in actual operation different W.O.S.B.s employed different standards, and to some extent differed in the actual disposal judgements arrived at. While it was clear that this unreliability was often above the scientifically desirable minimum, it should also not be over-exaggerated. Certain gross cases were observed, but there were also many instances in which discrepancies did not appear to be serious, and where good agreement could reasonably be presumed to exist.

From the evidence of differing acceptance rates alone no inferences could be directly drawn about differences in standards. It was necessary to show to what extent the observed variance could be accounted for by differences in quality of candidate supply and differences in the Arms for which candidates were being selected. This proved exceedingly difficult to do. Some statistical evidence of this sort was obtained, but the most important evidence on the more serious cases came from a number of carefully designed experiments. In one of these, two Boards showing consistently different pass rates were chosen. They constituted the grossest case of apparent disagreement which could be found. A batch of candidates normally designed for one of these Boards was randomly split in two, one half of the sample being sent to each Board. The two sub-samples were compared with regard to those variables which could be assessed independently of the final judgement, and were shown not to differ significantly from each other in these respects. In this experiment one W.O.S.B. showed a pass rate of 23 per cent and the other of 48 per cent. This very large difference was not due to any one type of observer nor to any single cause but rather reflected the different patterns of judgement which existed at the two Boards, and which persisted throughout everything they did. It is of interest to note that the difference was found to concern, almost exclusively, assessment for suitability for the more combatant arms.

In another experiment two batches of candidates were assessed by each of two Boards. One batch went first to Board A, then on to Board B. The second batch proceeded in the reverse direction. A double assessment of each batch was thus obtained, and allowances could be made for any 'learning' effect. Significantly different acceptance rates were found. In 60 per cent of cases there was agreement as to disposal. Disagreement on a major issue of disposal was found in 25 per cent of the cases. This was regarded as a serious discrepancy.

Steps were taken to minimize such disagreements, but, for many reasons, mainly of policy, this proved an exceedingly intractable problem. In the opinion of the Research Staff, the root of the trouble lay in the lack of adequate selection of W.O.S.B. staff, and in the lack of a common and systematic training for all personnel engaged in the work. It was not till the end of the war that such a common training was instituted.

The Research Staff, holding that unreliability was mainly due to factors of this kind, rather than to inherent defects in the principles used, continually pressed for an opportunity to test this hypothesis experimentally. Such an opportunity was not granted till the summer of 1945, when the war was over. An elaborate and carefully designed experiment was then carried out. The personnel used were the best and most experienced available. They were given an initial period of common training. Common forms of reporting were introduced and a standard personality profile adopted. The basic design was as follows: Two Boards X and Y were set up. They lived and worked on the same premises but were sworn to have no intercourse relevant to their selection tasks, during the experiment. Each Board simultaneously observed the same candidates performing the same tests. In all 200 candidates were seen. Independent judgements were arrived at and subsequently compared by central research staff. From the vast mass of material available from this experiment, the following has been chosen as being a very small and limited, but representative, sample of the most important results.

177

Reliability and Intercorrelation of W.O.S.B.
Observers under Optimum Conditions

Reliability	Average Intercorrelation
Board X v. Board Y (Final Grade)	·80
President X v. President Y (Interview)	·65
Psychiatrist X v. Psychiatrist Y (Interview)	·65
M.T.O.s X v. M.T.O.s Y (Observer roles)	·86
Psychologists X v. Psychologists Y (Observer roles)	·78
Agreement between different members	
Presidents v. M.T.O.s	·60
Presidents v. Psychiatrists	·62
M.T.O.s v. Psychiatrists	·60
M.T.O.s v. Interviewers	·59

Note: All the coefficients are significant at the 1 per cent level.

These figures may speak for themselves. The most important is the first, Board X v. Board Y. A reliability coefficient of ·80 for W.O.S.B. procedure as a whole may justifiably be regarded as a high one. Further, no significant differences in standards (pass rates) or in the variances of grading distributions were found between Board X and Board Y. With only one or two exceptions no significant differences were found between the standards of any pair of observers, whether of the same or of different type. From these figures and the rest of the material available, to be published later, it may be concluded that under the optimal conditions of this experiment W.O.S.B. methods showed a satisfactory degree of reliability for work of this kind. Further, it was also shown that the different observers and parts of the procedure made significant contributions to the final assessments.

Conclusion

In evaluating the work of W.O.S.B.s as a whole it is necessary to consider their achievement in relation to the task which was set them and to the conditions under which they had to be set up, staffed and operated. It is necessary to distinguish what was accomplished under the emergency conditions of war and what was shown to be possible under more favourable conditions. There are considerable and demonstrable achievements to be recorded. Moreover, the deficiencies revealed and the many problems left unsolved have the merit of opening up a very large territory for investigation in the future.

In conclusion, a large debt exists to the many workers, psychologists and military personnel alike, of all ranks, who made this large-scale cooperative endeavour possible. Most of all a vote of thanks is due to those thousands of candidates for commissions who went cheerfully through the exacting, but, as they often confessed, stimulating experience, of living at a War Office Selection Board.

References
1. Garforth, F. I. de la P.: War Office Selection Boards (O.C.T.U.) *Occupational Psychology*, 1945, *19*, 97–108.
2. Munro Fraser, J.: An Experiment with Group Methods in the Selection of Trainees for Senior Management Positions. *Occupational Psychology*, 1946, *20*, 63–7.
3. Munro Fraser, J.: New Type Selection Boards in Industry, *Occupational Psychology*, 1947, *21*, 170–8.
4. Bridger, H. and Isdell-Carpenter, R.: Selection of Management Trainees. *Industrial Welfare*, 1947, *29*, 177–81.
5. Wilson, N. A. B.: The Work of the Civil Service Selection Board, *Occupational Psychology*, 1948, *22*, 204–12.
6. Beverstock, A. G.: Group Methods Applied to Youth Leader Selection. *British Journal of Educational Psychology*, 1949, *19*, 112–20.
7. Bartlett, R. J.: *Measurement in Psychology*, Presidential Address to Section J (Psychology), British Association for the Advancement of Science, Dundee, 1939.
8. Morris, B. S.: Community Studies and Community Education in Relation to Social Change. *Occupational Psychology*, 1949, *23*, 129–39.
9. Pearson, Karl: *The Grammar of Science*. London, 1892, Everyman Edition, 1937. Chap. 10.
10. Feigl, Herbert: Logical Empiricism, in *Twentieth Century Philosophy*; edited by Dagobert D. Runes. New York, Philosophical Library, 1947.
11. O.S.S. Assessment Staff: *Assessment of Men*. New York, Rinehart, 1948.

THE NATURE AND NURTURE
OF CREATIVE TALENT

The war-time selection procedures described in the last two articles were unique in respect not only of the scale on which they were conducted, but also, possibly, in that the nature of the abilities being sought was unusually hard to define. The topic of Dr MacKinnon's paper is more circumscribed, and perhaps also more in line with current trends in psychology at large.

Present-day interest in 'creativity' may be related to dissatisfaction with conventional conceptions of 'intelligence'. Unpublished work by the editor of this book has suggested that outstanding students of psychology are not (not even 'not necessarily'!) those with the highest 'ability', as measured by intelligence tests. Hudson (2) takes the story a stage further and claims that 'degree class as a predictive index . . . should be viewed with scepticism'.

Excellent (and in some ways, complementary) discussions of creativity will be found in recent books by Barron (1) and Taylor (5).

A word may be added on vocational guidance – the other side of occupational psychology, in contrast to selection. Many psychologists believe that it is more difficult to choose the job for the man than the man for the job. More depends, perhaps, on interest than on aptitude, though the two are bound to be inter-related. Dr MacKinnon refers to the 'Strong Vocational Interest Blank'; a rather different approach, making use of a forced-choice technique similar to that of the Study of Values (see p. 193, below) is that of the 'Kuder Preference Record' (3).

Many books have been written on vocational guidance, at various levels. The one by Super and Crites (4) may be recommended, as having stood the test of time.

References
1. Barron, F., Creativity and Psychological Health. New York and London: Van Nostrand. 1963.

2. Hudson, L., Degree Class and Attainment in Scientific Research. *British Journal of Psychology, 51*, 67–73. 1960.
3. Kuder, G. F., *Kuder Preference Record – Vocational Manual.* Chicago: Science Research Associates, 1960.
4. Super, D. E. and Crites, J. O., *Appraising Vocational Fitness by means of Psychological Tests.* Revised edition. New York and London: Harper and Row. 1962.
5. Taylor, C. W. (ed.), *Creativity. Progress and Potential.* New York and London: McGraw Hill, 1964.

8 D. W. MacKinnon

The Nature and Nurture of Creative Talent*

American Psychologist, 1962, Vol. 17. pp. 484-94

[. . . .]

Whatever light I shall be able to shed on the nature and nurture of creative talent comes in the main from findings of researches carried on during the last six years in the Institute of Personality Assessment and Research on the Berkeley campus of the University of California, and supported in large part by the Carnegie Corporation of New York.

In undertaking such a study one of our first tasks was to decide what we would consider creativity to be. This was necessary, first, because creativity has been so variously described and defined, and second, because only when we had come to agreement as to how we would conceive creativity would we be in a position to know what kinds of persons we would want to study.

We came easily to agreement that true creativeness fulfills at least three conditions. It involves a response or an idea that is novel or at the very least statistically infrequent. But novelty or originality of thought or action, while a necessary aspect of creativity, is not sufficient. If a response is to lay claim to being a part of the creative process, it must to some extent be adaptive to, or of, reality. It must serve to solve a problem, fit a situation, or accomplish some recognizable goal. And, thirdly, true creativeness involves a sustaining of the original insight, an evaluation and elaboration of it, a developing of it to the full.

Creativity, from this point of view, is a process extended in time and characterized by originality, adaptiveness, and realization. It may be brief, as in a musical improvization, or it may involve a considerable span of years as was required for Darwin's creation of the theory of evolution.

The acceptance of such a conception of creativity had two important consequences for our researches. It meant that we would not seek to study creativity while it was still potential but only after it had been realized and had found expression in clearly identifiable creative products – buildings designed by architects, mathematical proofs developed by mathematicians, and the pub-

*The Walter Van Dyke Bingham Lecture given at Yale University, New Haven, Connecticut, 11 April, 1962.

lished writings of poets and novelists. Our conception of creativity forced us further to reject as indicators or criteria of creativeness the performance of individuals on so-called tests of creativity. While tests of this sort, that require that the subject think, for example, of unusual uses for common objects and the consequences of unusual events, may indeed measure the infrequency or originality of a subject's ideas in response to specific test items, they fail to reveal the extent to which the subject faced with real life problems is likely to come up with solutions that are novel and adaptive and which he will be motivated to apply in all of their ramifications.

Having thus determined that we would limit our researches to the study of persons who had already demonstrated a high level of creative work, we were still confronted with the problem of deciding from which fields of creative endeavor we would seek to recruit our subjects.

The fields which we finally sampled were those of creative writing, architecture, mathematics, industrial research, physical science, and engineering.

If one considers these activities in relation to the distinction often made between artistic and scientific creativity, it may be noted that we have sampled both of these domains as well as overlapping domains of creative striving which require that the practitioner be at one and the same time both artist and scientist.

Artistic creativity, represented in our studies by the work of poets, novelists, and essayists, results in products that are clearly expressions of the creator's inner states, his needs, perceptions, motivations, and the like. In this type of creativity, the creator externalizes something of himself into the public field.

In scientific creativity, the creative product is unrelated to the creator as a person, who in his creative work acts largely as a mediator between externally defined needs and goals. In this kind of creativeness, the creator, represented in our studies by industrial researchers, physical scientists, and engineers, simply operates on some aspect of his environment in such a manner as to produce a novel and appropriate product, but he adds little of himself or of his style as a person to the resultant.

Domains of creative striving in which the practitioner must be both artist and scientist were represented in our researches by mathematicians and architects. Mathematicians contribute to science, yet in a very real sense their important creative efforts are as much as anything else personal cosmologies in which they express themselves as does the artist in his creations. So, too, in architecture, creative products are both an expression of the architect and thus a very personal product, and at the same time an impersonal meeting of the demands of an external problem.

If in reporting the findings of our researches I draw most heavily upon data obtained from our study of architects (Mac-Kinnon, 1962), it is for two reasons. First, it is the study for which, in collaboration with Wallace B. Hall, I have assumed primary responsibility. Second, it is in architects, of all our samples, that we can expect to find what is most generally characteristic of creative persons. Architecture, as a field of creative endeavor, requires that the successful practitioner be both artist and scientist – artist in that his designs must fulfill the demands of 'Delight', and scientist in that they must meet the demands of 'Firmnesse' and 'Commodity', to use the words of Sir Henry Wotton (1624). But surely, one can hardly think that the requirements of effective architecture are limited to these three demands. The successful and effective architect must, with the skill of a juggler, combine, reconcile, and exercise the diverse skills of businessman, lawyer, artist, engineer, and advertising man, as well as those of author and journalist, psychiatrist, educator, and psychologist. In what other profession can one expect better to observe the multifarious expressions of creativity?

It should be clear that any attempt to discover the distinguishing traits of creative persons can succeed only in so far as some group of qualified experts can agree upon who are the more and who are the less creative workers in a given field of endeavor. In our study of architects we began by asking a panel of experts – five professors of architecture, each working independently – to nominate the 40 most creative architects in the United States. All told they supplied us with 86 names instead of the 40 they would have mentioned had there been perfect agreement among them. While 13 of the 86 architects were nominated by all five panel members, and 9 nominated by four, 11 by three, and 13 by two, 40 were individual nominations each proposed by a single panel member.

The agreement among experts is not perfect, yet far greater than one might have expected. Later we asked 11 editors of the major American architectural journals, *Architectural Forum*, *Architectural Record*, the *Journal of the American Institute of Architects*, and *Progressive Architecture*, to rate the creativity of the 64 of the nominated architects whom we invited to participate in the study. Still later we asked the 40 nominated creative architects who actually accepted our invitation to be studied to rate the creativity of the invited 64 architects, themselves included. Since the editors' ratings of the creativity of the architects correlated + ·88 with the architects' own ratings, it is clear that under certain conditions and for certain groups it is possible to obtain remarkable agreement about the relative creativeness of individual members of a profession and thus meet the first requirement for an effective study of creative persons.

A second requirement for the successful establishment of the traits of creative individuals is their willingness to make themselves available for study. Our hope was to win the cooperation of each person whom we invited to participate in the research, but as I have already indicated in the case of the architects, to obtain 40 acceptances, 64 invitations had to be sent out.

The invitation to this group, as to all the creative groups which we have studied, was to come to Berkeley for a weekend of intensive study in the Institute of Personality Assessment and Research. There, in groups of ten, they have been studied by the variety of means which constitute the assessment method – by problem-solving experiments; by tests designed to discover what a person does not know or is unable or unwilling to reveal about himself; by tests and questionnaires that permit a person to manifest various aspects of his personality and to express his attitudes, interests, and values; by searching interviews that cover the life history and reveal the present structure of the person; and by specially contrived social situations of a stressful character which call for the subject's best behavior in a socially defined role.

The response of creative persons to the invitation to reveal themselves under such trying circumstances has varied considerably. At the one extreme there have been those who replied in anger at what they perceived to be the audacity of psychologists in presuming to study so ineffable and mysterious a thing as the creative process and so sensitive a being as a creative person. At the other extreme were those who replied courteously and warmheartedly, welcoming the invitation to be studied, and manifesting even an eagerness to contribute to a better understanding of the creative person and the creative process.

Here we were face to face with a problem that plagues us in all our researches: Are those who are willing to be assessed different in important ways from those who refuse? With respect to psychological traits and characteristics we can never know. But with respect to differences in creativeness, if any, between the 40 who accepted and the 24 who declined our invitation, we know that the two groups are indistinguishable. When the nominating panel's ratings of creativity were converted to standard scores and the means for the 24 versus the 40 were compared, they were found to be identical. When the editors' ratings were similarly converted to standard scores, the mean for the nonassessed group was slightly higher (51·9) than for the assessed sample (48·7), but the difference is not statistically significant.

Certainly we cannot claim to have assessed the 40 most creative architects in the country, or the most creative of any of the groups we have studied; but it is clear that we have studied a highly creative group of architects indistinguishable in their creativity from the group of 24 who declined to be studied, and so with the other groups too.

A third requirement for the successful determination of the traits of highly creative persons in any field of endeavor is that the profession be widely sampled beyond those nominated as most creative, for the distinguishing characteristics of the restricted sample might well have nothing to do with their creativeness. Instead they might be traits characterizing all members of the profession whether creative or not, distinguishing the professional group as a whole but in no sense limited or peculiar to its highly creative members. In the case of the architects, to use them once again as an example, two additional samples were recruited for study, both of which matched the highly creative sample (whom I shall now call Architects I) with respect to age and geographic location of practice. The first supplementary sample (Architects II) had had at least two years of work experience and association with one of the originally nominated creative architects. The second additional sample (Architects III) was composed of architects who had never worked with any of the nominated creatives.

By selecting three samples in this manner, we hoped to tap a range of talent sufficiently wide to be fairly representative of the profession as a whole; and we appear to have succeeded. The mean rating of creativity for each of the three groups – the ratings having been made on a nine-point scale by six groups of architects and experts on architecture – was for Architects I, 5·46; for Architects II, 4·25; and for Architects III, 3·54, the differences in mean ratings between each group being statistically highly significant.

So much for method and research design. I turn now to a discussion of the nature of creative talent as it has been revealed to us in our researches.

Persons who are highly creative are inclined to have a good opinion of themselves, as evidenced by the large number of favorable adjectives which they use in self-description and by the relatively high scores they earn on a scale which measures basic acceptance of the self. Indeed, there is here a paradox, for in addition to their favorable self-perceptions the very basic self-acceptance of the more creative persons often permits them to speak more frankly and thus more critically and in unusual ways about themselves. It is clear, too, that the self-images of the more creative differ from the self-images of the less creative. For example, Architects I, in contrast to Architects II and III, more often describe themselves as inventive, determined, independent, individualistic, enthusiastic, and industrious. In striking contrast Architects II and III more often than Architects I describe themselves as responsible, sincere, reliable, dependable, clear thinking, tolerant, and understanding. In short, where creative architects more often stress their inventiveness, independence, and individuality, their enthusiasm, determination, and industry, less creative members of the profession are impressed by their virtue and good character and by their rationality and sympathetic concern for others.

The discrepancies between their descriptions of themselves as they are and as they would ideally be are remarkably alike for all architects regardless of their level of creativeness. All three groups reveal themselves as desiring more personal attractiveness, self-confidence, maturity, and intellectual competence, a higher level of energy, and better social relations. As for differences, however, Architects I would ideally be more sensitive, while both Architects II and III wish for opposites if not incompatibles; they would ideally be more original but at the same time more self-controlled and disciplined.

As for the relation between intelligence and creativity, save for the mathematicians where there is a low positive correlation between intelligence and the level of creativeness, we have found within our creative samples essentially zero relationship between the two variables, and this is not due to a narrow restriction in range of intelligence. Among creative architects who have a mean score of 113 on the Terman Concept Mastery Test (1956), individual scores range widely from 39 to 179, yet scores on this measure of intelligence correlate —·08 with rated creativity. Over the whole range of intelligence and creativity there is, of course, a positive relationship between the two variables. No feeble-minded subjects have shown up in any of our creative groups. It is clear, however, that above a certain required minimum level of intelligence which varies from field to field and in some instances may be surprisingly low; being more intelligent does not guarantee a corresponding increase in creativeness. It just is not true that the more intelligent person is necessarily the more creative one.

In view of the often asserted close association of genius with insanity it is also of some interest to inquire into the psychological health of our creative subjects. To this end we can look at their profiles on the Minnesota Multiphasic Pe sonality Inventory (MMPI) (Hathaway & McKinley, 1945), a test originally developed to measure tendencies towards the major psychiatric disturbances that man is heir to: depression, hysteria, paranoia, schizophrenia, and the like. On the eight scales which measure the strength of these dispositions in the person, our creative subjects earn scores which, on the average, are some 5 to 10 points above the general population's average score of 50. It must be noted, however, that elevated scores of this degree on these scales do not have the same meaning for the personality functioning of persons who, like our subjects, are getting along well in their personal lives and professional careers, that they have for hospitalized patients. The manner in which creative subjects describe themselves on this test as well as in the life history psychiatric interview is less suggestive of psychopathology than it is of good intellect, complexity and richness of personality, general lack of defensiveness, and candor in self-description – in other words, an openness to experience and especially to experience of one's inner life. It must also be noted, however, that in the self-reports and in the MMPI profiles of many of our creative subjects, one can find rather clear evidence of psychopathology, but also evidence of adequate control mechanisms, as the success with which they live their productive and creative lives testifies.

However, the most striking aspect of the MMPI profiles of all our male creative groups is an extremely high peak on the *Mf* (femininity) scale. This tendency for creative males to score relatively high on femininity is also demonstrated on the Fe (femininity) scale of the California Psychological Inventory (CPI) (Gough, 1957) and on the masculinity-femininity scale of the Strong Vocational Interest Blank (Strong, 1959). Scores on the latter scale (where high score indicates more masculinity) correlate —·49 with rated creativity.

The evidence is clear: The more creative a person is the more he reveals an openness to his own feelings and emotions, a sensitive intellect and understanding self-awareness, and wide-ranging interests including many which in the American culture are thought of as feminine. In the realm of sexual identification and interests, our creative subjects appear to give more expression to the feminine side of their nature than do less creative persons. In the language of Jung (1956), creative persons are not so completely identified with their masculine *persona* roles as to blind themselves to or to deny expression to the more feminine traits of the *anima*. For some, to be sure, the balance between masculine and feminine traits, interests, and identification, is a precarious one, and for several of our subjects it would appear that their presently achieved reconciliation of these opposites of their nature has been barely effected and only after considerable psychic stress and turmoil.

The perceptiveness of the creative and his openness to richness and complexity of experience is strikingly revealed on the Barron-Welsh Art Scale of the Welsh Figure Preference Test (Welsh, 1959), which presents to the subject a set of 62 abstract line drawings which range from simple and symmetrical figures to complex and asymmetrical ones. In the original study (Barron & Welsh, 1952) which standardized this scale, some 80 painters from New York, San Francisco, New Orleans, Chicago, and Minneapolis showed a marked preference for the complex and asymmetrical, or, as they often referred to them, the vital and dynamic figures. A contrasting sample of nonartists revealed a marked preference for the simple and symmetrical drawings.

All creative groups we have studied have shown a clear preference for the complex and asymmetrical, and in general the more creative a person is the stronger is this preference. Similarly, in our several samples, scores on an Institute scale which measures the preference for perceptual complexity are significantly correlated with creativity. In the sample of architects the correlation is $+ \cdot 48$.

Presented with a large selection of one-inch squares of varicolored posterboard and asked to construct within a 30-minute period a pleasing, completely filled-in 8″ × 10″ mosaic (Hall, 1958), some subjects select the fewest colors possible (one used only one color, all white) while others seek to make order out of the largest possible number, using all of the 22 available colors. And, again citing results from the architects, there is a significant though low positive correlation of $+ \cdot 38$ between the number of colors a subject chooses and his creativity as rated by the experts.

If one considers for a moment the meaning of these preferences on the art scale, on the mosaic test, and on the scale that measures preference for perceptual complexity, it is clear that creative persons are especially disposed to admit complexity and even disorder into their perceptions without being made anxious by the resulting chaos. It is not so much that they like disorder *per se*, but that they prefer the richness of the disordered to the stark barrenness of the simple. They appear to be challenged by disordered multiplicity which arouses in them a strong need which in them is serviced by a superior capacity to achieve the most difficult and far-reaching ordering of the richness they are willing to experience.

The creative person's openness to experience is further revealed on the Myers-Briggs Type Indicator (Myers, 1958), a test based largely upon Jung's theory of psychological functions and types.

Employing the language of the test, though in doing so I oversimplify both it and the theory upon which it is based, one might say that whenever a person uses his mind for any purpose, he performs either an act of perception (he becomes aware of something) or an act of judgement (he comes to a conclusion about something). And most persons tend to show a rather consistent preference for and greater pleasure in one or the other of these, preferring either to perceive or to judge, though every one both perceives and judges.

An habitual preference for the judging attitude may lead to some prejudging and at the very least to the living of a life that is orderly, controlled, and carefully planned. A preference for the perceptive attitude results in a life that is more open to experience both from within and from without, and characterized by flexibility and spontaneity. A judging type places more emphasis upon the control and regulation of experience, while a perceptive type is inclined to be more open and receptive to all experience.

The majority of our creative writers, mathematicians, and architects are perceptive types. Only among research scientists do we find the majority to be judging types, and even in this group it is interesting to note that there is a positive correlation ($+\cdot25$) between a scientist's preference for perception and his rated creativity as a scientific researcher. For architects, preference for perception correlates $+\cdot41$ with rated creativity.

The second preference measured by the Type Indicator is for one of two types of perception: sense perception or sensation, which is a direct becoming aware of things by way of the senses versus intuitive perception or intuition, which is an indirect perception of the deeper meanings and possibilities inherent in things and situations. Again, everyone senses and intuits, but preliminary norms for the test suggest that in the United States three out of four persons show a preference for sense perception, concentrating upon immediate sensory experience and centering their attention upon existing facts. The one out of every four who shows a preference for intuitive perception, on the other hand, looks expectantly for a bridge or link between that which is given and present and that which is not yet thought of, focusing habitually upon possibilities.

One would expect creative persons not to be bound to the stimulus and the object but to be ever alert to the as-yet-not-realized. And that is precisely the way they show themselves to be on the Type Indicator. In contrast to an estimated 25 per cent of the general population who are intuitive, 90 per cent of the creative writers, 92 per cent of the mathematicians, 93 per cent of the research scientists, and 100 per cent of the architects are intuitive as measured by this test.

In judging or evaluating experience, according to the underlying Jungian theory of the test, one makes use of thought or of feeling; thinking being a logical process aimed at an impersonal fact-weighing analysis, while feeling is a process of appreciation and evaluation of things that gives them a personal and subjective value. A preference for thinking or for feeling appears to be less related to one's creativity as such than to the type of materials or concepts with which one deals. Of our creative groups, writers prefer feeling, mathematicians, research scientists, and engineers prefer thinking, while architects split fifty-fifty in their preference for one or the other of the two functions.

The final preference in Jungian typology and on the test is the well-known one between introversion and extraversion. Approximately two-thirds of all our creative groups score as introverts, though there is no evidence that introverts as such are more creative than extraverts.

Turning to preferences among interests and values, one would expect the highly creative to be rather different from less creative people, and there is clear evidence that they are.

On the Strong Vocational Interest Blank, which measures the similarity of a person's expressed interests with the known interests of individuals successful in a number of occupations and professions, all of our creative subjects have shown, with only slight variation from group to group, interests similar to those of the psychologist, author-journalist, lawyer, architect, artist, and musician, and interests unlike those of the purchasing agent, office man, banker, farmer, carpenter, veterinarian, and interestingly enough, too, policeman and mortician. Leaving aside any consideration of the specific interests thus revealed we may focus our attention on the inferences that may be drawn from this pattern of scores which suggest that creative persons are relatively uninterested in small details, or in facts for their own sake, and more concerned with their meanings and implications, possessed of considerable cognitive flexibility, verbally skillful, interested in communicating with others and accurate in so doing, intellectually curious, and relatively disinterested in policing either their own impulses and images or those of others.

On the Allport-Vernon-Lindzey Study of Values (1951), a test designed to measure in the individual the relative strength of the six values of men as these values have been conceptualized and described by the German psychologist and educator, Eduard Spranger (1928), namely, the theoretical, economic, esthetic, social, political, and religious values, all of our creative groups have as their highest values the theoretical and the esthetic.

For creative research scientists the theoretical value is the highest, closely followed by the esthetic. For creative architects the highest value is the esthetic, with the theoretical value almost as high. For creative mathematicians, the two values are both high and approximately equally strong.

If, as the authors of the test believe, there is some incompatibility and conflict between the theoretical value with its cognitive and rational concern with truth and the esthetic value with its emotional concern with form and beauty, it would appear that the creative person has the capacity to tolerate the tension that strong opposing values create in him, and in his creative striving he effects some reconciliation of them. For the truly creative person it is not sufficient that problems be solved, there is the further demand that the solutions be elegant. He seeks both truth and beauty.

A summary description of the creative person – especially of the creative architect – as he reveals himself in his profile on the California Psychological Inventory (Gough, 1957), reads as follows:

He is dominant (Do scale); possessed of those qualities and attributes which underlie and lead to the achievement of social status (Cs); poised, spontaneous, and self-confident in personal and social interaction (Sp); though not of an especially sociable or participative temperament (low Sy); intelligent, outspoken, sharp-witted, demanding, aggressive, and self-centered; persuasive and verbally fluent, self-confident and self-assured (Sa); and relatively uninhibited in expressing his worries and complaints (low Wb).

He is relatively free from conventional restraints and inhibitions (low So and Sc), not preoccupied with the impression which he makes on

193

others and thus perhaps capable of great independence and autonomy (low Gi), and relatively ready to recognize and admit self-views that are unusual and unconventional (low Cm).

He is strongly motivated to achieve in situations in which independence in thought and action are called for (Ai). But, unlike his less creative colleagues, he is less inclined to strive for achievement in settings where conforming behavior is expected or required (Ac). In efficiency and steadiness of intellectual effort (Ie), however, he does not differ from his fellow workers.

Finally, he is definitely more psychologically minded (Py), more flexible (Fx), and possessed of more femininity of interests (Fe) than architects in general. [....]

Having described the overall design of our studies, and having presented a selection of our findings which reveal at least some aspects of the nature of creative talent, I turn now, but with considerably less confidence, to the question as to how we can early identify and best encourage the development of creative potential. Our findings concerning the characteristics of highly creative persons are by now reasonably well established, but their implications for the nurture of creative talent are far from clear.

It is one thing to discover the distinguishing characteristics of mature, creative, productive individuals. It is quite another matter to conclude that the traits of creative persons observed several years after school and college characterized these same individuals when they were students. Nor can we be certain that finding these same traits in youngsters today will identify those with creative potential. Only empirical, longitudinal research, which we do not yet have, can settle such issues. Considering, however, the nature of the traits which discriminate creative adults from their noncreative peers, I would venture to guess that most students with creative potential have personality structures congruent with, though possibly less sharply delineated than, those of mature creatives.

Our problem is further complicated by the fact that though our creative subjects have told us about their experiences at home, in school, and in college, and about the forces and persons and situations which, as they see it, nurtured their creativeness, these are, after all, self-reports subject to the misperceptions and self-deceptions of all self-reports. Even if we were to assume that their testimony is essentially accurate we would still have no assurance that the conditions in the home, in school, and society, the qualities of interpersonal relations between instructor and student, and the aspects of the teaching-learning process which would appear to have contributed to creative development a generation ago would facilitate rather than inhibit creativity if these same factors were created in today's quite different world and far different educational climate.

In reporting upon events and situations in the life histories of our subjects which appear to have fostered their creative potential and independent spirit, I shall again restrict myself to architects. One finds in their histories a number of circumstances which, in the early years, could well have provided an opportunity as well as the necessity for developing the secure sense of personal autonomy and zestful commitment to the profession which so markedly characterize them.

What appears most often to have characterized the parents of these future creative architects was an extraordinary respect for the child and confidence in his ability to do what was appropriate. Thus they did not hesitate to grant him rather unusual freedom in exploring his universe and in making decisions for himself – and this early as well as late. The expectation of the parent that the child would act independently but reasonably and responsibly appears to have contributed immensely to the latter's sense of personal autonomy which was to develop to such a marked degree.

The obverse side of this was that there was often a lack of intense closeness with one or both of the parents. Most often this appeared in relation to the father rather than to the mother, but often it characterized the relationship with both parents. There were not strong emotional ties of either a positive or a negative sort between parent and child, but neither was there the type of relationship that fosters overdependency nor the type that results in severe rejection. Thus, if there was a certain distance in the relationship between child and parent, it had a liberating effect so far as the child was concerned. If he lacked something of the emotional closeness which some children experience with their parents, he was also spared that type of psychological exploitation that is so frequently seen in the life histories of clinical patients.

Closely related to this factor of some distance between parent and child were ambiguities in identification with the parents. In place of the more usual clear identification with one parent, there was a tendency for the architects to have identified either with both parents or with neither. It was not that the child's early milieu was a deprived one so far as models for identification and the promotion of ego ideals were concerned. It was rather that the larger familial sphere presented the child with a plentiful supply of diverse and effective models – in addition to the mother and father, grandfathers, uncles, and others who occupied prominent and responsible positions within their community – with whom important identifications could be made. Whatever the emotional interaction between father and son, whether distant, harmonious, or turbulent, the father presented a model of effective and resourceful behavior in an exceptionally demanding career. What is perhaps more significant, though, is the high incidence of distinctly autonomous mothers among families of the creative architects, who led active lives with interests and sometimes careers of their own apart from their husbands'.

Still other factors which would appear to have contributed to the development of the marked personal autonomy of our subjects were the types of discipline and religious training which they received, which suggest that within the family there existed clear standards of conduct and ideas as to what was right and wrong but at the same time an expectation if not requirement of active exploration and internalization of a framework of personal conduct. Discipline was almost always consistent and predictable. In most cases there were rules, family standards, and parental injunctions which were known explicitly by the children and seldom infringed. In nearly half the cases, corporal punishment was not employed and in only a few instances was the punishment harsh or cruel.

As for religious practices, the families of the creative architects showed considerable diversity, but what was most widely emphasized was the development of personal ethical codes rather than formal religious practices. For one-third of the families formal religion was important for one parent or for both, but in two-thirds of the families formal religion was either unimportant or practised only perfunctorily. For the majority of the families, in which emphasis was placed upon the development of one's own ethical code, it is of interest to inquire into the values that were most stressed. They were most often values related to integrity (e.g., forthrightness, honesty, respect for others), quality (e.g., pride, diligence, joy in work, development of talent), intellectual and cultural endeavor, success and ambition, and being respectable and doing the right thing.

The families of the more creative architects tended to move more frequently, whether within a single community, or from community to community, or even from country to country. This, combined with the fact that the more creative architects as youngsters were given very much more freedom to roam and to explore widely, provided for them an enrichment of experience both cultural and personal which their less creative peers did not have.

But the frequent moving appears also to have resulted frequently in some estrangement of the family from its immediate neighborhood. And it is of interest that in almost every case in which the architect reported that his family differed in its behavior and values from those in the neighborhood, the family was different in showing greater cultural, artistic, and intellectual interests and pursuits.

To what extent this sort of cultural dislocation contributed to the frequently reported experiences of aloneness, shyness, isolation, and solitariness during childhood and adolescence, with little or no dating during adolescence, or to what extent these experiences stemmed from a natural introversion of interests and unusual sensitivity, we cannot say. They were doubtless mutually reinforcing factors in stimulating the young architect's awareness of his own inner life and his growing interest in his artistic skills and his ideational, imaginal, and symbolic processes.

Almost without exception, the creative architects manifested very early considerable interest and skill in drawing and painting. And also, with almost no exception, one or both of the parents were of artistic temperament and considerable skill. Often it was the mother who in the architect's early years fostered his artistic potentialities by her example as well as by her instruction. It is especially interesting to note, however, that while the visual and artistic abilities and interests of the child were encouraged and rewarded, these interests and abilities were, by and large, allowed to develop at their own speed, and this pace varied considerably among the architects. There was not an anxious concern on the part of the parents about the skills and abilities of the child. What is perhaps most significant was the wide-spread definite lack of strong pressures from the parents towards a particular career. And this was true both for pressures away from architecture as well as for pressures towards architecture by parents who were themselves architects.

The several aspects of the life history which I have described were first noted by Kenneth Craik in the protocols for the highly creative Architects I. Subsequently, in reading the protocols for Architects II and III as well as Architects I, a credit of one point for the presence of each of the factors was assigned and the total for each person taken as a score. The correlation of these life history scores with rated creativity of the architects is $+.36$, significant beyond the .005 level of confidence.

And now I turn finally to a consideration of the implications of the nature of creative talent for the nurturing of it in school and college through the processes of education.

Our findings concerning the relations of intelligence to creativity suggest that we may have overestimated in our educational system the role of intelligence in creative achievement. If our expectation is that a child of a given intelligence will not respond creatively to a task which confronts him, and especially if we make this expectation known to the child, the probability that he will respond creatively is very much reduced. And later on, such a child, now grown older, may find doors closed to him so that he is definitely excluded from certain domains of learning. There is increasing reason to believe that in selecting students for special training of their talent we may have overweighted the role of intelligence either by setting the cutting point for selection on the intellective dimension too high or by assuming that regardless of other factors the student with the higher I Q is the more promising one and should consequently be chosen. Our data suggest, rather, that if a person has the minimum of intelligence required for mastery of a field of knowledge, whether he performs creatively or banally in that field will be crucially determined by nonintellective factors. We would do well then to pay more attention in the future than we have in the past to the nurturing of those nonintellective traits which in our studies have been shown to be intimately associated with creative talent.

There is the openness of the creative person to experience both from within and from without which suggests that whether we be parent or teacher we should use caution in setting limits upon what those whom we are nurturing experience and express.

Discipline and self-control are necessary. They must be learned if one is ever to be truly creative, but it is important that they not be overlearned. Furthermore, there is a time and place for their learning, and having been learned they should be used flexibly, not rigidly or compulsively.

If we consider this specifically with reference to the attitudes of perceiving and judging, everyone must judge as well as perceive. It is not a matter of using one to the exclusion of the other, but a question of how each is used and which is preferred. The danger for one's creative potential is not the judging or evaluating of one's experience but that one prejudges, thus excluding from perception large areas of experience. The danger in all parental instruction, as in all academic instruction, is that new ideas and new possibilities of action are criticized too soon and too often.

Training in criticism is obviously important and so widely recognized that I need not plead its case. Rather I would urge that, if we wish to nurture creative potential, an equal emphasis be placed on perceptiveness, discussing with our students as well as with our children, at least upon occasion, the most fantastic of ideas and possibilities. It is the duty of parents to communicate and of professors to profess what they judge to be true, but it is no less their duty by example to encourage in their children and in their students an openness to all ideas and especially to those which most challenge and threaten their own judgements.

The creative person, as we have seen, is not only open to experience, but intuitive about it. We can train students to be accurate in their perceptions, and this, too, is a characteristic of the creative. But can we train them to be intuitive, and if so how?

I would suggest that rote learning, learning of facts for their own sake, repeated drill of material, too much emphasis upon facts unrelated to other facts, and excessive concern with memorizing, can all strengthen and reinforce sense perception. On the other hand, emphasis upon the transfer of training from one subject to another, the searching for common principles in terms of which facts from quite different domains of knowledge can be related, the stressing of analogies, and similes, and metaphors, a seeking for symbolic equivalents of experience in the widest possible number of sensory and imaginal modalities, exercises in imaginative play, training in retreating from the facts in order to see them in larger perspective and in relation to more aspects of the larger context thus achieved – these and still other emphases in learning would, I believe, strengthen the disposition to intuitive perception as well as intuitive thinking.

If the widest possible relationships among facts are to be established, if the structure of knowledge (Bruner, 1960) is to be grasped, it is necessary that the student have a large body of facts which he has learned as well as a large array of reasoning skills which he has mastered. You will see, then, that what I am proposing is not that in teaching one disdain acute and accurate sense perception, but that one use it to build upon, leading the student always to an intuitive understanding of that which he experiences.

The independence of thought and action which our subjects reveal in the assessment setting appears to have long characterized them. It was already manifest in high school, though, according to their reports, tending to increase in college and thereafter.

In college our creative architects earned about a B average. In work and courses which caught their interest they could turn in an

A performance, but in courses that failed to strike their imagination, they were quite willing to do no work at all. In general, their attitude in college appears to have been one of profound skepticism. They were unwilling to accept anything on the mere say-so of their instructors. Nothing was to be accepted on faith or because it had behind it the voice of authority. Such matters might be accepted, but only after the student on his own had demonstrated their validity to himself. In a sense, they were rebellious, but they did not run counter to the standards out of sheer rebelliousness. Rather, they were spirited in their disagreement and one gets the impression that they learned most from those who were not easy with them. But clearly many of them were not easy to take. One of the most rebellious, but, as it turned out, one of the most creative, was advised by the Dean of his School to quit because he had no talent; and another, having been failed in his design dissertation which attacked the stylism of the faculty, took his degree in the art department.

These and other data should remind all of us who teach that creative students will not always be to our liking. This will be due not only to their independence in situations in which nonconformity may be seriously disruptive of the work of others, but because, as we have seen, more than most they will be experiencing large quantities of tension produced in them by the richness of their experience and the strong opposites of their nature. In struggling to reconcile these opposites and in striving to achieve creative solutions to the difficult problems which they have set themselves they will often show that psychic turbulence which is so characteristic of the creative person. If, however, we can only recognize the sources of their disturbance, which often enough will result in behavior disturbing to us, we may be in a better position to support and encourage them in their creative striving.

References

Allport, G. W., Vernon, P. E., & Lindzey, G. *Study of values: Manual of directions.* (Rev. ed.) Boston: Houghton Mifflin, 1951.

Barron, F., & Welsh, G. S. Artistic perception as a possible factor in personality style: Its measurement by a figure preference test. *J. Psychol.*, 1952, *33*, 199–203.

Bruner, J. S. *The process of education.* Cambridge, Mass.: Harvard Univer. Press, 1960.

Gough, H. G. *California Psychological Inventory Manual.* Palo Alto, Calif.: Consulting Psychologists Press, 1957.

Hall, W. B. The development of a technique for assessing aesthetic predispositions and its application to a sample of professional research scientists. Paper read at Western Psychological Association, Monterey, California, April 1958.

Hathaway, S. R., and McKinley, J. C. *Minnesota Multiphasic Personality Inventory*. New York: Psychological Corporation, 1945.

Jung, C. G. *Two essays on analytical psychology*. New York: Meridian, 1956.

MacKinnon, D. W. The personality correlates of creativity: A study of American architects. In G. S. Nielsen (Ed.), *Proceedings of the XIV the International Congress of Applied Psychology, Copenhagen 1961.* Vol. 2. Copenhagen: Munksgaard, 1962. Pp. 11–39.

Myers, Isabel, B. *Some findings with regard to type and manual for Myers-Briggs Type Indicator, Form E.* Swarthmore, Pa.: Author, 1958.

Russell, W. A., & Jenkins, J. J. The complete Minnesota norms for responses to 100 words from the Kent-Rosanoff Word Association Test. Technical Report No. 11, 1954, University of Minnesota, Contract N8 onr-66216, Office of Naval Research.

Spranger, E. *Types of men.* (Trans. by Paul J. W. Pigors) Halle, Germany: Max Niemeyer, 1928.

Strong, E. K., Jr. *Manual for Strong Vocational Interest Blanks for Men and Women, Revised Blanks (Form M and W).* Palo Alto, Calif.: Consulting Psychologists Press, 1959.

Terman, L. M. *Concept Mastery Test, Form T manual.* New York: Psychological Corporation, 1956.

Welsh, G. S. *Welsh Figure Preference Test: Preliminary manual.* Palo Alto, Calif.: Consulting Psychologists Press, 1959.

Wotton, Henry. *The elements of architecture.* London: John Bill, 1624.

THE EXPRESSION OF PERSONALITY
AND MALADJUSTMENT
IN INTELLIGENCE TEST RESULTS

Early writing on 'individual differences' tended perhaps to distinguish too sharply between 'intelligence' on the one hand and 'personality' on the other. There is no reason why intelligence should not be regarded as an aspect of personality, but the dichotomy to some extent survives. Not even the simplest intelligence test item can be entirely 'personality-free', if one may coin the term on the analogy of 'culture-free'. The implications for consideration of 'objectivity', and the like, are far-reaching, but need not concern us here.

Reference has already been made (see 6, above) to the origins of the writer's own interest in what are sometimes called the qualitative aspects of intelligence test performance. A full account of techniques specifically designed to exploit these has been given by Semeonoff and Trist (4). The work received part of its impetus from some of the earlier publications from the Menninger Clinic, Topeka, Kansas, which later became the basis of Rapaport's two-volume *Diagnostic Psychological Testing* (9, 1). This work to some extent perpetuates the dichotomy mentioned above, in that Volume I deals with 'Diagnostic Psychological Testing and Concept Formation', while Volume II covers 'Personality and Ideational Content'. This latter volume covers a Word Association Test, the Rorschach, and the TAT, and so might well have appeared in the bibliographies to the articles in the next section of this book of Readings.

The main topics in Volume I are the diagnostic use of the Wechsler-Bellevue scale, and of concept-formation, stemming from the work of Vygotsky (5) and of Goldstein and Scheerer (2). Work in this latter field might perhaps have formed a separate section of the present book; an example of the use of 'Object-sorting' techniques in personality is given by Eysenck (1 Vol. 2,) and, in a selection context, by Semeonoff (3).

The best-known and most important work in the general field under discussion, however, has been done in relation to the Wechsler intelligence tests. Copyright difficulties prevented inclusion of the most recent account (6), but the general trend is well expressed in the article that follows.

References

1. Eysenck, H. J. (Ed.), *Experiments in Personality* (2 vols.) London: Routledge and Kegan Paul, 1960.
2. Goldstein, K. and Scheerer, M., Abstract and Concrete Behaviour: an Experimental Study with Special Tests. *Psychological Monographs. 53*, no. 2 (whole no. 239). 1941.
3. Semeonoff, B., Projective Techniques in Selection for Counselling. *Human Relations, 11*, 113–22. 1958.
4. Semeonoff, B. and Trist, E. L., *Diagnostic Performance Tests: a Manual for use with Adults.* London: Tavistock. 1958.
5. Vygotsky, L. S., Thought and Language. Trans. by Eugenia Haufmann and Gertrude Vakar. London and New York: Wiley, 1962.
6. Wechsler, *The Measurement and Appraisal of Adult Intelligence.* 4th edition. Baltimore: Williams and Wilkins: London: Ballière, Tindal & Cox. 1958.

9 R. Schafer

The Expression of Personality and Maladjustment in Intelligence Test Results

Annals of the New York Academy of Sciences, 1946, Vol. 46, Article 7 pp. 609–623.

Introduction

Intelligence testing has long remained a technique for determining mental ages or I.Q.s, but has remained unconcerned with the impairments of specific intelligence-functions called into play by the different test-items. For example, it has remained unconcerned with whether the vocabulary score is high and the learning efficiency score low, or *vice versa*, as long as the total score remains the same. This gross approach leaves intelligence testing a technique in no way helpful in assessing personality and maladjustment.

In recent years, interest has begun to swing to scatter-analysis, that is to say, to the analysis of the distribution of passes and failures within the test, or the unevenness of achievement in the test as a whole. For the most part, these studies have been concerned with finding a good gross quantitative measure of the amount of scatter or unevenness within the test. But even these procedures do not advance intelligence testing as a technique for exploring personality and maladjustment. At best, they can demonstrate a statistical trend, which may be of theoretical significance or may lend itself to mechanical-diagnostic attitudes, but which does not relate, in any palpable way, to the characteristics and individual variability of any specific case.

In order that intelligence testing may become a technique for detecting manifestations of personality-organization and maladjustment, a number of assumptions have to be made and thought through, about intelligence-functions and intelligence tests.

First of all, it is necessary to recognize that, in thinking about any individual's 'intelligence' for diagnostic purposes, one must think in terms of a variety of intelligence-functions such as judgment, anticipation, concentration, etc.

Secondly, it is necessary to recognize that different intelligence-functions underlie achievement on the different item-groups in an intelligence test, and that, consequently, it is necessary to establish what each of these functions may be.

Thirdly, it is necessary to recognize that the development and efficiency of each of these intelligence-functions are integral parts of the individual's personality development, and are regulated in their development by the vicissitudes of his needs and drives with all their emotional derivatives. From the time of Kraepelin (2) up to today, standard clinical descriptions of the different psychiatric disorders or personality types have always referred, explicitly or implicitly, to manifestations of symptomatology or modes of adjustment in the person's thought processes and intelligence-functioning. However, these attempts have been, in the main, descriptive, and have not related the development and efficiency of intelligence-functions to the dynamics of specific illness or personality. Specifically, the patterning of intelligence-functions does not relate directly to needs, wishes, and drives, but rather to preferred modes of control of these, or limitations of the expressions of these. It is by these modes of control that we know the individual. However, this general thesis must be made specific by recourse to data on the pathological conditions under which each of these functions becomes profoundly impaired, temporarily impaired, remains well retained, or is even heightened in its scope and efficiency. An integration of these data with the psychiatrist's descriptions of the dynamics of the cases studied will then become the condition for inferring personality characteristics or maladjustment from intelligence test results.

At this point, intelligence testing may appear to become a projective technique, in the broad sense that it can be seen to elicit expressions of personality through the medium of the intelligence-functions. However, intelligence testing remains an essentially non-projective technique, in that it does not use the medium of individual organization, manipulation, and elaboration of *unstructured* test materials. The subject must cope mainly with directly meaningful material and explicit requirements, and he may safely fall back upon verbal stereotype and memory, unlike any of the standard projective tests.

Finally, for using intelligence tests as non-projective tests of personality, it is necessary to recognize that there exist, in the general 'normal' population, trends to have specific relationships between achievements on different kinds of subtests. These relationships should be considered norms, deviations from which are significant for the individual case. If Z-scores or derivatives of Z-scores are used to denote achievement on each subtest, then discrepancies between the subtest scores in any individual case become crucial diagnostic data.

Consequently, it is necessary to devise quantitative methods of analysis of intelligence test results, in order to explore and refine, with their help, qualitative methods of analysis. These quantitative methods not only utilize the test results to their full diagnostic advantage, but render them 'objective' and easily communicable. The intelligence test, of choice, is one which lends itself more readily to such analyses. We chose the Wechsler Bellevue Scale (3). Before describing our methods of analysis, it will be necessary to describe briefly the test itself.

The Bellevue Scale

The Bellevue Scale comprises eleven subtests, each containing relatively homogeneous, but increasingly difficult, items.* The subject's achievement on each subtest obtains an independent score from 0 to 17; these scores are equated-scores, that is, they are derived from Z-scores and are therefore intercomparable. Thus, a score of 15 on one subtest and a score of 9 on another indicate a definite superiority of the development and efficiency of the function underlying achievement on the former. The scale includes six Verbal subtests, counting the Vocabulary subtest, and five non-verbal or Performance subtests. Recognition is thereby taken of the fundamental differences between the thought processes underlying achievement on items requiring verbal, and those requiring visual and/or motor, performance.

Methods of Analysis

Personality and maladjustment can be traced in the intelligence test results from three points of view, i.e., by three main methods: 1. In terms of relative impairment or superiority of a function; 2. in terms of its temporary inefficiencies; 3. in terms of the subject's manner of verbalizing his responses.

(1) *Impairment or Superiority of Functions*

The impairment or superiority of the different intelligence-functions involved in the intelligence test is established by scatter analysis. Scatter analysis, as used here, is analysis of the quantitative differences between the weighted subtest scores of the Bellevue Scale. Several different types of comparisons are possible: a comparison of the Verbal score-level to the Performance score-level; a comparison of the achievement on any Verbal test to the general level of the remaining Verbal tests, and similarly for the Performance tests; a comparison of the achievement on subtests

*The only exception is the Digit Symbol Subtest.

vulnerable to maladjustment with the relatively sturdy Vocabulary score; and intercomparisons of specific subtest scores, which clinical experience has indicated to be a fruitful source of diagnostic indications.

Scatter analysis is dependent upon establishing baselines from which to estimate impairments or superiorities; our experience shows that three main baselines may be profitably used:

(a) *Vocabulary scatter*. Vocabulary Scatter is based on the well-known finding (4) that, of all intelligence test scores, the Vocabulary score offers the greatest resistance to impairment by maladjustment. In almost all clinical cases, it is the Vocabulary score from which the premorbid level of intelligence development – before pathology impaired intelligence-functioning – can best be inferred. The remaining scores show greater or lesser vulnerability to maladjustment, and, therefore, comparison of these scores to the Vocabulary score as a baseline will indicate the extent of impairment. A slight amount of variability of the subtest scores below the Vocabulary score is frequent even in the normal range, but in this range the Comprehension, Information, and Similarities scores, in general, stay on the same level as Vocabulary.

(b) *Mean scatter*. It is also necessary to see how the more vulnerable scores compare to each other. Mean Scatter measures the difference between the score on any subtest and the general level of the scores on the remaining subtests. Thus, if all the scores excepting Vocabulary are pushed down markedly, Mean Scatter may demonstrate that the Comprehension score, for example, is especially impaired, as it is, frequently, in chronic schizophrenics. Analysis of Mean Scatter should be pursued separately for the six Verbal subtests and five Performance subtests.

(c) *Specific subtest comparisons*. Also crucial to scatter analysis are the specific comparisons of pairs of subtest scores other than the Vocabulary score, aimed at answering such questions as: 'How does the subject's judgment compare to his fund of information?', 'How does his capacity for attention compare to his capacity for concentration?' etc.

Thus, scatter analysis traces the relationship of the score on one subtest to the Vocabulary score, in order to estimate extent of impairment; to the general level of other scores, in order to estimate especial impairment; and to single other scores, the relationship to which is a crucial datum for the understanding of the personality and maladjustment of the subject.

(2) *Temporary Inefficiency*

Inasmuch as each of the Bellevue Scale subtests comprises homogeneous items of varied degrees of difficulty, item-analysis of the sequence of passes and failures within each subtest clarifies the smoothness and efficiency of the function or functions underlying achievement on that subtest. It is important to know whether the final subtest score derives from failures on the 'easy' items and successes on the 'difficult' ones (in which case we speak of temporary inefficiency), or whether the failures first set in on difficult items and mark the point where the subject's development is no longer adequate to cope with the new items. The difficulty of items can be statistically established by the incidence of failure on each in the general population.

Inefficiencies may be due either to intense anxiety or to a psychotic process. When anxiety is their source, the responses are characterized by uncertainty, false choice between the correct and an incorrect alternative, and quick or delayed correction of wrong answers. Furthermore, these failures on the relatively easy items will tend to be few and to occur on those items which, although 'easy', are frequently missed by other cases showing inefficiency. For example, in the Information subtest, the capital of Italy may be Naples, the average height of American women may be 5 feet 2 inches, there may be 4 pints in a quart and 48 weeks in a year, etc. Intense anxiety can prevent knowledge or ideas, once acquired, from emerging into consciousness and may lead to false and inaccurate responses. However, anxiety, alone, does not account for answers so incorrect as to be absurd. Both of these, especially when accompanied by a degree of bland confidence, are indications of a psychotic process. Furthermore, if the subject knows what ethnology and the Apocrypha are, and yet does not know where Brazil is, this, too, is a psychotic indication: the discrepancy between retained and lost information here is too great to be accounted for merely on the basis of anxiety-determined, temporary inefficiency.

(3) *Analysis of Verbalization*

Thus far, we see that departure from gross statements about I.Q. is accomplished by scatter analysis, as described above; that scatter analysis is amplified by item-analysis, as described above; and now amplification of the test results, in general, is accomplished by qualitative analysis of the subject's verbalization of his responses. In verbalization, we can follow the subject's intelligence *at work* and, thus, we often see in it, in clear form, the expressions of the subject's maladjustment or of the main aspects of his personality make-up. This analysis is concerned with *how* the subject failed or passed the test-items; that is, were doubt and indecision characteristic, were more or less bizarre ideas expressed, was impulsiveness prevalent, etc.?

It must be remembered that, although the correct responses to the test-items are fixed by common agreement, the routes to these, as well as to the incorrect responses, are not fixed. Thus, the subject's manner of reasoning out Comprehension or Similarities or Arithmetic items, his speed and confidence in delivery of his responses, his anxiety or blandness about incorrect responses, are all revealing of him. For example, when an otherwise intelligent subject states blandly that the capital of Italy is Constantinople, that a dog and a lion are alike because both have cells, etc., the diagnosis of schizophrenia is strongly indicated. When a subject lists five alternative courses of action or explanations on some of the Comprehension items, three similarities on some of the Similarities items, and gives extensive and quibbling definitions on the Vocabulary items, etc., obsessive character make-up or obsessive pathology must seriously be considered. This occurs in paranoid cases, too, but in these the circumstantiality or pedantry will become peculiar in places. If wild guessing occurs on every item, no matter how difficult and obviously beyond the subject's level of ability it may be, psychopathic trends are likely to be present.

Furthermore, on a number of the Bellevue Scale items, common agreement or consensus of opinion are not knowable to a subject and here verbalization may become especially revealing of him. This is true, for example, of the difficult Picture Arrangement items, where distorted anticipations may be verbalized in explaining the sequence of pictures offered. One paranoid subject saw a woman rejecting a man's attentions by signalling to another man, although it was the same man in both pictures and no indications of any signalling are present in the pictures.

In the course of experience with any test, an examiner becomes familiar with the usual forms of verbal expression used by subjects, and with the usual errors or failures. It is against this subjectively-retained experience as a baseline that he may detect deviant verbalizations, that is, verbalizations the form or content of which stems from a specific maladjustment type or personality-organization. To date, however, verbalization is the least explored and systematized of all the material elicited by intelligence tests, and, for that matter, by tests in general.

Sample Analyses

Let us analyze, by the techniques outlined above, the Bellevue Scale records of a few cases. Their scores are presented in Figures 1–4.

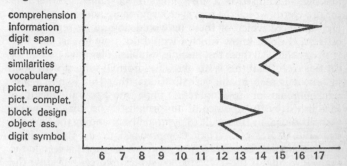

Figure 1

Case 1 is an obsessive-compulsive neurotic. If we look first at the scatter, its outstanding aspects are the impairment of the Comprehension score and the superiority of the Information score. In everyday experience, this pattern of verbal achievement is repeatedly encountered in the records of cases of obsessive character make-up or of those with obsessional symptoms; furthermore, our statistical analyses show this scatter pattern to significantly differentiate obsessive cases from other neurotics[1]. The rationale of this diagnostic pattern is the following: the superior Information score must represent an especial inclination to pick up facts, knowledge, general information; and hence refers to an intellectualizing mode of adjustment. This becomes confirmed in analysis of verbalization. Many responses of the following type of exhaustiveness occur: the subject defines *diamond* as 'a carboniferous gem found mostly in South Africa, it is mined, it can be used as an adornment or on machine tools', and then asks confidently, 'Do you want more?'. Furthermore, the low score on Comprehension refers to an impairment of judgment, that is, of the ability quickly and definitively to make decisions harmonious with the objective as well as affective aspects of a situation. The form of appearance of this type of impairment of judgment is seen in the characteristically obsessive, doubt-ridden, and indecisive verbalization about any course of action or result of reasoning. In accord with the inclination to know all the facts and angles, too many alternatives come to mind

211

at once, judgments are formed full of reservations, so much so that they do not really qualify as 'judgments', and a final decision is hampered, if not altogether avoided. When asked, 'What should you do if while sitting in the movies you were the first person to discover a fire?', the subject replied, 'Either ring the fire-alarm, or tell the manager, or jump up and shout "fire".' He was asked which of these he would do and he replied with distress, 'I don't know which I would do: how honest can I be with myself?' All these test findings establish obsessive pathology for this case. That this is no obsessive, normal subject with poor judgment is seen in the verbalizations; that this is not a pre-schizophrenic or schizophrenic impairment of judgment is established by the absence of any irrealistic (peculiar or queer) verbalizations, by the results of item-analysis, and by the minimal scatter of scores other than Comprehension and Information. Further support for the obsessive neurosis diagnosis is seen in the slight lowering of the Performance subtest scores, reflecting the hampering of action by doubt, excessive caution, and meticulousness.

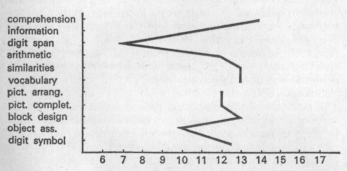

Figure 2

Case 2 is a conversion hysteric. If we look first at the scatter, its outstanding aspects are the impairment of Information and Digit Span; Comprehension, i.e., judgment, is well retained. In everyday experience and in our statistical analyses, this pattern of achievement is typical for hysterical neuroses (1). The rationale of this diagnostic finding is the following: Digit Span, to our understanding, is a test of attention, that is, of the capacity for the free intake of stimulation. Digit Span does not correlate with tests of immediate memory, nor is its material meaningful, and, therefore, it is not considered a memory item by us. As a test of attention,

Digit Span is especially vulnerable to impairment by anxiety. We have data to show that, even within the normal range, the Digit Span score progressively drops with increasing degrees of anxiety, as assessed by clinical observation (1). Hence, our first inference about the case is that intense anxiety is present: there is a 6 unit difference between the Digit Span and Vocabulary scores. In regard to the low Information score, our understanding is this: at the core of hysterical neurosis is a pathologically excessive use of repression as a mechanism of defence. Effects of repression become widespread, when knowledge, information, extensive, and speculative thinking all may become dangerous to the hysterical adjustment and, therefore, have to be avoided; otherwise, these thoughts might, in some more or less distant way, touch upon the repressed ideas and thereby mobilize further anxiety. As a result of the widespread repression, the function underlying acquisition of information suffers, and the Information score becomes low. Item-analysis amplifies this point: it is not that all information suffers, but rather that there are sudden gaps in the information retained. For example, this subject knew who discovered the North Pole and who wrote *Huckleberry Finn*, but said that there are four pints in a quart, calculated that there are 48 weeks in a year, and could say of the heart only, 'It beats'. Analysis of verbalization shows that, in regard to the fire in the movie house, the subject would 'yell "fire" and run to the exit'. The contrast of this impulsive response and the high Comprehension score indicates the characteristically hysteric-like affective lability. All these indications establish the diagnosis of hysteria.

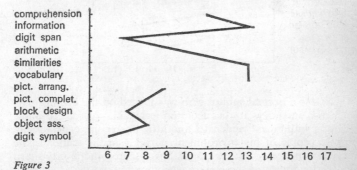

Figure 3

Case 3 is a neurotic depressive. Outstanding in the scatter is the great discrepancy between the Verbal and Performance subtest scores, and this discrepancy we have found to be a statistically significant, and therefore diagnostic, indication of depression (1). The rationale of this finding is the following: depression becomes manifest in intellectual functioning, by a retardation of perceptual and associative processes. The relatively complex visual organization and visual-motor coordination required by the Performance subtests put too great demands upon the slowed-down depressive. Furthermore, in contrast to the untimed Verbal subtests, the Performance subtests have time-limits on each item and even give extra credit for speed. Consequently, depressives not only do not obtain extra credit, but exceed the time limit on many items. For this case, item analysis confirms the retardation by showing that, on Picture Completion and Block Design, a number of items were failed only because they exceeded the time limit. To return to the scatter, the impairment of Digit Span or attention is also striking and reflects the presence of intense anxiety accompanying the depression. The mild impairment of Arithmetic is referable to an inability to meet the time-limits and gain time-bonuses on the items of this subtest. In verbalization, much self-deprecation, as well as indirect criticism of the test and examiner, are evident. The diagnosis of depression is clear.

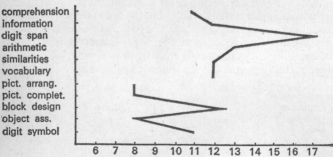

Figure 4

Case 4 is a normal subject who was judged on the basis of psychiatric interview to be definitely schizoid, that is, to show strong withdrawal tendencies and little interest in, or fellowship with, people of his environment. Striking in the scatter is the great superiority of the Digit Span score; the overly-sharp attention indicated thereby we have found in our data to show a significant correlation with schizoid trends in the normal range. The Performance subtests show more than the average amount of scatter, with Block Design being the highest score. This total scatter pattern is often encountered in the records of preschizophrenics and acute schizophrenics, but differential diagnosis here is made by recourse to item-analysis and analysis of verbalization. The absence of irrealistic thinking or performance, and the persistently good achievement on the easy items of each subtest speak against any acute pathology. Instead, we see a schizoid normal subject with excellent attention (Digit Span), some weakness of ability to make correct anticipations (Picture Arrangement and Object Assembly), and some impairment of concentration (Picture Completion).

These few analyses have been presented to illustrate the methods of analysis of, or ways of looking upon, intelligence test results which we found to be the most useful for the diagnostic application of these tests. To repeat: know the underlying functions, use scatter analysis, item-analysis, and analysis of verbalization. Knowing the functions underlying achievement on the different item-groups is the main safeguard against mechanical application of diagnostic scatter analysis. Mechanical application is a hazard, because intelligence test records are not always as diagnostically clear as in the few cases described above; there are cases whose scatter in no way reflects their diagnoses and even points away from the correct one. Special environmental educational advantages or disadvantages, mood swings, or a generalized anxiety state accompanying the crucial diagnostic symptoms, etc., may all obscure the significance of the test findings. Furthermore, the maladjustment may find other avenues of expression than in the shaping of intelligence-functions. Due to specific conditions, an hysteric can have excellent information and poor judgment, an obsessional neurotic can have a fund of information inferior to his other achievements, a depressive can have great scatter with high scores on some of the Performance subtests, etc. If a battery of projective and nonprojective tests is used, the atypical variations of scatter will not dismay the examiner, but will be used by him to draw out the specific flavor of the individual case. The other tests will establish the diagnosis.

The Criteria for Diagnostic Intelligence Tests

From this analysis, the following ideals may be derived for the development and application of an intelligence test as a nonprojective test of personality and maladjustment: (1) The test must include homogeneous item-groups. (2) The intelligence-function or functions underlying achievement on each item-group must be known to the examiner, so that he can reconstruct a psychologically meaningful and differentiated picture of the subject's intelligence. (3) Within each item-group, there should be a carefully established sequence of increasing degree of difficulty of the items, so that item-analysis can be pursued. (4) The final score on each item-group or subtest must be translated into an equated score which will be directly comparable to the equated scores on the other subtests. (5) The range of the equated score-scale should be sufficiently wide to allow for representation of fine, as well as great, differences in achievement. (6) One of the item-groups must be a Vocabulary test, because, thus far, the score on this has been found to be the most reliable indicator of the subject's potential, or premorbid, level of achievement. (7) The test must include verbal and non-verbal item-groups. (8) The specific item-groups, other than Vocabulary, must be selected to call into play intelligence-functions which are specifically vulnerable to, or specifically regulated by, different kinds of maladjustment and personality organization. This selection must be based on a scrutiny of clinical descriptions of the various psychiatric disorders for statements about differentially diagnostic impairments of specific intelligence-functions; and it must be based on a scrutiny of results, obtained with intelligence tests already extant, to detect the kind of items which are most effective in establishing differential diagnoses. (9) The items finally selected or invented must be tested on a large number of clinical cases of all the classical diagnoses, as well as on a large number of normal cases with different types of personality organization and maladjustment tendencies. In other words, the traditional ideal of using merely a large number of 'normal subjects in general' must be abandoned, and the diagnostic intelligence test must be standardized and validated, not only on normal subjects in general, but on specific kinds of normal subjects and on clinical cases, too.

An intelligence test, meeting or approximating all these criteria, allows for the most fruitful scatter-, item-, and verbalization-analyses and, therefore, allows for a reliable reconstruction of the subject's characteristic mode of intelligence-functioning.

One final ideal must be discussed here. Traditionally, the content of each item in an intelligence test has been selected only on its ability to differentiate levels of intelligence. Exactly *what* the examiner was asking and *what* the subject was reasoning about have not been held relevant considerations, except, perhaps, in the qualitative analyses pursued by the individual clinician. However, intelligence-functions do not operate in a vacuum, nor are they consistently on one level of efficiency. The questions the psychologist must ask himself are: Information about what? Good judgment when? Planning ability with respect to what? In other words, the content of the test-items must be selected to refer to different areas of ideation, and affect above and beyond the ability of these items to differentiate levels of intelligence. Such a selection would allow for considerably richer analyses of verbalization than are possible with the already existing tests.

To be specific: it is apparent that acquisition of information is largely a selective process. Some things we must all know, but others we know only if we care to, and remember only if we are able. Hence, a random selection of the content of test-items allows, for example, only for statements about the subject's fund of information *in general*, and allows little room for inferences about characteristic inclinations or modes of accumulating information. Therefore, tests of information should be designed in which information pertaining to a variety of different areas of ideation is measured. For example, the items might inquire about things sexual, aggressive, practical, abstract, esthetic, scientific, everyday, remote, etc. From the discrepancies between the achievements within each of these areas of information, personal interest and inclination could be inferred, and statements about the subject's information could gain a profitable degree of differentiation. These same considerations hold for vocabulary and for all subtests where the subject must cope with meaningful material. To take other examples, Picture Arrangement could present sets of pictures dealing with danger, with fear, with expression of hostility, with sexually-toned situations, with humorous situations, etc.; tests of learning efficiency (unfortunately lacking in the Bellevue Scale) could present a similar variety of material to be remembered.

Needless to say, a test or an experimental study, using such varieties of content, would offer invaluable material, not only for assessment of personality-organization and maladjustment, but for the general psychology of thinking and of verbalization of thinking. It would offer data to show how the development of some intelligence-functions is speeded or retarded in general, or is speeded or retarded with respect to only specific conditions. It would also have data to offer on how the subject's characteristic mode and efficiency of using his intelligence-functions vary in different kinds of situations or in connexion with different problems. The final picture of intelligence drawn from the material of such a test would be a living one, pertaining directly to personality-organization and maladjustment-type, and would not be a statistical skeleton of scores and score-comparisons. Nonprojective testing of personality through the medium of intelligence tests will have come of age.

References
1. Rapaport, D., Gill, M. and Schafer, R. 1945. *Diagnostic Psychological Testing*. Chicago: Yearbook.
2. Kraepelin, E. 1917. *Clinical Psychiatry*. New York: William Wood.
3. Wechsler, D. 1941. *The Measurement of Adult Intelligence*. Baltimore: Williams & Wilkins.
4. Babcock, H. 1930. An experiment in the measurement of mental deterioration. *Arch. Psychol.* 117.

[. . . .]

THE FORM INTERPRETATION TEST

Although work in related fields had already appeared in print
the publication, in 1921, of Rorschach's
Psychodiagnostics (4) marks the real beginning of what has
sometimes been called Projective psychology. Rorschach died
the next year, 1922, leaving only one other major work dealing
with his 'experiment', the lecture embodying a detailed case
study, reprinted here. This was edited by Rorschach's friend
and colleague Emil Oberholzer, and appeared originally as
an article in 1923 in the *Zeitschrift f.d.ges. Neurologie und
Psychiatrie*, Vol. 82, pp. 240–74, and in an English translation
as 'The Application of the Interpretation of Form to Psychoanalysis' in the *Journal of Nervous and Mental Disease*, 1924,
Vol. 60, pp. 225–48; 359–79. Subsequently a different
translation appeared as an Appendix to the second English
edition of the *Psychodiagnostics*, and it is this translation that
has been used as the basis of the present version. However, in
certain passages renderings from the earlier translation have
been preferred as apparently closer to Rorschach's original
meaning, and other minor modifications have been introduced.

This article is of particular interest in that it gives
Rorschach's own statement of the main points in his rationale,
which he included since not all members of his audience were
familiar with his work. Furthermore, it presents a unique
example of the author of a technique interpreting in 'blind'
and minute detail a test record from a patient for whom full
psychiatric data were also available.

Rorschach's early death prevents us from knowing how he
would have developed a technique which he himself saw as
'a mere beginning'. There is now, of course, an immense
literature on the subject, and it is perhaps unfortunate that
to some extent divergent 'schools' of Rorschach psychology
have emerged. While the general principles remain common
to all, writers differ in their detailed use of scoring categories
and symbols. The best-known systems in English-speaking
countries are those of Klopfer (3) and of Beck (2). Theodora
Alcock, under whose direction training courses in the

Rorschach are offered at the Tavistock Clinic, London,
follows Klopfer in her recent book (1), which represents
the major British contribution in this field to date.

References
1. Alcock, T., *The Rorschach in Practice.* London: Tavistock, 1963.
2. Beck, S. J., *Rorschach's Test.* Vol. I. Basic Processes. New York: Grune and Stretton, 1944.
3. Klopfer, B. *et al. Developments in the Rorschach Technique.* New York: World Book Co.; London: Harrap. Vol. I. Technique and Theory, 1954. Vol. II. Fields of Application. 1956.
4. Rorschach, H., *Psychodiagnostics* Second Edition. Berne: Huber 1942.

10 H. Rorschach

The Form Interpretation Test

H. Rorschach, 'The Application of the Interpretation of Form to Psychoanalysis', published posthumously by E. Oberholzer, *Journal of Nervous and Mental Disease*, 1924, Vol. 60.

[. . . .]

Two years ago I presented to you my first report on the form-interpretation test. The experiment has developed a great deal in that time. The Plates and the methods of making records have remained the same but there has been further development in the application of results, in the evaluation of the symptomatic indications of the factors, and in the manner of interpretation. There has, however, been little progress in the development of the theory of the experiment.

Today I should like to present one case in order to illustrate the computation of the factors, the interpretation of the results and the method of making a diagnosis. I should also like to acquaint you with a fresh aspect of the test which may come to have great importance in psychoanalysis.

1. The Test Protocol
(Formulation of the Interpretations and Computation)

The following record was sent to me by my friend, E. Oberholzer, for 'blind' diagnosis. Only the age and sex of the patient was indicated on the record. The subject was a man of forty. He gave the following interpretations for the ten plates.

Plate 1

1. 'A bat'. Formula for this interpretation is W F+ A P. W indicates that the plate was apperceived as a whole. This apperceptive mode stands in contrast to D, Dd, S, and Do, all of which, with the exception of Do will be encountered later.*

D (detail) indicates that only a part of the plate was used in the interpretation, particularly one of those parts which, because of the configuration of the picture, attracts the eye most easily, or, because of its position on the plate, is most easily apperceived. These parts are, at the same time, the most common detail responses statistically.

* Do (oligophrenic small detail) is used by Rorschach for those interpretations in which only parts of human figures are given where other subjects give complete figures which are clearly visualized.

Dd (small detail) indicates that the part interpreted is not one of those usually interpreted, i.e., is unusual and uncommon.

S (space form) is the symbol for interpretations in which the black parts of the figures are neglected in favour of the white spaces they outline.

F indicates that the form of the blot alone determined the response and that neither kinaesthetic nor colour factors contributed. The plus sign indicates that the form was clearly visualized, even though this conclusion does not agree with my subjective estimation. The quality of form perception does not depend on subjective estimation, but on statistical frequency of responses. Plate I is frequently interpreted as 'bat' by intelligent normals as well as unintelligent subjects. In fact, 'bat' is one of the 'popular responses', i.e., it belongs to a group of interpretations which are given by one in every three normal subjects. I have designated such responses by the symbol P.

Finally, A (animal) indicates that the response was an animal figure.

2. The second interpretation was, 'bony structure'.* The subject referred to the upper half of the middle part of the plate. This is an apperception of a detail and a form response, but the form is poorly visualized. The formula is D F— At.

3. 'A skeleton in a light wrapping.' D F+ At. This response may be designated as a clearly visualized form because the middle part which is here taken as a complete figure is frequently interpreted as a human figure. It is quite possible that kinaesthetic factors influence this response but we cannot be sure. Equally uncertain is the influence of shading in 'wrapping'. In such cases, where it remains a question whether we deal with a simple form interpretation or with a combination of factors we are forced to give the response the symbol F temporarily, correcting it later, if necessary, after comparing it with all the other responses.

4. The plate is again interpreted as a whole: 'A flying creature'. The bat and the draped skeleton are combined to form a new interpretation. If there were kinaesthetic factors in play at all they were certainly of secondary importance. The formula is W F+H. H indicates that a human figure was interpreted.

Plate 11

1. 'Two Clowns': W M+ H |P. This is a movement response whether the subject says anything about the clowns being in motion or not. Comparative studies of many cases have shown that a kinaesthetic factor is necessary in this interpretation.†

---

* German: *Knochengerüst*.

† In the *Psychodiagnostics* Rorschach defines kinaesthetic responses as follows: 'Kinaesthetic responses are those interpretations which are determined by form perceptions plus kinaesthetic factors. The subject imagines the object interpreted to be in motion ... The following may be taken as a rule: Responses may be considered as movement determined

2. 'And yet it may also be a wide parkway (space form) lined by beautiful dark trees (black), and it loses itself in the distance in a fence (middle black); it is all quite in perspective.' This interpretation is determined not only by form but by shading as well. Black and white are given value as colors. Such color responses are not equivalent to genuine color interpretations and must be evaluated differently, as chiaroscuro responses, as we shall see later. These responses have one general characteristic peculiar to the group, namely, that they emphasize space and perspective, though this emphasis may not be actually stated. I designate such responses by putting the color symbol, C, in brackets. This answer also approaches the Original interpretations, those which appear but once in about 100 test records. The formula for the response is, then, S F(C)+ Landscape.

3. 'And here it is red; it is a well of fire which gives off smoke. The smoke billows up to the top where the flames break out again.' This, too, is a W response, determined in the first instance by the color and secondarily by the form. The formula is, therefore, W CF Fire and smoke O.

Plate III

1. 'Two dandies who bow and greet each other according to the prescribed forms of etiquette. They are in dress clothes and carry their top hats in their hands.' I designate this as a whole response even though the red parts are not taken into consideration. The black figures are the essential parts of the plate. The formula is: W M+ H P.*

2. 'It is as if that red thing in the middle were a force separating the two sides, preventing them from meeting.' This interpretation can hardly be designated other than D ? Abs. (Abstraction).

---

only when human figures are seen.' But even then the responses are not always M. The question always is, does the movement indicated play a primary role in the determination of the response? Is it really a feeling of movement and not merely the apperception of a form which is only secondarily interpreted as being in motion? Kinaesthetic responses may be, as in the case of the forms, subdivided into well and poorly visualized M's. Those which do not correspond well to the form of the figures are scored M—. (See pp. 25, 26.)

* This is not only a 'popular' response but is, at the same time, a kinaesthetic one. I refer to Rorschach, who says in the *Psychodiagnostics*, p. 25: 'Plate III is important for this consideration. It is usually interpreted as "two waiters carrying a champagne bucket" or some similar answer is given. In this interpretation the black fish-shaped forms below and laterally are thought of as the legs of the waiters, and the legs are, as may be seen, separated from the body. Primary kinaesthetic factors are very probably necessary to make the abstraction represented by overlooking this separation. Such answers are, then, to be considered as kinaesthetically determined.'

Plate IV

1. 'A column of smoke which shoots up through the middle, divides, and loses itself at the top.' W F(C)+ Smoke O. This formula is given because color or rather white-black (chiaroscuro) and form together determine the interpretation.

2. 'It might also be two human figures in a bent-over position with their legs hanging down (the snake-like lateral extensions); there is the head (the black area just above the hump which marks the insertion of the lateral extension), the face is turned up (the hump just described), and the arms (the thin line at the side which, with the lateral extensions, encloses a white space).' This is a D interpretation, nearly a Dd. It is a true kinaesthetic response and, in addition, an original answer. The formula is D M+ H O.

3. 'On the whole it gives me the impression of something powerful in the middle to which everything else clings.' This interpretation, again, cannot be put into a formula.

At the end the patient repeated his first impression: 'A typical smoke formation; I don't see anything else.'

Plate V

1. 'It is a symmetrical body in a flying position, with two feelers.' It appears that he means a flying animal so that the formula becomes W F+ A.

2. 'At the side here there is the lower part of a human body; there are legs, one is a wooden leg.' D F+ Hd.

Plate VI

1. 'It is a symmetrical figure with a strongly marked mid-line axis. Everything is remarkably arranged around the axis.' This is, again, an interpretation which cannot be formulated. It belongs in the category of descriptive responses.

2. 'The pelt of a wild animal. The tracing of the backbone is particularly marked.' A popular response: W F+ A P.

3. 'I don't see anything else. Yet this white line in the middle is interesting; it is a line of force around which everything else is arranged.' This, again, is a half descriptive, half abstract, response, one of those interpretations which does not allow classification. Such are rather uncommon. In the interpretation of the findings they will be discussed in detail.

4. 'The whole thing is an insect spread out, quite flattened out.' W F+ A.

Plate VII

1. 'This is a typical pelvis again' (the confluent parts): D F− At.

2. 'The center part (confluent part as before) from which rise thick clouds of smoke. The smoke takes on forms': W F(C)+ Smoke.

3. 'These are gargoyles; they are like rodents.' Formula: D F+ Ad P.

4. 'And here are two more of them' (upper third). Formula: D F+ Hd. 'H' is used here because these parts are usually interpreted as human faces.

Plate VIII

There was no response for quite a while. There is a lack of associations which appears when the colored plates are presented. I designate this reaction 'color-shock'. The subject then proceeded:

1. 'It is again in the category of animals, a sort of bear or dog, with a well-developed body and short legs, and the tail hanging down into the lower part of the picture.' D F+ A P.

2. 'Another typical vertebra, like a spinal column': D F+ At.

He studies the plate a while, then says he sees nothing more.

Plate IX

There was a long pause as before; it was even longer on this plate. The subject shook his head and said:

1. 'At best all one can say is two animal heads with turned-up snouts.' (In the green where it is confluent with the brown.) D F+ Ad.

2. 'The rest is just a figure you can't do much with.'

3. 'This is just like the Norwegian coast. It lies just like that and is heavily shaded; that would be the mountains. Here (outer part of the brown) is Sweden which is less mountainous.' Dd F(C) + Geog O. This is a small detail apperception – the brown figure is usually interpreted as a whole.

4. 'There is that projection in the middle part, like a fountain.' D F+ Fountain.

The subject again explains, 'I don't know, nothing much comes to me', expressing the associative inhibition due to colour-shock.

Plate X

Here again some hesitation.

1. 'From a distance it looks like a collection of colored beetles.' W FC+ A. This is one of those interpretations where it is difficult to decide whether it was primarily the form, particularly the distribution of forms, which was the primary determinant of the response, or whether the color was primary and the form secondary. In such cases it is wise to remember that rigid classification is not possible, and that even with great experience and careful consideration subjective conclusions based on analogy cannot be entirely avoided. It is quite possible that color had no influence at all in this interpretation and that it would have been the same had the plate been black instead of colored.

2. 'These are polyps, but they are blue' (blue lateral). D F+ A.

3. 'Here we have something like newts' (grey lateral). D F+ A.

4. 'These things standing up are two little animals with their feelers. They are standing on their hind legs' (upper grey). D F+ A.

5. 'The whole thing is like a path in a park and the dark parts are the trees (upper dark gray). There is a path in the middle; stretching a long, long way.' S F(C)+ Landscape O.

6. 'It is like an arm of the sea' (white between the red, the lower half). Interpretation of intermediate figure. Like the previous responses of this kind, it takes into consideration the borders. S F— Geog.

7. '... the waves are breaking on this steep coast' (red). D F(C)+ Geog.

8. 'The dark part in this blue star-shaped figure is a little man who is holding on to the red here. He is taking a step' Formula: Dd M+ H O. Clearly a movement response and also a small detail interpreta- tion using only a part of the blue radial figure. This figure is usually interpreted as a whole (cf. the second response this subject gave to this plate).

9. '... and behind him there is a squirrel trying to follow him; it is sitting upright on these branches (squirrel – upper part of blue; branches – horizontal extensions below).' Dd F+ A O.

10. 'And this is like a distorted face (lower green), with two long plaits hanging down.' D F— Hd.

11. 'These two yellow parts are like barking dogs, two terriers standing guard as if someone was trying to come into a house – they would come through this passage – and the dogs would bark at them.' D F+ A.

Summing the interpretations that can be expressed in formulae we obtain the following figures:

1. Manner of Apperception

W	11	i.e., responses interpreting the plate as a whole were given 11 times.
D	17	i.e., responses using normal details were given 17 times.
Dd	3	i.e., small and unusual details were picked out three times. It should be noted that several of the 17 Ds were nearly Dds. No absurd small details were used, however, as is characteristic of schizophrenics.
S	3	None of these is a pure space interpretation since all use adjacent parts of the figures.
	34	

2. Quality of the Responses

F	22	i.e., 22 of the 34 responses given for the ten plates were form interpretations. Of this number, 5 are minus in sign, i.e., poorly visualized, making F+ % = 77. The number of F+ is rather higher than usual.
M	4	i.e., 4 interpretations were determined by kinaesthesias. The fact that several other interpretations might possibly have

been kinaesthetically determined must not be overlooked, however, so that 4 may be reckoned as too small rather than too large a count in this case. Further, there is a tendency to give 'small M' responses and secondary Ms. The symptomatic value of these movement responses has not yet been entirely clarified.*

FC 1 i.e., there is only one such interpretation, and that rather doubtful – the 'beetle collection' in Plate X – in which form is the primary determinant though color also has influence.

CF 1 i.e., a single interpretation – 'Well of fire which gives off smoke' (Plate II) – which is determined primarily by the color of the blot though form is not entirely neglected.

C 0 There is, however, a tendency towards such 'primary' color responses as seen in the interpretation last mentioned. In C responses, the form of the figure has no part whatever.

F(C) 6 i.e., 6 responses in which light and shade were the primary determinants rather than actual color.

—
34

3. Content of the Responses

H	5
Hd	3
A	11
Ad	2
At (Anatomy)	4
Fountain	1
Geography	3
Landscape	2
Smoke	2
Fire	1
	—
	34

Relative Numbers

Besides the F+ percentage already computed, experience has shown several other relationships of this sort to be of value in interpretation.

* Subsequently to the publication of the *Psychodiagnostics*, Rorschach designated kinaesthetic interpretations of small and unusual parts of the figures as 'small M', differentiating them from the other M responses which are Ws or Ds. In this he was probably guided by the experience that, as a rule, only interpretations involving the whole or the normal details of the figures involve kinaesthetic influences. 'Small Ms' are, for the most part, not experienced as kinaesthesias in the primary interpretation, but are added and felt secondarily. Sometimes they are purely confabulatory ornamentations of the interpretation and appear to indicate pleasure in confabulating and vivid affective life in the subject. Cf. H. Behn-Eschenburg, *Psychische Schüleruntersuchungen mit dem Formdeutversuch*. Inaug.-Diss., Zurich, 1921.

1. Percent animal responses – in this case 38% of all interpretations deal with animals or part of animals.

2. 'Popular' responses, i.e., those interpretations given by one person in three. In this case they form 21% of the total.

3. Original responses are rare interpretations which occur once in a hundred records. Here, these too amount to 21%. This number might be judged actually higher rather than lower; the same is true for the Popular responses.

There are, furthermore, a few individual responses, i.e., responses which have been given only by this patient. These are the fire and smoke interpretations of Plate II and the bowed figure of Plate IV, as well as the unformulated abstract responses, the line of force in the centre, etc.

4. The Apperceptive type, which in this case is: $\overline{W} - D - (Dd + S)$.

This formula is intended to express the approximate proportion of the modes of apperception to each other. The normal formula is $W - D$; if the number of responses were the same as in this case, the distribution would be approximately: 8 W, 23 D, 2 Dd, and 1 S. In our case the number of W's is proportionately too large, the number of D's too small, and there are too many Dd's and S's. Consequently, we must underline the W and place Dd and S in parentheses.

Succession is orderly, or, at most, only slightly loose. This means that, in general, the subject tends to interpret first W, then D, and then Dd, so that there is a certain logical sequence of the mode in apperception.

The figures obtained by calculations based on the record are by no means to be considered as absolute. A general view of the total findings must be retained so as to avoid being misled by the figure for a particular factor: On the other hand, these figures form the basis of the interpretation of what I have called the 'psychogram'. I consider it quite impossible to obtain a definite and reliable interpretation from the records alone, even after a great deal of experience and practice, unless the calculations are made.

2. The Interpretation

In view of the extraordinary variability of the findings, no definite directions can be given as to which factor would be the easiest and most convenient to use in starting the interpretation. It is, however, generally safest to begin with the color responses; these responses have been found empirically to be the representatives of the affectivity, the total affective responsiveness. A still more reliable point of departure might be the unusual status of any one factor in the experiment, or any unusual correlation between the factors. This method offers many opportunities to arrive at definite conclusions quickly. For instance, if well-visualized forms constitute 100% of the responses, that is, if all the forms have been chosen carefully, and, in addition, there is a definite tendency to interpret Do, pedantic small details, then it is fairly obvious that we are dealing with a compulsion neurosis or a depression. If there are many whole interpretations, especially wholes made up by combining normal details (D), and at the same time many Ms, then the subject is certainly imaginative. If the experience type is extratensive, i.e., if the color responses predominate over the M interpretations, and if there is a high percentage of well-visualized forms and a high percent animal response, then the subject is a skillful and alert worker, adaptable, but somewhat stereotyped. If the sequence of W, D, etc., is maximally rigid, i.e., if the subject interprets a W, then a D and then a few Dd regularly for each plate, then the subject certainly is a skillful logician but an unaccommodating systematist, etc. Thus it is seen that there are a large number of correlations which can be grasped very quickly and thereby permit the establishment of the main lines of the psychogram without great difficulty. When no such correlations are present the task is not so easy. When the factors tend towards average values and the findings approach the normal it is more difficult to analyse the record. Too many 'averages' make the records rather colorless.

The findings in the present case deviate from mere medium values in more than one particular and, in addition, exhibit a phenomenon which at once clarifies the problem to a certain extent. This is the sudden lack of ideas and the long pauses which occur when the subject encounters the colored plates, whereas previously, on the black blots, he had interpreted very freely. This is 'color-shock'.

The symptom value of color interpretation lies in the field of affectivity. The FC responses represent adaptable affectivity; CF and C, on the other hand, represent non-adaptable, egocentric affectivity. The proportions of the various types of color responses to each other make it possible to draw conclusions concerning the emotional dynamics of the subject. Color-shock also contributes to such conclusions. It invariably indicates neurotic repression of affect. Suppression of color responses as expressed in color-shock is a pathognomonic sign of neurotic repression of affect.

There are other means of demonstrating this process of suppression. When the color responses are suppressed, kinaesthetic factors are usually, probably always, suppressed as well. My previous researches have shown that kinaesthesias represent the capacity for 'inner' life, i.e., introversion. Plate I has been so selected that it allows interpretation in terms of M if the subject is at all kinaesthetically inclined. In fact, normal subjects tend to give kinaesthetically-determined responses for Plate I beginning with the second or third response, if, indeed, not with the very first. If it is found that the total record indicates some kinaesthetic tendencies and that, in spite of this, no M responses have been given for Plate I, then it is certain that kinaesthetic factors are being suppressed. The present subject gave kinaesthetic responses only after the first plate, and similarly we find that true color responses to the colored plates also appear late (in Plate X). It follows, therefore, that both color and kinaesthetic factors are being partially suppressed in this case and that the kinaesthetic (introversive) as well as the affective (extratensive) side of the experience type is narrowed or 'coartated' by processes of neurotic repression.*

There is a third sign of repression. In the absence of repression the subject interprets movement and color in the plates in a more or less haphazard fashion. This free mixing of movement, form and color responses appears to be characteristic of persons who are free of 'complexes'. This undoubtedly means that the normal dynamics of human experience cannot be expressed simply by the terms introverted and extraverted. There is a to and fro swing between introversiveness and extratensiveness. This free oscillation between introversion and extratension is restricted in the presence of repressive processes. In the experiment, this

* With reference to the concepts 'introversion' and 'extratension', see pp. 72–87 of the *Psychodiagnostics*. I add a statement for superficial orientation. Rorschach reserved the usual expression 'introverted' or 'introvertedness' for the state in which the subject is turned in upon himself, and he calls the person showing a marked preponderance of M, introversive, M responses being representative of 'inner' life or of living within oneself. Persons with a high predominance of CF and C responses tend more to 'outward' life and show more motor excitability and affective lability. These Rorschach designates as extratensive. In this he wishes to express the fact that these are not fixed traits but mobile potentialities, not contrasting but different psychic mechanisms, the first being represented by kinaesthesias and the second by color responses. The adjective 'introverted' would, then, indicate the *rigid* preponderance of introversive tendencies over the non-introversive or extratensive tendencies. The terms 'introversiveness' and 'extratensiveness' would denote the *capacity for*, and 'introversion' and 'extratension' the *process of*, becoming introverted or extratended, or turning towards oneself or towards the outside world. In any given case, the range between introversivity and extratensivity is the experience type (Erlebnistypus). Rorschach calls the experience type coartated if the values for M and C responses approach zero; when both introversive and extratensive capacities are present to a marked degree, the experience type is designated as broadened or dilated.

restriction is shown by the fact that a normal subject with kinaesthetic tendencies gives color responses when confronted with the colored plates, but soon returns to kinaesthetic interpretations, perhaps after giving four or five responses. (Color responses usually begin with Plate VIII, the first that is fully colored.) The repressed subject is virtually chained to color. In the present case the first M interpretation is the eleventh response, an evidence of the fact that the fluid relationship between the factors of 'inner' life and those of outwardly directed affect is disturbed by neurotic repressive processes, evidence that the normal, free and unobstructed flow between introversion and extratension is disturbed in this subject.

At this stage it can be concluded definitely that we are dealing with a neurosis, and that further investigation is possible. There is obviously no psychosis – at least no manifest psychosis – for in psychoses color shock never appears. The subject shows 4M : $1\frac{1}{2}$ CF.* This would be the formula for his experience type. The M's outweigh the colors even though factors other than rigid adherence to these numbers are considered. As was noted above, more of the F responses could be considered as influenced by kinaesthetic determinants than were influenced by color. In other words, the tendency to give kinaesthetic interpretations is stronger than the urge to interpret color; the experience type of the individual is, therefore, more introversive than extratensive. Recalling the processes of suppression we have already shown to be present in the patient, this conclusion might be expressed more correctly by saying that the introversive features of the experience type were more resistant to repression than the extratensive features. The constriction, or coartation, has affected the extratensive features more profoundly than it has the introversive.

In my experience the general findings with regard to the neuroses indicate that in the more extratensive experience types hysterical symptoms predominate while in introversive types neurasthenic and psychasthenic symptoms are dominant. The nearer the experience type approaches ambiequality, i.e., the more nearly equal the number of movement and color responses become, the more compulsion phenomena appear in the neurotic picture. The clearcut compulsive neurosis lies midway between

* Rorschach found it practical to balance unit M against unit CF. He felt theoretically justified in this practice since in both M and CF responses form enters into consideration in addition to the primary determinants of movement and color. FC responses were evaluated as one-half, and primary Cs as one and one-half units.

231

the hysterical and psychasthenic pictures. Therefore, it may be expected that our patient will show neurasthenic and psychasthenic symptoms, and it may be assumed that there will be some compulsion phenomena since the experience type is not too far from ambiequality. To review, then, we have concluded from the existence of color-shock that there is a neurosis, and from the experience type that the neurosis is of a particular form, namely, psychasthenia with compulsive (obsessive) features.

Returning to the computations, it will be seen that the relationships referring to the affect are at first rather vague. F(C) responses predominate. These are interpretations in which color values do not have determining influence, but are replaced by light and shade values. The symptomatic indications inherent in such interpretations are not yet entirely clear; the interpretations appear to have something to do with the capacity for affective adaptability, but also indicate a timid, cautious and hampered sort of adaptability. Further, they indicate self-control, and especially a tendency towards a fundamentally depressive disposition which the subject tries to control when others are present. On the other hand, we have at least one interpretation which reveals markedly egocentric affectivity, namely, the first color response, 'fire and smoke' (Plate II). When the first color response is egocentric and is then followed by equivocal responses, as is the case in our patient, a violent and impulsive affectivity is generally indicated; nevertheless, this violent affectivity is subject to control. In this case, then, we see conscious rather than unconscious repression of affect, and less actual repression than conscious struggle against the subject's own affective reactions. Hence, for the time being, we can only conclude that there are two affective tendencies opposed to each other in our patient: 1. a depressive one outwardly controlled and rather timidly adapted, and 2. an egocentric-impulsive trend which is controlled to the utmost degree both outwardly in the presence of others and inwardly as well.

The color responses do not allow any further conclusions at this time, and we now turn to other factors. The problem of intellectual rapport and adaptability furnishes a starting point, the solution of which may be sought in a number of factors.

Apperceptive type and sequence will be discussed first. The apperceptive type is that of an individual who neither loses himself in small details (Dd) nor rigidly sticks to giving whole perceptions (W). The entire test shows, rather, that he first tries to give a whole response to each plate before turning to the D's and that the sequence is quite orderly without being maximally rigid. This means that there is no scattering nor any programmatic rigidity in his method of thinking, but that in general his thinking displays common sense, that is, is capable of adapting itself to the task in hand, discriminating important from side issues. On further examination, however, the sequence does show an individual peculiarity additional to the fact mentioned above, namely that the number of D's is rather small for the large number of W's and Dd's. This will be discussed later.

In Plate I the subject first gives a whole response, then turns to the middle of the plate and interprets a bony structure, then the skeleton, and finally reverts to a whole response in reporting the flying creature with its body lying in the centre line. With the second plate the first response is again a whole; then he turns to the middle as before and interprets a landscape and, after that, starting again with the middle part of the figure, the subject constructs a W, the well of fire with the columns of smoke above from which the flames burst out. Again in the third plate a W is given first, then the subject turns again to the middle, giving the interpretation, 'It is as if that red thing in the middle were a force separating the two sides, preventing them from meeting'. The sequence, first W, then a detail from the middle, then an inclusive interpretation starting from the middle, a W or a response composed of several Ds (DW). This sequence reveals quite definitely a sort of programmatism in the thinking processes.

Several points are to be observed in this connection. First, this sequence furnishes an insight into the manner in which the subject first takes a general reconnoitering view, then fastens on the central detail, and finally develops the whole from this central detail, a sort of construction. The first Ws, the reconnoitering ones, are usually rather abstract; they are ideas which the subject himself does not trust very much. Indeed, the first interpretation for each plate is neither very original nor very clearly perceived. The later interpretations for each plate, however, all show a constructive tendency. The first abstract whole interpretations are as indefinite, hazy and uneven as these later constructive ones are definite, even and convincing. We can thus conclude that the subject reasons better inductively than deductively, better synthetically than analytically, and better concretely than abstractly. The fact that the first interpretation is abstract in spite of all this, allows the conclusion that while the subject certainly attempts to make a survey of the whole problem in every case by

233

making a rapid reconnoitering review of it, he is nevertheless not satisfied with this and does not feel at ease until he can turn to the details and to a constructive production arising out of them.

The sequence permits one further deduction. The subject pays close attention to details, but not to those details which draw attention by virtue of their prominent position in the plate. He disregards a number of normal details which are easy to interpret, especially avoiding those which are placed laterally, and usually turns to the middle of the plate for his details. Even when he has nothing concrete to report his attention still hovers around the center of the figure. Looking over these interpretations again, we see that they fall into the group that cannot be classified: 'the force separating the two sides, preventing them from meeting', 'the line of force on which everything depends', 'the power around which everything is grouped', 'the well of fire and smoke'. All these have been constructed from a medial detail. Here again we see a programmatic kind of thinking. Despite the predominance of concrete reasoning he has a tendency towards the abstract. This tendency must be psychogenetically determined since we cannot be deceived into believing that abstractive reasoning is easier for this subject than constructive thinking. Furthermore, it has been demonstrated that abstract interpretations generally are conditioned by 'complexes'. This would be particularly true in this case where they always arise from things in the center line. The individual peculiarity of the sequence in our subject is, then, 'complex determined'. It would appear that a more or less compulsive overemphasis of abstract reasoning is present here, and that this stands in opposition to the actual and natural disposition to be more concrete than abstract, more constructive than abstractive.

Consideration of the apperceptive type leads us a step further. As was mentioned in connection with the computation of the factors, the number of W's and Dd's is somewhat too high, and the number of D's rather too low. Neglecting the sequence for the moment, this apperceptive type would indicate that the subject shows a certain tendency to overlook the most tangible and essential things in the plates, the D's. These details are always the expression of the sense for grasping the immediate, essential considerations in any problem. The tendency to give W's, representing a tendency towards making generalizations, is somewhat over-emphasized. The tendency to get lost in details – to choose Dd's in the test – is also over-emphasized. There is, then, a contradiction here, in that the subject, on the one hand, tends to seek out far-fetched connections but, at the other extreme, also tends to brood over incidental niceties. This same contradiction which is found here in the field of intellectual processes has already been noted in the emotional processes. There the subject was found to have a strong though somewhat restrained egocentric-impulsive trend but, at the same time, a depressive trend and timid adaptation, which he covers up. We might at this point continue on this line of investigation and attempt to find further relations between this pair of contradictions and the responses from which these parts of the psychogram are derived. The method would be practicable but circuitous; it is, furthermore, very important in making interpretations not to get too far away from the only basis of any interpretations, namely, the protocol and the computations made from it. If this precaution is not observed there is danger of deriving too much from a single factor and of building one structure on top of another.

For this reason it is necessary to search for another factor which will furnish further indications concerning the intellectual adaptability of the subject. Such a factor is number of popular responses – 21 % in our case – and their distribution. The popular responses represent the subject's share in the collective or common way of sensing or perceiving things. The number of popular responses is low even when responses which approach the popular are included. On this basis, we conclude that the subject does not share in the common mode of perceiving to any great extent. We will now relate this small percentage of popular responses to the already established fact that the subject gives too few D interpretations, which indicates that his sense of what is tangible and essential is somewhat reduced by a need, perhaps an obsessional one, for indulging in abstract processes of reasoning. Indeed, among the popular responses which are present, there are none which make use of Ds. The number of detail responses, and these are the ones which are also frequently popular, is small in this case. Here, again, is a contradiction: even though the subject interprets concretely and constructively he lacks, nevertheless, a certain simple skill and readiness in adapting the quick wit of the practical man who, because of his freedom to grasp any opportunity, can see through and master any situation. It is the genuine opportunism of the practical adjustment to the matter in hand and self-assured efficiency in conceiving and handling a situation.

The Original interpretations are the opposite of the popular responses, and in this case the two are equal in amount – 21 %. It must be emphasized that his is a genuine originality. It is not the originality of the shop-talker, nor does it consist in hair-splitting differentiations, but is rather representative of well-developed individuality with an independent way of looking at things. This is apparent in the primary conceptions as well as in the elaboration of the responses, and is especially in evidence in the constructive elaboration of the original impression. Many of these responses are not only original, but individual, that is, are responses given by this patient alone. These will be discussed later.

The percentage of form and form-color interpretations are the last factors to be mentioned in this connection. This subject gave 77% clearly visualized forms. If the F(C) responses – the black-white interpretations – are added, these being closely allied with form and all sharply apperceived, the $F+\%$ rises to 80 or 85. Furthermore, two of the poorly visualized forms which depress the $F+$ percentage are anatomical interpretations. In subjects who are not physicians such responses indicate either a complex impelling the subject to try to give an impression of 'intelligence' or a tendency to hypochondriacal brooding, or to both. An $F+\%$ of 80 to 85 is a good average finding. Higher figures approaching or reaching 100% of well-chosen forms are seen only in outspoken pedants and grumblers among normal people, those subjects who try to be most rigidly objective in their interpretations. This leads to the production of only 2 or 3 whole responses, or to giving D and Dd responses exclusively; they do not dare to venture on constructive or combinatory trains of thinking. Our patient, in spite of the anxious and cautious predilection noted, is far removed from this type.

The FC responses represent the capacity for affective rapport and adaptability, a kind of combination of affective and intellectual adaptability. They are, in general, characteristic of the normal individual who is both well adapted and capable of making new adaptations. Our subject gave only one form-color response and that a questionable one. Here indeed is the gap in the patient's emotional life: on the one hand he is expansively egocentric in his affectivity; on the other, he shows the too consciously cautious adaptation represented by the chiaroscuro interpretations. His wish to apply himself to the task and his capacity to do so are beyond all question; Dr Oberholzer states that he showed this trait to a marked degree during the application of the test.

Before going further with the investigation, it would be well to summarize briefly what we have been able to learn thus far in the interpretation of the record. This is a neurosis in an introversive experience type; hence predominance of psychasthenic features. There are probably compulsive (obsessive) phenomena. There is deficiency of freedom in affective adaptation. Two contradictory tendencies exist. First, a depressively colored, all-too-conscious and highly intellectualized manner of adaptation; and second, an expansively egocentric trend in affective life. The intelligence is, on the whole, good, keen, original, more concrete than abstract, more inductive than deductive, although there is a contradiction in that the subject exhibits a rather weak sense of the obvious and the practical. This, too, represents a gap; on the one hand, there is obsessive compulsion in the direction of abstract, generalizing patterns of thought; on the other, a compulsion to begin his constructive pattern, not with what is practical and essential, but with a central point chosen on the basis of a 'complex'. He thus gets held up by trifling and subordinate details, embroiling himself in them. There is, however, no incoherence; affective and intellectual self-discipline and mastery are apparent.

Of the remaining factors, we have yet to discuss the three space responses. Space responses always indicate some sort of oppositional trend. When the experience type is extratensive, this takes the form of some 'outward' opposition, defiance, a tendency to indulge in polemics, to make contradictions and to be aggressively stubborn. In an ambiequal experience type, this oppositional tendency is directed against the subject's own consciousness and gives rise to skepticism, doubt, hesitancy, vacillation, and indecision as well as emotional ambivalence and ambitendencies. Obsessional thoroughness, a desire to collect things, and a compulsion in the direction of completeness in all things are also not infrequently present. When the experience type is introversive, the space interpretations appear to indicate opposition to the subject's own 'inner' life, resulting in constant self-distrust, feelings of insufficiency of every sort, self-criticism and circumstantiality; frequently there is an admixture of phlegm and asceticism.

Our patient shows an experience type definitely introversive, but close to the ambiequal. Hence there will be a predominance of ideas of insufficiency, referring particularly to the innermost self, the productive sphere of the personality, a distrust of himself and of his efficiency and capacity. We shall also have to expect the phenomena of the ambiequal type, for in our subject both introversive and extratensive features are repressed, and the resulting coartation tends in the direction of ambiequality.

Skepticism, doubt and ambivalence will, therefore, be present along with the characteristics mentioned above. We may assume that both the tendency towards opposition to the inner self and opposition to the more conscious life combine to result in the following picture: fretting and doubts about his own intelligence, indecision, phantasies of insufficiency, compulsive meticulousness, obsessive thoroughness, a drive to view things from all angles, the need to hear the other side of the story every time, with rigid objectivity and pedantic self-correction almost to the extent of becoming an ascetic. The neurotic element herein is much more clearly demonstrated now than hitherto. It is striking to note how the study of the space responses defines the neurotic aspects of the record. This is frequently the case, though I am, as yet, unable to say why this should be. The space responses frequently furnish such clues, and it is probable that other factors would also contain clues for the investigation; this will be known only through further experience.

There is another characteristic of the space responses in this case which makes them specific for this subject, makes them individual. At least two are used in the elaboration of chiaroscuro interpretations, and both in a quite similar manner. I refer to the roads in perspective seen in Plates II and X. Two quite different situations are revealed in these interpretations. If we start by considering the space responses we arrive at the conclusion that there are ideas of insufficiency in the subject; if we start with the other half of the formula, namely the chiaroscuro interpretation, we come to the conclusion mentioned above, that the affective adaptations are made carefully and are cautiously guarded. Thus it cannot be denied that there is a very close relationship between the ideas of insufficiency and the patient's methods for correcting them on the one hand, and this trend towards measured affective adaptations on the other. It may also be assumed that each of these factors, S and F(C), also has a relation to the content of the interpretation; according to the findings in previous similar cases I have seen, this is indeed the case. Those subjects who gave striking chiarosucro interpretations also showed definite signs that the content was influenced by 'complex' material and this appeared in the form of correction of this influence, that is to say, as wish-fulfillments. Our subject's interpretations of this kind are landscapes, or rather architectonic landscapes. Other individuals see castles and towers, temples and arches, etc. When such responses occur in a record it is safe to conclude that the subject considers himself disrupted in his 'inner' (mental) life, weak, out of joint, inwardly inharmonious; he projects these feelings in the form of wish-fulfillments into the test, responding with constructions, streets, temples and arches. The feelings of insufficiency, the feeling of having built badly in his own life, betrayed in introversive subjects by the space responses, and the trend towards depression and caution in the affectivity shown in the chiaroscuro responses, appear to be the unconscious basis for seeing buildings, such interpretations representing compensations or corrections.

There is one final noteworthy characteristic of these interpretations. These chiaroscuro responses more than any of the other interpretations emphasize depth as a dimension of the picture. Our subject also stresses perspective and in his other interpretations of this kind notes a three-dimensional quality. According to my experience, this indicates that a peculiar type of psychological correlation is functioning here. There is a special talent for the appreciation of spatial relationships, of depth and distance which appears to be correlated with cautious, guarded affectivity with depressive nuances. Frequently, perhaps always, this talent is correlated with feelings of insufficiency, in the form of feelings of loss of solidity, of instability, of being 'out of joint with the times'. Black and white interpretations which deal with architectural structures and which are original or approach originality permit us to infer that the subject possesses a marked ability to visualize objects in space and has a talent for construction. I drew this conclusion in this case and it proved to be correct though I had no inkling of the patient's profession and he did not reveal it in the manifest content of his interpretations. Dr Oberholzer gave me the record of the analysis later. It contains a number of remarks about the pattern (*Formale*) of his psychological personality and these confirm the presence of constructive talent. He has demonstrated this talent more than once by creative inspiration in his work as a mechanical engineer. In the same way, the notes of the analysis confirm the presence of the ability to visualize in space which is so well developed in this subject. He can tell, before any drawings are made, and by mental visualization alone, whether or not a proposed construction can actually be reduced to drawings. Building plans become alive for him and give him a plastic image of the finished structure. On the other hand, he himself is unable to conceive a new and original form.

In relation to this matter of constructive thinking we are brought to consider the W responses, which prove, in many instances, to be made up of details. These constructive whole responses alone do not allow the conclusion to be drawn that the subject has technical constructive talents, but only indicate the ways in which the subject arrives at intellectual conclusions. A subject who shows constructive W responses will build up his conclusion from one or another detail and will have a tendency to adjust his whole according to the detail he first perceived. He will create surprising conceptions but at times will lapse into the productions over-burdened with ideation. If sufficient intuition is available to the subject he will be able to survey large masses of material and organize them with remarkable certainty. On the other hand, should this intuition fail him, he will be blindly one-sided in his constructions and will tend to treat all things in the same way. But if it can be established that constructive talents as described above are present and if there are also a number of well-balanced constructive whole apperceptions, then it can be stated that these two mental capacities – constructive thinking and an actual talent for technical construction – may be combined to produce outstanding achievements.

I have just mentioned intuition. If a subject produces clever Ws particularly rapidly, and if abstract and constructive as well as combinatory associative processes are intermingled in their production, we can infer with certainty that he has intuitive capacities. In this record the fire and smoke interpretation of Plate II most clearly suggests the presence of intuition. To be sure, construction is preponderant, but the apperception of this interpretation appears to have been the result of a *single* glance. It can be demonstrated that such intuitive interpretations are rich in 'complex' material. On the other hand, it is almost exclusively persons with dilated experience type, those who furnish many movement and color responses, who give intuitive interpretations. The fewer Ms and the fewer Cs, the more rare are these intuitive interpretations, because neurotic repressions eventually stifle the intuitive powers. Not every intuition, however, has the full value of an intuition. To have this value, there must be capacity for coartation as well as for dilatation, for the forms first arise as the result of the conscious use of that part of the mind the function of which is the production of clear, self-limited forms. There must, then, be capacity for dilatation and coartation in the 'organ' which serves to connect introversion and extra-tension functionally. Intuition can be of value only when the subject has the ability to grasp and hold the intuition represented by the dilated reaction; that is to say, he must be able to shift from dilated to coartated type quickly, and only if this is possible will the intuitions be of value. The value is liable to be reduced under two conditions, first, when there is too little capacity for coartation, and second, when the habitual coartation is too marked. If there is too little ability to coartate, the intuition will remain sketchy and have the character of an aphorism, of a castle of dreams, of an unrealizable Utopia. On the other hand, when the habitual experience type is one of too great coartation, i.e., when logic alone is dominant, or when coartation is too great because of neurotic repressions, intuition becomes paralysed. This last is the case with our subject whose neurosis paralyses the freedom of his inner productivity, as so often happens. Obviously this is nothing new. What is new, however, is the fact that we are able by means of the test to follow the conflict between the repressing conscious and the repressed unconscious, and observe how the neurotic repressions narrow the productive sphere and to see how freedom of 'inner life' is completely stifled by conscious restraints and by compulsive hypercriticism. On this basis we are able to understand why it is that our patient always plunges at once into abstract thinking and does it in so inadequate a manner, and to understand why he allows himself to be led by complex determined conceptions rather than his own adequate constructive disposition. The reason lies in a compulsive state arising out of depressive feelings of insufficiency.

And finally, a correction. Up to now we have paid too much attention to the introversive features in our patient and have neglected the extratensive side. The fact that the patient produced an almost intuitive color-form interpretation with the first plate containing any color (Plate II) indicates that the simple computation of the color responses undervalues the extratensive features. Introversive features certainly predominate, but extratensive features are not as weak as at first appeared, and it may be safely assumed that at least occasionally it is possible for this experience type to swing towards the extratensive side. When subjects have had or still have extratensive periods of some duration, the psychogram, and with it the diagnosis, must be changed. During extratensive periods the patient must necessarily be capable of showing defiance, spite and revolt, and impulsive actions and aggressive adjustments, and at such times the quality of the neurosis must change so that hysterical conversion symptoms replace psychasthenic symptoms, and the compulsive phenomena take on a different character. Compulsive acts and feelings and possibly compulsive movements may appear.

Nevertheless, the whole personality receives a certain

stabilization in that the introversive and rather autistic attitude towards the external world will not be broken through easily, in spite of a strong desire in the patient to apply himself in this sphere. For the most part the patient is a psychasthenic, always at odds with himself, dissatisfied with his accomplishments, easily upset but recovering again because of his need for application. He finds little full, free affective rapport with the world about him, and shows a rather marked tendency to go his own way. The dominant mood, the habitual, underlying affective tone is rather anxious and depressed and passively resigned. Thanks to adequate intellectual capacity all these conditions can be and are controlled to the greatest possible extent.

3. The Findings and Psychoanalysis

The relationship between the findings of this experiment and psychoanalysis, the real topic of this paper, will be discussed in the following pages. This relationship may be demonstrated best by means of a Table in which the interpretations given by our subject are arranged in the following order:

The middle column of the Table lists those interpretations which are pure form responses (F). The column to the extreme left contains the interpretations which were kinaesthetically determined (M). The column between these two lists those interpretations which may have a kinaesthetic determinant (F tending to M). The extreme right column lists the pure color interpretations (C), at the bottom above these come the color-form responses (CF), and at the top of the column, the form-color interpretations (FC). The fourth column, between the last mentioned and the form column, contains those FC interpretations in which the C is placed in parentheses, that is, the chiaroscuro responses, those in which a form interpretation tends in the direction of color. P indicates the popular responses, O the original responses, and the individual responses are printed in italics.

This grouping conforms closely to one which I have been using for a long time and which recurs constantly in the *Psychodiagnostics*. The middle column represents the conscious functions; the F percentage is an indicator of the clarity of the associative processes and, at the same time, of the extent of the span of attention and the subject's capacity for concentration. The left of the Table represents the introversive, and the right the extratensive features in the person tested. From the relations between the two parts of the Table, i.e., between M and (CF + C)

M
Two Clowns – P
Two dandies bowing – P
Two human figures in bent-over position – O
A little man holding on to the red – O

F tending towards M
A skeleton in a light wrapping.
A flying creature.
Bears or dogs with well-developed body and short legs – P
Two little animals with feelers standing on their hind legs.
A squirrel sitting on a branch – O
Two barking dogs standing guard.

F
Bat – P
Bony structure.
Symmetrical figure with accentuated midline axis.
Pelt of a wild animal – P
An insect spread out.
Rodent gargoyle.
Human gargoyles.
Typical vertebra, like a spinal column.
Animal heads.
Polyps.
Newts.
Arm of the sea.
Distorted face with two plaits hanging down.

Abstractions

As though that red thing in the middle were a force separating the two sides.

Something powerful in the middle to which everything else clings. The white line in the middle as a line of force around which everything is arranged.

F tending towards C
A wide parkway lined by beautiful dark trees.
All in perspective.
A column of smoke which divides – O
A typical smoke formation.
Norwegian coast and Sweden – O
Path in park; dark parts are trees.
Path in middle runs off a long way – O
Steep coast.

FC
Collection of colored beetles.
CF
A well of fire giving off smoke,
C
Fire.

243

certain obvious inferences concerning the extent and activity of autistic thinking may be drawn. The clarity of the forms and the orderliness of the sequence indicate the balancing factor, namely, the extent and effectiveness of disciplined thinking. In relating the concepts of the conscious and unconscious as used in psychoanalysis to the experimental factors, it is obvious that, with regard to symptom-values, the M and C and FC responses are more closely related to the unconscious than the form interpretations and that individual and original responses – in so far as we deal with genuine originality and not with 'shop' – reveal more about the individual strivings of the subject and thus have more psychoanalytic meaning than the popular answers.

In our case it can hardly be mere chance that the most original M response should be two men stooping, and that the most original color interpretation should be such a peculiarly constructed, almost intuitive, picture of fire with thick smoke and flickering flames. There must be a definite relationship between the interpretation of the stooping men and the introversive content, and between the fire picture and the subject's affective tone. The subject cannot be conscious of this for he is not concerned with whether he gives M, F, or C interpretations. The most striking and therefore the most individual interpretations, as I have pointed out in the section on interpretation, namely the abstract ones which could not be expressed in a formula, must have a background in the unconscious, however rationalized they appear to be. If any of the interpretations reveal 'complex' material it must surely be in these original and individual responses which include M and C factors, for in these there are definite relations between the formal and content categories.

This assumption is first demonstrated in the M interpretations. The actual object interpreted is not important – any more than the manifest content of a dream is of importance in dream interpretation – but rather the particular kind of kinaesthesia. Subjects who see predominantly extensor movements, figures stretching or rising, are significantly different from those who see bent and bowed, burdened and twisted figures, or figures in kneeling or recumbent positions. The former are active individuals with strong drives towards importance and activity although they frequently show neurotic inhibitions. Those who see flexion kinaesthesias have passive and resigned natures. Thus in Plate V, holding the plate with the narrow edge as the base, a representative of the first group saw a danseuse leaping upwards and making passionate movements. In the same plate one of the second group saw a stooped old woman carrying two umbrellas under her arm. In the protocol of a politician which I received recently, the only kinaesthetic interpretation was two gigantic gods clinging to something. This man also gave several original color responses which always repeated the same theme, namely, the inside of the earth, the centre of a volcano, the core of the earth, etc. He also, like our present subject, gave several abstract interpretations in which the centre line and middle parts of the plate formed the stimulus for variations on a single theme: the germ out of which all things shall develop. Hence on the one hand we have gigantic gods and on the other the inside of the earth and the germ from which all grows. These interpretations arouse the suspicion that there are present phantasies of remaking the world; they explain how he became a politician, particularly how he became a constructive organizer. Such experiences have taught me that the content of interpretations can have meaning, a meaning which is determined primarily by relationships which exist between form and content.

We return now to our patient whom Dr Oberholzer has analysed, to see what was demonstrated by means of the psychoanalytical-historical material and the results of the analysis.

(a) The M Interpretations

The M responses represent introversion, the 'inner life'. The greater the predominance of kinaesthetic interpretations over color interpretations, the more introversive is the subject and the greater the role of introversive mechanisms in his psychic life, with a tendency to regression and to react against the world.

In our case there is a clear predominance of flexion kinaesthesias. Indeed, the most original M interpretation of the whole test is the peculiar twisted figure of Plate IV. The conclusions drawn from the consideration of the whole test are borne out by this special type of M response; the subject is not only introversive, but flexion kinaesthesias play an important role in his introversion. There must, then, exist an unconscious passive attitude. The experiment allows us to approach the unconscious to this extent.

If we follow Dr Oberholzer and approach the record with knowledge of the results of the analysis, thus reversing the process of interpretation, we arrive at the following:

The flexion kinaesthesias reveal the patient's profoundest adjustment to his life experience. They are the expression of his passivity and of the feminine part of his sexuality. This passivity is the result of a turning against his own person* which took place early in his life and which was due to an originally sadistic urge. Later the passivity was combined with the sex instincts to produce the feminine attitude. The original sadism is not only found in traits of cruelty in his dreams but also made itself felt early, and later as well, in his life in occasional outbursts during which the patient would strike out blindly, afterwards being unable to understand the flaring up of his temper. The sadistic tendency was also expressed in occasional lack of consideration bordering on brutality in the pursuit of his business aims and interests, or in sudden outbursts of anger against his subordinates in which his ' master-nature ' comes to the fore; this in contrast to his habitually strong self-control and his conscious dislike of all crude instincts. A part of his personality was not mastered during the transition into passivity and masochistic sufferance, and this part gave rise, in the prepubertal period, to an initial compulsion neurosis which took the form of obsessional thinking; in earlier childhood this part of the personality had given rise to phantasies of mastery. The initial neurosis dictated the later obsessional character of the patient who tried to regulate his elementary instinctive functions.

The M series is, therefore, what is 'lived' (*gelebt*). I purposely avoid saying 'experienced' (*erlebt*) in order not to imply that the patient knows the nature of this experience. M is the compulsion determining what is lived, and how it is lived. The patient sacrificed eight years of his life in what he knew was a futile battle to save his father's business. It was a struggle against most unfavorable circumstances which included the brutal selfishness of his own brothers. One of these brothers, remarkable for his fine, strong teeth, constantly appeared in the patient's dreams as a father substitute. In the face of constant disappointments and bitternesses the patient 'carried the burden' in memory of his father and because it was his father's wish – for the sake of his father. After the inevitable liquidation of the business, which put an end to the eight years of suffering, the neurosis broke out, continuing the 'hammer-blows' of the earlier years.

The flexion kinaesthesias, therefore, belong to the deepest unconscious, and their content can hardly be called content in the usual sense of the word. The proof of this in this case, when considered in view of and in connection with the symptom values of other factors, becomes most remarkable; the relation of the kinaesthesias to the unconscious should occupy the first place in any theoretical foundation attempted in dealing with the findings of the experiment.

The kinaesthesias, when they become the determinants of the interpretation of the record, as they have in this case, do actually bring unconscious things to the light of day; the analysis establishes the fact that they must stand in the closest relation to

* Freud, Triebe und Triebschicksale. *Internat. Zeitschr. f. Psychoanalyse*, 1915.

what is generally spoken of as the unconscious. The passive nature of the patient demonstrated by the analysis explains, on the basis of information from within the patient himself, other traits which appeared in the psychogram in the course of the interpretation. These are the ascetic tendencies in the patient's living, the ideas of insufficiency, and his distrust of himself, particularly with regard to his own productivity. We are able to understand to some extent the source of the contradictions in his make-up.

(b) The C Interpretations

In the *Psychodiagnostics* I defend the view that the color interpretations, especially the Cs and CFs, are in some way related to egocentric affectivity, to unmodified, almost instinctive affectivity. On the other hand, the content and the relation of the content to the general pattern remained obscure for a long time, although it was obvious that the content could not be independent of the accompanying affective tone. If a subject produces a series of genuine C interpretations (representative of impulsive affect) and the content of these interpretations turns ever and again to the topic of fire and blood, it must be assumed that the strong affects of his psyche must have something to do with fire and blood, and that fire and blood have some relation to his predominant emotions. It will also make a difference whether a patient interprets the red in a plate as an open wound, whether he sees rose petals, or syrup, or a slice of ham. The question of how much the content of such interpretations belongs to the conscious and how much to the unconscious cannot be decided except in relation to specific responses. One such case was that of the politician, the world builder, mentioned above. He reported the centre of the earth, chaos, the inside of the earth, these being C responses; on the kinaesthetic side there are the gigantic gods. From these we can deduce that he himself wants to construct the earth anew. But this is only the manifest content; the latent content indicates something else. These gigantic gods are in an extraordinary position – the kinaesthetic interpretation suggests the foetal position. The core and interior of the earth may, then, signify something quite different, perhaps the mother's womb. This would mean that the color responses extend much more deeply into the 'complexes' than at first appeared and that the egocentric affectivity actually has its source in the most highly emotionally toned psychic mechanisms. Evidently the content of the color interpretations is to be evaluated like the manifest content in dream interpretation where the latent content is brought to light only in dream analysis.

How does this problem appear when approached in the light of the analysis? I quote Dr Oberholzer again:

Smoke and fire form a part of the childhood experience of the patient. The forge, which at that time was still a part of his father's workshop, is linked with his most important childhood memories of his father. He, the father, was a master at the art of tempering, a special process to which he owed his reputation; these facts were known to the patient early in life. Even when he was hardly able to climb the steps he would slip into the shop again and again, or, if he were put out, would look in longingly for hours at a time regardless of wind or weather. This workshop, as well as the large factory which later grew out of it, with its machines and parts of machines, are the most frequently occurring elements in the manifest content of the patient's dreams. These furnished important sexual symbols from which, in the course of the analysis, it was possible to draw conclusions regarding his early sexual curiosity directed towards his parents and the feminine adjustment to his father. In one such dream he was watching a big boiler being put into its foundation under a scaffold; in another, he saw cast iron standards being lowered into round concreted holes.

The content of the color interpretations is, then, a part of the conscious symbolic material through which the analysis worked as it proceeded, the true significance and the relationships of these symbols being unknown to the patient. It is to be expected that with a larger number of C responses a correspondingly larger part of the symbolic material could be elicited.

Here again we have proof furnished by the analysis. If during dream analyses motifs appear which are reminiscent of the content of color interpretations we shall be able to ascribe special significance to them, and give them a central position in the analysis.

(c) The Abstract Interpretations

The abstract responses are not actually form interpretations but originate in the fact that the picture has a central part, a middle area or a line in the middle. There is no perception of form associated with a visual engram as in other interpretations, but rather a description of an impression produced by the midline in relation to what surrounds it. The most definitely descriptive interpretation given by this patient, and that most closely related to the abstract responses we are now discussing, is the first one in the column of the Table where the abstract responses are listed. Such descriptions are always the expression of phenomena of repression, a demonstration of negation. The purely abstract interpretations carry similar implications, although they also reveal a strongly affect-laden application to the task in hand.

Let us review all the interpretations built up on the theme of the central line:

First in Plate I, the 'bony structure', then the 'skeleton in a wrapping'. Interpretations of bones and skeletons, etc., are found chiefly in neurotics who complain of inner emptiness, of loneliness, of (emotional) coldness. Shroudings, coverings, and masks not infrequently reveal a tendency to conceal something. We have already seen, in the subject's chiaroscuro interpretations, this tendency to depressive feelings of emptiness and want of internal harmony occurring in conjunction with a tendency to conceal this depressive feature. The skeleton in the wrapping already mentioned is such a chiaroscuro interpretation. Thus in Plate I the mid-line is to some extent associated with affective poverty and depression, with a concomitant wish to conceal and dissimulate the affective situation in question.

In the second plate, the mid-line interpretation is a landscape seen in perspective; this is a chiaroscuro response also, but it is, as it were, a positive, constructive one. With some justification we can say that the affect described above is sublimated in this interpretation. However, there follows the interpretation 'a well of fire' in this same plate; this is a C response which is flung out with almost the force of an intuition.

Abstract responses first appear in the third plate: 'the force which separates the two figures and won't allow them to come together'. In it the mention of two movement-motifs, a centripetal and centrifugal, illustrates the ambivalence associated with the mid-line.

In the fourth plate there is again a cloud of smoke, and then the impression of the power in the middle, to which everything clings. In the fifth plate there is the half-descriptive interpretation, the symmetrical body. In the sixth, a purely descriptive response, the symmetrical figure with the marked central axis around which everything is arranged. This is followed by another abstract interpretation, that concerned with the white line in the middle, 'the line of force about which everything revolves'. In the seventh plate there is first the section of the skeleton; there follows another response of fire and smoke with emphasis on the center. The eighth plate yields the response, 'a part of a skeleton'. The response to the ninth plate is a geographical interpretation of the chiaroscuro type, and, secondly, the half-descriptive response, the fountain-like figure rising from the center. To the tenth plate he responds, 'a path in a park', again a chiaroscuro interpretation. There follow, towards the end, a few unimportant interpretations, but finally he stresses the mid-line again in reporting the passage-way guarded by the barking dogs.

We see also that the interpretations associated with the mid-line are conditioned by a wide variety of factors. There are descriptive and abstract responses, color responses of the most intense as well as the most dilute type (C and FC), and, most important, chiaroscuro responses. These interpretations demonstrate the two fundamental affective dispositions of the patient, the depressive adaptation and the egocentricity. Both are related to the mid-line in content as well as position, the former in the interpretations of parts of the skeleton and the 'path in the park', the latter in those dealing with the 'well of fire'. The ambivalence associated with the mid-line is also demonstrated in the opposing directions of the movement in Plate III. In these interpretations associated with the mid-line, there is a tendency to give S and Dd responses. The Ws, especially those which are constructive, also belong to the mid-line group of responses. The normal D response, the 'inbetween' factor in the experience type, is crowded out by the Ws, the Ss and the Dds. This finding is in agreement with the absence of the moderating values in affectivity, the FC responses, which represent the free play of affective intercourse with the environment. All the 'complex' reactions are summarized in the mid-line interpretations; it is here that all the contradictions (of personality) are knotted together. The most powerful affect, finding its expression in the CF responses, and the most severe coartation and affective repression, expressed in the purely descriptive responses, are both associated with the mid-line of the plates. All this presents a mass of alternatives and contrasts which appears quite incapable of analysis; the solution of the problem probably lies in the abstract interpretations, since these are the most extraordinary and individual responses.

In connection with these abstract interpretations the question of the relation of the mid-line to the surrounding parts is always cropping up; it is always the mid-line 'which holds everything to it', etc. The mid-line appears to attract the patient's attention with a sort of magical power. Suppose we visualize this relationship kinaesthetically; does the mid-line hold on to the other parts, or do the surrounding parts of the figure actively grasp the mid-line? It is possible to answer this question by considering the genuine kinaesthesias; none of these deal with the mid-line but always with lateral parts – witness the clowns, the dandies, the little men taking hold of the red parts of the figure – all exhibit movement towards the center. This implies that the subject saw the lateral parts as those which were actively clinging. The wording of the abstract interpretations bears this out: the 'power' in the middle to which everything is attached, the line of force about which everything is arranged, the middle axis around which it all revolves. If any movement is sensed in this connection, it is obviously not the mid-line which holds actively to the surrounding parts, but the surrounding parts which hold on to the mid-line, reach for the mid-line, strive to strengthen their grip on the mid-line. The mid-line is the abstract, magical power which supplies something to hold on to. These deductions reiterate statements already found in the psychogram, namely, that the subject shows a relative incapacity to maintain a grip on a central thought and that he is passively orientated and lacks an active central force or power.

This is as much as can be gathered from the test. The analysis should clarify matters considerably, and it actually does so with startling success. I quote Dr Oberholzer's statements regarding the abstract interpretations:

In these interpretations, everything is concerned with power – a central line of power, a middle point of power, a center of power. The same situation exists in the analysis. The central point was the father and the father was the power; this was true also in the symbolism of his dreams. In one of these dreams the father was symbolized as the queen ant who maintains the integrity of the ant state. In the dream the queen ant stings the patient on the finger. It will be recalled that after the father's death this son tried vainly to prevent the collapse of the estate. In another dream he thought that he awoke during the night and saw the stars following their courses, and he drew their courses, which were curves passing through a central point. This dream recalled to him the first period of insomnia which preceded the development of the obsessional phenomena mentioned above and which had its onset after he had seen the performance of two tight-rope walkers. Later the associations led to a period as a boy of three to five years when there was the active desire to see the father's "spitzli" (a child's term for the genitalia) and when he would frequently awake in terror during the night. In the analysis he described the "power" as stocky in form so that I was able to say quite definitely that his father had been a stocky, thick-set man.

In this connection I must return to the first interpretation for the first colored plate, Plate VIII. The subject interpreted the red figures at the sides as a sort of animal, bears or dogs, described as

251

having a 'thick-set body and short legs'. From what has been said above, it can be assumed that this is not merely a coincidence, more especially since we are dealing with a red detail of the plate.

Without knowledge of my deductions, Oberholzer continued:

The M and C factors run concurrently in the abstract responses. The content of these – it is always the same, this 'power' – reveals the nature of the symbolic relationships of the color response; these relationships are unknown to the patient. We discover what he wants to experience. Ultimately it is the desire to experience the power of his father's genitalia; this appeared as a wish-fulfillment in many dreams both before and during the analysis.

The introversive and the most strongly affective content are amalgamated in the abstract responses, and the flexion kinaesthesias and the abstract responses fit each other like a lock and key. The striving of the kinaesthesias to 'live' the content of the abstract interpretations is the deepest source of the yearning with which this patient is possessed, of his basic depressive and anxious mood, of the habitual pattern of his affect. From this source springs all that is found in the psychogram, the ideas of insufficiency, the sense of internal disharmony, the inability to control himself and bring unity into his being; it is the source of the yearning for peace, for a something strong to hold on to, for unity within himself.

The test has shown, then, that the power which is repeatedly mentioned in the abstract interpretations is something which the patient longs to possess for himself and that it carries the deepest affect with it; it is, so to speak, the object and goal of the kinaesthesias. Furthermore, it has been discovered that his adjustment to this power is a passive one and that the unconscious seeks support from this power. Further, this power actually exercises a sort of magical influence by means of the unconscious affective control and signifies a kind of center in the patient's life; at the same time, however, in his deepest unconscious he does not wish to control this power actively, but wants to suffer passively under it. The analysis has only to substitute the real object, and it can be stated definitely that this power is the father. This key opens a number of doors at once. The most unconscious attitudes are now apparent. With the discovery of a fundamental attitude so pregnant with possibilities one can probably offer a prognosis for the analysis: if this power can also signify the analyst, then a transference must work miracles in the case.

This was actually the situation here. The patient had certain hysterical symptoms consisting in periodic violent attacks of dizziness leading to falls, which, at their zenith, were accompanied by vomiting, diarrhoea, and complete deafness in the left ear.

The presence of hysterical symptoms can be read from the record of the test. Dr Oberholzer reports that these paroxysms ceased after the first analytic period and recurred as a serious attack only once again and in a much later phase of the analysis. At this time the growth of the transference out of the deep, unconscious fundamental adjustment was in progress. The patient had been paying his tribute to this fundamental attitude by these attacks of dizziness and left ear deafness ever since the liquidation of his father's business. The left side, as is so often the case, proves to be feminine and the fact that his mother had been hard of hearing in the left ear for as long as he could remember explained the identification of the mother in the symptom complex.

(d) The Form Interpretations

There remain only the form interpretations, and these, so far as Dr Oberholzer can gather from the analytic material, exhibit no important or distinct 'complex' relationships. This is theoretically plausible, for the form interpretations are the work of consciousness; the purer the form, the more certain that the response is determined by conscious thinking. The share of the unconscious in these interpretations is infinitely less than it is in the kinaesthetic and color responses. In practice, however, this is not always the case, for there are neurotics whose 'complexes' are related to the form interpretations. In any case, however, these complexes do not appear unmodified but are changed; an example is found in the towers which were included in the form responses of the politician discussed above, which probably reflect narcissistic desires. But there are subjects in whom unmistakable signs of 'complexes' can be demonstrated on the basis of the F series. These are irrational types in whom unconscious material is constantly seeping into the conscious, and subjects who are in especially good humor at the time of the test; the good humor dilates the experience type and permits material, otherwise repressed, to get smuggled into consciousness. The stronger the repressions, the less capable is the subject of getting into a lighter mood, and the more definitely are all complexes excluded from the sphere of form interpretation; but then it is more certain that these complexes will be represented in the kinaesthetic and color interpretations.

Thus we see that the kinaesthetic interpretations furnish a deep insight into the unconscious. They reveal the unconscious tendencies of the subject, the basic attitude, whether it be active or passive. The color interpretations are symbols corresponding to the symbols in dreams. In the unconscious they represent something else, namely, the latent content, revealing the tremendous affective relationships of the latent content. The form responses are usually free of 'complex' material; the stronger the repressions in the subject, the less complex material in the form responses; the less subjective, the more objective they are. The abstract responses furnish relationships between the kinaesthesias and the color responses, between the unconscious attitudes and the affect-laden goals of the unconscious. The practical value of this discussion can be confirmed only on the basis of more material; on the other hand, the facts obtained by purely empirical methods should offer significant contributions to the theory of the relationships between the conscious and the unconscious.

Summary

The Formal Psychogram: I designate as the formal psychogram all those conclusions drawn from the formal qualities of the protocol alone, excluding consideration of the content of the interpretations, and obtainable irrespective of whether the subject is known to the examiner or not. In our subject the formal psychogram reveals that we are dealing with a neurosis in which psychaesthenic symptoms must be predominant, since the experience type is more introversive than extratensive, though approaching ambiequality. Because of this latter fact the neurosis must also show compulsion (obsessional) phenomena and at least periodic symptoms of hysteria. The main features of the neurotic character are ideas of insufficiency, feelings of inner disharmony, inability to integrate himself, brooding about himself, distrust of his own efficiency, ambivalence, vacillation between broad-mindedness and pedantry, impulsiveness and passion which alternate with scrupulousness and anxious, depressive attitudes, a tendency to autistic fantasies and inferences, especially to autistic systematizations, and finally, a tendency to asceticism and inability to make decisions. The form of the specific bodily symptoms cannot be determined from the record.

Alongside the neurosis other traits were found, namely, good intelligence, original thinking, particularly concrete thinking, but a slight weakness in the field of abstract thinking. There was a significant disposition for constructive thought processes and – which is not the same – a talent for construction, though there was little combinatory imagination. The psychogram also revealed a marked ability to apply himself and a tendency to neglect the essential and practical in order to concentrate on large systems or, in contrast, to get held up by small details. On the whole, the capacity for sharing common modes of perceiving is reduced; there are individual peculiarities, and a tendency to be seclusive. There is a reduction in the freedom of affective adjustment; there are fluctuations of affect between egocentric moods and feelings of oppression, depression and anxiety. It might be said that the basic principles of his adaptability are expressed in the chiaroscuro responses. The whole record, because of the compulsive tone throughout, indicates a rather obsessional fundamentality in thinking along with a sort of mild fanaticism, or at least a certain zeal in the defense of basic principles. This conception has been expressed in the discussion of the programmatic nature of his thinking already referred to.

The Comparison of the Formal Psychogram and the Content: The test by itself leads to the conclusion that the patient's unconscious expectancy is that he will be passive in the experiences that come to him. From the color responses we conclude that there are powerful, affect-charged complexes which must be repressed. From the abstract interpretations and their relation to the kinaesthesias it can be concluded that the unconscious is seeking a power to cling to. From the relationship of this last fact to the color responses, it can be stated that this power must be expressed symbolically in the content of the color responses. These conclusions are fundamentally 'formal' in character, and arise out of a comparison of the scorable factors and content of the interpretations. The psychoanalytical conclusions allow us to complete the formal psychogram in a few words. The abstract interpretations represent the desires of the patient, the desires he wishes to 'live'. The power referred to in these responses is the goal of the passive attitude, the power of the father which he unconsciously longs to experience. This is indicated in the color responses, where the force is symbolic of the father and his power. The neurosis results from the conflict of this unconscious longing and the conscious repression of it. We do not know what earlier and more primitive attitudes and tendencies may have played a role in the production of the neurosis.

PSYCHOLOGICAL PREMISES
UNDERLYING THE RORSCHACH

This article appeared as Chapter One of *Rorschach Psychology* (London and New York: Wiley, 1960) edited by its author. The book is, to quote its dust-cover, 'devoted to an examination of the major working principles of the Rorschach in the light of general psychological thinking'. Sections are devoted to the various 'categories of Analysis' (i.e., Location, Determinants, Content); one to 'The Test Pattern'; and a final section to 'Problems of Scientific Appraisal'. Of the two articles in this last section, the second is a long discussion of Validity, the scope extending beyond the validity of the Rorschach.

The preceding article is a much shorter one on Reliability, which presents special problems in relation to the Rorschach. Split-half reliability would appear on *prima facie* grounds to be difficult to demonstrate, but the present writer's finding has been that at least for some categories it can yield surprisingly satisfactory results. An alternative, which interested Rorschach himself, although its wide application has largely been allowed to lapse, is the use of parallel series. The best-known of these is the Behn–Rorschach (3). The Zulliger Test (4) is a 'Rorschach' consisting of three cards. Neither of these (nor any of the other alternative series which have been published) can be regarded as exactly equivalent to the original Rorschach. Techniques designed for group administration (particularly those based on forced-choice responses) are still further removed from normal Rorschach practice and are not, in general, to be recommended. On the other hand, the Holtzman technique (2) which takes a much more explicitly psychometric standpoint, has much to commend it.

Similar in scope to *Rorschach Psychology* is *Rorschach Science* (1), a book of Readings, spanning the period 1934–56. Much of the comment is frankly critical, and, as a measuring instrument, the Rorschach emerges with little to its credit. Nevertheless, the book (as one reviewer put it) 'provides many provocative ideas about relationships between phenomenal experience and personal development'.

References
1. Hirt, M. (Ed.), *Rorschach Science: Readings in Theory and Method.*
   New York: Free Press of Glencoe, 1962.
2. Holtzman, W. H., Thorpe, J. S., Swartz, J. D. and Henon, E. W.,
   Inkblot Perception and Personality: Holtzman Inkblot Technique.
   Austin, Tex.: University of Texas Press, 1961.
3. Zulliger, H., *The Behn-Rorschach Test.* Bern and Stuttgart: Huber,
   1956.
4. Zulliger, H., *Der Zulliger-Tafeln-Test.* (Tafeln-Z-Test.) Bern and
   Stuttgart: Huber, 1962.

11 M. A. Rickers-Ovsiankina

Psychological Premises Underlying the Rorschach

M. A. Rickers-Ovsiankina, *Rorschach Psychology;* John Wiley, New York, 1960.

[. . . .]

The most outstanding virtue of the Rorschach method is generally recognized to lie in its power for providing an integrated pattern of the total personality, and for at once articulating this pattern in specific quantitative ways into a manifold of personality dimensions. This accomplishment, still unique among assessment procedures, was made possible to a considerable degree by the way in which Rorschach defined his task from a systematic point of view. His primary interest was in getting at the nature of the basic modes of functioning, underlying all of an individual's psychic activity. He was quite explicit in emphasizing that his goal was to uncover *how*, rather than *what*, the person experiences. This meant looking, e.g., not so much for the particular content of a subject's preoccupations, hopes, and fears as for the modes by which these psychic events come about: whether they are experienced as impulsive upsurges, as all pervading emotional states, as lively resonances to the surrounding atmosphere, or as rationally controlled reactions. The concern is more with the formal or functional than with the contentual, substantive aspects of the personality.

It was Rorschach's conviction that a person's perceptual responses to the ink blots were capable of serving as clues to such basic tendencies so long as the responses were viewed consistently in the frame of this systematic orientation. Accordingly, when abstracting from the complex test performance certain components for analysis, he concentrated primarily on formal categories and only secondarily on content categories. With the formal test dimensions thus providing the basic structure or scaffolding of the equally formal personality configuration, the actual content of day-to-day experiences then, but only then, becomes important in lending individuality and concreteness to the formal representation. The outcome is a formalized, yet alive, picture of the complete personality.

Besides Rorschach's choice of categories of analysis, his manner of employing these variables is of equal importance for a full appreciation of what Rorschach has given psychology with his instrument. While taking full advantage of the amenability of these categories of analysis to precise identification and measurement, he never interpreted any one of the categories by itself, but always as dependent upon the others, thus adhering to his basic principle of interaction among psychological functions right at the level of their correlates within the test data.

Over and over again Rorschach impresses upon the reader the importance of observing this principle. Each scoring category is viewed in relation to the other extant categories – whether the numerical pattern of the whole protocol or a single test response is under consideration. An individual response acquires its true meaning only when perceived against the background of the total cross-sectional psychogram, and when considered in terms of its place in the longitudinal sequence of the test performance. It is a matter of wholes and sub-wholes of a horizontal-structural and of a temporal nature. This emphasis on the pattern or configuration, however, never leads to vague globality, since each component scoring category is given a great deal of attention *per se*, each being recorded and evaluated in careful and very specific detail. The Rorschach worker has to be constantly attuned to handling the sub-units now as dependent parts and now as gestalten in their own right. In other words, the test as envisioned by its founder constitutes a true *unitas multiplex*.

For an understanding of how such unified, formalized, yet richly individual personality pictures derive from a set of responses to ink blots, we must turn our attention to the ·psychological meaning of the test components, both singly and in their interplay. Inasmuch as these components constitute the cornerstones of the method, it is only through an illumination of their respective roles in the test pattern that this pattern in its deeper personality implications will acquire full significance. The manner in which Rorschach relates specific aspects of percepts, represented by the scoring categories, to those basic personality dimensions that were of major concern to him, reflects well the origin of the test; empirical generalizations, rational deductions, artistic intuition, hunches, and flashes of ideas intermingle in providing the foundation for this multifaceted system of inter-related functioning. Unravelling this isomorphism of percept and personality is complicated by the fact that the correspondences do not constitute simple one-to-one equivalents. Every category of test performance taps more than one psychological function and, conversely, a psychological characteristic is derived from a combination of several test categories.

Categories of Analysis

A response to the ink blots is classified under four major headings:

Location refers to the area of the plate chosen, to whether the area is whole or part, and to what kind of part.

Determinant comprises the specific properties of the blot that according to the testee prompted the response, such as the form of the blot, its color, shading, kinesthetic features.

Content identifies the subject matter of the response in broad categories; e.g., human, animal, landscape.

Popularity-originality represents the opposite poles of frequency in the identification of a certain blot area with a certain content.

Under each of these four major classes Rorschach employed a set of differential scoring categories. In essence, his classification system is still followed in contemporary practice. Since the test has been used so widely, a considerable number of modifications have naturally evolved around certain aspects of the scoring system, resulting in additional scores, in subdivisions, and in reformulations. Inasmuch as these particularities of scoring lie outside the focal orientation of this book, they will not be discussed in the present synopsis.

Location

The location scores deal with such configurational properties of a percept as extension, connectedness, and segregation in visual space. The main distinctions derived from these features rest on the question as to whether the response pertains to the whole blot (*W*), to a readily isolated, frequently apprehended blot detail (*D*), to a less obvious blot detail (*Dd*), or whether the subject reverses figure and ground, selecting the white space for an interpretation (*S*). Within these classifications a good deal of attention is paid to such qualitative considerations as to whether a certain whole response is aimed at embracing the totality of the given material to the neglect of details, or whether the response constitutes an effort to combine into a meaningful whole as many of the details as possible.

The numerical constellation of location scores, supplemented by these kinds of qualitative elaborations, is considered to reveal the fundamental orientation of a person's mental functioning. This orientation refers to the relative weight of organization versus articulation, of synthesis versus analysis in the subject's cognitive activities, and to the degree of generality, complexity, and specificity that characterizes these activities. Although primarily indicative of such variations in intellectual ability, the psychological significance of the location scores is not limited to the cognitive area. In a way typical of Rorschach's thinking, the location measures reflect also some volitional factors of effort or intent towards cognitive display.

Here, then, essential psychological functions are identified effectively for diagnostic purposes on the basis of structural characteristics of a person's perceptual behaviour. Quite independently, such properties of the perceptual process have been studied and conceptualized by the laboratory psychologist. The challenge of following up this parallel between the Rorschach and perception psychology is close at hand. [....]

Determinants

The test is introduced by the examiner's question, 'What might this be?' The subject's task is thus formulated as one of recognition. We know from psychology of memory that the occurrence of an experience of recognition presupposes the existence of a certain degree of similarity between the incoming stimulus complex and a system of memory traces left behind by an earlier perceptual process. According to gestalt theory (11) this correspondence does not imply absolute similarity, or similarity based on identity of elements, but rather similarity of gestalt character.

Instruction to the subjects to draw their percepts results in a considerable range of variations in apparently the same responses to the same blot or blot detail (12). As Brosin has pointed out, a response like 'bat' is given with high frequency to several of the cards, which are neither identical in their perceptual features, nor does any one of them represent an accurate image of a real bat. What seems to elicit this response is that 'these cards have a batlike character, ... the gestalt quality of a bat' (5, p. 4). The question arises as to what it is that conveys to one subject a batlike character in a certain ink blot, or that makes another subject see the same blot as a crouching giant?

In Rorschach's thinking these problems occupy a central position. In the analysis of a person's perceptual performance he considers them under a separate classificational grouping called *determinants*, subdivided into *form*, *color*, *chiaroscuro* (*shading*), *movement*. In the following, these categories will be identified, first, in terms of the perceptual processes involved in each determinant and, second, in terms of the psychodiagnostic implications accorded to a determinant within the test procedure.

Perceptual processes. The description of the perceptual processes underlying the respective determinant will begin with the autochthonous properties of these processes and will then evolve from these properties the type of person-environment interplay and the activity level characteristic of the particular perceptual process.

FORM (*F*). When the interpretation given by the subject is based primarily on the shape or form of the chosen blot area, as 'bat' or 'aeroplane' for all of card I, the determinant is indicated by the *Form* score (*F*). The perceptual process involved in this type of reaction can be readily represented as an instance of proficiency in perceptual organization. Structural gestalt principles as symmetry, contour, and closure operate in producing the figural quality that is perceived by the testee as a certain object. Individual parts are utilized according to their place within the overall percept. The emerging gestalt character of the perceived figure is viewed in relation to another organized pattern, that of a memory trace complex; or, to state it a little differently, a 'hypothesis' is checked against the input information (6). The more accurately these organizational principles are applied in bringing about the particular interpretation, i.e., the greater the figural 'goodness' or the *prägnanz* of the percept, the higher, in Rorschach terminology, the form level of the subject's functioning.

In achieving such a *prägnant* percept, the subject has to exert a certain amount of effort. We know from the psychology of perception that the activation of organizational processes consumes energy. In establishing gestalt similarity between the visual figure before him and an appropriate memory image, the person has to apply himself actively and deliberately. He has to select, weigh, and evaluate. His reactions are controlled and guided by objective features of the given material. They are stimulus-bound. In keeping with this nature of the task, the observer's activity level may be characterized as relatively high, and the prevailing subject-environment relation as object-determined, detached, and impersonal.

MOVEMENT (*M*). There is a type of response in which the gestalt character does not follow strictly from the forms of the two-dimensional card but implies, as it were, a third dimension. This occurs when the perceived configuration is no longer static for the subject, as in form-determined responses, but has a dynamic character, direction, figural incompleteness, tension. As Arnheim

263

has demonstrated, 'gradients of perceptual qualities ... oblique forms, shadings' are apt to create the impression of movement (1, p. 271). On the Rorschach test such dynamic effect, when apprehended by a person, usually leads to an interpretation of a human or animal figure seen in motion. Accordingly, the determinant for this group of reactions is designated as *Movement* or *kinesthetic response*. Rorschach maintained that some kind of kinesthetic element actually enters into the experience of a genuine movement percept. From a theoretical point of view, this assumption is noteworthy since it anticipates in an interesting way present-day organismic models of perception (9, 22).

In the movement response we have, then, a situation where the subject manipulates the structural features of the stimulus manifold freely and autonomously in the course of his perceptual production. He is less stimulus-bound and less closely dependent on the objectively given than in the case of a form response. In contrast to the latter, when bringing about the relatively complex movement response, the testee puts more of himself into the task, drawing on broader and deeper personal resources. Correspondingly the subject-environment relation is no longer detached and object-controlled, but is marked by spontaneity and ego involvement, while the activity level of the observer remains as high as in form perception.

COLOR (*C*). When the gestalt character of the percept is evoked either solely or in conjunction with form by the hue of the blot ('flowers, fire') the determinant of *Color* (*C*) is used in the scoring of the respective response. Whereas, with both form and movement interpretations, the subject is actively at work on an organizational process consuming energy, when color serves as the carrier of the gestalt character the situation is quite different in this respect. As the author has pointed out elsewhere (17), apart from the circumstance that color differences might demarcate different regions within the visual field and thereby bring into play the factor of form with its organizational properties, color perception as such does not involve complex processes of articulation and organization. Characteristically, the experience of color is of undifferentiated nature. It is a much more direct sense datum than is either form or movement. The person becomes aware of color at once, without an intermediate step of reflecting, organizing, or evaluating processes. Colors, particularly the warm or hard hues, impress themselves in an immediate, one might say personal, manner. They affect us, speak to us, in a simple, rather primitive, fashion. This impact is rarely experienced as neutral. Colors strike us as pleasing, displeasing, exciting, or soothing. They attract or repel us. Because of this vivid, emotionally toned quality, the author has referred to color experience as physiognomic (17). Similarly, Bash (3) has recently pointed out that color perception fits Metzger's identification of an entity's gestalt character in terms of its intrinsic nature or essence (*Wesen*).*

The object's physiognomy or essence is thrust upon the observer in a specific, individualized fashion. The direction of the action goes from object to subject. This latter aspect of the interplay, together with its immediacy and forcefulness has led to characterizing the subject's position in color perception as receptive, passive (19, 20), or as a state of surrender (9). The perceptual process that underlies the color determinant, then, may be characterized as a state of passivity regarding the activity level, and as a condition of being subjectively affected by the essence of a particular outside object with respect to the person–environment relation.

CHIAROSCURO (*Ch.*). Akin to the color is the *Chiaroscuro* or *shading* determinant. It is used when the gestalt character of the percept is brought about exclusively, or in combination with form, by transitions within the achromatic light-dark continuum. Unlike the chromatic response, however, the chiaroscuro interpretation is not evoked by single colors. A shading reaction is rather produced by a diffuse total impression of the manifold of lightness nuances blurring into each other. The darkness, or haziness, or fluffiness of this impression typically leads to percepts of a synesthetic nature, such as 'fur', 'storm clouds', 'rocks'. Following Bash's application of Metzger's classifications one might, therefore, identify the gestalt character of the chiaroscuro determinant as based chiefly on the substance or fabric of the perceived material (see footnote below), or one might say with Koffka (11) and Gibson (8) that the response derives from the microstructure (grain, texture) of the stimulus constellation. Although the subject is in the case of the shading response equally,

* Metzger (16) differentiates the following three modes by which the gestalt character of an entity may become apparent: (a) Structure (*Struktur*) or organization (*Gefüge*), referring to all types of spatial-temporal formation and patterning; (b) global quality (*Ganzqualität*) or substance (*Ganzbeschaffenheit*), comprising all characteristics of material or fabric; (c) essence or intrinsic nature (*Wesen*), including all expressive, physiognomic features.

if not more than in the case of the color response, at the mercy of the environment, the components of the interaction stand out less, no part of the field acquires figure character, there is only ground. The situation is not experienced as one of being affected by the essence of an individual object in the environment, but rather as a generalized state of finding oneself in the atmosphere or the mood emanated by the material substance of the environmental setting. The diffuseness and lack of clear-cut articulation within the setting has an overpowering, frequently disquieting or threatening, effect upon the observer. Because of the pervading quality of this effect, the subject feels submerged, enveloped by its atmosphere. Similarly to color experience, the person feels passively affected, acted upon by the environment, with the important difference, however, that now there is no one particular environmental object affecting the observer. Instead, there is a general blurring of boundaries, not only in the visual field but also in the person-versus-environment differentiation.

Psychodiagnostic implications

By thinking of the response determinants in the light of the perceptual processes underlying these determinants, it becomes psychologically meaningful, if not actually compelling, how these determinants can be understood as being functionally dependent on certain personality characteristics.

FORM. Rorschach saw in the form level not only a measure of the directly observable ability for appropriate structuring of visual stimulus material but, moreover, an index of the person's total rational equipment for comprehending and grasping relations. Such a generalization should make sense to those students of psychology who view all modes of cognitive functioning as governed by the same fundamental organizational laws, and who consider precision and versatility in structuring a crucial factor in evaluating any intellectual performance.

When, furthermore, the subject–environment relation described above for the *F* determinant is taken into consideration, it becomes clear that possession of a certain level of intellectual ability is not likely by itself to result in a corresponding level of form perception on the test. To adhere to the given reality of the test material throughout the examination, there has to be not only ability for accurate perception but also the power to apply oneself consistently to the task in a critical and objective manner. The exercising of such a power requires control over interference from internal pressures of an emotional–motivational nature, a constellation of forces dynamically referred to as ego strength.

MOVEMENT. Rorschach contended that the ability to employ the movement factor in interpreting the ink-blots implies mental productivity, a creative potential and, in a more extended sense, a tendency toward inner living. Viewing *M* as an indicator of creativity falls in line with gestalt psychological principles since structuring activity that depends for its completion on components not explicitly given (the type of structuring found in the movement response) is in gestalt literature equated cognitively with creativity and inventiveness rather than with mere comprehension (10). If, in addition, we accept the organismic dictum that no cognitive behavior is without supporting conative-emotional components (21), then it is to be expected that these components would be particularly evident in as complex a cognitive process as the movement response; and the spontaneous, ego-involving character of the subject–environment relation, prevailing in the 'creating' of an *M* response, will further the participation of relatively central inner-personal regions. It is, then, inherent in the specific fashion by which the *M* determinant comes about that the study of such responses should be capable of providing clues not only regarding the subject's creative potential but also of supplying insights into the general realm of his inner living. [. . . .]

COLOR. In Rorschach practice the color determinant is related specifically to the emotional sphere and, more generally, to a person's environmental reactivity. The isomorphism of chromatic color perception and emotionality has been forecast by our earlier description of the perceptual properties of the color determinant. In a situation where an environmental object impresses its physiognomy or essence upon the observer in an immediate and impelling fashion, allowing for no emancipative distance, there can be no place for active reflection or sober evaluation, so fundamental in the exercise of purely intellectual functions of the human mind; the behavior will tend rather toward receptive and relatively primitive forms. If, furthermore, one wanted to identify these forms of behavior in terms of a conventional psychological function, the dimension of emotionality naturally suggests itself. As pointed out above, chromatic colors affect us with quite individualized, directed, and provocative qualities, and we know from general psychology that the experience of being affected in such ways by an environmental event is considered by authorities on the subject (2) to be equivalent to experiencing emotion.

Although matters of person–environment interaction play a cardinal role in most field-theoretical personality systems, Lewin's (13) treatment of the problem seems most appropriate to this discussion. In his conceptual model, both the extent of accessibility of inner personal regions to outside influences and the facility of outward expression of these regions depend on the degree of permeability of the individual's outside boundary. The greater the functional permeability of the outer boundary, the freer the interplay between the person and his immediate environment. Applying this line of thinking to our discussion of color perception, one could say that the freedom of interplay is manifested equally in the subject's being easily impressed, affected, provoked by the essence of outside objects, and in his reacting to such 'intrusions' in a spontaneous, immediate, and more or less uncontrolled fashion. Among the latter reactions, emotionality is but one mode, yet the clearest. From this point of view, color responses on the Rorschach become indicators of a very basic personality variable – the degree of permeability of the subject's outside boundary.

It would thus appear that the diagnostic role assigned by Rorschach to the color determinant readily lends itself to fruitful treatment within more contemporary theoretical frames. [. . . .]

CHIAROSCURO. The diffuse total impression of shading on the Rorschach finds its laboratory parallel in the total homogeneous field. The latter, when produced under controlled 'pure' conditions, is experienced phenomenologically as moving toward the subject and as oppressing him (15). This finding corresponds well to the earlier cited observations, emphasizing the depressive, discomfort- and anxiety-arousing states that seem to overpower the perceiver of the achromatic light-dark continuum. Psychiatrically, the emotional state of anxiety has been frequently likened to a condition of being lost in a world that has no discernible organization or, in a phrase of the existentialists, that engulfs the person by its nothingness. Correspondingly it has become Rorschach practice to interpret the chiaroscuro responses on the test as signs of generalized emotional states or moods (chiefly of a dysphoric nature) in contradistinction to the specifically object-oriented emotions that are associated with the chromatic color determinants.

In his original volume Rorschach did not consider the shading of the ink blots as a separate test variable, and in his posthumous publication he merely introduced one score for it. Here was, then, a natural area for further development. In view of the extensive usage of the test, it is not surprising that such developments have proceeded through the years along a diversity of lines, both in classificational criteria applied to the shading element and in the interpretative significance coordinated to these criteria.

One system, of which the research and theoretical potentialities are relatively unknown in English-speaking countries, is that of Hans Binder, a student and co-worker of Rorschach (4). The distinguishing feature of this classificational system lies in the fact that it is consistently based on the methodological principles of psychological phenomenology, and that it is linked to a theory of emotions, also phenomenological.*

Binder's treatment of the shading determinant shows the phenomenological procedure on two levels. Through painstaking qualitative analysis of a large number of subjects' responses and introspections to the shaded areas of the blots, he endeavored to discern the intrinsic personal meanings inherent in this material. After casting the salient trends of his analysis into a set of classificational categories, he was able to spell out the diagnostic significance of the different categories by relating them to the concepts of the Munich phenomenological theory of emotions. In addition to providing a demonstration of psychological phenomenology in Rorschach usage, the exposition of Binder's ideas on the chiaroscuro determinant acquaints the reader with a scheme for conceptualizing emotive phenomena in a somewhat more differentiated and subtle manner than is habitual in standard clinical practice.

American commentaries on the phenomenological approach

* Phenomenology is an orientation that emphasizes less the conceptualization of data than a way of approaching them. It stresses the importance of viewing psychological phenomena at their own face value. When dealing with new material, the psychologist is urged to cast aside any previously acquired frame of reference and to contemplate his task with a fresh and unbiased attitude. By observing carefully and recording with meticulous accuracy what is before him, he is taking the first, indispensable step toward his ultimate goal of discovering the intrinsic psychological nature of the phenomenon under consideration. 'It (phenomenology) reveals meaning as the very stuff of experience, and it invites the psychologist to turn his attention to the meaningful aspects of the world' (14, p. 228). The approach has been developed most fruitfully in Western continental Europe where its application to the cognitive areas of thinking and perception has yielded rich and penetrating descriptive insights.

in psychology (14) usually point to the desirability for phenomenology to parallel its contributions to the cognitive field by similar accomplishments in the emotional-motivational realm, and to the advisability of strengthening its scientific respectability by some form of quantification. It is the writer's opinion that Binder's chiaroscuro system constitutes a positive step in both these directions, particularly since some of his hypotheses would appear quite amenable to experimental manipulation.

EXPERIENCE TYPE ($M:C$). Besides the interpretative significance accorded the M and the C determinants separately, even greater significance is ascribed to their interrelationship. This interrelationship is represented by a variable, called the experience type (*Erlebnistypus*). It is expressed numerically as the ratio of the M to the sum C scores. When viewed in the frame of this configuration, the impact of the two determinants, their qualitative nuances, and, primarily, their broader personality implications, all undergo reciprocal modifications. Since M and C represent opposite forms of the subject-environment relation, Rorschach looked upon their numerical constellation as an expression of the fundamental polarity of an individual's stance to his surrounding world: his inwardly determined strivings versus his outwardly stimulated reactions. Depending on whether the balance in the ratio is tipped toward the movement or toward the color side, the experience type is designated as 'introversive' or 'extratensive' respectively. When the two sides approximate each other, either in abundance or in impoverishment, the experience type becomes 'dilated' in the first place and 'coartated' in the second. Considering how many intermediary combinations are possible, it is clear that this schema provides for a wide range of individualized patterns of basic orientations.

For Rorschach these patterns do not correspond to mutually exclusive personality types. Their poles are universal psychological functions, present in varying degrees in every person. He felt that the totality of a person's enduring features is most pertinently conceived when organized around this nuclear pattern, 'the inmost, intimate capacity of resonance to life experiences' (7, p. 203), as Ellenberger has aptly defined the experience type. In evolving the ultimate personality picture from the test, all other variables are viewed in the light of this catalytic factor, or the 'axis' as Rorschach liked to call it.

Because of the psychologically challenging problems that

are entailed in the far-reaching significance attached to the experience type, a good deal of thinking has revolved around it.

Content

The last category of analysis to be sketched here deals with the ideational content of the subject's responses in contrast to the foregoing categories, which derive from formal aspects of the perceptual process. As noted earlier, Rorschach was explicit in ascribing to the formal features the primary power in his diagnostic method: 'The actual content of the interpretations comes into consideration only secondarily' (18, p. 181), and 'the content of the interpretations offers little indication as to the content of the psyche until it is considered in relation to the psychogram' (tabulation of all scores) (18, p. 122). These two quotations convey succinctly Rorschach's position: Although unquestionably subordinated to the formal components, the content factor plays an integral role, provided that it is treated as closely embedded into the total test analysis.

In spite of the usual recognition of the desirability of taking into account both the formal (function) and the substantive (content) aspects in personality representation, contemporary theories have been relatively unsuccessful in attaining an intrinsic synthesis of these two conceptually divergent avenues of personality exploration. In contrast, Rorschach's psychodiagnosis stands out by genuinely integrating both approaches, not in the loosely additive manner of an afterthought, but in a sense that takes seriously the implications of such synthesis at every level of test interpretation. Thus the evaluation of an individual response always incorporates along with the formal characteristics the respective content as an essential factor that is not only modified in its significance by the formal categories but also, in turn, can influence the meaning of these categories. To give just one example, the color determinant is interpreted quite differently according to whether it serves as basis for the content 'fire' or for 'rose water'.

The location, determinant, and content categories, introduced so far, cover Rorschach's major test components with the exception of the popularity-originality dimension. The latter is omitted from discussion because, in addition to constituting the least novel aspect of Rorschach's psychodiagnostic method, it has failed to stimulate a notable amount of either research or theoretical speculation.

The Test Pattern

Our presentation of the psychological tenets of the Rorschach method moves now to a higher level of generality by focusing on the over-all pattern that results from the interplay of the test components.

At the outset of this paper, emphasis was placed on the point that the test interpretation involves a complex process of integration, of handling the part processes at times as relatively independent units and in other contexts as dependent parts. An idea of how these interpretative principles operate in reality can be gleaned from the implications of the M and the C determinants, when considered separately and when viewed within the experience type. As described earlier, by virtue of the particular perceptual features underlying each of these determinants, their individual roles as representatives of certain personality dimensions are accrued to them. The treatment, on the other hand, of the same determinants as juxtaposed in the experience type cogently brings out the power of organizational principles in the Rorschach.

The observation that the respective weights of either M or C are reciprocally accentuated, dampened, or blocked reflects the principle of interdependence of subwholes within a larger whole. The fact that the new whole – the experience type – carries new, broader psychological implications than either of its constituent components did by themselves, illustrates the principle that the whole is greater than the sum of its parts. Finally, the circumstance that this integrated whole – the experience type – emerges as the catalytic factor of the superordinate whole – the total personality configuration – impressively exemplifies the principle of organization of a larger whole around a nuclear subunit or strong part, to use a gestalt term.

Full appreciation of how this complex method of interpretation shifts back and forth from one level of organization to another would perhaps best be conveyed by following a Rorschach worker through the elaborate procedure of studying a test record on all levels and in all detail: Viewing the combination of scores on an individual response as a unit in its own right; analyzing the temporal pattern of these responses in the sequence of the entire record and in relation to accompanying behavioral data; scrutinizing the cross-sectional configuration (psychogram) of all the scoring categories; and, after all this sorting, weighing, relating, arranging, and rearranging has been done, observing the evolution of the final *unitas multiplex* of the Rorschach personality picture. [....]

Problems of Scientific Appraisal

An enterprise dealing with the place of the Rorschach within the broader orbit of psychology would be incomplete without consideration of an issue that recently has aroused a vast amount of argumentation: the dependability and trustworthiness of the Rorschach method as a diagnostic tool. The problem itself is certainly a legitimate one, recognized by every serious psychologist with respect for scientific standards. The controversy centers not around the need for such demonstration of worth, but around the question as to just what means of demonstration may be accepted as scientifically irreproachable.

Psychometric practice, influenced in its basic philosophy by behavioristic tradition, relies for such purposes on the two time-honored indicators – reliability and validity. For the readily isolable and accurately measurable variables of psychometric assessment, these indicators constitute an entirely appropriate means of establishing in correspondingly dissective and quantitative fashion the respectability of a test. As the reader realizes by now, the Rorschach, and for that matter any projective technique, having grown up in a distinctly different theoretical climate, has very little in common with psychometric tests either in objectives or in actual test composition, or in underlying premises. It hardly can be surprising, therefore, that its organismically integrated configuration of variables does not yield smoothly to evalutation by the traditional procedures of reliability-validity probing.

The recognition of this difficulty, however, should in no sense be interpreted as denial of the problem. The implication is rather a quest for recasting the criteria for establishment of the scientific worth of a projective method in a way that is syntonic to the intrinsic nature of the diagnostic tool. To the same extent to which a truly scientific spirit requires us to stand ready constantly to revise our knowledge, so this spirit compels us to modify correspondingly our means of evaluating the growing and changing body of knowledge. One might say that what should remain unquestioned with projective as with any other assessment techniques is the genotype of scientific standards, whereas the phenotype of carrying out these standards through the conventional psychometric procedures of reliability-validity testing constitutes a social lag in need of revision [....]

Bibliography

1. Arnheim, R. Perceptual and aesthetic aspects of the movement response. *J. Personal.*, 1951, **19**, 265–81.
2. Arnold, Magda. The status of emotion in contemporary psychology. In: A. A. Roback (ed.). *Present-day-psychology.* New York: Philosophical Library, 1955.
3. Bash, K. W. Ganzeigenschaften als Determinantenträger im Rorschach Versuch. *Schw. Z. f. Psychol. und ihre Anw.*, 1957, **16**, No. 2, 121–6.
4. Binder, H. Die Helldunkeldeutungen im Psychodiagnostischen Experiment von Rorschach. *Schweiz Arch. Neurol. Psychiat.*, 1933, **30**, 1–67; 233–86.
5. Brosin, H. W. and Fromm, E. Some principles of gestalt psychology in the Rorschach experiment. *Rorschach Res. Exch.*, 1942, **6**, 1–15.
6. Bruner, J. S. Personality and the process of perceiving. In: R. R. Blake and G. V. Ramsey (eds.). *Perception – an approach to personality.* New York: Ronald Press, 1951.
7. Ellenberger, H. Hermann Rorschach, M.D., 1884–1922: A biographical study. *Bull. Menn. Clin.*, 1954, **18**, 173–219.
8. Gibson, J. J. The perception of visual surfaces. *Amer J. Psychol.*, 1950, **63**, 367–84.
9. Goldstein, K. *The organism.* New York: Am. Book Co., 1939.
10. Koehler, W. Das Wesen der Intelligenz. In: A. Keller (ed.). *Kind und Umwelt, Anlage und Erziehung.* Leipzig: Deuticke, 1930.
11. Koffka, K. *Principles of gestalt psychology.* New York: Harcourt Brace, 1935.
12. Levine, K. and Grassi, J. The relation between blot and concept in graphic Rorschach responses. *Rorschach Res. Exch.*, 1942, **6**, 71–3.
13. Lewin, K. *Principles of topological psychology.* New York and London: McGraw-Hill, 1936.
14. Macleod, R. B. The place of phenomenological analysis in social psychological theory. In: J. H. Rohrer and M. Sherif (eds.). *Social psychology at the crossroads.* New York: Harper, 1951.
15. Metzger, W. Optische Untersuchungen am Ganzfeld. II. Zur Phänomenologie des homogenen Ganzfelds. *Psych. Forsch.*, 1930, **13**, 6–29.
16. Metzger, W. *Psychologie.* 2nd ed. Darmstadt: Steinkopf, 1954.
17. Rickers-Ovsiankina, Maria. Some theoretical considerations regarding the Rorschach method. *Rorschach Res. Exch.*, 1943, **7**, 41–53.
18. Rorschach, H. *Psychodiagnostics* (5th ed.). Bern: Huber, 1951.
19. Schachtel, E. On color and affect. Contributions to an understanding of Rorschach's test. II. *Psychiatry*, 1943, **6**, 393–409.
20. Shapiro, D. Color-response and perceptual passivity. *J. proj. Tech.*, 1956, **20**, 52–69.
21. Sheerer, M. Personality functioning and cognitive psychology. *J. Personal.*, 1953, **22**, 1–16.
22. Werner, H. Motion and motion perception: a study on vicarious functioning. *J. Psychol.*, 1945, **19**, 317–27.

A METHOD FOR INVESTIGATING FANTASIES: THE THEMATIC APPERCEPTION TEST

Among projective techniques the Thematic Apperception Test (TAT) alone approaches the Rorschach in popularity, or, as Bell (see Further Reading A4) puts it 'in quantity and quality of research and use'. The two techniques are not, however, to be thought of as in rivalry with one another; rather, their functions are complementary. The Rorschach aims at analysis of personality structure; the TAT throws light on the here and now, the specific interpersonal and other situations which are 'pressive' or 'significant' for the individual.

The present text presents the authors' original description of the technique, but widespread interest in the TAT may be said to date from Murray's account (1) of its use as part of a very varied battery of procedures used in the intensive study at the Harvard Psychological Clinic of several groups of male college students.

A fuller description of the 'official' method of presentation, along with 'norms' based on the student population just mentioned is given in the Manual for the test (2). It must be stressed that such norms cannot be regarded as valid for other groups of subjects; indeed satisfactory quantification is something that is lacking for the TAT even more than for the Rorschach.

A full TAT series as at present used consists of 20 cards, with variations according to the age and sex of the subject. Some are specifically intended for use with children, but many psychologists are of the opinion that it is better to have an entirely separate series for this purpose (see also introduction to 13, below).

Unlike the Rorschach, the TAT does seem to lend itself to group administration, and following the precedent set at the British War Office Selection Boards (see 7, p. 165), it has been very widely used in this form, usually with a much smaller number of pictures. While strict psychometrists rightly condemn the indiscriminate use of 'new' or unstandardized TAT pictures, users of the technique have sometimes found the standard pictures unsuited to their needs, and have experimented with others. In particular, the absence of colour has been said to detract from the attractiveness or stimulating quality of the pictures. The Object Relations Technique (ORT) (3), a device little used as yet other than at the Tavistock Clinic, introduces colour, and other variables, with the express intention of applying a measure of Rorschach rationale to a TAT-type procedure, and so to some extent bridging the gap between the two leading projective techniques.

References
1. Murray, H. A. *et al.*, *Explorations in Personality*, New York and London: Oxford University Press, 1938.
2. Murray, H. A., *Thematic Apperception Test Manual*, Cambridge, Mass.: Harvard University Press, 1943.
3. Phillipson, H., *The Object Relations Technique*, London: Tavistock, 1955.

12 C. D. Morgan and H. A. Murray

A Method for Investigating Fantasies: The Thematic Apperception Test

C. D. Morgan & H. A. Murray, *Archives of Neurology and Psychiatry* 34; American Medical Association, 1935, Vol. 34, pp. 289–94.

Psychoanalysis attempts to represent the underlying dynamics of personality as an interaction of forces. Each force is a need which impels the individual person to pursue a certain course of activity – a course of activity which usually involves a certain kind of object. An inhibited or repressed force with its associated impressions of objects may manifest itself in the guise of a fantasy which the subject can report on, or its presence may be inferred by the analyst on the basis of other phenomena. In the latter case the analyst is apt to speak of it as a repressed unconscious fantasy. Since the exposition of such hidden fantasies is one of the fundamental aims of analysis and since, at best, the customary technique for accomplishing it calls for a long period of watchful waiting, it seems that it would be helpful if a more expeditious method could be devised. For, if the analyst were cognizant at the very start of the fundamental fantasy constructions of his patient he should be in a better position to apperceive and to interpret the dynamic relations of what, in the beginning of an analysis, is ordinarily fragmentary and obscure. He might also, at a later state, have a better idea of what might be considered irrelevant as well as what important latent trends had yet to be disclosed.

The method which is to be described is based on the well recognized fact that when someone attempts to interpret a complex social situation he is apt to tell as much about himself as he is about the phenomena on which attention is focused. At such times the person is off his guard, since he believes that he is merely explaining objective occurrences. To one with 'double hearing', however, he is exposing certain inner forces and arrangements – wishes, fears and traces of past experience. Another fact which was relied on in devising the present method is that a great deal of written fiction is the conscious or unconscious expression of the author's experiences or fantasies. The process involved is that of projection – something well known to analysts. It is utilized in the Rorschach test.

Procedure

The procedure which suggested itself was this: to present subjects with a series of pictures, each of which depicts a different dramatic event, with the instructions to interpret the action in each picture and give an imaginary reconstruction of the preceding events and the final outcome. It was anticipated that in the performance of this task a subject would necessarily be forced to project some of his own fantasies into the material and so reveal some of his more pressing underlying needs.

Since for purposes of comparison it is desirable to make such a procedure as uniform as possible, that is, to present every subject with similar stimuli and similar instructions for response, the attempt was made to find a standard set of pictures. Each picture should suggest some critical situation and be effective in evoking a fantasy relating to it. The set should also be comprehensive. Ideally, there should be a picture which would act as a trellis to support the growth and unfolding of every root of fantasy. It was considered, and the idea was later confirmed by experience, that there should be at least one person in each picture with whom the subject could easily identify himself. Such an object may be termed an evoker, that is, one who evokes empathy in another. Thus, there should be a separate set of pictures for males and females, and also for children, young adults and elderly persons. Since in the present experiments the subjects were all young men between the ages of 20 and 30, most of the pictures to be described included at least one figure of that sex and age. After a preliminary selection from several hundred pictures and an elimination of those which on repeated trials proved unproductive, we found a set of twenty which gave good results. This test was one of many to which fifty subjects were exposed. It formed a part of a comprehensive study of personality in which about twenty experimenters participated.

The subject was seated in a comfortable chair with his back to the experimenter, and the following directions were read to him:

'This is a test of creative imagination. I am going to show you a picture, and I want you to make up a plot or story for which it might be used as an illustration. What is the relation of the individuals in the picture? What has happened to them? What are their present thoughts and feelings? What will be the outcome? I want you to do your very best. As this is a test of literary imagination you may make your story as long and as detailed as you wish.'

The subject was then handed picture 1, and the experimenter wrote down everything that he said. If, in giving his story, the subject omitted the antecedent circumstances or the outcome, he was reminded of it by such remarks as, 'What led up to this situation?', 'How will it end?' etc. When the subject finished his story he was handed picture 2 and asked to proceed as before. There were twenty pictures in the series, but as the test was stopped after an hour most of the subjects did not have time to make up stories for more than two thirds of them.

The test was given once to forty subjects as a group test, the stories being written. The time saved by this method was considerable, but the results were less satisfactory.

After a few days had elapsed each subject was interviewed. This time the experimenter explained that he was studying the imaginative process in the construction of literary plots and that he wished to know if what professional writers had told about their creative experiences was true for everyone. The subject was then asked if he would cooperate by trying to remember whether his story had come from something which he had seen or read; whether it had come out of the experience of friends or relatives, or whether it had come out of his own private experience. The subject was then reminded of the plot of each story in turn and encouraged to speak freely and openly.

Results

An examination of the stories concocted by our subjects in conjunction with material obtained from introspections, autobiographies, hours of free association, interviews, etc., reveals the fact that there were four chief sources from which the plots and the items of the plots were drawn: (1) books and moving pictures, (2) actual events in which a friend or a member of the family participated, (3) experiences (subjective or objective) in the subject's own life and (4) the subject's conscious and unconscious fantasies.

Although the material from the first two of these four sources may seem at first blush to be of little importance, it was discovered that even here much of significance was revealed. This, it seems, may be explained by referring to the tendency exhibited by most subjects to enjoy observing most and to remember best the external events which resemble their underlying fantasies. Thus, when a subject gives a vivid account of an occurrence one may profitably consider whether or not the theme of the event is a clue to his latent personality.

That every subject almost immediately projects his own circumstances, experiences or preoccupations into the evoker was only too obvious. For instance, in one experiment six of the eleven college men who took the test said that the youth in picture 4* was a student, whereas none of the twelve non-college men who acted as subjects described him as such. One subject, whose father had been a ship's carpenter, wanted to go to sea himself, to travel and see the world. This was his dominant fantasy. Three of his scenes in his stories were laid on board a ship and two were in the Orient. In regard to picture 17†, which illustrates a middle-aged man talking to a younger man, the subject said: 'The older man is educated and has traveled a lot. He convinces the other to travel, to take a job that will take him to different places.' In commenting on a picture which illustrates a young man sitting in a chair brooding rather disconsolately, this subject said: 'This is a businessman who runs quite a business in town. He is weighing the possibility of a European trip. He has been arguing with his wife on the subject. She got angry because he would not go and finally took up her hat and left. He is thinking it over. He changes his opinion, goes out and buys tickets.' In interpreting another picture, illustrating two laborers engaged in conversation, the same subject said: 'These two fellows are a pair of adventurers. They always manage to meet in out-of-the-way places. They are now in India. They have heard of a new revolution in South America, and they are planning how they can get there.... In the end they work their way in a freighter.'

Many other examples of this sort of thing could be cited. No subject failed to exemplify it. Some of them, in fact, gave stories which were frank and unabashed autobiographies, one example of which will be sufficient.

When presented with picture 5‡, depicting a young lad gazing pensively at a violin which is resting on a table before him, our subject said: 'A very sensitive boy – sensitive lips – who is musical by nature. His mother wants him to be a violonist, but his father, who is in business, is averse to it. The father came home one night and heard him squeaking – "squeaking" to him but beautiful to the mother – and told him to stop. He is a highly irritable father with a bad temper, and he partially destroys the violin. The boy is rudely shocked. He is over his grief now, but is studying the violin with tenderness and sorrow. This upset makes

* Picture 14 in the current series.

† An earlier variant of picture 7BM in the current series.

‡ Picture 1 in the current series.

him all the more fervently musical. It gives him new sorrow, making him more mature. It takes away the light spirit of a child and makes him a better artist. His mother buys him a new violin in spite of the father. He continues his playing and so goes on to the life of an artist. By this experience he will have nothing in common with other children of his age. He is more sensitive and will find his greatest happiness in solitude. He becomes a genius, appears at concerts and is acclaimed by critics because he is so precocious. Then his popularity wanes. He deviates to musical expression through the medium of language – literature. He becomes a poet. At fourteen or fifteen he has had none of the contacts of ordinary youth. He is called a sissy and is quite unhappy. But he glories in the happiness of the consciousness of his own superiority. Others of his age he thinks are silly. School is a limitation. He feels its thorns. His father is interested in his marks rather than in the development of his mind. His mother wants him to be what she couldn't be, but she doesn't influence his intellectual development. She is a pillar of strength to fall back upon, but she doesn't feel deeply. The boy looks on her as inferior but necessary. He goes into philosophy and the arts. If he is not careful he will become sexually abnormal. At nineteen he has written great poetry with great imagination and imagery. He puts deep philosophic thoughts into great language ...'

In his introspections this subject admitted: 'All of this story is autobiographical.' He said further: 'My father isn't like that, but he could be. Only by keeping my mouth shut (the subject did not speak until he was three years old) is it possible to keep the atmosphere one of indifference. The conflict of the businessman and the poet (the subject himself has written poetry and intends to dedicate his life to this calling) is so intense that it could flame out between us as great hostility. There is a lot in it about sorrow. Well, I'll tell you, though you will probably think it foolish. You see I feel that I really want to be like Byron. I want to be highly sensitive as he was. You know the girls in high school ridiculed me when I read them my poetry. I want to expose myself to their scorn and ridicule. I want to be sensitive and expose myself in order to suffer, because it is only through the greatest suffering that we can know anything of life and be strong....'

In his autobiography the subject said: 'I have no close attachment to the family and (as a corollary to this condition) no favorite parent. Probably I do favor my mother, however, because I see more of her but the attachment is inconsequential. ... I was timid and easily beaten in fist fights. I suffered from the barbaric joys of young boys.... My favorite story and hero was Robinson Crusoe, lonely and self-sufficient.... Writing is my chief aim of the immediate and distant future. I also aim to develop more mature sex relationships. I do not care to try to remodel the world; it is much more intriguing to fathom the one I have found. If I could remodel it, I would like to be the greatest writer – equivalent to prophet – and receive the acclaim of an intelligent populace. Above all, I would like to have the world more alive to and aware of its own beauty.'

Although some of this material is suggestive of certain under-lying infantile experiences and fantasies, it is not to demonstrate such trends that this case is cited. It is our intention merely to indicate how much important biographic data may sometimes be obtained from a single story and the introspections which follow it. This kind of information, however, can often be obtained by direct questioning, and the preset test would be quite unnecessary if it were only this that one wished to discover. What we have to show is that subjects project their deepest fantasies into such dramatic pictures and thereby reveal directional tensions of which they are quite unconscious. Though some of their stories are elaborations of conscious fantasies, others are not recognized by the subjects as having any personal reference. It is these – in which the personal reference is suggested by other data – that have been ascribed to unconscious fantasies. Of course, the stories as given are conscious fantasies. Like dreams, they must be interpreted if one is to arrive at the unconscious trends which determine them. Before presenting typical case histories to support this assumption, however, it will be necessary to outline the conceptual scheme which we have adopted for the classification of fantasies.

Psychoanalysts have found it convenient to name some of the more common fantasies – the oedipus fantasy, king-slave fantasy, foster-parent fantasy etc. This naming represents the beginning of a classification – the initial step in the construction of any science – and the practice should be continued until all important fantasies have been so recognized. If this is to be done in a systematic fashion every fantasy must be analyzed into the factors which compose it, so that the groupings may be made in terms of similar fundamental elements.

Our own reflections have led us to the conclusion that every fantasy may be analyzed into a series of events, each event, in turn, being an occurrence which is usually analyzable into: (1) a driving force (or fusion of forces in the subject), (2) an object (or group of objects) towards which or away from which the force is directed, and (3) the outcome of their interaction expressed in terms of subjective feeling – satisfaction or dissatisfaction. This mode of analysis is applicable not only to a fantasy but to an actual event as well. Sometimes it is preferable to speak first of the object, i.e., the environment press or stimulus situation, and second of the subjective trend, i.e., the response. Stated in this way, our mode of representation resembles the familiar S-R formula of the behaviorists, except that with us the stimulus is more than a single sensation or perception. It is a temporal Gestalt of stimuli which bear the same dynamic meaning – the *press* (p). And with us the response is ordinarily represented not as a particular muscular movement or reflex but as a *need* (n) or general course of action, the tendency of which is to produce a certain effect.

To incorporate fantasies into a scientific system of psychology, then, we propose to classify them according to the single events which compose them, every event, as we have pointed out, being classified according to its essential structure. To refer to the dynamic structure or plot of a fantasied event – or, for that matter, of an actual event – we have found it convenient to use the term *thema* (th). A simple thema we shall define as the abstract formula for a single event. It consists of a particular press–need combination. The term complex thema may be used to describe a commonly encountered temporal association of simple themas, some of which may be dominant and some subsidiary.

In some events only the press is known or the press is of primary importance (something happens or an object does something and the subject merely experiences it or adapts to it), whereas in other events nothing is known of the press or the press is merely the usual environment and it is the subject's action which is significant. In the former case the press alone will constitute the thema, and in the latter case, the need alone. For instance, 'p punishment' will describe an event in which the subject is punished by an object, and 'n punishment' or just 'punishment' will describe an event in which the subject punishes an object. Strictly speaking, a thema is the structure of a momentary event, but the term may also be used to describe a long continued press followed by a long continued response, provided the intervening events are more or less irrelevant. For instance, 'p family discord' may be used to describe the fact that a child is frequently exposed to quarrels between his father and his mother, and 'revenge' may be used to describe a subject's long enduring resentment and a series of retaliative actions.

This brief exposition of the concept of thema (th) was necessary, it seemed, in view of the fact that we have analyzed our material in this way and have proposed a name for every significant thema which would be clearly identified. The names, of course, should be regarded merely as suggestions, for they may prove to be inadequately descriptive when more fantasies of the same kind are examined.

Since the subjects who take this test are asked to interpret each picture, that is, to apperceive the plot or dramatic structure exhibited by each picture, we have named it the 'thematic apperception test'. [. . . .]

THE TAT AS A PROJECTIVE METHOD

The introduction to the previous article called attention to *ad hoc* modifications in TAT procedure. The present text discusses more radical attempts to reformulate TAT rationale; it stops short at the point in the author's opening chapter of her book at which she introduces her own method of analysis, involving a rather complex but apparently objective scoring system.

Comment has already been made on the absence of a universally accepted method of 'scoring' the TAT. Much depends on the purpose for which the TAT is applied: for non-clinical use Wyatt's system (4) has much to recommend it. Bellak (1) has proposed a clinically-biased method, not unlike Arnold's in general conception. Bellak's book also describes his Children's Association Test (CAT) in which animals take the place of human beings, on the grounds that children will empathize more readily with animal figures. Evidence on this point is conflicting, and the whole question of TAT for children is open to some doubt: it should be borne in mind that according to earlier standardizations of the Stanford–Binet tests, spontaneous *interpretation* of pictures could not be expected before year XII.

A simple method of analysis for adult use, with much illustrative material is offered by Stein (3).

Murstein (2) provides a very full survey of research in the TAT, along with a consideration of underlying theory.

References
1. Bellak, L. *The Thematic Apperception Test aud the Children's Apperception Test in Clinical Use*. New York: Grune and Stratton, 1954.
2. Murstein, B. I. *Theory and Research in Projective Techniques*, (emphasizing the TAT). New York and London: Wiley. 1963.
3. Stein, M. I. *The Thematic Apperception Test: an Introductory Manual for its use with Adults*. Cambridge, Mass.: Addison-Wesley, 1955.
4. Wyatt, F. 'The scoring and analysis of the Thematic Apperception Test'. *J. Psychol.*, **24**, 319–30. 1947.

13 Magda B. Arnold

The TAT as a Projective Method

M. B. Arnold, Story Sequence Analysis; Columbia University Press,
New York, 1962, pp. 3–13.

Since the time Morgan and Murray first published the Thematic
Apperception Test (TAT) in 1935 and Murray brought out the
final manual in 1943, a great many psychologists have attempted
to improve upon Murray's scoring of needs and press, while
others were content to use the test merely for clinical diagnosis.
According to Murray, a man is likely to reveal his motivation,
that is, his needs, wishes, hopes, and fears, while interpreting an
ambiguous social situation, such as is portrayed in each of the
TAT pictures. In the first version, the instructions were simply to
interpret each picture, to guess what went before and what was
the final outcome. Increased experience gradually modified the
instructions. Now the subject is asked to tell a story about each
picture.

This modest beginning has flowered into a vast array of research papers and books. I do not intend to review the many
studies that deal with the TAT and other storytelling tests
modeled on it. What I do want to discuss is the assumptions
upon which work with this test has been based. Wyatt and Veroff
(1956) point out that the TAT presupposes three kinds of theory:
a theory of fantasy, a theory relating fantasy to individual
behavior, and a theory of personality. The theory of personality
used by TAT interpreters from Murray to the contributors to a
recent symposium (Kagan and Lesser, eds. 1961) has usually been
psychoanalytic theory. This proposes that instinctive drives or
impulses are the real motivating forces of man which are modified
by ego-processes in overt behavior, but reveal themselves in
fantasy. This is possible because in fantasy the primary process
stemming from these drives is concealed from the ego by various
defense mechanisms (projection, identification, etc.). Early TAT
workers, particularly, assumed that TAT stories, like fantasy in
general, express the storyteller's needs or drives. This theoretical
framework seemed validated by Morgan and Murray's report
that the material revealed in the TAT of one subject could be
verified in five months of psychoanalysis.

Unfortunately for this neat scheme, later research findings did not support it. They looked promising at first: When people were hungry, their TAT stories showed more food themes than when they were sated. But, on further investigation, it was found that the curves indicating the relation between hunger and TAT themes of food and eating were either negatively accelerated or shaped like an inverted U; that is, there was a positive correlation between mild hunger and food imagery, but it often became negative when hunger was prolonged (see Sanford, 1936, 1937; Atkinson and McClelland, 1948; McClelland and Atkinson, 1948; Levine, Chein, and Murphy, 1942; Lazarus *et al.*, 1953). Levine and his co-workers suggested that this curve represents the functioning of the primary process during the first half of the curve, when food is fantasied; while the second leg of the curve reveals the operation of a reality-oriented process which represses such fantasies because they would be unduly disturbing. This explanation might hold for a study like that of Brozek *et al.* (1951), who found that men who had been semi-starved for some time did not reveal excessive food imagery in their TAT.

A similar pattern was found in TAT studies on aggression. Though aggressive themes increased when the storytellers were subjected to annoyance or frustration before the test, they increased principally in the group that scored low on a Manifest Hostility Scale, while the high scorers tended to have fewer aggressive themes (Hokanson and Gordon, 1958). And, Sanford *et al.* (1943) reported that the number of aggressive themes in the TAT stories of aggressive adolescents was no greater than in the stories of well-adjusted boys. However, Mussen and Naylor (1954) found that aggressive boys told many stories of aggression but few in which aggression was punished. In contrast, well-behaved boys told many stories in which aggression was punished. We may conjecture that aggressive personalities could be distinguished by the way in which they treat aggressive themes in their stories.

Research in achievement motivation (McClelland *et al.*, 1953) shows an even more confused pattern. When a task was given to students with the simple instruction to do it as a favor to a graduate student (relaxed condition), those with high scores on *n* Achievement (derived from TAT stories) did not do as well as those with low *n* Achievement scores. But, when the experimenter described the task as a measure of intellectual ability and urged the students to do their best, high scorers did better than low scorers. The same differences were found in a number of tasks, though these differences were not always significant.

In a group of thirty college men, high n Achievement scorers also had higher average college grades during the semester in which the test was taken and in the two succeeding semesters. The correlation coefficient of $+\cdot51$ was, however, reduced to $+\cdot39$ when the scores on a verbal and mathematical Scholastic Aptitude Test were partialled out. Other groups of college students showed much lower correlations of n Achievement scores with college grades ($+\cdot05$ and $-\cdot14$, see McClelland *et al.*, 1953, pp. 237–41). Lazarus and his co-workers also reported negative or insignificant trends when n Achievement was correlated with task performance plus 'behavioral evidence of achievement striving' (1961, p. 54). And, Elizabeth French has shown that increased performance can be produced by instructions that arouse not the need for achievement but the affiliative motive (1955).

Moreover, McClelland's n Achievement scores of women do not show the same relation to performance as do men's scores. Veroff admits that 'obtaining valid achievement motivation scores for women has always been a problem for this apperceptive technique' (1961, p. 102). There is legitimate doubt whether n Achievement scores reflect real-life achievement motivation, unless we want to say that women just are not motivated toward achievement. Even the fact that men in high status occupations show higher n Achievement scores than men in lower status occupations (Veroff, 1961) is not convincing proof that this score really indicates achievement motivation. It could be that high status men are more articulate or that they are more preoccupied with their work than are low status men – or, for that matter, than women, whether career women or housewives.

A look at McClelland's scoring may clear up some of the mystery. To determine n Achievement, McClelland scores each story for unrelated, doubtful and achievement imagery. Unrelated imagery is scored -1, doubtful imagery is scored zero. Achievement imagery is scored $+1$ when the hero is engaged in competitive activity, is concerned about doing well, and has a unique accomplishment to his credit or shows long-term involvement in a task. Additional scores of $+1$ are given to the same story for each of the following themes: when there is another reference to achievement (category TI); when the story character desires achievement (n); when overt or mental activity is directed toward a goal, whether that is successful ($I+$), unsuccessful ($I-$), or doubtful ($I?$); when the character thinks or dreams of success ($Ga+$), or thinks, dreams, or anticipates failure ($Ga-$);

when an obstacle to achievement is described, whether that is personal (Bp) or external (Bw); when positive affect is connected with mastery ($G+$), or negative affect is connected with failure ($G-$); when someone aids, helps, encourages the story character (Nup); when achievement becomes the central theme of the story ($AchTh$) even when that is only described as a daydream. Accordingly, the n Achievement score for a single story may reach $+11$ if the story contains all the above themes and has no unrelated imagery.

From this brief survey of McClelland's scoring, it is clear that the longer the story, the better the chance of a high score. Even expectation of failure is scored under n Achievement ($Ga-$), so is mere dreaming of success ($Ga+$), withdrawal on meeting an obstacle (Bw), or despair on incurring failure ($G-$). In our own studies, such story imports were found in records of low achievers, while high achievers told stories in which failure is overcome, success is achieved by work rather than dreaming, and obstacles are met by resourceful action. It seems likely that McClelland's n Achievement score indicates a preoccupation with the problem of success or failure rather than enduring motivation to achieve excellence. This would explain, for instance, why Veroff's survey (1961) showed that young professional men (but not young unskilled workers) have high n Achievement scores, while older unskilled workers who are increasingly concerned with their livelihood as their families grow eventually reach and even surpass the scores of older professional men who at that time in life are established and need no longer be exclusively preoccupied with their work.

At any rate, all these studies attest that the drives and affects that are assumed to be projected upon the story characters are not a sure guide to the kind of motivation that leads to action in everyday·life. As a result of such findings, later theorists began to say that TAT stories could not be called 'fantasy' in the accepted (psychoanalytic) sense. Wyatt and Veroff (1956) insisted that a story is an 'intentional wide-awake act of expression' and is neither an instinctual discharge nor the repetition of unconscious patterns. Holt (1961) pointed out that stories are not like daydreams; when they are, the storyteller is sick. For Holt, the strength of the TAT lies in the fact that stories reveal not only primary process thinking but also defenses and ego-processes. He insists that stories are not fantasies and claims that we have 'gotten away with calling TAT stories "fantasies" for so many years *because nobody checks*' (1961, p. 40, original emphasis).

In accord with these objections, later TAT experts have argued that the relation between needs and their TAT expression is neither direct nor simple. For Lazarus (1961), needs and need imagery are positively related only when the need is not expressed or satisfied in action. If it is adequately expressed in behavior, it will not appear as TAT imagery 'except under special circumstances which are not yet clear' (p. 66). When needs and need imagery occur together, he postulates low levels of blocked needs; when blocked needs become very urgent, ego-defenses are brought into play and prevent fantasy expression because this would only intensify the disturbance created by the blocked need. In this way, Lazarus hopes to explain the finding that semi-starved men or sexually aroused students show no increase of hunger or sex imagery in their TAT stories (Brozek *et al.*, 1951; Clark, 1952). But it should be noted that Brozek's subjects thought and talked about food incessantly, fantasied sumptuous dinners, even wanted to become cooks or restaurant owners. This does not suggest reduced food fantasy. What needs to be explained is why these men did have increased food imagery all during the day but did not express it in the TAT stories. Our suggestion that such themes in the TAT indicate preoccupation but not genuine striving might solve the difficulty. Such preoccupation will be expressed in story themes, provided that the storyteller's convictions do not prevent their expression; and provided that the theme has not become so familiar through long rumination that the TAT pictures constitute a welcome diversion.

Actually, the storyteller's motivation is illustrated not by the story themes but by the story outcome and the way the story is told. For instance, Lazarus mentioned that strong sexual arousal (measured by the psychogalvanic reflex) produced stories with little sex imagery while moderate arousal produced stories with extensive imagery, when he instructed his subjects 'to tell the most erotic story they could'. He gave examples of both types of story. In the first story, which reveals little imagery, the storyteller implies that the young couple give in to their desire out of love and are soon to be married; in the second, that they enjoy an experience in which the girl is encouraged by her mother who wishes she could be in the daughter's place. In the first story, the emphasis is on love and marriage; in the second, on enjoyment of the sex act – which easily accounts for the difference in imagery. Lazarus's conclusion is that the TAT is the end result of the interaction between needs and ego-control processes. For this reason, he thinks it impossible 'to make clear inferences about either needs or ego-control processes' from the TAT alone (1961, p. 68).

Among the ego-control processes that are assumed to modify fantasy expression of needs is *anxiety*. McClelland *et al*. (1953) mentioned that 'individuals with fairly high (achievement) motivation will fail to express it even in fantasy because of basic anxieties about achieving' (p. 326). And Feshbach (1961) concedes that anxiety, as a result of an approach-avoidance conflict, may result in blocking the expression of approach motivation or may result in stories that combine these motives with expressions of anxiety. Like Lazarus (1961) and Atkinson (1958, 1961), Feshbach insists that we must know the conditions under which a motive is aroused before we could expect a correlation between TAT themes and behavior. Feshbach sums up his discussion: 'It is by now evident that we should not expect a simple, uniform relationship between "covert" fantasy expression of a motive and "overt" behavioral expressions. The proper question is not "what is the relationship?" but rather "under what conditions would we expect to find a positive, inverse, or negligible correlation?"' (1961, p. 137).

This bird's eye view of recent opinions seems to indicate that both the clinical and the research-oriented view of the TAT has profoundly changed since the test was first introduced. Today, clinicians as well as research workers seem agreed that the TAT is not 'fantasy' in the sense of 'primary process'; that it reveals not only impulses, needs, or affects projected on the character with whom the storyteller identifies but also defensive and adaptive processes. Holt goes so far as to say that 'most of the inferences about personality structure that we can draw from the TAT depend on these non-fantasy aspects' (1961, p. 37).

This new emphasis on an organizing, synthetic function of the ego which produces TAT responses (Wyatt, 1958) has led to a renewed preoccupation with the stimulus properties of the TAT pictures (see Murstein, 1961; Kenny, 1961), for it is the picture that provides the stimulus for ego-controlled 'apperception'. This endeavor has its own pitfalls: the problem of determining the 'absolute' stimulus value of each TAT picture, of which the question of the 'ambiguity' of the picture is a major part. From the first, it was assumed that the stimulus has to be ambiguous to allow responses that will reveal individuality – just as the Rorschach inkblots, for instance, are ambiguous. But inkblots, like fire or clouds, are ambiguous in the sense that they portray nothing definite so that a great many things may be seen in them.

This is not the ambiguity of TAT pictures. Here, the term seems to mean that a great many stories can be told about pictures that have definite outlines and unmistakably portray people and things. This is not really *stimulus* ambiguity. Rather, it is a difference in the way the stimulus is *used* to create a story.

This brings us to the assumption underlying the scoring methods developed thus far. It is the notion that the story is an aggregate of themes, and these themes must be isolated before scoring is possible. Themes may be categorized in a variety of ways, from Murray's needs and press, Tomkins' vector and level analysis, to Kagan's affect states; but in every case, the scoring is based on isolated parts of the story. This assumption leans on Freud's notion of fantasy, as exemplified by his dream analysis: fantasy images are conceived as the end product of a causal chain stemming from drives aroused by the original traumatic experience. For Freud, every fantasy is a wish fulfillment, an image of the object cathected by the drive. Influenced by Freud, most modern psychologists seem to think of fantasy as a series of personal memories, strung together haphazardly, connected up and cleverly disguised by the superego. For this reason, Tomkins, for instance, suggests that we need a theory of memory to explain how TAT pictures are related to stories (Kagan and Lesser, eds., 1961, p. 312).

This view of the TAT story as a patchwork of personal memories has not changed, despite the changing view of what it is that is expressed in it. At least this is the conclusion that seems to be implied by the unanimous agreement of TAT experts to score each story theme individually. Despite Henry's insistence that 'there is no single element in a given TAT record that has any meaning in and of itself' (1961, p. 117), the themes are scored one by one; and the variables supposedly revealed in these themes remain similarly isolated. Veroff (1961), for instance, reports that he found no correlation between *n* Achievement, *n* Affiliation, *n* Power, in a nationwide survey of a representative sample of 1,619 men and women. Since McClelland's system is one of the best worked-out scoring methods, it is not likely that we may expect better success from other systems if they are based on the same assumptions.

If it were true that the themes represent the storyteller's needs, drives, or affects when they are not blocked by ego-processes, and that ego-processes have a similar connexion with themes, we should be able to use TAT themes for predicting behavior at least in those cases where fantasy expression is not blocked by ego-defenses. In such cases, the storyteller's actions should duplicate the hero's actions; the storyteller should have the same desires, the same anxieties and inhibitions he ascribes to the hero or, as Piotrowski (1950) and Wyatt and Veroff (1956) would have it, the same affects he ascribes to *all* story characters. Unfortunately for prediction, but perhaps fortunately for this hypothesis, we never can tell whether themes revealed in the TAT accompany behavior or are an alternative to behavior; whether themes missing in the TAT indicate lack of the corresponding need, its blocking by ego-defenses, or its being acted out in reality. It almost seems as if we had to agree with Lazarus, who insists that we will never be able to predict behavior from the TAT alone.

Before we subscribe to such a pessimistic conclusion, we might consider another possibility. Perhaps neither drives nor ego-processes are revealed in story themes. Perhaps motivating tendencies, whatever they are, shape the story *action* and are expressed in the story *outcome*.

Of course, several interpretive techniques are using the outcome in addition to story themes (see McClelland *et al.*, 1953; Eron, 1951; Hartman, 1951; and many others). But surely the outcome is not just another theme like aggression, hostility, affiliation, and the like. The outcome caps the plot, and the plot integrates various themes into a unified whole. A story is not a collection of themes nor is it a string of memory images. A story is a *creative reorganization* of past sense impressions, a *new product* of human imagination, very different from personal memories recalled in the original sequence and pattern. The story has a meaning which cannot be discovered from the meaning of the individual themes into which it can be analyzed. It is another example of the truism that a structured whole is not the sum of its parts. Whatever score we may assign to such parts, and however we may manipulate or categorize the elements into which we have divided the story, we are disregarding *the story* so long as we deal with themes rather than plot and outcome. If it were possible to score *what the story* is saying, and include *all there is to the story*, we would discover a new dimension in the TAT which might allow very different correlations with behavior.

Elsewhere* a method of story analysis is proposed which does just that. Each story is condensed into an import that leaves out incidental details but preserves the kernel – the meat of the story. When all the imports are read in sequence, a picture of the

* In Chapters 4–9 of *Story Sequence Analysis*, the work in which the present text appears as Chapter 1.

individual emerges that does portray his attitudes, his intentions for action. Every story makes a point, expresses a conviction. It describes an action that may be headed for success or failure, may exemplify cooperation or hostility, may be an attempt to cope with adversity or betray spineless acceptance of whatever may come. Or, the story may speak of hopes and dreams rather than actions and depend on fate or luck to make them come true. In every case, emotions may influence the action, but the outcome is primarily an expression of the storyteller's convictions, garnered from experience and reflection. The plot sets a problem, the outcome solves it. [....]

References

Atkinson, J. W. 1961. Discussion of Dr Lazarus' paper. In: J. Kagan and G. S. Lesser, 1961 *q.v.*

Atkinson, J. W., ed. 1958. *Motives in fantasy, action and society*. New York: Van Nostrand.

Atkinson, J. W. and McClelland, D. C. 1948. The projective expression of needs: II. The effect of different intensities of the hunger drive on thematic apperception. *J. Exp. Psychol.*, **38**, 643–58.

Brozek, J., Guetzkow, H., and Baldwin, M. V. 1951. A quantitative study of perception and association in experimental semistarvation. *J. Pers.*, **19**, 245–64.

Clark, R. A. 1952. The projective measurement of experimentally induced levels of sexual motivation. *J. Exp. Psychol.*, **44**, 391–9.

Eron, L. 1951. Chapter 7 in: E. S. Shneidman *et al.*, eds. *Thematic test analysis*. New York: Grune & Stratton.

Feshbac, S. 1961. The influence of drive arousal and conflict upon fantasy behavior. In: J. Kagan and G. S. Lesser, 1961 *q.v.*

French, E. G. 1955. Some characteristics of achievement motivation. *J. Exp. Psychol.*, **50**, 232–6.

Hartman, A. A. 1951. Chapter 9 in: E. S. Shneidman *et al.*, eds. *Thematic test analysis*. New York: Grune & Stratton.

Henry, W. E. 1961. Discussion of Dr Veroff's paper. In: J. Kagan and G. S. Lesser, 1961. *q.v.*

Hokanson, J. E. and Gordon, J. E. 1958. The expression and inhibition of hostility in imaginative and overt behavior. *J. Abnorm. Soc. Psychol.*, **57**, 327–33.

Holt, R. R. 1961. The nature of TAT stories as cognitive products: a psychoanalytic approach. In: J. Kagan and G. S. Lesser, 1961. *q.v.*

Kagan, J. and Lesser, G. S., eds. 1961. *Contemporary issues in thematic apperceptive methods*. Springfield, Thomas.

Kenny, D. T. 1961. A theoretical and research appraisal of stimulus factors in the TAT. In: J. Kagan and G. S. Lesser, 1961. *q.v.*

Lazarus, R. S. 1961. A substitutive-defensive conception of apperceptive fantasy. In: J. Kagan and G. S. Lesser, 1961. *q.v.*

Lazarus, R. S., Yousem, J., and Arenberg, D. 1953. Hunger and perception. *J. Pers.*, **21**, 312–28.

Levine, R., Chein, I., and Murphy, G. 1942. The relation of the intensity of a need to the amount of perceptual distortion. *J. Psychol.*, **13**, 282–93.

McClelland, D. C. and Atkinson, J. W. 1948. The projective expression of needs: I. The effect of different intensities of the hunger drive on perception. *J. Psychol.*, **25**, 205–22.

Morgan, C. D. and Murray, H. A. 1935. A method for investigating fantasy. The Thematic Apperception Test. *Arch. Neurol. Psychiat.*, **34**, 289–306.

Murray, H. A. 1943. *Thematic Apperception Test manual.* Cambridge, Harvard University Press.

Murstein, B. I. 1961. The role of the stimulus in the manifestation of fantasy. In: J. Kagan and G. S. Lesser, 1961. *q.v.*

Mussen, P. H. and Naylor, M. K. 1954. The relationships between overt and fantasy aggression. *J. Abnorm. Soc. Psychol.*, **49**, 235–40.

Piotrowski, Z. 1950. A new evaluation of the Thematic Apperception Test. *Psychoanal. Rev.*, **37**, 101–27.

Sanford, R. N. 1936. The effect of abstinence from food upon imaginal processes: a preliminary experiment. *J. Psychol.*, **2**, 129–36.

—— 1937. The effect of abstinence from food upon imaginal processes: a further experiment. *J. Psychol.*, **3**, 145–59.

Sanford, R. N., Adkins, M. M., Miller, R. B., Cobb, E. A., and others. 1943. Physique, personality and scholarship. *Monogr. Soc. Res. Child Dev.*, **8**, No. 1 (Serial No. 34).

Tomkins, S. S. 1947. *The Thematic Apperception Test.* New York: Grune & Stratton.

Veroff, J. 1961. Thematic apperception in a nationwide sample survey. In: J. Kagan and G. S. Lesser, 1961. *q.v.*

Wyatt, F. A. 1958. A principle for the interpretation of fantasy. *J. Proj. Techn.*, **22**, 229–45.

Wyatt, F. and Veroff, J. B. 1956. Thematic apperception and fantasy tests. *Progr. Clin. Psychol.*, **2**, 32–57.

A BLIND ANALYSIS OF A CASE
OF MULTIPLE PERSONALITY
USING THE SEMANTIC DIFFERENTIAL

'Alternating' or multiple personality is a theme which many people have found particularly fascinating. R. L. Stevenson's *Dr Jekyll and Mr Hyde* ranks of course as science fiction, and transcends physical possibility, but actual recorded cases are scarcely less dramatic. The classical study, by Morton Prince (4) was first reported as far back as 1901, but more recently an equally interesting case attracted even more attention, even serving as the basis of a commercially-released film (*The Three Faces of Eve*).

The present article, however, is reprinted here (in slightly abridged form) primarily for its methodological interest. Osgood's systematic treatment (3) of his 'semantic differential', designed as an instrument for the 'measurement of meaning' appeared in 1957. It had been preceded, by two years, by Kelly's *Psychology of Personal Constructs* (2), a work which at the time made comparatively little impact, whereas the semantic differential caught on quickly, perhaps because of its implications for disciplines outside psychology, notably linguistics. The two approaches are very similar; both require the subject to allocate scale-positions to concepts, or 'objects' (in the widest sense). Interest has grown very rapidly in recent years; the first half of the sixties may even be said to be the era of concept analysis, much as the fifties were the period of projective techniques and the forties that of factor analysis.

Kelly's *Role Construct Repertory Test* has been described by Bannister (1). The main difference from the semantic differential is that the technique allows the subject to define his own scales, and that the ratings are applied to persons. For these and other reasons Kelly's approach is sometimes said to be more 'psychological' than Osgood's: it was, in fact, specifically designed for clinical use.

Mention may also be made of Stephenson's Q-sort technique (6) in which statements, possibly questionnaire items from standardized inventories, have to be rated according to the degree to which they are characteristic of the subject, usually oneself. All these techniques may be classed as self-report methods. Self-description of a less structured kind was included in the WOSB 'projective battery' (7, 2); since then Semeonoff (5) has attempted some measure of validation, in another context.

References
1. Bannister, D., Personal Construct Theory: a Summary and Experimental Paradigm, *Acta Psychologica*, **20**, 104–20, 1962.
2. Kelly, G. A., The Psychology of Personal Constructs (2 vols.). New York: Norton, 1955.
3. Osgood, C. E., Suci, G. J. and Tannenbaum, P. H. *The Measurement of Meaning*. Urbana, Ill.: University of Illinois Press. 1957.
4. Prince, M., *The Dissociation of a Personality*. New York: Longmans Green, 1906.
5. Semeonoff, B., Self-description as an Instrument in Personality Assessment, *British Journal of Medical Psychology*, **35**, 165–75. 1962.
6. Stephenson, W., *The Study of Behavior: Q-technique and its Methodology*. Chicago: University Press, 1953.

14   C. E. Osgood and Z. Luria

A Blind Analysis of a case of Multiple Personality using the Semantic Differential.

C. E. Osgood and Z. Luria, *Journal of Abnormal and Social Psychology*, 1954, Vol. 49, pp. 579-91.

The Semantic Differential

The semantic differential is a combination of association and scaling procedures designed to give an objective measure of the connotative meaning of concepts. The underlying logic (1) can be summarized as follows: (*a*) The process of description or judgment can be conceived as the allocation of a concept to a set of experimental continua defined by pairs of polar terms. Thus the connotative meaning of a linguistically complex assertion, such as 'My father has always been a rather submissive person', can be at least partially represented as

$$1 \quad 2 \quad 3 \quad 4 \quad 5 \quad 6 \quad 7$$

MY FATHER active—:—:—:—: × :—:—passive
MY FATHER   soft—: × :—:—:—:—:—hard

The greater the strength of association, e.g., '... extremely submissive, a regular doormat', the more polarized, towards 1 or 7, the allocation (2). Since many scales of judgment are highly intercorrelated (e.g., *good–bad*, *fair–unfair*, *honest–dishonest*, *kind–cruel*, and so forth all reflect mainly the single 'evaluative' factor in judgments), a limited number of such continua can be used to define a semantic space within which the connotative meaning of any concept can be specified. This clearly indicates some variant of factor analysis as the basic methodology in developing such an instrument. Two such analyses have been completed, both providing evidence for three general factors, 'evaluation', 'potency', and 'activity', and some unknown number of specific factors that are probably denotative in nature.

The form of semantic differential we have been using in studying psychotherapy is based on this factor analytic work. In the 10 scales used, it gives approximately equal weight to the first three factors isolated. These scales and their factor loadings are given in Table 1. The 15 concepts used in this form of the differential were selected after consultation with clinicians and pretesting for their differentiating power. Ideally, they should sample the major persons and problems involved in therapy-in-general; we are not entirely satisfied with the present set, however, and more work should be done here. The concepts used are also shown in Table 1. In the test form itself, concepts are rotated against scales in such a way that each concept appears once with each scale, but with a maximum interval between successive appearances of both. The subject is instructed to do his checking rapidly, without struggling over particular items, to give his 'immediate impressions'. A 150-item form such as this usually takes less than 10 minutes to complete.

Table 1
Concepts and Scales Used in This Analysis

Concepts		
Love	Mental Sickness	Self-control
Child	My Mother	Hatred
My Doctor	Peace of Mind	My Father
Me	Fraud	Confusion
My Job	My Spouse	Sex

Scales and Their Factor Loadings			
Scales	Evaluation	Activity	Potency
valuable-worthless	·79	·13	·04
clean-dirty	·82	·03	— ·05
tasty-distasteful	·77	— ·11	·05
fast-slow	·01	·70	·00
active-passive	·14	·59	·04
hot-cold	— ·04	·46	— ·06
large-small	·06	·34	·62
strong-weak	·19	·20	·62
deep-shallow	·27	·14	·46
tense-relaxed	— ·55	·37	— ·12

Reordering the raw data for a single subject on a single testing yields a matrix of N columns (here, 15 concepts) and i rows (here, 10 scales). The *meaning* of a particular concept to the subject, as defined by the operations of measurement here, is the profile of numbers in its column (or, more efficiently, the position in the

n-dimensional space defined by the projection of these numbers onto the factors). *Difference in meaning* for two concepts is defined by the distance between their positions in this space, as computed by the generalized distance formula, $D = \sqrt{\Sigma d^2}$, in which d is the difference in allocation of the two concepts on a single scale (2). The more similar any two concepts are in connotative meaning, the smaller will be the value of D. *Change in meaning* (of the same concept at different times during therapy, or in different 'personalities') can be defined by the same operation, except that d here refers to the differences in allocation of the same concept on the same scale at different testings. The mathematical properties of this formula also allow us to represent the *semantic structure* of an individual in a concise form; computation of the distance, D, of every concept from every other concept yields an N/N matrix (here, 15/15) of distances which have the property of plotting within a space having dimensionality equal to the number of factors. To the extent that the individual subject being studied uses the same three factors isolated in our general factor work, his data will plot accurately in three dimensions.

The Semantic Data

At this point we should state exactly what information we have about this case.* We know that we are dealing with a case of triple personality, and these have been labelled for us (presumably by the therapists who collected the semantic data) 'Eve White', 'Eve Black', and 'Jane'. We suppose that the 'White' and 'Black' have some connotative significance – certainly, as will be seen, the quantitative semantic data distinguish sharply between them. We also know, of course, that the patient is a woman, presumably participating in some kind of therapy; we do not know the stage of therapy or whether or not she is hospitalized. We considered it also fair to ask (from J. McV. Hunt) about the following items of sociological status, because they contribute to the meaningful interpretation of certain concepts: Concept CHILD – does this woman have a child? Yes, she does. Concept SPOUSE – is this woman married? Yes, she is. Concepts FATHER and MOTHER – are her parents alive? The mother is, but Hunt doesn't know about the father. Concept MY JOB – has this woman had a job outside of homekeeping? Yes, she has. This is the sum total of our external information about the case.

* The case was originally reported by Thigpen and Cleckley (3), and later described more fully, in book form, by the same authors (4).

The semantic differential was given to this woman twice while 'in' each of her three personalities; a period of about two months intervened between the two testings. The roman numerals I and II refer to first and second testings respectively. Since the form given at each testing was actually a double form (each item repeated once), we were able to estimate the reliability of these data. The immediate test–retest reliability coefficients for each of the testings are as follows: Eve White I, ·82; Eve White II, ·90; Eve Black I, ·65; Eve Black II, ·89; Jane I, ·89; Jane II, ·94. These coefficients indicate (a) a generally satisfactory level of reliability, (b) a consistent trend in all three personalities toward greater stability through time, and (c) that Jane is the most consistent or stable personality over short intervals of time and Eve Black is the least.

To obtain measures of semantic similarity and structure, we computed the matrices of D for each concept with every other concept, for each personality and testing. These 'distances' are based on application of the formula given earlier across all 10 scales. For convenience in plotting the models which appear as Fig. 1–6, the data for scales contributing to each of the three factors were averaged and new D's computed. This, in effect, forces those data into three dimensions and, hence, into solid models that have no error. The very slight amount of distortion, or loss of information, resulting from this averaging process and restriction to three dimensions can be seen from the following correlations between original (10 scale) and 'factor' D matrices (3 average scales): Eve White I, ·91; Eve White II, ·93; Eve Black I, ·96; Eve Black II, ·98; Jane I, ·86; Jane II, ·92. In other words, nearly all of the variance in this woman's judgments can be accounted for in terms of three factors. Figures 1–6, then, provide quite accurate representations of the ways various concepts are related in each of the personalities; the smaller the distance between any two concepts the more similar in connotative meaning they are.

The Three Personalities and Their Changes Through Time

The general assumption we are following is that 'mental illness' is essentially a disordering of meanings or ways of perceiving from those characteristic of people judged 'normal' in our society, and that the process of psychotherapy from the patient's point of view is essentially a reordering and changing of these meanings. Within the limitations of our type of measurement and our sampling of concepts, the locations and relations among concepts shown in

Figs. 1–6 can be thought of as pictures of how this woman perceives herself, the significant people about her, and certain modes of action – when functioning 'in' her several personalities.*

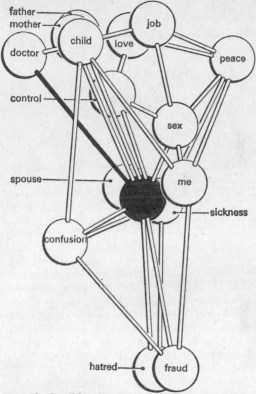

Figure 1 Eve White I

We assume that this woman is receiving some kind of treatment through the period covered by our two samplings, I and II, and therefore look particularly for the types of changes in meaning that are taking place in the three personalities, as well as at the general nature of their organization. For purposes of ready comparison, all of the models are oriented in respect to the

* The authors wish to thank Professor Jozef Cohen for his help in preparing these figures.

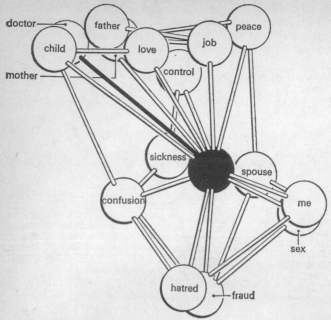

Figure 2 Eve White II

concept MY DOCTOR, which stays practically constant in meaning (*good*, *strong*, and *quite active*) through both time and personalities; spatially, in the figures, *good* is up and *bad* down, *active* to the left and *passive* to the right, and *strong* is away from the viewer; the solid ball represents the origin of the space, e.g., a hypothetical 'meaningless' concept that would result from checking all 4's.

Eve White

Semantic structures for Eve White I and II are shown in Figs. 1 and 2. The most general characterization would be that *Eve White perceives 'the world' in an essentially normal fashion, is well socialized, but has an unsatisfactory attitude towards herself*. Here the usual societal 'goods' are seen favourably – MY DOCTOR, MY FATHER, LOVE, SELF-CONTROL, PEACE OF MIND, and MY MOTHER are all *good* and *strong* whereas FRAUD, HATRED, and to some extent CONFUSION are *bad*. The chief evidence of disturbance in the personality is the fact that ME (the self concept) is considered a little *bad*, a little *passive*, and definitely *weak*. Substantiating evidence is the *weakness* of her CHILD, as she sees him (or her), and the essential meaninglessness to her of MY SPOUSE and SEX. Note also the wide evaluative separation between LOVE and SEX. In the interval between testings I and II ME and SEX become more *bad* and *passive* and simultaneously become almost identical in meaning to her – and note that her conceptions of LOVE (a good, strong thing) and SEX (a bad, weak thing like herself) have moved still further apart.

Eve Black

Semantic structures for Eve Black I and II are shown in Figs. 3 and 4. The most general characterization here would be that *Eve Black has achieved a violent kind of adjustment in which she*

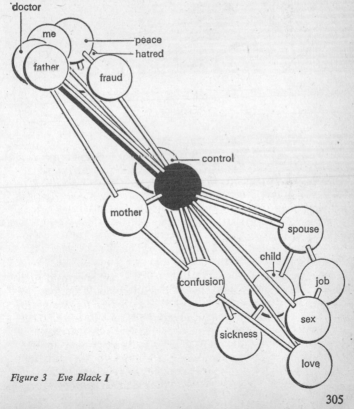

Figure 3 Eve Black I

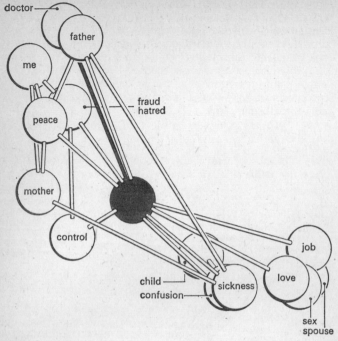

Figure 4 Eve Black II

perceives herself as literally perfect, but, to accomplish this break, her way of perceiving 'the world' becomes completely disoriented from the norm. The only exceptions to this dictum are MY DOCTOR and PEACE OF MIND, which maintain their *good* and *strong* characteristics, the latter, interestingly enough, also becoming *active* on II. But if Eve Black perceives herself as being *good*, then she also has to accept HATRED and FRAUD as positive values, since (we assume) she has strong hatreds and is socially fraudulent. So we find a tight, but very un-normal, favorable cluster of ME, MY DOCTOR, PEACE OF MIND, HATRED, and FRAUD. What are positive values for most people – CHILD, MY SPOUSE, MY JOB, LOVE, and SEX – are completely rejected as *bad* and *passive*, and all of these except CHILD are also *weak* (this may be because CHILD was weak in Eve White and much of the change here is a simple 'flip-flop' of meanings). Note that it is MOTHER in this personality that becomes relatively meaningless; FATHER, on the other hand, stays *good* but shifts completely from *strong* (in Eve White) to *weak* – possible implications of these familial identifications will be considered later. Note also that in this personality LOVE and SEX are closely identified, both as *bad, weak, passive* things.

Jane

Semantic structures for Jane I and II are shown in Figs. 5 and 6. The general characterization is that *Jane displays the most 'healthy' meaning pattern, in which she accepts the usual evaluations of concepts by her society yet still maintains a satisfactory*

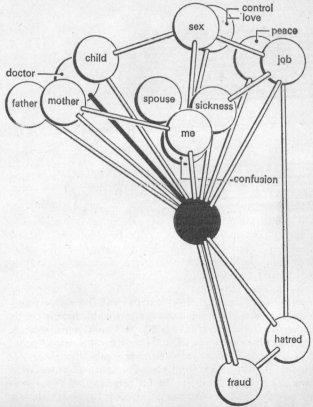

Figure 5 Jane I

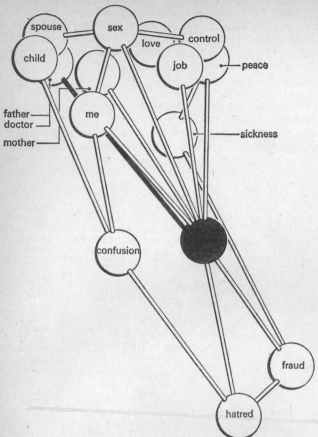

Figure 6   Jane II

evaluation of herself. MY FATHER, MY MOTHER, MY CHILD, and MY DOCTOR – most of the significant persons in her life – are seen as *good, strong,* and *active.* The major modes of behavior, PEACE OF MIND, LOVE, SELF-CONTROL and MY JOB, are seen as equally *good* and *strong,* but *somewhat passive* – as if these ways of behaving and thinking were simply accepted without stress. The two socially agreed-upon evils, HATRED and FRAUD, are put in their proper places. The most significant characteristics of Jane's meaning system, however, are these: The self concept, ME, while still not *strong* (but not *weak*, either) is nearer the *good* and *active* directions of the semantic space; note also the close identification of ME and MENTAL SICKNESS, which here is *not* an unfavorable concept to her. Her attitude towards her husband, MY SPOUSE, is for the first time meaningful (unlike Eve White) and tending toward the *good, strong, active* directions, like the other significant persons (unlike Eve Black). And LOVE and SEX (quite unlike Eve White) are both favorable and quite closely identified. The changes from testings I to II are simply such as to strengthen the 'healthy' pattern evident in the first view. ME becomes considerably more *good* and *active*; MY SPOUSE for the first time becomes completely identified connotatively with MY DOCTOR and MY FATHER (and loses its tie with CONFUSION); and LOVE and SEX become intimately identified with each other and close in meaning to SELF-CONTROL and PEACE OF MIND.

The thumbnail semantic sketches of each personality just given make it intuitively evident that the semantic differential does draw sharp distinctions between the three personalities inhabiting one nervous system. It is possible to demonstrate these distinctions quantitatively by intercorrelating D matrices between personalities and over time. If two of our models are generally similar in structure, such that large and small distances between concepts in one are reflected also in the other, then the r will be high. Table 2 gives these correlations. The first thing to note is that the correlation of each personality with itself (e.g., testings I and II) is regularly much higher than the correlation of that personality with any other personality (with the single exception of Eve White I and Jane I). This is quantitative justification for the

Table 2
Correlations of D-Matrices between Personalities and over Time

	White I	White II	Black I	Black II	Jane I	Jane II
White I	—					
White II	·73	—				
Black I	— ·06	—	—			
Black II	—	— ·02	·86	—		
Jane I	·73	—	— ·26	—	—	
Jane II	—	·53	—	— ·08	·92	—

statement that the semantic differential does differentiate between the several personalities of this woman. Whether it differentiates in a valid way is a matter that can be judged only by relating our analysis to the detailed case history material available elsewhere (3).

Another important thing to note about these correlations is that Eve White and Jane (the two 'socialized' personalities) are fairly highly correlated whereas the correlations of Eve Black with the other two are definitely low, even negative. In other words, Eve Black is clearly the most deviant and disordered personality. Finally, it should be noted that these three personalities differ somewhat in their stability, as indexed by the I/II correlations, Eve White being the least stable and Jane the most.

Changes in Meaning of Specific Concepts

As noted earlier, the meaning of a specific concept is operationally defined as its profile against the differential (e.g., its position in semantic space). Change in meaning between testings I and II can be measured directly by the D between I and II profiles for the same concept. These D values are given under 'Within Personalities, Between Testings' in Table 3. Changes in meaning between personalities for the same concepts can be measured directly by the D between profiles for the same concept but as judged in two different personalities; these D values are given under 'Between Personalities, Within Testings' in Table 3.

Semantic Stability Through Time

In general, although the differences are not great, Eve Black is the least stable personality through time and Jane the most stable (cf., columns 2–4 in Table 3). The concept-by-concept data thus confirm the stability of Jane as shown in the structural data given above. For Eve White the most unstable or labile concepts are CHILD, MY MOTHER, FRAUD, HATRED, MY FATHER, CONFUSION, and SEX. For Eve Black the most labile concepts are LOVE, CHILD, MY JOB, MY MOTHER, MY SPOUSE, MY FATHER, and CONFUSION. For Jane the most unstable notions are ME, MY JOB, MY MOTHER, MY SPOUSE, HATRED, CONFUSION, and SEX. We note that the family constellation – mother, father, spouse, child – tend to be more susceptible to change through time within these personalities, but that the self concept stays relatively constant within personalities (e.g., the location of the self concept, in a sense, defines these three personalities). HATRED, SEX, and CONFUSION also seem to be points of stress.

Semantic Stability Between Personalities

The data given in columns 5–10 in Table 3 make it clear that

Table 3
hanges in Meaning of Specific Concepts

Concept	Within Personalities, Between Testings			Between Personalities, Within Testings					
	$D_{\text{I-II}}$ Eve White	$D_{\text{I-II}}$ Eve Black	$D_{\text{I-II}}$ Jane	$D_{\text{W-B}}$		$D_{\text{W-J}}$		$D_{\text{B-J}}$	
				I	II	I	II	I	II
Love	·42	·67	·23	1·58	1·44	·35	·57	1·62	1·81
Child	·71	·96	·37	1·65	1·40	·68	·54	1·47	1·41
My Doctor	·15	·05	·27	·23	·23	·28	·25	·30	·12
Me	·36	·32	·42	1·21	1·40	*·60*	*·88*	·83	·77
My Job	·27	·62	·42	1·30	1·43	·49	·43	1·19	1·54
Mental Sickness	·45	·45	·19	1·24	1·38	·40	·32	1·30	1·47
My Mother	·54	·78	·46	·71	·78	·66	·23	1·02	·68
Peace of Mind	·40	·35	·41	·86	·66	·21	·?8	·81	61
Fraud	·64	·12	·40	1·46	1·35	·73	·34	1·29	1·22
My Spouse	·30	·62	·47	·67	·96	*·61*	*·89*	1·04	1·75
Self-control	·32	·25	·24	·78	·80	·34	·39	·92	1·01
Hatred	·51	·19	·44	1·54	1·31	·51	·23	1·37	1·19
My Father	·53	·71	·09	1·06	·60	·25	·43	1·06	·43
Confusion	·64	·67	·44	·86	·96	·71	·42	·98	·88
Sex	·62	·34	·47	1·10	·62	*·63*	*1·20*	1·45	1·76

Note — Numbers in Italics indicate concepts that serve best to characterize differences between Eve White and Jane.

concept meanings in general shift more between Eve Black and the other two than between Jane and Eve White, this again substantiating the over-all correlations between total structures. The only concept that remains strictly constant in meaning through the personality changes in this woman is MY DOCTOR, although PEACE OF MIND and CONFUSION show greater stability than most others. It is interesting to note which concepts serve best to characterize the differences between Eve White and Jane (Eve Black shows gross differences on almost all concepts). These two 'socialized' personalities differ from one another chiefly on ME, MY SPOUSE, and SEX, and these differences are increasing in magnitude through time. This clearly suggests this woman's sexual life as a core problem, Eve White being highly critical of all three concepts and Jane accepting them as positive values. It is also interesting to note in this connexion that semantic differences between Eve White and Jane on CHILD, MY MOTHER, FRAUD, HATRED, and CONFUSION are decreasing through time.

Interpretations of These Semantic Data

The analyses of these personalities and their changes given so far have been descriptive rather than interpretive for the most part. In a sense, we have merely put into words what this woman herself, in her several personalities, has indicated by her check marks. The treatment of semantic differential data, from the patterns of check marks to construction of the models shown in Figs. 1–6, is completely objective, and any investigator starting from the same data and following the rules would have to end up with the same pictures we have.

Making interpretations and predictions about this case on a 'blind' basis is another matter entirely. In this section we go far beyond the objective data, and we are consequently much less confident about our statements. For one thing, neither of the writers is an experienced clinician – certainly not experienced with respect to the dynamics and characteristics of multiple personality. For another thing, we do not know at what stage in therapy our two testings were made, and interpretation would certainly vary greatly in terms of such information. It should also be pointed out that in the ordinary use of the semantic differential as a clinical tool (as compared with a blind analysis) many other sources of information would be available to support certain alternative interpretations and render others farcical. Let it be understood, then, that what follows is a flight into conjecture, in contrast with the preceding, factual reporting of semantic data.

Interpretive Descriptions of the Three Personalities

Eve White is the woman who is simultaneously most in contact with social reality and under the greatest emotional stress. She is aware of both the demands of society and her own inadequacies in meeting them. She sees herself as a passive weakling and is also consciously aware of the discord in her sexual life, drawing increasingly sharp distinctions between LOVE as an idealized notion and SEX as a crude reality. She maintains the greatest diversity among the meanings of various concepts. She is concerned and ambivalent about her CHILD, but apparently is *not* aware of her own ambivalent attitudes towards her MOTHER – and seems to become more resistant to this by testing II. Those psychoanalytically inclined may wish to identify Eve White with dominance of the *superego*: certainly, the superego seems to view the world through the eyes of Eve White, accepting the mores or values of others (particularly her mother) but continuously criticizing and punishing herself. If this case came to the psychotherapists with a voluntary, self-initiated plea for help, then it seems likely that Eve White was dominant at the time.

Eve Black is clearly the most out of contact with social reality and simultaneously the most self-assured. To rhapsodize, Eve Black finds PEACE OF MIND through close identification with a God-like therapist (MY DOCTOR, probably a father symbol for her), accepting her HATRED and FRAUD as perfectly legitimate aspects of the God-like role. Naturally, she sees herself as a dominant, active wonder-woman and is in no way self-critical. She is probably unaware of her family situation. Those psychoanalytically inclined could say that the *id* looks out at the world through the eyes of Eve Black. Like a completely selfish infant, this personality is entirely oriented around the assumption of its own perfection. Actually, Eve Black seems to be more harmonious with the Adlerian than with the Freudian model, since personal perfection is apparently the demand acceded to rather than sexuality. If the case was committed to an institution, it seems likely that this personality was the reason for commitment.

Jane is the most puzzling of the three personalities, and our interpretation will have to depend upon assumptions about the stage of treatment (see below). Superficially, Jane is a very healthy personality: 'all's well with the world, and day by day I'm getting better and better'. Thus we find all the people in her life perceived as *good* and *strong* and *active* and all the socially approved modes of action perceived as *good* and *strong* and *passive*; SEX is LOVE-ly, her SPOUSE is becoming more like the noble DOCTOR all the time, and she is coming to perceive herself even, as a pleasant and reasonably active (if somewhat weak and submissive) person. But all this is a little too rosy, a little too pat. We note that Jane is becoming more and more 'simple-minded' – all of her judgments tending to fall along a single factor of *good–strong* vs. *bad–weak* – which makes the Jane II model the most restricted and undiversified of all. Those psychoanalytically inclined may wish to view this personality as representing dominance of a self-deceptive *ego* which has woven a web of repression as to the state of reality; or, they may wish to view Jane as an essentially strong, healthy, and improving ego-dominated personality. In any case, we doubt if Jane would have either come for therapy or have been institutionalized – as such.

Possible Dynamisms Operating in the Case

Identification mechanisms. We say the patient 'identifies' with some other person when her meaning of herself, ME, is semantically close to her meaning of the other person; e.g., if she sees her father as a kind, active, relaxed, etc. person and describes herself in the same terms, we infer identification. However, the pattern of identifications displayed by this patient seems unusual. Only in Eve Black, the obviously disoriented personality in terms of her values, is there clear differential identification – with her FATHER (and this may reflect the semantic tie-up between FATHER and MY DOCTOR). Jane shows some slight tendency towards closer identification with MOTHER, but it is not close. Eve White shows none with either parent. The fact that identification with FATHER (and MY DOCTOR) in Eve Black is accompanied by rejection of MOTHER to meaninglessness is suggestive of an underlying conflict in identifications. Note also, in this connexion, that in Eve Black I the ascendancy of ME to the *good, strong, active* position is accompanied by making FATHER weak – as if she were taking over her father's role and putting her mother in her own previous place. And, interestingly enough, the concept SELF-CONTROL suffers the same fate as MOTHER. This picture of Eve Black is certainly suggestive of an *Electra complex* as the underlying dynamism. In 'real' life, her MOTHER is or was the dominant, threatening figure – moralizing, demanding standards and SELF-CONTROL – and in Eve Black this woman escapes the pressure by rendering both MOTHER and SELF-CONTROL meaningless and simultaneously identifying with and taking her FATHER's place (via the therapist). Thus, the raw data (not reproduced here) shows that MOTHER is consistently *colder* than FATHER and usually more *tense* and *fast* (e.g., Factor 3). Identification of the self with the therapist in Eve Black is perfect, of course. The concept MY DOCTOR is the only personal concept to show perfect stability both between personalities and through time. The patient thus displays what might be called maximal *positive transference* in all three personalities; there is no sign of any negative transference at either testing, which may be indicative of the stage of therapy (e.g., early).

Significance of the patient's sexual life. Although Jane shows a rosy acceptance of normal sexual patterning – with LOVE and SEX linked and passively favorable, Eve White clearly displays awareness of a basic conflict in this area – SEX is clearly somewhat more distasteful than LOVE and becomes distinctly distasteful and dirty by testing II. In Eve White also we find ME and MY SPOUSE becoming linked with SEX in this unpleasant location. Eve Black, on the other hand, rejects both SEX and LOVE – but closely links them in her thinking. If we were to relate these facts with the Electra situation described above, the interpretation would be that her persisting conflict with her mother and attempts to identify with her father make it impossible for her to experience normal sexual satisfactions with her husband and to carry out the normal mother-wife-home role. Eve White is aware of this, in a sense, but Jane clearly is not. The concept MY JOB is interesting in this connexion: its persistent linkages with LOVE, PEACE OF MIND, and SELF-CONTROL in the two 'socialized' personalities, coupled with its linkage with SEX and MY SPOUSE in Eve Black, clearly suggests to us that this woman is interpreting MY JOB in the sense of 'my job as a mother, wife, and homebuilder' rather than in terms of her outside work (which we understand she has). In any case, there is clear evidence of involvement with her sex life as a major problem, and this may have been the presenting problem when she began therapy.

Repression and amnesia. Knowing that we are dealing with a case of multiple personality – usually characterized by complete dissociation between states – it is interesting to speculate on what meanings are repressed in the several personalities. It will be recalled that, operationally, meaninglessness of a concept is defined by its closeness to the origin (the solid balls in the models). This is probably to be interpreted as 'connotative deadness' or 'damping of affect' with respect to the concept involved. Within the matrix of our instrument, however, there is another way in which repression or amnesia may show up, and that is via a complete shift in meaning of the concept being judged (e.g., CHILD may shift from the personal reference of 'my own youngster' to 'children-in-general'). Looking back at the semantic data with these points in mind, we hazard the following guesses: Eve White probably has the best contact with reality and may not be amnesic at all (except for the other personalities); Eve Black may be amnesic for her mother and her own role as a mother and wife; Jane in Pollyanna fashion may be amnesic for her own problems, e.g., MENTAL SICKNESS and CONFUSION, and the indiscriminate way in which she lumps all socially favorable concepts at least suggests that she is judging CHILD, MOTHER, etc. in the abstract rather than as MY CHILD, MY MOTHER, and so forth.

Interpretation I – Assumed Early Stage of Therapy

The 'original' personality, in the sense of being most characteristic of the woman her friends and relations knew, was Jane. The first testing of this personality shows a relatively weak ME that is associated with MENTAL SICKNESS; i.e., she was dimly aware of her own inadequacies but was striving to maintain a rigid acceptance of the real world and maintain an adequate home life. The people about her, with the exception of her husband, were seen as strong and active (perhaps threatening) in relation to herself, and her love life was regarded as a sort of deliberate, controlled duty. She was completely unaware of her (repressed) emotional ambivalence toward her mother, husband, and child. The things being hidden in this personality, and providing the force behind the eventual split, were (*a*) her Electra complex, (*b*) her repugnance for sexual relations with her husband, and (*c*) her ambivalent attitude towards herself. We suspect that she had a position in society that demanded 'good front'.

We must assume strong and about equal pressures toward solving the Electra complex, (*a*) by identifying with FATHER and asserting the self (id?), and (*b*) toward solving it by identifying with MOTHER and devaluing herself (superego?). This produces a two-way split away from the Jane pattern, one into Eve Black where selfish needs for superiority and playing the father role are achieved and another into Eve White where societal needs for submission and playing the mother role are achieved. This split, and the subsequent availability of the other roles, allows Jane to shift toward the 'sweetness and light' view of the world, and this is clearly demonstrated by the changes between Jane I and Jane II. Eve White continues to become more simply and rigidly self-critical and Eve Black continues to become more simply and rigidly self-satisfied.

Assuming successful therapy is possible – which seems questionable – it will involve less and less time being spent in being Jane and Eve Black and a consequent shift into Eve White, where better contact and differentiation seems to be maintained. But here it will be necessary to bring Eve White to understand the reason for her depression, the role of her ambivalence towards her mother in her problem – which shows no signs of happening yet – and thence a gradual restructuring in which ME becomes more favorable, along with SPOUSE and SEX, and identifications with FATHER and MOTHER are reassigned. This will probably involve a period of negative transference, with MY DOCTOR and MOTHER becoming closely identified and being temporarily shifted to *bad*, *strong*, and *active* directions of the semantic space. In other words, successful treatment will mean increasing time spent in, and a gradual restructuring of, Eve White to the point where it incorporates what is now Jane, but with a realignment of significant persons. On the other hand, if this woman is in a mental institution and remains there, it seems likely that Eve Black will become the dominant house she lives in. In either case, it is probable that Jane will appear less and less.

Interpretation II – Assumed Late Stage of Therapy

If we assume that we are seeing the terminal stages of therapy with a case of this sort, then a quite different interpretation is necessary. The difference in interpretations hinges upon Jane, either as a deceptive and vanishing original personality (interpretation I) or as an increasingly healthy and augmenting personality (interpretation II). In the latter case we would assume that Eve White had been the 'original' personality as people knew her – a socially acceptable wife and mother, but one laden with conflicts, anxieties, and self-criticism. The split in this case – into one personality in which the self-criticism completely disappears via irrationality (Eve Black) and another in which self-criticism vanishes via rationality (Jane) – seems less sensible, however. Jane seems unnecessary at this stage and really should have developed out of Eve White rather than being contemporaneous. If we assume there was a split in any case, Jane is clearly the most healthy personality, since LOVE and SEX are identified, the world is viewed in acceptable fashion, and the self concept is becoming more favorable all the time. The prediction here would be increasing time spent in Jane and less in the others. The stumbling blocks in the way of this interpretation are (*a*) the lack of any realignment of the system of parental identifications, and (*b*) the fact that Jane is becoming *less* diversified semantically (more 'simple-minded') rather than the reverse. This second interpretation was actually the one we first adopted – because of the superficial 'healthiness' of Jane – but consideration of all the evidence seems to favor the first interpretation. However, it should be noted that *if* this case is near the end of successful therapy, Jane is the only personality that combines both a normal view of the world and reasonable (increasing) acceptance of the self.

Interpretation III – Combination of I and II

It is possible to combine interpretations I and II by assuming that Jane is both the original personality which broke apart and the terminal personality which is being developed out of therapy. In this case, the early development of the case, probably in childhood, would be the same as that given under interpretation I – the conflicting parental identifications (id and superego determined respectively) were of about equal strength and finally became too intense to be contained within the self-deceptive personality organization of Jane. During the middle course of the case, when therapy was undertaken, we thus find all three personalities oscillating, temporary dominance of the mother and wife role being represented by Eve White, temporary dominance of the self-gratifying father role being represented by Eve Black, and temporary dominance of the face-saving, problem-solving ego being represented by Jane. Intentionally or unintentionally, the effect of therapy may be to strengthen the self-deceptive organization of Jane without resolving the underlying conflicts dramatized by Eve White and Eve Black. The over-simplified, Pollyanna-like ways of perceiving herself as *good* along with all the other significant persons in her life yields a superficially happy person who views the world in an acceptable, if rigidly stereotyped, fashion. If the present combined interpretation approximates the actual situation, then we feel compelled to predict another breakdown at some later period in this person's life. In other words, the effect of therapy (whatever type it may have been) seems to have been further to strengthen the self-deceptive original organization of Jane, while making this personality even more rigid and insensitive to subtle differences in meaning and without resolving the underlying conflicts which created the original disturbance.

What Price Therapy?

It is impossible to tell from our semantic data whether the increasing simplification in structure characteristic of all three personalities is due to therapy itself or is happening despite therapy. However, a number of specialists in psychotherapy have from time to time expressed concern over the 'hidden' effects of therapy even in so-called successful cases – particularly reduction in initiative, creativeness, and flexibility of the patient. Certainly in the present case we are witnessing an over-all reduction in differentiation of meanings. If overt behavior is in considerable part determined by meanings, as we believe it is, then we must expect Jane (if she is the terminal personality) to be now even less capable of behaving differentially to her mother, father, spouse, and child – they are all essentially undifferentiated 'strong-active-goodness' to her. This would also be true, but to a lesser extent, of Eve White, although here we would assume an earlier stage of therapy and hence a possibility of secondary elaboration of semantic diversity under sensitive therapy.

Is rigidity of this sort a necessary price of therapy? In striving to achieve the goals of societal acceptability and individual happiness, does the therapist have to sacrifice the richness, individuality, and subtler adjustiveness of the patient? These are serious questions raised by the data of this single case – but not answered by them, of course. From the larger sample of cases we are presently working on, better answers may be forthcoming, but the cases are generally less severe. One other interesting phenomenon in the present cases should be mentioned: Despite the gross changes in meaning of concepts in the several personalities, and the over-all reduction in diversity, the semantic judgmental frame of reference remains constant. In other words, all three of the personalities in this woman utilize semantic scales in the same ways – the correlations between scales are the same for all three personalities and reduction in diversity in all of them is accomplished by a coalescence of *good*, *strong*, and *active* into a single evaluative dimension. Thus it would appear that the level of scale meanings is below that at which concepts vary, and common to all three personalities.

References
1. Osgood, C. E. The nature and measurement of meaning. *Psychol. Bull.*, 1952, **49**, 192–237.
2. Osgood, C. E. and Suci, G. J. A measure of relation determined by both mean difference and profile information. *Psychol. Bull.*, 1952, **49**, 251–62.
3. Thigpen, C. H. and Cleckley, H. A. A case of multiple personality. *J. abnorm. soc. Psychol.*, 1954, **49**, 135–51.
4. Thigpen, C. H. and Cleckley, H. A. *The Three Faces of Eve.* London: Secker & Warburg. 1957.

PERSONALITY STRUCTURE: THE LARGER DIMENSIONS

As Professor Mace explains in his editorial Foreword to the Pelican Original from which this chapter has been reprinted, Dr Cattell is a British psychologist, working in the United States, who stands in the direct succession, through Spearman, of the work of Galton and Karl Pearson (7, 9).

It is difficult to isolate any part of Cattell's teaching for separate presentation, since his writing is closely reasoned but with an interlocking of parts which necessitates a good deal of cross reference. The present extract has been chosen because it relates the author's basic position to its historical background, and makes reference to the principal instruments of personality measurement which have been developed on the basis of the research carried out in Cattell's laboratory. Particulars of the current editions of the tests referred to on pp. 336 and 339 are as follows:

Cattell, R. B. and Eber, H. W., *The 16 Personality Factor Test and Handbook*, 3rd edition, 1963.

Porter, R. B., Cattell, R. B., and Schaie, H. W., *The Child Personality Questionnaire and Handbook*, 2nd edition, 1966.

Cattell, R. B. and Nuttall, R. L., *The High School Personality Questionnaire*, 2nd edition, 1966.

– all published by the Institute for Personality and Ability Testing, 1602 Coronado Drive, Champaign, Illinois.

Numerous articles have been published by Cattell and his co-workers on the development of these tests and their applications. Two of the most important are listed below (1, 2), along with a more general statement in book form (3).

The distinction between source traits and surface traits, briefly dealt with in the present article, is an important one, and has been developed mainly by Cattell. Surface traits are, almost by definition, of less interest to psychologists than source traits, although they are more easily identifiable. Cattell uses the terms 'source trait' and 'factor' or 'dimension' almost interchangeably, but the first is perhaps the best term, since it suggests that it refers to something not directly observable. For the same reason he prefers to coin neologisms as labels for his traits or factors.

Omitted in the present reprint is a short passage explaining how a correlation coefficient is calculated. The principles of factor analysis, basic to this paper and the next, are variously treated by different authors; Cattell himself, in the work quoted, recommends Thomson's account (4).

References
1. Cattell, R. B., 'The main personality factors in questionnaire, self-estimate material', *J. Social Psychol.*, 31, 3–38, 1950.
2. Cattell, R. B., 'Validation and intensification of the Sixteen Personality Factor Questionnaire', *J. Clinical Psychol.*, 12, 205–14, 1956.
3. Cattell, R. B., *Personality and Motivation Structure and Measurement.* New York: Harcourt, Brace and World, London: Harrap, 1957, 1958.
4. Thomson, G. H., *The Factorial Analysis of Human Ability.* London: University of London Press, 1951.

15 R. B. Cattell

Personality Structure: the Larger Dimensions

R. B. Cattell, *The Scientific Analysis of Personality*, Penguin, Harmondsworth, 1965, pp. 53–75.

The Use of Types and Traits in Describing Personality

[. . . .] Every science has had to develop through a stage of accurate measurement, of ability to describe the dimensions of an event. Psychology is also somewhat belatedly developing its taxonomic (classificatory) and descriptive technique. To get some 'practical' psychologists and psychiatrists to face the difficult theoretical issues of measurement, it has been necessary to reiterate that dependable laws about how personality grows, changes, and operates are to be found only after we can accurately refer to this 'given personality at a given moment'. Similarly, we are able to see the dynamic movement of people in a movie film only because the instantaneous 'frames' which rush through at sixteen a second are themselves each descriptively exact.

As a first approximation to description, we may accept the concept of 'traits' as popularly understood. The novelist, for example, uses nouns to indicate particular traits, and then becomes implicitly quantitative by introducing adjectives to indicate more or less of each trait. In this implicit quantifying, fortunately for his peace of mind, he does not have to 'test' his measurements, for he can, and frequently does, make his characters do impossibly inconsistent things – even in the most valued literature. The literary tradition of personality description also uses types, as when Hamlet calls his uncle a villain. What is a villain? He, and every other type, is a *whole pattern of traits* which are uniquely combined and which are seen to repeat themselves often enough to justify the utility of a label.

Description by trait and description by type are therefore not opposed systems. Traits are conceived through abstracting from experience of many types, as the colour brown is abstracted from our experience of many diverse brown objects. Reciprocally, types can be and must be fixed in terms of traits, as when we describe an 'adolescent type' as having unusual enthusiasm, naïveté, impulsiveness, altruism, shyness, etc. The description of personality has long made use of types. For example, as early as the reign of Edward I in England a distinction was made between the 'born fool' and the lunatic who 'by grief or other cause hath lost his reason'. Psychologists and psychiatrists have oscillated in their techniques between use of traits and use of types. For example, at one time psychiatrists were satisfied if they could pigeon-hole any given patient under a type rubric such as an hysteric, a manic depressive, a schizophrenic, etc. But later they had doubts, consequent upon disagreements between one hospital and another (about one quarter of one psychiatrist's classifications are changed by the next). Obviously, there are intermediate cases, and although intermediates can be handled by types ('He is three quarters fool and one quarter rascal'), they can be more easily handled by traits, duly quantified.

Indeed, the term type, at least in the precise notion of 'species type' (as in the distinct species of animals) also implies *discontinuity*. There is nothing – if we set aside the myth of centaurs – existing half-way between a man and a horse. But types are not particularly apt for most personality description because the great majority of human traits appear to be continuous. In intelligence, for example, our population represents every gradation from the level of genius to that of idiocy. For this and other reasons the basic techniques for description and measurement of personality have developed more around *trait* concepts. Types, where they exist, have later been defined as *patterns of trait measures*, any one such type being singled out because it occurs in our populations with some peculiar, useful frequency.

The Invention of Correlation and Factor Analysis

However, the trouble with measuring traits is that there are too many of them! Allport and Odbert (1936), at Harvard, searched the dictionary and found over 3,000 trait words for describing personality. The tendency in the past has been for a psychologist to fancy some particular trait, such as 'authoritarianism', 'extraversion', 'flexibility-*vs*-rigidity', 'intolerance of ambiguity', etc., and to concentrate on its relations to all kinds of things. Even such devotion or addiction does not solve the problem. Thousands of traits are still neglected and the prejudices and preferences of individual psychologists lead to a system which tries to handle at least as many traits as there are psychologists! For example, when Scheier and the present writer began their researches on anxiety they found over 400 published researches on anxiety. The studies showed almost as many different shades of meaning and ways of measuring it, so that the studies could not be integrated. What a tower of Babel would arise in chemistry if every chemist had a different test for the presence of, say, chlorine, and, indeed, no really common conception of what chlorine is!

The answer to this problem, though it has technical complications which are still not fully straightened out by many of its users, is in the statistical method of *factor analysis*. Prior to factor analysis some psychologists reached such a stage of desperation that they were ready to fix traits if necessary by fiat, by setting up a commission to say what the important traits are and how they should be defined. Factor analysis, on the other hand, believes that there are natural, unitary structures in personality and that it is these traits, rather than the endless labels in the dictionary, on which we should concentrate. In other words, if there are natural elements in the form of functional unities, logically equivalent to an element in the physical world, then it would be far better to begin our studies – our comparisons and developmental understandings – on measures of such traits.

The problem which baffled psychologists for many years was to find a method which would tease out these functionally unitary influences in the chaotic jungle of human behaviour. But let us ask how, in the literal tropical jungle, the hunter decides whether the dark blobs which he sees are two or three rotting logs or a single alligator? He watches for movement. If they move together – come and disappear together – he infers a single structure. Just so, as John Stuart Mill pointed out in his philosophy of science, the scientist should look for 'concomitant variation' in seeking unitary concepts.

When it came to putting this philosophical notion into practice, psychologists were for a while baffled, until the statisticians came to their help. For it is rare for two manifestations literally to go together *every* time they are observed. They become 'by chance or nature's changing course untrimmed'. How *much* observed going together does there have to be for us to conclude that, but for other interfering circumstances, these two (or more) behavioural manifestations would always constitute a single trait?

The answer to this appeared in the form of the correlation coefficient, which Sir Francis Galton conceived when he was sheltering, on his daily walk, from a passing shower. The English statistician Pearson and the French mathematician Bravais polished it up, and it became known as the Bravais-Pearson correlation coefficient. [. . . .]

From the basic correlation coefficient the beginnings of factor analysis were developed by Charles Spearman, reader and professor in psychology at the University of London between 1907

	a	b	c	d	e	f	g
a		+·7	+·8	+·8	−·1	·0	·0
b			+·9	+·7	·1	·2	·0
c				+·8	−·2	−·1	−·1
d					·0	−·1	·2
e						·6	·7
f							·7
g							

Figure 1. *Correlation matrix*

The lower left would, of course, be an image of the upper right and is not entered.

By adding together the scores on a, b, c, and d, we could get an estimate of the underlying source trait X, and similarly, but not quite so reliably, of Y from e, f, and g.

Trait X covers a, b, c, and d.

Trait Y covers e, f, and g.

and 1931. From his interest in giving a better basis to the I.Q. he asked, 'Is intelligence a single power or a collection of several independent powers, that is, is it a unitary trait?' Instead of taking behavioural measures two at a time, as had hitherto been done with the correlation coefficient, he took a very large number of supposed manifestations of mental ability and intercorrelated them in every possible way, in a correlation matrix as in Fig. 1.

Here it will be seen that manifestations *a*, *b*, *c*, and *d* 'go together' in every possible way, having substantial correlations (above 0·7) of *a* with *b*, *b* with *c*, *a* with *c*, etc. They make a single functional unity. Similarly, *e*, *f*, and *g* go together in a single cluster, but *e*, *f*, and *g* are practically uncorrelated (no connexion being above 0·2) with *a*, *b*, *c*, and *d*. Thus among these seven behaviours we can say there are really only two underlying functional unities, which we can call *X* and *Y*. A matrix is thus a condensed means of showing all the possible relations among a set of behaviour – or, for that matter, any other kinds of measurement made over a sample of cases or occasions.

Factor analysis is actually a very complex mathematical technique, and goes beyond the mere recognition of clusters as in the above example, but this shows its essence. The factor X is said to 'load' a, b, c, and d, and Y to load e, f, and g. From the nature of these loadings we can begin to infer what the underlying influences X and Y really are. Conversely, if we know how much of X or Y a person has, we can make an estimate from the loadings of what a, b, c, etc., would be. Thus, from the above, approximately:

$$c_i = 0 \cdot 9 X_i$$

where c^i is the standard score of individual $_i$ on behaviour c, and X_i is his endowment in the factor trait X.

For example, Spearman found that a factor which covered most 'intelligent' performances (and, therefore, constituted some kind of general ability) loaded most highly such tasks as completing verbal analogies, perceiving the nature of arithmetical series, and so on. From this he concluded that intelligence is the 'capacity to perceive relationships' and he was able to make up tests which measured this particular X factor with increasing reliability and validity. No longer was there any excuse for different intelligence test constructors to make up arbitrary definitions or to disagree about the relative validity of different kinds. For on factoring a lot of ability measures, all investigators would finish with the same general factor and the relative loading or correlation of any two competing tests with this general capacity could be found experimentally. Thurstone (1887–1940), an American psychologist who independently made great contributions to factor analysis, entering ability research with more specific, 'narrow' measures, showed several 'primary abilities' were also involved, such as numerical, spatial, verbal, and logical abilities. But these were only, as it were, 'branches' of the truly general intelligence factor underlying all of them. (The terms 'first order' and 'second order' factor will later be used in our account to describe this kind of narrower and broader factor relation.)

Factor analysis was extensively applied to clearing up the structure of human abilities from 1905 onwards, but it was not until about 1930 that any very systematic application began with respect to personality structure. People were at first much too easily satisfied with clinical guesses about structure, or their own colourful intuitions, to feel the need for the more objective methods which ultimately had to come. Indeed, only as insoluble differences of opinion arose among these confident clinical assertions did it become evident that scientific psychology had to use trait concepts different from those long used in popular, literary, or clinical naming.

The Three Data Bases of Psychometry

To get correlations we have to start with measures of the two things that have to be correlated (or the many that enter a correlation matrix). Some people object to the idea that the mind can be measured, and we have replied that whatever exists must exist in some degree. Nevertheless, the demonstrating of this degree and the development of principles for measuring traits can become extremely complex. Indeed, a whole science has grown up, as a special branch of psychology, called *psychometry*.

The psychometrist of personality, if he is to get an unbiased picture of the whole, must have some concept of the totality of human behaviour, which we shall call the *personality sphere*. This may be roughly defined as what people do over a sample twenty-four-hour period, and it will vary somewhat with different ages and culture. Such behaviour we can observe and record broadly in three ways: (1) By ratings made by observers on the frequency and intensity with which specific kinds of behaviour occur in the people they observe. (2) By questionnaires which are answered by the person himself, from his own self-observation and introspection. (3) By *objective* tests, i.e., miniature situations set up for a person to react to, in which he does not really know on what aspect of his behaviour he is being scored (hence 'objective').

Technically the first is called '*L*-data' or 'life-record' because it deals with behaviour in the actual, everyday-life situation. Ideally it would include behaviour which can be scored without employing the intervening judgement of a rater, and such specific behaviours can be found, for example, in 'number of automobile accidents over twenty years', 'frequency of engagements', 'number of societies to which the person belongs', 'marks in school', and so on. However, such 'hard data' is difficult to get and the psychologist commonly takes his life-record data 'second-hand' in the form of a rating by someone who knows the person well. Thus a person may be rated on a 1 to 10 scale by two or three observers on such trait elements as 'sociability in school', 'emotional stability on the playing field', 'conscientiousness in performing duties', and so on, with reliabilities we shall discuss later.

The second source of data for personality calculations – that offered by questionnaires – has been called *Q*-data. Information offered in the medical, psychiatric consulting-room has essentially the same properties. It depends on introspection and is liable to distortion by imperfect self-knowledge, delusions about the self, or an intention deliberately to 'fake'. Although a questionnaire looks like a simple series of questions to which a person underlines a brief answer, such as 'yes', 'no', 'generally', etc., actually a great deal of art enters into the psychologist's choice of words, the direction of the question, the use of adjectives to ensure that all alternatives are well used, and so on. [. . . .]

The third type of evidence used for getting at personality structure lies in *objective tests*, called *T*-data for short. Occasionally questionnaires are called objective by teachers who are used to the essay type of examination, but the only thing objective about them is the scoring. That is to say, the scoring is done by a key, not by the subjective judgement of the psychologist. This degree of dependability in scoring is possible only if the tests have what is called 'closed end', or multiple choice answers, i.e. given answers between which the subject chooses. If he were free to *write down* any answer he liked in an open-ended or inventive answer test, obviously different psychologists would be likely to score each response differently. The multiple choice questionnaire type of test is better called *conspective* than *objective*. Conspective means 'seeing together', since two examiners are guaranteed to see the same answer and assign the same score when they have a key and a selective rather than inventive answer form. By contrast, the objective test in the sense of a behavioural miniature situation is truly objective, in that the subject is not being asked to evaluate himself, but is simply behaving in a standard situation, and his behaviour is being objectively observed and measured. [. . . .]

Personality Factor A:
The Cyclothyme–Sizothyme Temperament Dimension

[. . . .] If one takes two or three hundred young men or women and arranges for them to be rated by people who know them well, on each of, say, sixty different trait elements, such as the ten shown in Table 1 below, a basis is obtained for calculating a correlation matrix, as shown in Fig. 1. [. . . .]

When such a set (matrix) of correlations (covering the whole personality sphere, by perhaps fifty bipolar elements, not just a sample ten as in Table 1) is factor analysed, the result is usually that one gets evidence that between twelve and twenty independent factors or source influences must be at work. Furthermore, one gets recognizably the same factors from repeating the process at different age levels, except that a few of the differentiating dimensions which exist at the adult level are found not to have much

329

Table 1
List of ten rating traits

1. *Adaptable:* flexible; accepts changes of plan easily; satisfied with compromises; is not upset, surprised, baffled, or irritated if things are different from what he expected. *vs* *Rigid:* insists that things be done the way he has always done them; does not adapt his habits and ways of thinking to those of the group; nonplussed if his routine is upset.

2. *Emotional:* excitable; cries a lot (children), laughs a lot, shows affection, anger, all emotions, to excess. *vs* *Calm:* stable, shows few signs of emotional excitement of any kind; remains calm, even underreacts, in dispute, danger, social hilarity, etc.

3. *Conscientious:* honest; knows what is right and generally does it, even if no one is watching him; does not tell lies or attempt to deceive others; respects others' property. *vs* *Unconscientious:* somewhat unscrupulous; not too careful about standards of right and wrong where personal desires are concerned; tells lies and is given to little deceits; does not respect others' property.

4. *Conventional:* conforms to accepted standards, ways of acting, thinking, dressing, etc.; does the 'proper' thing; seems distressed if he finds he is being different. *vs* *Unconventional, eccentric:* acts differently from others: not concerned about wearing the same clothes or doing the same things as others; has somewhat eccentric interests, attitudes, and ways of behaving; goes his own rather peculiar way.

5. *Prone to jealousy:* begrudges the achievement of others; upset when others get attention, and demands more for himself; resentful when attention is given to others. *vs* *Not jealous:* likes people even if they do better than he does; is not upset when others get attention, but joins in praise.

6. *Considerate, polite:* deferential to needs of others; considers others' feelings; allows them before him in line, gives them the biggest share, etc. *vs* *Inconsiderate, rude:* insolent, defiant, and 'saucy' to elders (in children); ignores feelings of others; gives impression that he goes out of his way to be rude.

Table 1 (*contd*)
List of ten rating traits

---

7. *Quitting:* gives up before he has *vs* *Determined, persevering:* sees a job through in spite of difficulties or temptations; strong-willed; painstaking and thorough; sticks at anything until he achieves his goal.
   thoroughly finished a job; slipshod; works in fits and starts; easily distracted, led away from main purposes by stray impulses or external difficulties.

8. *Tender:* governed by sentiment; *vs* *Tough, hard:* governed by fact and necessity rather than sentiment; unsympathetic; does not mind upsetting others if that is what has to be done.
   intuitive, empathetic, sympathetic; sensitive to the feelings of others; cannot do things if they offend his feelings.

9. *Self-effacing:* blames himself *vs* *Egotistical:* blames others whenever there is conflict or things go wrong; often brags; quick to take credit when things go right; has a very good opinion of himself.
   (or nobody) if things go wrong; reluctant to take credit for achievements; does not seem to think of himself as very important or worthwhile.

10. *Languid, fatigued, slow:* lacks *vs* *Energetic, alert, active:* quick, forceful, active, decisive, full of pep, vigorous, spirited.
    vigour; vague and slow in speech; dawdles, is slow in getting things done.

---

contribution at earlier levels. Since it is most desirable to look at these new patterns without prejudice from earlier clinical notions or traditional popular terms, the first investigators in the 1930s and 1940s decided simply to symbolize the dimensions by letters of the alphabet. The investigators of vitamins did just the same, in a parallel situation, where the entities could be identified and partially described for some years by their *effects* before truly interpretive chemical labels could be attached to them. In the present area the letter *A* was given to the factor of greatest contribution to the totality of individual differences (the 'variance' of all ratings) and so down the alphabet to smaller factors.

As it happened, the largest factor turned out to be a dimension for differentiating individuals which had already been recognized as very important by the German psychiatrists Kraepelin and Kretschmer, and the Swiss, Bleuler, in their studies of mental hospital cases half a century earlier. Kraepelin first defined *dementia praecox* (now called schizophrenia) as a special 'withdrawn' pattern of behaviour. Following this Bleuler had pointed out that functional insanities, i.e., those not due to observable brain damage, fall into two exclusive and to some extent opposed types, called the cyclic insanities and schizophrenia. The former are characterized by a gross disturbance of emotional mood, towards extreme depression, on the one hand, or manic elation on the other, with some tendency to swing between the two. The latter show no marked abnormality of mood, except for a certain dullness and inaccessibility, but manifest a disconnexion of thoughts and feelings, a general silliness and ineptness of emotional expression, and commonly an obstinate seclusiveness. (This 'splitting' gave rise to the use of 'schizophrenia', from *schizo*, to split or cut.) Schizophrenia is somewhat more likely to strike people for the first time around adolescence, whereas manic-depressive, cyclic insanity is more frequent around middle age and more frequently clears up naturally, at least for a time.

Kretschmer, (1921), pointed out that the types recognized by Bleuler also existed in less extreme forms in normals and he called them the cyclothyme and schizothyme temperaments. (Thus insanity might strike anyone, but the form which it would take was expected to depend on the individual's prior temperament.) He added that this temperament had some relation to body build and that schizothymes tended to be thin and slight in build whereas cyclothymes were stocky and rounded. Table 2 shows the ratings most strongly affected by (loaded in) factor *A* and a comparison of these with those clinically described by Kretschmer shows a striking agreement. In Table 2 each trait element is given in bipolar opposites, as the axis of the earth might be fixed by north and south poles, and the rater spreads people out from those high in the trait (on the left-hand side) to those showing mostly the trait on the right. Consequently the factor which derives from these must also be considered bipolar, the positive or high score corresponding to the label on the left-hand side here. However, the reader should recognize from the outset that no value judgement is implied by calling cyclothymia 'positive' and schizothymia 'negative'. Each has its good uses and its bad consequences and the direction of scoring is purely arbitrary.

Table 2
Source trait A. Affectothymia-*vs*-sizothymia in ratings

A+ (Positively Loaded)		*A*− (Negatively Loaded)
Good-natured, easy-going	*vs*	Critical, grasping
Cooperative	*vs*	Obstructive
Attentive to people	*vs*	Cool, aloof
Soft-hcarted	*vs*	Hard, precise
Trustful	*vs*	Suspicious
Adaptable	*vs*	Rigid

In connexion with this naming, in spite of Kretschmer's using *schizothyme* to distinguish the normal temperament from the schizophrenic, the general public continues to regard 'schizo' as indicating abnormality. And since the tests we shall describe for this factor are likely to be recorded for schoolchildren and discussed with parents, it has seemed best to avoid misunderstandings by using finally the new title for it now adopted, namely *sizothymia*, instead of schizothymia, for *sizo*, deriving from the same root as 'size' in painting, means 'flat' and refers to what psychiatrists call the 'flatness of affect', i.e., the absence of lively and vibrant emotion, in the sizothyme. And it is this coldness and aloofness which, more than anything else, characterize the *normal A* (minus), i.e., the sizothyme person. Henceforth, with normal behaviour, we shall therefore characterize this basic division, so central in all personality differences, as sizothymia. Perhaps it will also recommend itself to psychologists to refer to the cyclothyme, when normal, as an *affectothyme*, because the primary characteristic is affect or emotion, not merely the cyclical ups and downs of elation and depression which occur in the abnormal, cyclically insane person.

If one runs one's eye over the group of trait elements which come together at this normal, 'lower' sizothyme pole, one sees a detached, shut-in, emotionally inexpressive type, which is quite healthy and normal in itself; however, if such an individual became abnormal, e.g., by having hallucinations and losing control, it is easy to see that he would behave as in schizophrenia. Similarly, as Kretschmer has pointed out, the warm-hearted, gentle, full emotionality of the affectothyme could develop, under unusual stress and exhaustion, that loss of mood control, and that abnormal domination of thought by elation or of pervasive depression which one sees in the 'affective' psychoses (insanities).

The Measurement of Source Trait A by Questionnaire

What comes out by the statistical calculations of factor analysis, as a unitary dimension or factor, is best characterized psychologically as a *source trait*. For it operates as an underlying source of observed behaviour. However, not all observed behaviour which correlates together can be identified with a source trait. Sometimes things go together by reason of overlap of several influences. Then we speak of a *surface trait* or *syndrome* (if it is abnormal). Thus a bunch of behaviour elements cluster together to constitute neuroticism, e.g., anxiety, indecision, inability to concentrate, irrational fears, etc., but neuroticism is due to a conjunction of several factors, not one. Or again, among men in the street there is a correlation cluster or surface trait among such things as larger vocabulary, some understanding of mathematics, of history, etc. We recognize that a person high in this surface trait is likely (*a*) to have had longer education, (*b*) to be naturally more intelligent, and (*c*) to have a studious temperament. Here three distinct factors of personality and personal history combine to give a single pattern.

It is important to distinguish source traits from surface traits. Right in the present area of behaviour there exists what some psychologists consider a broad surface trait – extraversion–introversion. We have reason to believe it is a 'second-order factor',* but regardless, it should not be confused with the primary source trait of 'affectothymia-*vs*-sizothymia' which we are now recognizing. The term extraversion–introversion, due to the Swiss psychiatrist Jung, is now so battered by popular usage that it may mean anything from sociability to good emotional adjustment, depending on the background of the user. If we accept, however, the unique definition by the second-order factor above, in which case we may prefer more precisely to call it 'exvia-*vs*-invia', then the statistical analysis shows that affectothymia-*vs*-sizothymia is only one component (along with the factors below labelled *F* and *H*) in this total exvia–invia temperament difference.

With this rejection of a possible false identification, let us note that a good deal more is now known about source trait *A*. First, it has quite an appreciable hereditary determination and some relation to broad and thin body-build difference. Second, it is

* Correlations between primary factors can be factor analysed in the same way as those between specific behaviours. When we do this we obtain *second-* or *higher-order factors*.

significantly higher in women than men, which accounts for some of the more expressive emotionality and tenderness of women, and is connected with the known higher rate of manic-depressive disorders of women and of schizophrenic disorders in men. Thirdly, there are marked differences of level between occupations: teachers and social workers are higher than average (affectothyme) and electricians and engineers, among others, lower (sizothyme).

It has been stated as one of the aims of modern scientific psychology to proceed to measurement in terms of natural functional unities in personality, not of arbitrary, artificial scales. Having discovered such a unity, and one contributing much to total personality differences, in affectothymia–sizothymia, describable in terms of behaviour ratings made on real life behaviours, we want to measure it. However, of the three 'media' of observation discussed above, only two of them – Q-data and T-data – are strictly *test* media. Behaviour rating is in one sense the *criterion* – the real behaviour – which the test has to predict. In any case, it is scarcely useful as a test, defined as 'a portable measuring device' because one cannot cart around the *same* judges from group to group. And unless we have the same judges, with the same standards, equal score figures on two people do not mean the same thing.

The first attempt at measuring personality was made in the questionnaire medium, which was well in use by 1920, in a number of 'scales'. However, it needs no great shrewdness to realize that self-evaluation, e.g., in responding to the question, 'Are you a worrying person?' is beset by systematic errors. The respondent does not *know* accurately where he stands relative to other people, not having been another person, and, if he did, he might not tell you when, for example, he wants to make a good impression in applying for a job. Also, people in different cultures show differing readiness to express private evaluations publicly. The French have a saying that words are given to us to disguise our feelings. And Freud has stressed that the barrier to the unconscious mind prevents our really knowing our desires and interests.

In spite of these shortcomings which can be commented upon systematically later, the questionnaire has worked tolerably well, when intelligently designed. The usual procedure is to present several 'items', generally from five to forty for *each* factor scale one wishes to measure. A person's score is the number out of the total array of questions, which he answers in the keyed way.

Usually, to get rid of effects from response sets, for example, tendency to say yes, or to choose the left answer, the items have to be balanced, i.e., made so that as many 'yes' or 'no' answers contribute to a positive score.

But how are the original question items chosen? In the construction of the Sixteen Personality Factor Questionnaire (Cattell and Stice, 1949), and of the corresponding Child Personality Questionnaires (Porter and Cattell, 1960), the dimensions found in ratings constituted the main framework. That is to say, the psychologist formed a conception of the unitary source traits in the normal personality *from the factor patterns of ratings*, as in affectothymia above, and made up the most potent questions he could to hit this target. But the patterns found in ratings were considered still only as *hypotheses*, not as guaranteed to reproduce themselves also in questionnaires. The structure of factors in questionnaire item responses had to be established independently, on its own merits. (If only for the reason that few psychologists can make up a question the answer to which will indeed correlate with that to other questions in the manner in which they intend it to do!) The difficulties which here mock intuition and blunt understanding are largely introduced by the need to construct questions so indirect that they gain some immunity to faking.

So the psychologist, though he is guided by hunches from rating factors, also adds many other items. In fact, he is guided by the original personality sphere notion – to represent as much of the totality of human behaviour as possible. Thus the procedure is to present hundreds – in the long run thousands – of carefully chosen items to large groups of normal persons. Each item is then correlated with every other to see which sets 'go together'. Factor analysis, usually pursued with the help of electronic computers, shows how many independent dimensions are required to account for the discovered connexions, and gives an indication of what these are, in terms of which items are loaded – just as we saw with rated trait elements. Actually, there quickly emerges a factor which seems to be a 'mental interior': a self view, corresponding to the affectothymia–sizothymia rating pattern seen above. The question items which it loads most highly are given in Table 3.

The warm sociability at one pole and the aloofness and unconcern with people at the other are as evident here as in the observers' ratings.

Table 3
Factor A in questionnaire responses

---

(1) I would rather work as:
      (a) an engineer   (b) *a social science teacher*
(2) I could stand being a hermit:
      (a) True   (b) *False*
(3) I am careful to turn up when someone expects me:
      (a) *True*   (b) False
(4) I would prefer to marry someone who is:
      (a) a thoughtful companion   (b) *effective in a social group*
(5) I would prefer to read a book on:
      (a) *national social service*   (b) new scientific weapons
(6) I trust strangers:
      (a) sometimes   (b) *practically always*

A person who answers all of the above in the indicated direction (*italic answers*) has a highly affectothyme temperament, but most will answer roughly a half.

The Source Trait C of Ego Strength

The striking – and encouraging – finding in these *Q*-data experiments is that despite different random samples of questions being used, one seems to get (*a*) approximately the same number of factors for 'mental interiors' as for 'behavioural exteriors', and (*b*) a very good alignment, in total meaning, of the two series of factors. This supports up to a point a theory of 'indifference of indicator'. That is to say, we seem to see the same 'shapes' despite the difference in the 'dress' (i.e. the form of expression or observation device), as a microscopist might expect to locate largely the same true objects, somewhat modified in appearance, despite using different wave lengths of light or different dyes.

There are some differences, to be sure, notably in that some factors like radicalism-*vs*-conservatism (Q_1), and internal self-sufficiency (Q_2), show up much more readily in the questionnaire than in gross behaviour. There are also some differences of emphasis, as when the sizothyme person describes himself in *Q*-data as slow and reserved, whereas people tend to see him rather (in ratings) as cold and arrogant. Similarly, high 'surgent' individuals describe themselves as gay and happy-go-lucky, whereas observers consider them as casual or even defective in conscience. But the failure of 'measures' on the same factor through two different media to correlate perfectly is now understood in terms of what are called 'instrument factors', that is, error intruding into one measure from a 'rating instrument' factor and into its 'twin' from a 'questionnaire instrument' factor, while a true common factor continues to exist.

In this connexion, one can see that it is a mistake to assume that all or most of the error is in the questionnaire, as some do, and that the behaviour rating is *the* 'criterion', i.e., that by which the questionnaire measure is to be validated. There are advantages and disadvantages on both sides. The interview, which is a form of rating – aided by a standard, if brief, situation – has been proved again and again by psychological experiment to be most unreliable, though interviewers will continue to fancy their talents. A major shortcoming of rating, as a technique, is that judges see subjects usually only in one place, e.g. the classroom, or the office, for a special part of the day, and from the position of a person in a particular role. Each of these three is an additional source of error. The questionnaire respondent, however, is *always* with himself, and sees a day and night sample of behaviour. On the other hand, especially in those things, e.g. worry, self-confidence, contempt, which people do not fully show openly, an individual, even if wishing to be truthful, lacks any firm standards of comparison from the inner life of others. For example, it is a commonplace that in social situations young people usually mistakenly believe other young people are more self-confident and less shy than they are themselves.

For these 'instrument factor' reasons, correlations of 'self-rated' and 'other-rated' estimates of what appears to be a factor identical in meaning in both tend to run numerically lower than would be expected – except where great care is taken to watch statistical and other conditions, as discussed elsewhere.

However, in the second largest source trait in ratings (which by its position is labelled *B*), there is no real difficulty. This looks like nothing less than general intelligence, and correlates well with actual test results. Although differences in the intelligence factor do tend to involve personality expressions, we must, since our concern is the main personality factors, skip *B* and pass on to the third factor, *C*, which is shown in Table 4 first in its rating and secondly in its questionnaire form. The meaning of this source trait seems to support the psychoanalytic concept of Ego Strength. Further, its demonstrated persistent negative correlation with neuroticism and anxiety, in various experimental groups in America and Britain, supports this interpretation. However, it will be noted that there are some 'viewpoint' differences in that the rater stresses emotionality, lack of responsibility,

Table 4
Source trait C. Ego strength-*vs*-emotionality and neuroticism, in *L*- and *Q*-data

Behaviour ratings by observer on these elements:

C+		C—
Mature	*vs*	Unable to tolerate frustration
Steady, persistent	*vs*	Changeable
Emotionally calm	*vs*	Impulsively emotional
Realistic about problems	*vs*	Evasive, avoids necessary decisions
Absence of neurotic fatigue	*vs*	Neurotically fatigued (with no real effort)

Questionnaire responses on these items:

Do you find it difficult to take no for an answer even when what you want to do is obviously impossible?
    (a) yes   (b) *no*
If you had your life to live over again, would you
    (a) *want it to be essentially the same?* (b) plan it very differently?
Do you often have really disturbing dreams?
    (a) yes   (b) *no*
Do your moods sometimes make you seem unreasonable even to yourself?
    (a) yes   (b) *no*
Do you feel tired when you've done nothing to justify it?
    (a) *rarely*   (b) often
Can you change old habits, without relapse, when you decide to?
    (a) *yes*   (b) no

and evasiveness of reality, whereas the *Q*-data stresses a little more of a sense of worthlessness, emotional fatigue, and inability to cope with reality.

This source trait is obviously one of the most important things for the clinician to measure, when he is attempting to size up the severity of a neurotic condition. But it also has importance in vocational guidance, in understanding school failures, and in many other ways. The essence of *C* factor appears to be an inability to control one's emotions and impulses, especially by finding for them some satisfactory realistic expression. Looked at from the opposite or positive pole, it sharpens and gives scientific substance to the psychoanalytic concept of 'ego strength', which it has come to be called. Measurements with the 16 P.F. (Sixteen Personality Factor Questionnaire) and the H.S.P.Q. (High School Personality Questionnaire) (Beloff and Cattell, 1962) show that almost all forms of neurotic, as well as alcoholics, narcotic addicts, and delinquents are abnormally low on this ego-strength factor. This also helps in its identification, for we would expect on dynamic grounds that the most widespread inadequacy among such a wide range of distinct abnormalities would be ego weakness. Occupationally, the scores are higher in persons belonging to callings requiring control and decision, as in airline pilots and firemen, and lower in such more sheltered occupations as clerical workers and janitors. Furthermore, there is evidence suggesting that ego-strength development is lower in clinical cases subjected to prolonged anxiety or given to excessive guilt proneness. This fits the psychoanalytic theory that excessive early demands by conscience can so add to the difficulties of finding suitable expression for emotional needs that the ego's capacity to handle impulses rationally is impaired.

As pointed out above, the mathematical nature of a factor is such that we should expect it to correspond to a single, scientific concept or influence, of which the elements listed, for example, in Tables 3 and 4 are expressions. The nature of this underlying power in C can be seen dynamically, as the self or ego, organized to give expression to the drives in a well-balanced way. But in other factors it may not be so easy. For example, how can we interpret the nature of the source trait underlying the A pattern? Much of the behaviour at the negative, sizothyme pole suggests a coldness and disillusionment about humanity. The natural warmth has been disciplined to a detached objectivity, an unwillingness to get much involved with people, and accompanied even by some degree of hostility. However, so far no one has found much evidence of $A-$ (henceforth, we will represent high and low on A by $A+$ and $A-$, and similarly for other factors) individuals having any more unfortunate experiences than others; while the body build and other evidence points to some appreciable constitutional determination. The constitutional influence could either be a lower emotionality – a greater natural detachment and disinclination to react, as is suggested by the term sizothyme (flatness of emotional life) – or some natural obstinacy of self-direction which begets frustration when people expect the individual to conform. This latter concept is not easy to develop in a short space, but if we suppose that some constitutional, temperamental, physiological condition makes some people's drives naturally more persistent and unchanging, this might account simultaneously for the greater natural emotional steadiness of the sizothyme and also for his greater sense of frustration, hostility, and withdrawal (since to have greater perseverance is also to experience greater thwarting) from an ordinarily unaccommodating environment. And what can be more unaccommodating and puzzling than people?

Regardless of the particular interpretation we adopt, it will be evident that a source trait as discovered by factor analysis is some kind of unitary influence in personality which affects a whole structure of responses. Even if psychology cannot immediately trace and interpret the nature of this unitary influence, we do well to represent it by a *symbol* and use it until interpretation is gained. For there is an immediate gain in economy alone in that by measuring a certain number of basic source traits we automatically describe a larger area of personality than if we measured the same number of arbitrary variables at random. What is perhaps even more important is that such traits are likely to have a functional unity and comparative independence in development, and in action, which makes them the most useful concepts around which to develop personality theory and experiment.

References

Allport, G. W. and Odbert, H. S. 1936. Trait-names: a psycho-lexical study. *Psychol. Monogr.* No. 211.

Beloff, H. and Cattell, R. B. 1962. The High School Personality Questionnaire. Champaign, Ill.: Institute for Personality and Ability Testing.

Cattell, R. B. and Scheier, I. H. 1961. *The Meaning and measurement of neuroticism and anxiety.* New York: The Ronald Press.

Cattell, R. B. and Stice, G. 1949. The Sixteen Personality Factor Questionnaire. Champaign, Ill.: Institute for Personality and Ability Testing.

Kretschmer, E. 1921. *Körperbau und Character.* Berlin: Springer; English trans. (1925): *Physique and Character.* London: Kegan Paul.

Porter, R. B. and Cattell, R. B. 1960. The Child Personality Questionnaire. Champaign, Ill.: Institute for Personality and Ability Testing.

DIMENSIONS OF PERSONALITY

Close parallels can be drawn between the work of Eysenck and of Cattell. Like Dr Cattell, Professor Eysenck has for many years headed a group of workers all engaged in unified research designed both to advance the frontiers of knowledge and to develop methods and material for practical use.

The fact that Eysenck's work and name have become better known, in Great Britain at least, to the layman as well as to the psychologist, is due to a combination of causes. First, the work has been carried out from an explicitly stated theoretical position (that of learning theory), and this fact has been publicized in his popular scientific writings; second, it has been closely associated with problems from the field of psychiatry; third, it has often been presented in conjunction with what can only be described as an attack, and not always a relevant one, on alternative orientations, notably psycho-analysis and 'dynamic' psychology generally.

These considerations do not, of course, affect the interest or importance of Eysenck's findings, and his predilection for describing personality variables by reference to orthogonal co-ordinates has the attraction of simplicity, if it lacks the descriptive power of Cattell's multivariate standpoint.

The present short summary of Eysenck's position has been chosen for its conciseness. It comes from a book with a specifically clinical bias, and it is worth noting that the closely integrated nature of Eysenck's work has resulted in the most important general references being relevant and noted even in this context. Little need therefore be added in the way of further suggested reading. Not mentioned, however, in the article is the important book, *The Dynamics of Anxiety and Hysteria* (2), the scope of which is wider than the title implies.

Much of Eysenck's work has been based on the application of the *Maudsley Personality Inventory* (MPI) (1). This was developed from, and superseded, the *Maudsley Medical Questionnaire*. It has been replaced in its turn by the Eysenck Personality Inventory (EPI) (3), to which a 'junior' version (4) has just been added. Little has as yet been published on work

343

with the EPI, but the MPI has been very widely used indeed, particularly as a basis for the choice of criterion groups in research. The value of the inventory for study of the individual case, however, has been questioned, e.g., by McGuire, Mowbray, and Vallance (5).

References
1. Eysenck, H. J., The Questionnaire Measurement of Neuroticism and Extraversion. *Rivista di Psicologia*, **50**, 113–40, 1956.
2. Eysenck, H. J., *The Dynamics of Anxiety and Hysteria*. London: Routledge and Kegan Paul, 1957.
3. Eysenck, H. J., and Eysenck, Sybil B. G. *Eysenck Personality Inventory*. London: University of London Press; 1963.
4. Eysenck, Sybil B. G., *The Junior Eysenck Personality Inventory*. London: University of London Press, 1965.
5. McGuire, R. J., Mowbray, R. M., and Vallance, R. C. The Maudsley Personality Inventory used with Psychiatric Inpatients. *British Journal of Psychology*, **54**, 157–66, 1963.

Dimensions of Personality

H. J. Eysenck and S. Rachman, *The Causes and Cures of Neurosis*.
Routledge and Kegan Paul, London; Robert R. Knapp, San Diego, 1965.

[. . . .]

As Watson (1930) once put it quite clearly, personality 'is the sum of activities that can be discovered by actual observation for a long enough period of time to give reliable information'. For many behaviourists, therefore, there is no room for personality in a natural science type of psychology.

However, it is becoming more and more widely recognized that between stimulus and response interposes an organism, and the formula S-O-R has pretty well superseded the old S-R paradigm. The recognition of the existence of an organism intervening between stimulus and response is made necessary by the very simple fact that identical stimuli applied to different organisms frequently lead to different responses, and even identical stimuli applied to the same organism do not always lead to similar responses. There are two possible causes for this, both involving the concept of an intervening organism. In the first place, individual organisms may differ with respect to their past reinforcement schedules; on this hypothesis, we are simply saying that past learning determines in part the reactions which we now make to different types of stimuli. There is nothing very novel in this, of course, and even commonsense recognizes the importance of past learning in present activities. However, the fact that this is so is incompatible with a simple-minded application of the principles of stimulus-response psychology. Equally interesting and important, and perhaps less widely recognized nowadays, is the fact that individual organisms differ innately with respect to many variables which may determine the responses to certain classes of stimuli. It is perhaps a little unfashionable to stress the importance of innate hereditary factors in behaviour, but the evidence regarding their importance is quite conclusive. We will return to this point in the next Chapter; it is raised here mainly to indicate the direction in which our discussion will be going. For the moment, therefore, let us simply note that the organism is an absolutely essential part of any stimulus-response type of psychology, because it is the organism which intervenes between the stimulus and the response, and organisms differ, both with respect to past reinforcement schedules and also with respect to innate potentiality and other variables.

Assuming, then, for the moment that the concept of personality may have some scientific value, we may go on to search for the main dimensions of personality in the hope that these may be related to different types of neurotic behaviour which we have discussed in the first Chapter. We may also hope that the discovery of these main dimensions of personality will help us in the problem of *nosology*, or classification of neurotic disorders. Classification is an absolutely fundamental part of the scientific study of human personality; a satisfactory typology is as necessary in psychology as was Mendeleyeff's Table of the Elements in physics. This has, of course, always been recognized by psychologists, and almost everyone is acquainted with the famous typological classification into melancholics, cholerics, sanguines, and phlegmatics dating back to Galen and even earlier. As this system still has much to teach us, we will present it here as Figure 1; it immediately confronts us with one of the main problems of classification. The first of these may be phrased in terms of the question: 'Categorical or dimensional?'. The famous German philosopher, Immanuel Kant, to whom this system owed much of its popularity during the last two hundred years, was quite specific in maintaining the categorical point of view, i.e., the notion that every person could be assigned to a particular category; he was a melancholic, or a phlegmatic, or a sanguine, or a choleric, but any mixtures or admixtures were inadmissible. This notion of categories is, of course, similar to the psychiatric notion of disease entities and their corresponding diagnoses; hysteria, anxiety state, paranoia, obsessional illness, and so on are often treated as categorical entities in this sense.

Opposed to this notion, we have the view that any particular position in this two-dimensional framework is due to a combination of quantitative variations along the two continua labelled 'introversion–extraversion' and 'stable–unstable'. Wundt (1903), who is the most notable proponent of Galen's system in modern times, favoured the dimensional view; he labelled the one axis 'slow–quick' instead of introversion–extraversion, and the other 'strong–weak' instead of unstable and stable.

It may be interesting to quote Wundt's very modern-sounding discussion: 'The ancient differentiation into four temperaments ... arose from acute psychological observation of individual differences between people ... The fourfold division can be justified if we agree to postulate two principles in the individual

346

reactivity of the affects: one of them refers to the *strength*, the other to the *speed of change* of a person's feelings. Cholerics and melancholics are inclined to strong affects, while sanguinics and phlegmatics are characterized by weak ones. A high rate of change is found in sanguinists and cholerics, a slow rate in melancholics and phlegmatics.

'It is well known that the strong temperaments ... are predestined towards the *Unluststimmungen*, while the weak ones show a happier ability to enjoy life ... The two quickly changeable temperaments ... are more susceptible to the impressions of the present; their mobility makes them respond to each new idea. The two slower temperaments, on the other hand, are more concerned with the future; failing to respond to each chance impression, they take time to pursue their own ideas.' (Pp. 637–8.)

There is no reason to believe that the notion of the *typology* presupposes a categorical system; both Jung and Kretschmer, who were probably the best-known typologists of the inter-war period, postulated a dimensional rather than a categorical system. The widespread notion that typologies implied discontinuities, bimodal distributions, and the like does not accurately represent the writings and views of modern typologists (Eysenck, 1960*b*).

Most writers on the subject of personality come down in favour of either the categorical or the dimensional point of view, without basing themselves on any experimental demonstration. It is, however, not impossible to devise experimental and statistical means for verifying the one and falsifying the other hypothesis. Eysenck (1950) has tried to do this in terms of the method of *criterion analysis*, which relies on separate factor analyses of intercorrelations between tests administered to two or more criterion groups (say, normals and psychotics), and a comparison of the factors emerging with the criterion column derived by biserial correlation between the tests and the criterion. The results of this method have, in every instance, supported the doctrine of continuity, and failed to support the doctrine of categorization, even when the latter seemed most firmly entrenched, as in the case of psychosis (Eysenck, 1952).

Assuming for the moment, therefore, the doctrine of dimensionality, we are required to build up, on an experimental and statistical basis, a quantitative system of personality description (Eysenck, Eysenck, and Claridge, 1960). The most widely used tool for this purpose is, of course, factor analysis, and the main results of the application of this tool are shown in Figure 1. The outer ring in this Figure shows the results of a large number

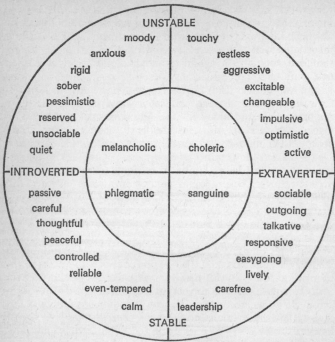

Figure 1   The inner ring shows the 'four temperaments' of Hippocrates and Galen; the outer ring shows the results of modern factor analytic studies of the intercorrelations between traits by Guilford, Cattell, Eysenck and others (Eysenck, 1963).

of factor analytic studies of questionnaires and ratings (Eysenck, 1960b). As is customary in these diagrams, the correlation between any two traits is equal to their scalar product, that is to say, in this case, the cosine of their angle of separation. The closer the two traits are together in the diagram, the higher is the observed correlation between them; the further apart are any two traits in this diagram, the lower is the correlation. If the angle between them exceeds ninety degrees, the correlation becomes negative.

Factor analysis has often been criticized on the grounds that different practitioners achieve different results, and that a method which is unreliable in the sense of failing to produce agreed results cannot be taken very seriously. Whatever may have been true twenty or thirty years ago, there can be no doubt that nowadays there is comparatively little disagreement between investigators in this field. Cattell's most recent book (Cattell and Scheier, 1961) shows him in firm agreement with the above-mentioned system first put forward in 1947 (Eysenck, 1947), and Guilford, too, now appears to recognize the existence of these two main factors in personality description which we have used as the major axes in Figure 1. Vernon (1953, p. 13) also puts forward a similar scheme, and factor analyses of a variety of questionnaires such as the MMPI (Kasselbaum *et al.*, 1959), the Gough California Personality Inventory (Mitchell and Pierce-Jones, 1960; Nicholls and Schnell, 1963) and the Murray List of Needs (Stern, 1962) all result in factors very closely resembling those noted in Figure 1. The agreement present nowadays is indeed impressive, and if failure to agree could be used as a criticism of the method of factor analysis, then the almost universal agreement existing at the present time can perhaps rightly be claimed as strong support for the usefulness of the statistical method in question.

Terms such as extraversion and introversion are used in our discussion in a sense strictly derived from empirical studies such as mentioned above; they should not be taken as having the same meaning here as they do in Jung's discussion. Jung, who is often erroneously credited with originating these terms which had been in use on the continent of Europe for several hundred years before he wrote his famous book on psychological types, has put forward a very complicated scheme of personality description; there would be no point in criticizing his scheme here. We merely wish to point out that our own use of these terms must stand and fall by empirical confirmation, and owes more to the work of factor analysts and early experimentalists like Heymans and Wiersma, than to Jung and his followers (Eysenck, 1960b). A brief description of typical extreme extraverts and introverts may be useful at this point, to show the reader precisely what we mean by these terms.

The typical extravert is sociable, likes parties, has many friends, needs to have people to talk to, and does not like reading or studying by himself. He craves excitement, takes chances, often sticks his neck out, acts on the spur of the moment, and is generally an impulsive individual. He is fond of practical jokes, always has a ready answer, and generally likes change; he is carefree, easygoing, optimistic, and 'likes to laugh and be merry'. He prefers to keep moving and doing things, tends to be aggressive and loses his temper quickly; altogether his feelings are not kept under tight control, and he is not always a reliable person.

The typical introvert is a quiet, retiring sort of person, intro-spective, fond of books rather than people; he is reserved and distant except to intimate friends. He tends to plan ahead, 'looks before he leaps', and mistrusts the impulse of the moment. He does not like excitement, takes matters of everyday life with proper seriousness, and likes a well-ordered mode of life. He keeps his feelings under close control, seldom behaves in an aggressive manner, and does not lose his temper easily. He is reliable, somewhat pessimistic and places great value on ethical standards.

These descriptions, of course, sound almost like caricatures because they describe, as it were, the 'perfect' extravert and the 'perfect' introvert; needless to say, few people closely resemble these extremes, and the majority of people undoubtedly are somewhat in the middle. This does not necessarily detract from the importance of these typological concepts, just as little as the fact that 50 per cent of the total population have I.Q.s of between 90 and 110 detracts from the importance of intelligence as a concept in psychology.

It is perhaps less necessary to give a detailed description of the typology implicit in the second major dimension of personality shown in Figure 1. We have there labelled the one end 'unstable'; this has often in the past been called a factor of *emotionality* or of *neuroticism*, and these terms adequately designate its meaning. At the one end we have people whose emotions are labile, strong, and easily aroused; they are moody, touchy, anxious, restless, and so forth. At the other extreme we have the people whose emotions are stable, less easily aroused, people who are calm, even-tempered, carefree, and reliable. Neurotics, needless to say, would be expected to have characteristics typical of the unstable type, normal persons typical of the stable type.

If we accept the principle of continuity, then we should be able to find a place for the major psychiatric classifications of neurotic disorders within our Figure 1. The theory has been put forward that dysthymic neurotics suffering from anxiety, reactive de-pression, obsessions, phobias, and so on would be found in the 'melancholic' quadrant, while hysterics, psychopaths, and per-haps juvenile delinquents and criminals generally, would be found in the 'choleric' quadrant (Eysenck, 1960b). Descriptively, there seems little doubt about the truth of this hypothesis; it is only necessary to look at the traits characterizing people in these two quadrants to realize that they might almost have been quoted from a psychiatric text-book, rather than being the result of factor analytic studies of normal people. Nevertheless, experimental support would seem to be required. Figure 2 shows the relative positions of different groups of neurotics and criminals, with respect to scores on various questionnaires of extraversion and neuroticism; the scales most frequently used in these studies have been the Maudsley Personality Inventory (Eysenck, 1959), the Cattell Personality Inventory (Cattell, 1957), and the Eysenck Personality Inventory (Eysenck and Eysenck, 1963). To make scores comparable, these have been turned into standard scores before plotting them in Figure 2. It will be seen that indeed, as

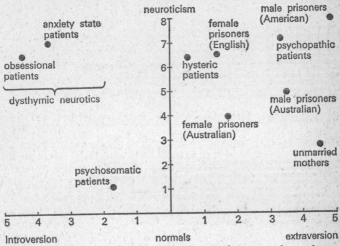

Figure 2   Position of various neurotic and criminal groups on the two factors of neuroticism and introversion-extraversion (Eysenck, 1964).

expected, patients suffering from anxiety, obsessional disorders, phobias, and so on, i.e., patients who have been called dysthymic by Eysenck (1947), do indeed fall into the melancholic quadrant and are strongly introverted, whereas psychopaths and criminals generally tend to fall into the choleric quadrant and be strongly extravert. Hysterics fall in between these two groups and are not significantly differentiated from normals with respect to extraversion–introversion, although they do, of course, have high scores on neuroticism. The position is well illustrated in Figure 3, which shows the results of a factor analysis of behaviour patterns observed in large groups of children referred to a child guidance clinic (Eysenck, 1960*b*). It will be seen that all the notations involved correlate together to define a factor of neuroticism, but that there is also another factor dividing the (introverted) *personality problems* from the (extraverted) *conduct problems*. Extraverted children swear, fight, are disobedient, destructive, play truant, steal, lie, are violent, rude, and egocentric, whereas introverted children are sensitive, absent-minded, depressed, seclusive, inefficient, have inferiority feelings, daydream, and are nervous. This is a very important and fundamental distinction, and is probably more useful in practice than the much more

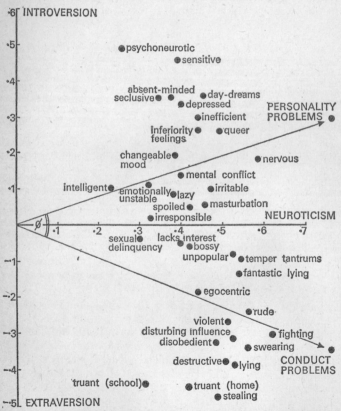

Figure 3   Results of a factor analysis of various conduct and personality problems shown by children (Eysenck, 1960b).

detailed psychiatric diagnostic nomenclature which is notoriously unreliable.

It may be asked just how closely psychiatric diagnosis, when reliably made by experienced psychiatrists, correlates with the results of psychological measurement, using questionnaires of the type described and short objective tests. The answer is given in an experiment carried out by Eysenck and Claridge (1962), who gave six such tests to sixteen normal, sixteen dysthymic, and sixteen hysteric patients. The results were treated by means of multiple discriminant function analysis. The theory we are dealing with predicts that if we carry out such an analysis, it should give us two significant latent roots; further, if we derive variance scores for the forty-eight subjects of our experiment, then these should be situated in a prescribed manner in a two-dimensional plane generated by the two significant variants. To put this prediction in its simplest form, we may say that the mean variance scores for the three groups should lie at the corners of an equilateral triangle. Figure 4 shows the outcome of the experiment. It will be seen that the prediction is verified, and that the first variant discriminates completely between the dysthymics and the hysterics. The second

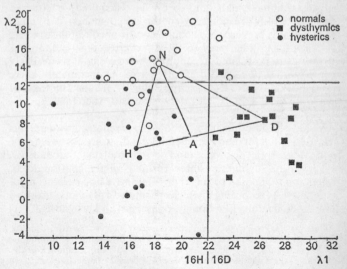

Figure 4 Position of 16 normal subjects, 16 dysthymic and 16 hysteric patients in a two-dimensional framework generated by a discriminant function analysis of their performance on 6 objective tests (Eysenck and Claridge, 1962).

variant, with only slight overlap, discriminates between the normal group on the one hand, and the neurotic group on the other. Similar success in achieving a 100 per cent agreement between diagnostic test and psychiatric diagnosis attended an earlier experiment by Eysenck, Eysenck, and Claridge (1960).

The discrimination between melancholics and cholerics, or, in modern terminology, between dysthymics and psychopaths, obviously corresponds, in some degree, with that between neurotic *disorders of the first kind*, and neurotic *disorders of the second kind**. Agreement is not quite complete, however; we have postulated that certain types of disorders, such as fetishism, homosexuality, and so forth are disorders of the second kind, yet we would [. , . .] regard people afflicted with these disorders as being more likely to be introverted than extraverted. We may say that in our general system introverts are postulated to condition more easily and, therefore, to acquire the conditioned anxieties and fears characteristic of the dysthymic more easily than other people, whereas psychopaths and prisoners generally are people who condition poorly and who, therefore, fail to acquire the conditioned responses characterizing the socialization process. Fetishists, homosexuals, and so on have acquired conditioned responses which are contrary to the social mores; it is quite likely that it is because they acquire conditioned responses easily that they have fallen prey to these perverted practices, and as introverts are postulated to condition more easily, it seems likely that they must be regarded as introverted. Unfortunately, there is very little empirical evidence regarding the personality traits of people in these groups, and very little can, therefore, be said about them from this point of view.

We have said nothing so far about the psychotic disorders. It is well known that for many psychoanalysts these are but an extreme form of neurotic disorders, and it is postulated that normal, neurotic, and psychotic states form a single continuum of 'regression'. Opposed to this is an alternative and perhaps more orthodox view, according to which neurotic and psychotic disorders differ fundamentally in aetiology, treatment, and prognosis. [. . . .]

Editor's note: Prof. Eysenck classes as *disorders of the first kind* those phobic reactions, anxiety states, etc., which 'are caused by conditioned autonomic fear responses and the reactions, skeletal, muscular and hormonal, of the organism of these conditioned responses.' He gives the name *disorders of the second kind* to those in which 'we postulate not the occurrence of a conditioning process leading to maladaptive habits, but rather the failure of a conditioning process to occur which would produce socially desirable habits.' (*The Causes and Cures of Neurosis*, pp. 6–7.)

It is possible to decide between these two hypotheses by means of factor analysis, and examples of this approach are given in the *Handbook of Abnormal Psychology* (Eysenck, 1960*a*, *c*). These results strongly favour the two-dimensional approach; two clear-cut orthogonal factors appear, one having high loadings on all the typical psychotic notations, the other on all the typical neurotic ones. Multiple discriminant function analysis, too, can be used to answer this question. In one such experiment, twenty normal controls, twenty neurotics, and twenty psychotics were tested on four objective laboratory tests (Eysenck, 1955). Multiple discriminant function analysis disclosed two significant latent roots, thus rendering impossible the assumption that one dimension was sufficient to incorporate the results. Figure 5

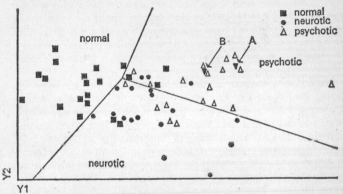

Figure 5   Distribution of 20 normal subjects, 20 neurotic and 20 psychotic patients in a two-dimensional framework generated by discriminant function analysis of objective test performance (Eysenck, 1955).

shows the actual position of the members of the three groups; the correlation ratio between the three groups and the two variants was 0·84, which indicates a refreshingly high validity for the tests used in predicting these psychiatric criteria. That this figure is not higher still is probably due to lack of reliability of the criterion. It will be seen in Figure 5 that two of the neurotics, labelled A and B, were grouped with the psychotics by the tests. Both were re-admitted later and diagnosed as psychotic. A similar study was carried out by S. B. G. Eysenck (1956), using a much larger population of subjects and a greater variety of tests; her results were similar to those just mentioned. It is interesting to note that cultural differences do not seem to affect the applicability of methods or conclusions to any considerable extent; Devadasan (1963) has duplicated many of the details of S. B. G. Eysenck's study on an Indian population in Kerala (Trivandrum) with almost identical results.

There are, of course, other ways in which theories of this type can be tested. One of these is the genetic method. If it is true that psychotic and neurotic disorders are orthogonal to each other, then we would expect that the children of psychotic parents should not show any greater degree of neuroticism than would the children of normal parents. This very interesting hypothesis was tested by Valerie Cowie (1961), and her results leave no doubt that the genetic implication of neuroticism in the children of psychotic parents is non-existent; if anything, they tended to be less neurotic. This finding may also serve as a warning to those who would overstress the importance of environment in giving rise to neurotic disorders; it is difficult to imagine a more severe stress to a child than having psychotic parents. All these studies, then, are in good agreement in stressing the complete separation between psychotic and neurotic disorders.

We can now summarize the main results of the discussion by saying that there are two main factors or dimensions which between them account for a good part of the non-cognitive aspect of personality. These two factors may be labelled extraversion–introversion, and neuroticism or emotionality as opposed to stability or normality. Psychotic behaviour trends are orthogonal to these dimensions and they may, therefore, be left out of account in a discussion of neurotic behaviour. Dysthymic neurotics, i.e. those exemplifying neuroses of the first kind, are found largely in the 'melancholic' quadrant, i.e., are both high on neuroticism and high on introversion. Psychopaths, criminals, and others exemplifying neuroses of the second kind tend to be high on extraversion as well as on neuroticism, with certain possible exceptions which were mentioned in the text. Hysteric patients tend to be intermediate between the dysthymic and the psychopathic groups, with introversion–extraversion scores on questionnaires which are not very much different from those of normals. On objective tests, however, as shown in Figure 4, hysterics tend definitely to group themselves on the extraverted side. For the purpose of the discussion, therefore, we shall henceforth treat them as extraverts, which is permissible perhaps also in view of the fact that, as compared with the dysthymic groups, they are always significantly more extraverted on questionnaires.

References

Cattell, R. B. 1957. *The sixteen personality factor questionnaire*. Champaign, Ill.: Institute for Personality and Ability Testing.

Cattell, R. B. and Scheier, I. H. 1961. *The meaning and measurement of neuroticism and anxiety*. New York: Ronald Press.

Cowie, V. 1961. The incidence of neurosis in the children of psychotics. *Acta Psychiat. Scand.*, **37**, 37–87.

Devadasan, K. 1963. Personality dimensions: a critical study. Unpublished Ph.D. thesis, University of Kerala. 27.

Eysenck, H. J. 1947. *Dimensions of Personality*. London: Routledge, Kegan Paul.

Eysenck, H. J. 1950. Criterion analysis – an application of the hypothetico-deductive method to factor analysis. *Psychol. Rev.*, **57**, 38–53.

Eysenck, H. J. 1952. *The Scientific Study of Personality*. London: Routledge, Kegan Paul. 18.

Eysenck, H. J. 1955. Psychiatric diagnosis as a psychological and statistical problem. *Psychol. Rep.*, **1**. 3-17.

Eysenck, H. J. 1959. *The Maudsley Personality Inventory*. London: University of London Press. San Diego: 1962. Educ. & Indust. Testing Service.

Eysenck, H. J. (Ed.). 1960a. *Handbook of abnormal psychology*. London: Pitman. New York: Basic Books.

Eysenck, H. J. 1960b. *The structure of human personality*. New York: Macmillan. London: Methuen.

Eysenck, H. J. 1960c. Classification and the problem of diagnosis. In: Eysenck, H. J. (Ed.). *Handbook of Abnormal Psychology*.

Eysenck, H. J. and Claridge, G. 1962. The position of hysterics and dysthymics in a two-dimensional framework of personality description. *J. abnorm. soc. Psychol.*, **69**, 46–55.

Eysenck, H. J. and Eysenck, S. B. G. 1963. *The Eysenck Personality Inventory*, San Diego. Educ. & Indust. Testing Service 1963. London: University of London Press.

Eysenck, S. B. G. 1956. Neurosis and psychosis; an experimental analysis. *J. ment. Sci.*, **102**, 517–29.

Eysenck, S. B. G., Eysenck, H. J. and Claridge, G. 1960. Dimensions of personality, psychiatric syndromes and mathematical models. *J. ment. Sci.*, **106**, 581–9.

Kasselbaum, G. G., Couch, A. S., and Slater, P. E. 1959. The factorial dimensions of the MMPI. *J. Consult. Psychol.*, **23**, 226–36.

Mitchell, J. V. and Pierce-Jones, J. 1960. A factor analysis of Gough's California Psychological Inventory. *J. consult. Psychol.*, **24**, 453–6.

Nichols, R. C. and Schnell, R. O. 1963. Factor scales for the California Psychological Inventory. *J. consult. Psychol.*, **27**, 228–35.

Stern, G. G. 1962. The measurement of psychological characteristics of students in learning environments. In: S. Messick and J. Ross (Eds.), *Measurement in personality and cognition*. London: J. Wiley & Sons, 27–68.

Vernon, P. E. 1953. *Personality tests and assessments*. London: Methuen.

Watson, J. B. 1930. *Behaviourism*. London: Kegan Paul. 14.

Wundt, W. 1903. *Grundzuge der Physiologischen Psychologie*. Leipzig: W. Engelmann. 5th Ed. Vol. 3.

THE MINNESOTA MULTIPHASIC PERSONALITY INVENTORY

Contrary to our usual practice, we have in this case used an original *Manual* as the basis of an article for inclusion in this book. The present text omits sections on 'Forms of the Inventory' and 'The Profile' and the list of the Test Items. Little need be added to the description here given, except to emphasize that in addition to its routine use, the Inventory has served as a pool of items for the development of a large number of other 'scales', the best known of which is probably the 'Taylor' or 'Iowa' Manifest Anxiety Scale (4). The *MMPI Handbook*, the standard text for the use of the technique (1) lists 213 scales, including the 'official' ones, and others have since been proposed. Between the publication dates of the Fifth and Sixth Mental Measurement Yearbooks (A5) the number of references to the MMPI cited has nearly doubled: the MMPI must in all probability rank as number one among non-projective tests of personality. Some of the most important studies are included in *Basic Readings on the MMPI* (5).

The MMPI has been criticized on a number of counts: the length of the test and the nature of the items; the nature of the profile scales; and its appropriateness as a basis for individual personality description.

To answer 550 items is certainly a formidable undertaking, but writing of the Tavistock Self-Assessment Inventory, which is more than half as long again, Sandler (3) has said that 'contrary to expectation the majority of patients find it neither dull nor irksome to work through such a large number of items.' This may be a suitable point at which to express a *caveat* regarding the application, in general, of psychological tests in other than a 'real' situation. To obtain worth-while results genuine motivation to take a test must be present. Students and others, if they have not been properly 'involved', sometimes find a test trivial, pointless or boring, whereas a patient seeking help or a candidate in a selection procedure might feel quite otherwise. In fact, absence of such involvement, when the situation is a 'real' one, can often itself be indicative of a relevant attitude or personality variable.

The fact that the majority of the main MMPI scales are clinical ones is a more serious point of criticism, since it tends to perpetuate the confusion between syndromes and personality variables, the distinction between which is a main theme of a recent book by Foulds (2).

Detailed discussion of the last of the criticisms noted above will be found in most general books dealing with psychological testing, e.g., those of Anastasi (see Further Reading, A2) or Cronbach (A7). A single sentence from the latter (p. 476) sums up the position rather well: 'There is no simple translation from MMPI information into descriptive terms.' This is not necessarily a damaging criticism; it merely emphasizes that the apparent 'objectivity' of inventory methods does not obviate the need for insight on the part of the tester any more than in the use of holistic or projective methods. Dependence on such insight is however minimized in the study of groups rather than of individuals, and it is to this latter purpose that inventory methods are particularly suited.

References

1. Dahlstrom, W. G., and Welsh, G. S., *An MMPI Handbook. A Guide to use in Clinical Practice and Research.* Minneapolis: University of Minnesota Press, 1960.
2. Foulds, G. A., *Personality and Personal Illness.* London: Tavistock, 1965.
3. Sandler, J., Studies in Psychopathology using a Self-Assessment Inventory. I. The Development and Construction of the Inventory *British J. of Medical Psychology*, **27**, 142–5. 1954.
4. Taylor, Janet A., A Personality Scale of Manifest Anxiety. *J. Abnormal and Social Psychology*, **48**, 285–90, 1953.
5. Welsh, G. S. and Dahlstrom, W. G. (Eds.), *Basic Readings on the MMPI in Psychology and Medicine.* Minneapolis: University of Minnesota Press, 1956.

17 S. R. Hathaway and J. C. McKinley

The Minnesota Multiphasic Personality Inventory

From S. R. Hathaway and J. C. McKinley, *MMPI Manual;*
Psychological Corporation, New York,
Copyright 1943, 1951, by the University of Minnesota,
Reprinted by special permission.

I. The Inventory

The *Minnesota Multiphasic Personality Inventory* is a psychometric instrument designed ultimately to provide, in a single test, scores on all the more important phases of personality (17). The point of view determining the importance of a trait in this case is that of the clinical or personnel worker who wishes to assay those traits that are commonly characteristic of disabling psychological abnormality. The instrument itself comprises 550 statements covering a wide range of subject matter – from the physical condition to the morale and the social attitudes of the individual being tested.

The subject is asked to sort all the statements into three categories: *True*, *False*, and *Cannot say*. After the subject has identified all the items he can as (mostly) *True* or (mostly) *False* about himself, his responses are counted so as to yield scores on four validity scales and nine clinical scales. There are a number of additional scales somewhat less widely used. The time required for administration varies, but is rarely longer than ninety minutes and is commonly as short as thirty minutes. Very little instruction and supervision are required: the examinee can, for example, work on the test as he sits in a waiting-room.

As a matter of convenience in handling and in avoiding duplication the items were arbitrarily classified under twenty-six headings, though it was not necessarily assumed that an item was properly classified merely because it had been placed in a given category. The arrangement was as follows:

1. General health (9 items)
2. General neurologic (19 items)
3. Cranial nerves (11 items)
4. Motility and coordination (6 items)
5. Sensibility (5 items)
5. Vasomotor, trophic, speech, secretory (10 items)
7. Cardiorespiratory system (5 items)
8. Gastrointestinal system (11 items)

 9. Genitourinary system (5 items)
10. Habits (19 items)
11. Family and marital (26 items)
12. Occupational (18 items)
13. Educational (12 items)
14. Sexual attitudes (16 items)
15. Religious attitudes (19 items)
16. Political attitudes – law and order (46 items)
17. Social attitudes (72 items)
18. Affect, depressive (32 items)
19. Affect, manic (24 items)
20. Obsessive and compulsive states (15 items)
21. Delusions, hallucinations, illusions, ideas of reference (31 items)
22. Phobias (29 items)
23. Sadistic, masochistic trends (7 items)
24. Morale (33 items)
25. Items primarily related to masculinity–femininity (55 items)
26. Items to indicate whether the individual is trying to place himself in an improbably acceptable light (15 items)

Personality characteristics may be assessed on the basis of scores on nine clinical scales originally developed for use with the Inventory. These scales are hypochondriasis, depression, hysteria, psychopathic personality, masculinity–femininity, paranoia, psychasthenia, schizophrenia, and hypomania. Other scales have been developed or are in the process of development (see paragraph II C). Although the scales are named according to the abnormal manifestation of the symptomatic complex, they have all been shown to have meaning within the normal range. In the presentation of the results the usual procedure is to translate the raw score of the measured trait into a standard score (the T score) and plot it on a profile chart. This procedure permits analysis of the relative strengths of the various phases, the pattern of which is usually more important than the presence of any one phase to an abnormal degree.

The basic concept assumes that among the 550 items there are some items that, when grouped, form numerous potential scales; those originally selected were merely the groups most easily derived. As it has been developed, however, the whole procedure permits the introduction of each new scale as it is derived without additional equipment other than a new scoring key and standards. Furthermore, since all the older record blanks can be scored on a new key, the clinician can immediately compare the scores on new scales with his clinical experience simply by a sampling of old records.

It is possible to separate from the 550 items those that do not occur in any scale so far derived. This will leave a group of somewhat fewer items that can be administered as a test in a shorter time. However, the shortened test is not recommended at present for two reasons: First, new scales are still being developed, and these will use some of the discarded items; second, the whole set of items forms a good research source that may be focused on the special problems of any new group or on any new application of the Inventory.

The fact that older records may be scored on any new key that may be derived makes it possible to present with each key standardization data on the same groups of normals and abnormals that have been used for earlier keys. The original normative data were derived from a sample of about 700 individuals representing a cross section of the Minnesota population as obtained from visitors to the University Hospitals. The sampling was fairly adequate for the ages sixteen to fifty-five and for both sexes. In addition to these data on normal individuals, data were available on 250 precollege and college students who as a group represented a reasonably good cross section of college entrance applicants. Data on several special groups, such as WPA workers and epileptic and tuberculosis patients, were also available.

The scales were developed by contrasting the normal groups with carefully studied clinical cases of which over 800 were available from the neuropsychiatric division of the University Hospitals when the test was published. The details of scale derivation are too variable and extensive for brief description, but several new methods were employed. The chief criterion of excellence was the valid prediction of clinical cases against the neuropsychiatric staff diagnosis, rather than statistical measures of reliability and validity.

Nevertheless, statistical studies regarding reliability and validity are of serious concern. For any psychological test, the reliability coefficient will vary with the population tested; i.e., using a group with a wide range of scores in the characteristic measured will yield a higher estimate of the reliability than will using a group with a narrow range of scores in the characteristic. When personality inventories are considered, the problem appears especially in the question of whether the group tested includes normals or hospitalized patients, or both. Presumably the personality patterns of normals should be more stable than the patterns of psychiatric patients. The problem is further aggravated when the inventories must measure personality traits which in themselves are known to be somewhat unstable (e.g., 'mood' or situational variables such as depression), or those which the therapist is attempting to modify.

In view of these difficulties, the data which have been reported on the reliability of the MMPI appear quite satisfactory. Hathaway and McKinley (18, 23, 25), using the Individual Form with unselected normals, reported test–retest coefficients for six of the clinical variables. The time between test and retest varied from three days to more than one year. Cottle (4) reported test–retest coefficients for unselected normals who took both the Individual Form and the Group Form within one week. Holzberg and Alessi (20) reported test–retest coefficients for unselected psychiatric patients who took both the complete version and a shortened version of the Individual Form within three days. Table I presents the data from these studies.* Since Cottle did not use the same form of the test for both testings, and Holzberg and Alessi did not use the same version, the coefficients they reported may provide a conservative estimate of the reliability of the MMPI.

As for validity, a high score on a scale has been found to predict positively the corresponding final clinical diagnosis or estimate in more than 60 per cent of new psychiatric admissions. This percentage is derived from differentiation among various kinds of clinic cases, which is considerably more difficult than mere differentiation of abnormal from normal groups. Even in cases in which a high score is not followed by a corresponding diagnosis, the presence of the trait to an abnormal degree in the symptomatic picture will nearly always be noted (24).

A detailed picture of the interrelationship of the clinical scales is available in *An Atlas for the Clinical Use of the MMPI* (19),† which has 968 short histories of clinical cases. Interpretation of scale intercorrelations, which vary widely, has been made simpler by these data on the dynamic interrelationships of the different clinical syndromes. For further data on validity and for the

* For the Si scale, which is not included in Table I, a test-retest reliability coefficient of +·93 has been found using 100 normals with intervals of one day to four months between testings (personal communication from L. E. Drake).

†*Editor's note:* See also p. 380, below. The *Atlas* is arranged in terms of 'coded profiles'. Raw scores are converted into T-scores. The 'high point code' and 'low point code' for a given individual summarize, respectively, those scales which have yielded T-scores of over 54 and under 46.

Table 1
Test-Retest Reliability Coefficients Reported for the
Minnesota Multiphasic Personality Inventory

Scale and Abbreviation	Hathaway and McKinley[1] Normals (N = 40—47)	Cottle[2] Normals (N = 100)	Holzberg and Alessi[3] Psychiatric Patients (N = 30)
Question (?)			·75
Lie (L)		·46	·85
Validity (F)		·75	·93
K (K)		·76	
Hypochondriasis (Hs)	·80	·81	·67
Depression (D)	·77	·66	·80
Hysteria (Hy)	·57	·72	·87
Psychopathic Deviate (Pd)	·71	·80	·52
Masculinity-Femininity (Mf)		·91	·76
Paranoia (Pa)		·56	·78
Psychasthenia (Pt)	·74	·90	·72
Schizophrenia (Sc)		·86	·89
Hypomania (Ma)	·83	·76	·59

1 Hathaway and McKinley used the Individual Form for both test and retest, with intervals of three days to more than one year between testings.

2 Cottle used the Individual Form alternately with the Group Form for test and retest, both testings occurring within one week.

3 Holzberg and Alessi used the complete Individual Form alternately with a shortened version of the Individual Form for test and retest, both testings occurring within three days.

actual intercorrelations of the various scales, the reader should consult the extensive bibliography in the *Atlas*.

The Inventory as a whole was designed partly to lessen the conflict between the psychiatrist's conception of the abnormal personality and that of psychologists and other professional workers who must deal with abnormality among more nearly normal persons. Many of the words in common usage, for example, apply to personality traits not easily carried over to the abnormal and not having clear-cut abnormal implications. The commonly used terms *introversion–extroversion*, *neuroticism* and *inferiority* are examples of concepts which rarely have specific value in practical psychiatry, but which may have value in describing the normal personality. The Inventory was also devised in the hope that it might be nearly universal in both its interpretation and its applicability to individual cases. It is for this reason that checks upon the validity of the answers given by each subject have been provided, so that scores may be interpreted with a fair degree of confidence even if they are obtained from individuals with very poor school experience, low mentality or incapacity due to psychological illness.

II. Description of the Scales

The following brief descriptions are intended merely as general guides to the meaning of the scales. The scales are based upon clinical cases that were classified according to conventional psychiatric nomenclature. To expand these brief statements the clinician may read reliable source books in the fields of psychiatry or abnormal psychology and should consult the *Atlas* previously cited. Naturally, the scales often discern more sharply and in a more restricted field than has been possible in the subjective formulation of a psychiatric category. Textbook descriptions of cases cannot show the complex mixture of abnormalities that is more common in clinical practice than the pure case. Some incidental data on the scales have clearly indicated, as a matter of fact, that the agreement between clinical judgement and measured trait strength is closely related to the amount of clinical experience and training of the clinician. [. . . .]

Because the basic over-all validity of the profile should be the first concern of the examiner, the validity scales will be considered first.

A. The Validity Scales

The question score (?). – The Question score is a validating score consisting simply of the total number of items put in the *Cannot say* category; the size of this score affects the significance of the other scores. Large Question scores invalidate all others. A 'borderline' Question score probably means that the subject's actual score, if he had not used the *Cannot say* category at all, would deviate farther from the average than his observed score indicates. In its own right the Question score is an indicator of personality factors, but no specific clinical material on it has been analysed. High scores have often been observed to occur in psychasthenic and retarded depression patients.

The lie score (*L*). – The L score is also a validating score that affords a measure of the degree to which the subject may be attempting to falsify his scores by always choosing the response that places him in the most acceptable light socially. A high L score does not entirely invalidate the other scores but indicates that the true values are probably higher than those actually obtained. In some cases the L score may be of interest in its own right as a measure of a special personality trend.

The validity score (F). – The F score is not a personality scale but serves as a check on the validity of the whole record. If the F score is high, the other scales are likely to be invalid either because the subject was careless or unable to comprehend the items, or because extensive scoring or recording errors were made. A low F score is a reliable indication that the subject's responses were rational and relatively pertinent. For further interpretive points see Section III.

The K score (K). – The K score is used essentially as a correction factor to sharpen the discriminatory power of the clinical variables measured by the Inventory. As such, K acts as a suppressor variable.*

If it is to be given any concrete non-statistical meaning, the K score is to be thought of as a measure of test-taking attitude, and is related to the L and F attitudes but is somewhat more subtle and probably taps a slightly different set of distorting factors. A high K score represents defensiveness against psychological weakness, and may indicate a defensiveness that verges upon deliberate distortion in the direction of making a more 'normal' appearance. A low K score tends to indicate that a person is, if anything, overly candid and open to self-criticism and the admission of symptoms even though they may be minimal in strength. A low K score can also result from a deliberate attempt to obtain bad scores or to make a bad impression ('plus-getting'). Users of the MMPI should become acquainted with the literature relative to K before making independent use of the variable.

B. The Clinical Scales

1. *The hypochondriasis scale (Hs).* – The Hs scale (22) is a measure of amount of abnormal concern about bodily functions. It is an improved revision of the original hypochondriasis scale H-CH. Persons with high Hs scores are unduly worried over their health. They frequently complain of pains and disorders which are

* For theoretical considerations, consult Horst (21), McNemar (26), Meehl (27), and Meehl and Hathaway (28).

difficult to identify and for which no clear organic basis can be found. It is characteristic of the hypochondriac that he is immature in his approach to adult problems, tending to fail to respond with adequate insight.

Hypochondriacal complaints differ from hysterical complaints of bodily malfunction in that the hypochondriac is often more vague in describing his complaint and in that he does not show such clear evidence of having got out of an unacceptable situation by virtue of his symptoms as does the hysteric. The hypochondriac more frequently has a long history of exaggeration of physical complaints and of seeking sympathy.

With psychological treatment a high score may often be improved, but the basic personality is unlikely to change radically. Common organic sickness does not raise a person's score appreciably, for the scale detects a difference between the organically sick person and the hypochondriac.

2. *The depression scale* (*D*). – The D scale (18) measures the depth of the clinically recognized symptom or symptom complex, depression. The depression may be the chief disability of the subject or it may accompany, or be a result of, other personality problems. A high D score indicates poor morale of the emotional type with a feeling of uselessness and inability to assume a normal optimism with regard to the future. In certain cases the depression may be well hidden from casual observation. This is the so-called 'smiling depression'. The depressive undercurrent is revealed in such cases by the subject's specific discourse and his outlook on the future. Often such persons insist that their attitude is the only realistic one, since death is inevitable and time passes. Though this may be true, the average person is – possibly erroneously – not so deeply concerned with the grim realities of life. A high score further suggests a characteristic personality background in that the person who reacts to stress with depression is characterized by lack of self-confidence, tendency to worry, narrowness of interests, and introversion. This scale, together with the Hs and Hy scales, will identify the greater proportion of those persons not under medical care who are commonly called neurotic, as well as individuals so abnormal as to need psychiatric attention.

Some high-scoring persons will change rather rapidly in response to improved environment or to pep talks and psychotherapy, but such individuals will be likely to remain subject to other attacks. The greater number, on the other hand, will not respond readily to treatment, but their scores will slowly tend to approach the normal level with the mere passage of time.

3. *The hysteria scale* (*Hy*). – The Hy scale (25) measures the degree to which the subject is like patients who have developed conversion-type hysteria symptoms. Such symptoms may be general systemic complaints or more specific complaints such as paralyses, contractures (writer's cramp), gastric or intestinal complaints, or cardiac symptoms. Subjects with high Hy scores are also especially liable to episodic attacks of weakness, fainting or even epileptiform convulsions. Definite symptoms may never appear in a person with a high score, but under stress he is likely to become overtly hysterical and solve the problems confronting him by the development of symptoms. It has been found that this scale fails to identify a small number of very uncomplicated conversion hysterias which may be quite obvious clinically and with a single or very few conversion symptoms.

The hysterical cases are more immature psychologically than any other group. Although their symptoms can often be 'miraculously' alleviated by some conversion of faith or by appropriate therapy, there is always the likelihood that the problem will reappear if the stress continues or recurs. As in the case of hypochondriasis, the subject with a high Hy score may have real physical pathology, either as a primary result of concurrent disease, such as diabetes or cancer, or as a secondary result of the long-time presence of the psychological symptoms. For instance, constant fears are a frequent background for the development of demonstrable ulcers of the stomach. This interrelationship is particularly important to the physician who undertakes therapy for the individual.

4. *The psychopathic deviate scale* (*Pd*). – The Pd scale (3, 16) measures the similarity of the subject to a group of persons whose main difficulty lies in their absence of deep emotional response, their inability to profit from experience, and their disregard of social mores. Although sometimes dangerous to themselves or others, these persons are commonly likable and intelligent. Except by the use of an objective instrument of this sort, their trend towards the abnormal is frequently not detected until they are in serious trouble. They may often go on behaving like perfectly normal people for several years between one outbreak and another. Their most frequent digressions from the social mores are lying, stealing, alcohol or drug addiction, and sexual

immorality. They may have short periods of true psychopathic excitement or depression following the discovery of a series of their asocial or antisocial deeds. They differ from some criminal types in their inability to profit from experience and in that they seem to commit asocial acts with little thought of possible gain to themselves or of avoiding discovery.

No therapy is especially effective in improving persons with high Pd scores, but time and careful, intelligent guidance may lead to an adequate adaptation. Institutionalization of the more severe cases is probably no more than a means of protecting society and the offender. Some active professional persons have high Pd scores, but their breaks, if any, are either disregarded by others or effectively concealed.

5. *The interest scale (Mf)*. – This scale measures the tendency towards masculinity or femininity of interest pattern; separate T scores are provided for the two sexes. In either case a high score indicates a deviation of the basic interest pattern in the direction of the opposite sex. The items were originally selected by a comparison of masculine with feminine males and of the two sexes. Some were inspired by Terman and Miles (30), and others are original.

Every item finally chosen for this scale indicated a trend in the direction of femininity on the part of male sexual inverts. Males with very high Mf scores have frequently been found to be either overt or repressed sexual inverts. However, homosexual abnormality *must not be assumed* on the basis of a high score without confirmatory evidence. Among females high scores cannot yet be safely assumed to have similar clinical significance, and the interpretation must be limited to measurement of the general trait.

The Mf score is often important in vocational choice. Generally speaking, it is well to match a subject vocationally with work that is appropriate to his Mf level.

6. *The paranoia scale (Pa)*. – The Pa scale was derived by contrasting normal persons with a group of clinic patients who were characterized by suspiciousness, oversensitivity, and delusions of persecution, with or without expansive egotism. The diagnoses were usually paranoia, paranoid state, or paranoid schizophrenia. Here again, however, we have observed a few very paranoid persons who have successfully avoided betraying themselves in the items of this scale

Persons with an excess of paranoid suspiciousness are common and in many situations are not especially handicapped. It is difficult and dangerous to institutionalize or otherwise protect society from the borderline paranoiac because he appears so normal when he is on guard and he is so quick to become litigious or otherwise to take action vengefully against anyone who attempts to control him. It should be needless to add that persons receiving very high scores on this scale must be handled with special appreciation of these implications. Although valid scores of 80 and above on this scale are nearly always significant of disabling abnormality, the range from 70 to 80 must also be checked by clinical judgment.

7. *The psychasthenia scale (Pt).* – The Pt scale (23) measures the similarity of the subject to psychiatric patients who are troubled by phobias or compulsive behavior. The compulsive behavior may be either explicit, as expressed by excessive hand washing, vacillation, or other ineffectual activity, or implicit, as in the inability to escape useless thinking or obsessive ideas. The phobias include all types of unreasonable fear of things or situations as well as over-reaction to more reasonable stimuli.

Many persons show phobias or compulsive behavior without being greatly incapacitated. Such minor phobias as fear of snakes or spiders and such compulsions as being forced to count objects seen in arrays or always to return and check a locked door are rarely disabling. Frequently a psychasthenic tendency may be manifested merely in a mild depression, excessive worry, lack of confidence, or inability to concentrate.

Pt is correlated to a negligible degree with the other scales, except for the Sc scale. There is an understandable tendency for depression to accompany abnormally high scores. The basic personality pattern of the psychasthenic individual is relatively difficult to change, but insight and relief from general stress may lead to good adjustment. As in the Pa scale the valid T scores above 80 are likely to represent disabling abnormality, but the range of 70 to 80 should be checked by clinical judgment since with a favorable environment or with other compensatory factors the subject may not be markedly handicapped.

8. *The schizophrenia scale (Sc).* – The Sc scale measures the similarity of the subject's responses to those patients who are characterized by bizarre and unusual thoughts or behavior. There is a

splitting of the subjective life of the schizophrenic person from reality so that the observer cannot follow rationally the shifts in mood or behavior.

The Sc scale distinguishes about 60 per cent of observed cases diagnosed as schizophrenia. It does not identify some paranoid types of schizophrenia, which, however, usually score high on Pa, and certain other cases which are characterized by relatively pure schizoid behavior. It is probable that one or two additional scales will be necessary to identify the latter cases, but this is not surprising in the light of the frequently expressed psychiatric opinion that schizophrenia is not a clinical entity but a group of rather heterogeneous conditions.

Most profiles with a high Sc score will show several other high points, and further clinical sorting will need to be carried out by subjective study of the case. Exceptional to other scale inter-correlations, the correlation of Sc with Pt for normal cases is ·84. Both experience and the fact that this correlation drops to ·75 on abnormal cases lead us to feel that, at least for the present, there is value in using both scales. Clinical experience shows that about twice as many cases diagnosed as schizophrenia obtain above borderline Sc scores as obtain such scores on Pt. An appreciable number of clinic cases not diagnosed as schizophrenia score high on the scale. These cases are nearly always characterized by complicated symptomatic patterns. *The clinician should be very hesitant to apply the diagnostic term schizophrenia because of its bad implications.*

9. *The hypomania scale (Ma).* – The Ma scale (25) measures the personality factor characteristic of persons with marked overproductivity in thought and action. The word hypomania refers to a lesser state of mania. Although the real manic patient is the lay person's prototype for the 'insane', the hypomanic person seems just slightly off normal. Some of the scale items are mere accentuations of normal responses. A principal difficulty in the development of the scale was the differentiation of clinically hypomanic patients from normal persons who are merely ambitious, vigorous, and full of plans.

. The hypomanic patient has usually got into trouble because of undertaking too many things. He is active and enthusiastic. Contrary to common expectations he may also be somewhat depressed at times. His activities may interfere with other people through his attempts to reform social practice, his enthusiastic stirring up of projects in which he then may lose interest, or his disregard of social conventions. In the latter connexion he may get into trouble with the law. A fair percentage of patients diagnosed psychopathic personality (see Pd) are better called hypomanic.

This scale clearly identifies about 60 per cent of diagnosed cases and yields a score in the 60 to 70 range for the remainder. For scores around 70 the problem of normality hinges more upon the direction of the overactivity rather than upon the absolute score. Even extreme cases tend to get better with time, but the condition tends to reappear periodically.

C. Additional Scales

As has been mentioned, the basic concept of the Inventory assumes that among the entire 550 items there are groupings of items that can form additional scales. The K-factor scale was developed in such a manner, and other scales have been – or may yet be – developed to meet special requirements. These scales may be applied to old records (where the full Inventory and not a shortened version has been used) and their value judged at once without waiting for the accumulation of new case material. The following scales have been developed under this hypothesis.

0. *The social I. E. scale (Si).* – The Si scale (5) aims to measure the tendency to withdraw from social contact with others. No appreciable sex differences were found for the standardization population (which consisted of college students).

The Si scale is not a clinical scale in the strict sense of being chiefly for use with hospitalized patients; it is, however, valuable for use with normals, and has been widely used in counselling and guidance work. High scores on the scale have, for example, been found to distinguish college women who engage in few extra-curricular activities from those who engage in many activities (6).

Other scales that have been developed for use with the MMPI cannot be fully described, and scoring keys and other information necessary to their application are not given here or included with the test materials when purchased. However, the references in the literature which describe their construction, usage and scoring are listed below for those who might have occasion to use them.

a. The dominance scale (Do). Aims to measure personal dominance in a face-to-face situation (14).

b. The low back pain scale (LBQ). Aims to measure psychological factors found in veterans with functional low back pain as distinguished from cases with organic pathology (15).

   c. The parieto-frontal scale (PF). Aims to differentiate cases with focal damage of the parietal lobe from those with frontal lobe lesions (1, 7).

   d. The prejudice scale (Pr). Aims to measure psychological factors associated with prejudices against minority groups, especially anti-Semitism (11).

   e. The Rc scale (Rc). A scale related to A.W.O.L. recidivism (2).

   f. The responsibility scale (Re). Aims to measure internalization of social and moral responsibility (13).

   g. The socio–economic status scale (St). Aims to measure certain inner psychological trends usually found associated with a person's socio–economic class (8, 9, 10).

   h. The neuroticism scale (Ne). Aims to differentiate normals from neurotics of mixed diagnoses (32).

While not new scales in the sense of those just mentioned, the development of 'subtle' (S) and 'obvious' (O) keys may merit attention (31). All of the items of the D, Hy, Pd, Pa, and Ma scales have been classified into these two categories, and it has been found that examinees who are psychologically sophisticated and have high intelligence ratings and high L scores are higher on the S than the O keys, and that the reverse is true of examinees who have lower intelligence ratings and lower L scores. High correlations (—·47 to —·78) have also been found between K scores and O minus S scores. While O items contribute largely to the validity of the Inventory for institutionalized groups, S items seem to have potential value in counseling relatively normal, sophisticated or superior populations.

III. General Principles for the Interpretation of Profiles

The MMPI was particularly designed to provide an estimate of symptomatic syndromes commonly recognized among persons with clinical problems. The clinical scales were derived at least in part from the general descriptive background of Kraepelinian terminology as modified and applied in American practice. The scales were not expected to measure pure traits nor represent discrete etiological or prognostic entities.

The MMPI profiles are not adequate as a basis for evaluation of the meaning of symptoms as factors in the client's environmental adjustment; and, for that reason, among others, the MMPI profile does not directly provide definitive evidence as to disability or diagnosis even with the majority of psychiatric patients. The profile must be subjectively evaluated by the clinician in terms of his concepts of the significance of the symptoms to the subject's self-concept, to the prognosis, and relative to the particular cultural milieu of the subject.

MMPI scales show considerable variability from one testing to another; often this variability occurs within a matter of hours. For personality factors subject to therapy or to variation from any source, it should be obvious that this would be so to the extent that the profiles reflect the changing personality pattern. As an example, a clinically significant depression may disappear almost in minutes where it has resulted as a reaction to some environmental stress that is suddenly relieved. The sensitivity of the paranoid person is also variable depending upon his conceptual view of his environment. With explanation of what to him were puzzling or threatening social factors, he may change from a suspicious and defensive individual into an open, warm, and friendly one (although he will likely be susceptible to new suspicions).

MMPI profiles may also follow the shifting patterns of symptomatology as the client progresses through therapy (29). At times the disappearance of a depression will be accompanied by the appearance of a definitely anti-social or psychopathic pattern of symptoms. Again, a hypomanic person may shift to depression; and all profiles indicating maladjustment tend to appear more and more normal as the individuals become improved. It should also, in this connexion, be kept in mind that the various specific syndromes are not equal in their disabling characteristics. Of two paranoid persons equally distorted in their thinking, one may be dangerously specialized and thus be considered committable; the other may be so generalized that he is not effectively dangerous and can remain free although he is known as a 'crank' or reclusive misogynist.

The MMPI also provides a number of checks upon the attitude of the patient as he takes the Inventory and upon the validity of his item responses. Obviously a subject who answers the items of the Inventory with the knowledge that the data may be used to his disadvantage, will tend to react differently than if he were answering the items in a completely permissive and unthreatening setting. Not infrequently, subjects will be defensive in what would seem to be an ideal setting to be frank. Paranoid individuals, for example, occasionally distort the most unthreatening surroundings, making every effort to conceal any response that might appear undesirable. Unfortunately, these varying attitudes with which a subject may take the test are not simple over-all affects;

for example, a client may be extremely defensive about physical symptoms that he thinks he may have, yet be entirely frank and unguarded regarding psychological symptoms. More often, the reverse of this is true. There is an unknown number of such variables in test-taking attitude that must be considered by the clinician when using the MMPI. Every effort should be made to gain the subject's confidence and to reassure him about the uses to be made of the individual item responses and the profile obtained.

It cannot be too strongly emphasized that the administration of an MMPI constitutes a professional act, and that with the administrator rests the responsibility for ethical practices in the use of data contained in the subject's responses. Answer sheets should never be made public property, and the profiles obtained from scoring answer sheets should be considered confidential. Such care and guardedness is essential and should be followed to the extent that often direct interpretation of the profiles should not be made even to the subject himself. It is most naive and ill-advised to attempt a diagnosis or make statements about a subject from his test data without some study of the person himself, and without consideration of the circumstances under which he answered the items or his environmental culture.

From the foregoing it should be clear that adequate use of the MMPI can only be achieved by persons with extensive clinical experience and particular training with the Inventory itself. For special purposes, it is often effective to use cutting point scores or other simple devices by which some validity for a particular purpose can be obtained by simple objective sorting of profiles. Even when such simplified methods are used, an experienced clinician should act as consultant and keep in touch with the practices.

A. The Problem of Validity

After scoring and coding, the interpretation of a profile begins with the problem of whether or not the responses of the subject have yielded a valid set of scores. Validity in this connexion refers chiefly to questions of attitude, candour, literacy, and the like, as these might affect the subject's responses and thus the scores on the various scales. Four primary checks are provided for the evaluation of validity, the ?, L, F, and K scores. Among these, various combinations may be used. Obviously the sorting of many items into the *Cannot say* (or ?) category will tend to have a depressing effect upon the elevation of clinical scores since the *Cannot say* items are never scored relative to a scale. The effect of

Cannot say items is, of course, proportional to the number of such items that occur in the subject's responses for each scale. If subjects cannot be induced to force most of their answers into the *True* or *False* categories, it is probably desirable, as has been suggested by a number of users of the M M P I, to identify the individual *Cannot say* items and note the per cent that might have contributed to each scale. Even when there are many *Cannot say* items, the per cent of these belonging to a given scale may be found negligible and thus not a significant factor. Some clinicians routinely assign all *Cannot say* responses of the subject to their respective scales in an arbitrarily adverse direction, thus obtaining a score on the scale which would have resulted if the adverse answer had been chosen by the subject for every one of the refused items. Although this practice *invalidates the T scores*, there may be value sometimes in the subjective use of such scores.

The chief complication in the interpretation of L, F, and K scores lies in the fact that they necessarily have two meanings. In the first implication, they are related to the test-taking attitude and general test-taking competency of the subject, and can be thought of as indicating, in varying degree, the validity of the clinical scales. However, it should be obvious that attitudes of the subject, as reflected in willingness to distort his answers, or over-candidness or defensiveness in responding, are aspects of his personality. If a subject takes the M M P I, rejecting all item responses that imply personal faults or that relate to his symptoms of personality difficulty, then a validity indicator that betrays him in this effort also tells us something about the kind of person he is. Interpretation then becomes a mixture of concern with the effect of his attitude on the values of the scales and the implications of his actions as they refer to the whole problem that prompted the testing in the first place.

Generally speaking, as is indicated in the descriptions of the scales, high L and high K scores tend to be indicators of one or another form of defensiveness. In a similar way, high F and low K scores are indicators of an attitude of self-criticism or a wish to appear in an unfavourable light, which may be either deliberate or unconscious. To a certain extent these various tendencies are corrected by use of the K correction of the five scales for which it was found to be a valid suppressor. In this way the profile is made interpretable without regard to the test-taking attitude. Many clinicians have felt, however, that the statistically applied K correction is incomplete, especially in the case of the more extreme deviations of K.

It has been found that the T scores for L and F were not appropriately chosen. This has led to the use of the raw scores instead of the T scores in interpretation and in the coding of profiles for these scales. Usage varies, but a raw score of 7 or more on L or one of 17 or more on F are probably very significant deviations that require interpretation, although not necessarily implying *a priori* invalidity of the findings. Illiteracy, scoring error, carelessness in subject responses, and the like, must always be considered as possible sources of high F scores and, unless one can be assured that these factors have not materially affected the profiles, the latter should be classed as invalid. Gough (12) has suggested that raw score F minus K should be used as a main indicator of test-taking distortion. For the use of this index the original papers dealing with it should be consulted.

Experience has shown the validity scores to be quite effective in detecting profiles that are distorted in the adverse direction (false positives, or 'plus-getting'). When distortion occurs in the good or 'normal' direction, the validity scales have proved definitely less effective for detection of the tendency. In this connexion, experienced users of the MMPI have tended to modify their thinking about the validity scores by attention to the clinical profile itself. High F scores, for example, are unlikely to be an indication of scoring error or of deliberate adverse falsification of a profile if several of the clinical scales show scores near a T score of 50. In the other direction, profiles with many low scores may be regarded with some suspicion even though the L and K scores are not greatly elevated.

The foregoing brief account does no more than hint at the complexities of interpretation relative to the test-taking attitudes and abilities of the subject. Unusual or inexplicable profiles should always be regarded with suspicion and interpretation should be routinely cautious.

B. The Clinical Profile

When the findings of the MMPI are to be interpreted in ways that directly affect the treatment, the social placement, or the personal reactions of individuals, the authors strongly recommend that interpretation should be made only by persons accredited in the general field of psychiatry, clinical psychology, personal counseling, psychiatric social work, or any field recognized as scientifically oriented in work with problems of psychological adjustment and maladjustment. In addition to this professional specialization, those who interpret profiles should be further qualified. They need special training in the use of the MMPI and supervised experience with the test. They should also be acquainted with the published literature on the use of the MMPI in the particular context of their clinical work.

It should be continually kept in mind that the great majority of persons having deviant profiles are not, in the usual sense of the word, mentally ill, nor are they in need of psychological treatment. Having no more information about a person than that he has a deviant profile, one should always start with the assumption that the subject is operating within the normal range. This assumption is, in an actuarial sense, more likely than not to be correct, since we have every reason to think that if a truly representative cross section of the population were to be tested, more deviant profiles would be obtained from persons not obviously abnormal (in clear need of professional help) than from persons having admitted or obvious difficulties. This is not because the per cent of deviant profiles from normals is greater, but simply because there are so many more normals in the general population.

Although American psychiatric practice strongly influenced the classifications implied by many of the scales, the MMPI profile is not to be regarded as being chiefly directed toward the psychiatric diagnosis of disorders. As has been emphasized above, the mere presence of unusual or deviant factors in a personality, even if validly indicated, does not necessarily mean that the person is handicapped. Kracpclinian-based thinking is useful, however, in the fact that it is almost universally understood and so far has not been seriously threatened by any other system of classification. The MMPI, being chiefly directed at the practice of clinical psychology, is a direct reflection of the importance of these patterns in clinical evaluation of both the hospitalized patient and the normal personality.

The psychiatric syndromes are not pure nor independent of one another. Any experienced clinician recognizes that the symptoms of moderately ill patients always show the patient as a mixed problem diagnostically. Depression, for example, is the most ubiquitous of the patterns seen in psychological abnormality. It may be present even in a person with many manic characteristics. For example, patients with cortical brain damage often have depressing insight into their disability, yet the very character of the lesions leads to fallacious judgment and impulsiveness that are characteristic of hypomanic patients. It is this variety in the symptomatic problems of patients that makes the selection of a particular diagnosis so seemingly unreliable. The several diagnoses given at different times also often relate to the shifting importance of the different syndromes as a patient reacts to his illness or environmental pressures.

An Atlas for the Clinical Use of the MMPI (19) is intended as a prime source book for interpretation of individual cases. Codes for given profiles may be traced so that a kind of clinical cross section of experience with persons having relatively similar codes will suggest tentative interpretations and lines of investigation relative to the person under consideration. Also, tables are provided that will give an actuarial indication relative to diagnostic categories, and, in a broader sense, relative to the frequency with which a given profile occurred among various populations.

MMPI users often wonder about the significance of low points as they occur in codes. Clinical experience has convinced many counselors that low points are valid (at least on some scales). Scales D, Pd, Mf, Pa, Pt, Sc, Ma, and Si may be meaningful when very low, but formal evidence should be awaited before more specific statements are made. A study of low points relative to case histories in the *Atlas* may help in the meantime.

When looking at the average drawn or coded profile, it is best to attend to the *several* highest (and lowest) points rather than the absolute standing of any one scale. This is because of the complex mixture of abnormalities that is found in most hospitalized patients, and which the Inventory reflects. Each clinical scale in the Inventory was based on a group of patients having a certain *primary* diagnosis; for example, the Sc scale was based on a group of patients diagnosed as being schizophrenic, the D scale on a group of patients diagnosed as being depressive, etc. Depression, however, is usually found in cases diagnosed as schizophrenic, and in fact the T score on D may well be higher than the T score on Sc for many schizophrenic patients. Nothing in the statistical derivation of the MMPI justifies our expecting that T scores on a given clinical scale will necessarily be higher than the T scores on all the other clinical scales, even for a group of patients whose primary diagnosis bears the same label as the scale. Thus while the Sc scale came from the responses of diagnosed schizophrenic patients, this does not mean that for such patients the T scores on Sc will always be higher than the T scores on D. Most of these patients will be depressed and will have high D scores. When they are paranoid, they may also have high Pa scores. (Some clinicians say the paranoid person tends to get either a high *or* a very low Pa score while normal persons are in the middle.) We do not yet have adequate statistical methods to express this 'pattern' validity properly but must rely upon counselor judgment based upon experience, or better, upon empirical indexes.

In a very broad way, the clinician may think of the profiles of both normal and abnormal persons as having some similarity to three generalized patterns. These three are the neurotic, the behavior problem, and the psychotic. With this in mind, the scales Hs, D and Hy (the neurotic triad) tend to be dominant among neurotic patients. Pt is usually also considered relative to neuroticism and is a fourth indicator. Behavior problem profiles are those dominated by the scales Pd, Mf and Ma, with Pa less clearly related. In psychotic profiles, the scales Sc and Pa become of greatest importance, with D and Ma also expressing the pattern. The importance of this broad classification is related to the varying clinical implications of the three categories. Neurotic persons, in general, are less handicapped and more amenable to treatment. Behavior problem persons are more likely to be in conflict with society; environmental considerations may be of great importance here. The psychotics are more deeply and obviously ill. Of course these generalizations are subject to many exceptions and are probably chiefly useful in the treatment of group data.

Interpretation of high scores should always be modified by the knowledge that statistical deviation on one scale has not been validated *relative to* a similar deviation on *other* scales. There is no certain way of saying how much abnormality is represented by a T score of 70 on Hs as contrasted to a T score of 70 on Pa. Both the clinical significance of the deviations and the validity of the scales will differ and theoretically ought to affect thinking along these lines.

Within certain limits, experience has indicated that the more scores found to be elevated and the higher these scores are, the more likely it is that the person is severely disturbed. There are probably outstanding exceptions, however, to even this rule. In some degree the scales Ma and Pd, for example, tend to have a kind of negative clinical relationship to Hs and D. Extreme elevation of one or both of the Pd and Ma scales alone may indicate a more profoundly and significantly disturbed individual than would be the case if the other two scales were also extremely elevated. This example does not relate an established fact but is meant to be merely illustrative of possible future developments in our understanding of the interrelationship of scales.

As a final emphasis, the interpretation of profiles should never be considered a final statement. The fact is that people get better and get worse clinically; or, if they are not clinical problems, they change in the relative significance of various factors in their personalities. Personality testing can never yield scores with stability comparable to that of aptitude and interest test scores. A test giving stable scores would probably be clinically of little use, at least for certain types of evaluation, no matter how valid it might be. With future research, it is not unlikely that we shall find a hierarchy of stability for various personality traits, some remaining quite constant, others being exceedingly variable. Even now we are certain that a factor like depression is an exceedingly variable one. The repeated emphasis given here to this variability is by no means an apology for the fact that variability of MMPI profiles is also attributable partly to invalidity and random or non-valid factors. Unfortunately, no adequate experimental demonstration has been devised to establish how much variance should be attributed to valid sources and how much to invalid or nonpertinent ones. The point should merely be emphasized that, such considerations aside, there is every reason to expect valid variance; and, therefore, interpretation should be based upon adequate clinical experience in modifying what might otherwise seem to be cold and final statistics.

References

1. Andersen, A. L. Personality changes following prefrontal lobotomy. *J. consult. Psychol.*, 1949, **13**, 105–7.
2. Clark, J. H. Application of the MMPI in differentiating AWOL recidivists from non-recidivists. *J. Psychol.*, 1948, **26**, 229–34.
3. Cleckley, H. *The mask of sanity*. St Louis: C. V. Mosby, 1941.
4. Cottle, W. C. Card versus booklet forms of the MMPI. *J. appl. Psychol.*, 1950, **34**, 255–9.
5. Drake, L. E. A social I. E. scale for the MMPI. *J. appl. Psychol.*, 1946, **30**, 51–4.
6. Drake, L. E. and Thiede, W. B. Further validation of the social I. E. scale for the MMPI. *J. educ. Res.*, 1948, **41**, 551–6.
7. Friedman, S. H. Psychometric effects of frontal and parietal lobe brain damage. Unpublished Ph.D. thesis, Univ. Minn., 1950.
8. Gough, H. G. A new dimension of status: I. Development of a personality scale. *Amer. sociol. Rev.*, 1948, **13**, 401–9.
9. Gough, H. G. A new dimension of status: II. Relationship of the St scale to other variables. *Amer. sociol. Rev.*, 1948, **13**, 534–7.
10. Gough, H. G. A new dimension of status: III. Discrepancies between the St scale and 'objective' status. *Amer. sociol. Rev.*, 1949, **14**, 275–81.
11. Gough, H. G. Personality correlates of social and ethnic attitudes among high school students. Unpublished Ph.D. thesis, Univ. Minn., 1949.

12. Gough, H. G. The F minus K dissimulation index for the MMPI. *J. consult. Psychol.*, 1950, **14**, 408–13.
13. Gough, H. G., McClosky, H., and Meehl, P. E. A scale for measuring social responsiblity. *J. abnorm. soc. Psychol.*, in press.
14. Gough, H. G., McClosky, H., and Meehl, P. E. A scale for measuring dominance. *J. abnorm. soc. Psychol.*, in press.
15. Hanvik, L. J. Some psychological dimensions of low back pain. Unpublished Ph.D. thesis, Univ. Minn., 1949.
16. Hathaway, S. R. The personality inventory as an aid in the diagnosis of psychopathic inferiors. *J. consult. Psychol.*, 1939, **3**, 112–17.
17. Hathaway, S. R., and McKinley, J. C. A multiphasic personality schedule (Minnesota): I. Construction of the schedule. *J. Psychol.*, 1940, **10**, 249–54.
18. Hathaway, S. R., and McKinley, J. C. A multiphasic personality schedule (Minnesota): III. The measurement of symptomatic depression. *J. Psychol.*, 1942, **14**, 73–84.
19. Hathaway, S. R., and Meehl, P. E. *An atlas for the clinical use of the MMPI.* Minneapolis: Univ. Minn. Press, 1951.
20. Holzberg, J. D., and Alessi, S. Reliability of the shortened MMPI. *J. consult. Psychol.*, 1949, **13**, 288–92.
21. Horst, P. The prediction of personal adjustment. *Soc. Sci. Res. Coun. Bull.*, 1941, No. **48**, 1–156.
22. McKinley, J. C., and Hathaway, S. R. A multiphasic personality schedule (Minnesota): II. A differential study of hypochondriasis. *J. Psychol.*, 1940, **10**, 255–68.
23. McKinley, J. C., and Hathaway, S. R. A multiphasic personality schedule (Minnesota): IV. Psychasthenia. *J. appl. Psychol.*, 1942, **26**, 614–24.
24. McKinley, J. C., and Hathaway, S. R. The identification and measurement of the psychoneuroses in medical practice: The MMPI. *J. Amer. med. Ass.*, 1943, **122**, 161–7.
25. McKinley, J. C., and Hathaway, S. R. The MMPI: V. Hysteria, hypomania, and psychopathic deviate. *J. appl. Psychol.*, 1944, **28**, 153–74.
26. McNemar, Q. The mode of operation of supressant variables. *Amer. J. Psychol.*, 1945, **58**, 554–5.
27. Meehl, P. E. A simple algebraic development of Horst's supressor variables. *Amer. J. Psychol.*, 1945, **58**, 550–54.
28. Meehl, P. E., and Hathaway, S. R. The K factor as a suppressor variable in the MMPI. *J. appl. Psychol.*, 1946, **30**, 525–64.
29. Schofield, W. Changes in responses to the MMPI following certain therapies. *Psychol. Monogr.*, 1950, **64**, No. 311.
30. Terman, L. M., and Miles, C. C. *Sex and personality.* New York: McGraw-Hill, 1936.
31. Wiener, D. N. Subtle and obvious keys for the MMPI. *J. consult. Psychol.*, 1948, **12**, 164–70.
32. Winne, J. F. A scale of neuroticism: an adaptation of the MMPI. *J. clin. Psychol.*, 1951, **7**, 117–22.

SOCIAL DESIRABILITY AND
PERSONALITY TEST CONSTRUCTION

It is of the nature of Inventory methods that the import of the questions they ask will be evident, at least in part, to any but a totally naïve subject. This point has already been mentioned in the Introduction (p. 11), and it is of course one of which makers of inventories are well aware. 'Lie' scales are indeed built into many inventories, as a safeguard, but one's concern is not only or even primarily with deliberate falsification, but rather with error due to desire to conform with a social norm, or to discrepancies between the 'self-concept' and the 'objective' self.

Also relevant here is the notion of response style, the most frequently quoted example of which is 'acquiescence', or 'yeasaying', to use a term made fashionable by Couch and Keniston (2). If a tendency to say 'Yes' to a questionnaire item, irrespective of its content, is indeed a personality variable, the effect on such measures as the MPI Neuroticism scale (see 16, above) where all items are keyed 'Yes', must be considerable. However, a recent provocatively-titled survey by Rorer (3) suggests that 'current opinion to the contrary notwithstanding' there is little or no evidence that response style ever seriously affects conclusions. Rorer distinguishes between 'response style', of which acquiescence would be an example, and 'response set', which would include such phenomena as responsiveness to the social desirability of inventory items.

The present text develops the theme of the author's standard work on the subject (18, 13). It appeared first in a collection of papers (1) originally read at a symposium at Louisiana State University in 1958. The orientation was largely theoretical; most relevant to the content of this book are the contributions by W. H. Holtzman on 'Objective Scoring of Projective Techniques' and B. M. Bass on 'An Approach to the Objective Assessment of Leadership'.

References
1. Bass, B. M., and Berg, I. A. (Eds.), *Objective Approaches to Personality*. New York and London: Van Nostrand, 1959.
2. Couch, A. and Keniston, K., Yeasayers and Naysayers: Agreeing Response Set as a Personality Variable, *J. abnorm. soc. Psych.* **60**, 151–74. 1960.
3. Rorer, L. G., The Great Response-Style Myth, *Psychological Bulletin*, **63**, 129–56. 1965.

18 A. L. Edwards

Social Desirability and Personality Test Construction

Bass, B. M., and Berg, I. A. (Eds.), *Objective Approaches to Personality;* Van
Nostrand, Princeton and London, 1959, pp. 101–16.

In the typical personality inventory, the number of possible responses available to the subject is fixed by the nature of the test so
that the subject must choose one of the several alternatives presented to him. I shall refer to these various alternatives as
response categories. An objective personality inventory may have
any number of response categories. However, we seldom find
inventories with more than five response categories and, in most
cases, the inventories in current use have only two or three
response categories. These are usually of the form: True-False,
Yes-No, Agree-Disagree, Like-Dislike, and so forth. When three
response categories are provided, the third category is typically an
Undecided category.

Although it is not a necessary condition for an objective personality inventory, we generally find that only one of the response
categories is keyed. By a keyed response, I shall mean the
response that is assigned a non-zero scoring weight. With a
True-False test, designed to measure a personality variable, the
keyed response is the one that we believe is more likely to be
given by those who have a greater degree of the variable than by
those who have a lesser degree. For example, in an inventory
designed to measure introversion, the following item might
appear: I keep in the background on social occasions. If we
believe, for one reason or another, that those who have a high
degree of introversion are more likely to answer True to this item
than those who have a lesser degree of introversion, the keyed
response would be True.

It will be convenient to confine the present discussion to those
objective personality inventories in which a limited number of
response categories are available to the subject and in which only
one of the possible responses is keyed. The points I wish to make,
however, have general implications and would, I believe, apply
also to those inventories in which differential weights are
assigned to multiple categories.

Methods Used in Developing Inventories

In constructing objective personality inventories, three somewhat different procedures have been followed. Cattell (4) and Guilford (16, 17), for example, have used factor analysis techniques in developing their personality inventories. The *Minnesota Multiphasic Personality Inventory* and the *Vocational Interest Blank*, on the other hand, were constructed by Hathaway and McKinley (20) and Strong (25), respectively, using a procedure which I shall call the method of criterion groups. Still a third approach is the one used by Allport, Vernon, and Lindzey (1) in constructing the *Study of Values*, and which I have also used in developing the *Personal Preference Schedule* (9). This latter approach, I shall refer to as the construct approach.

If the factor analytic approach is followed, one starts initially with a large pool of items. Subjects are asked to respond to each item and the responses to all possible pairs of items are correlated. The resulting intercorrelation matrix is factor analyzed in anticipation of obtaining a smaller number of factors than items. By rotation of the factor matrix, simple structure may be found. Then, those items with high loadings on a given factor and low loadings on all other factors are placed together. By examining the content of the items with high loadings on a single factor, an attempt is made to see what they have in common. These items, for the factor analyst, will constitute a scale for measuring a single personality variable. Thus Cattell (3, p. 81) has found a factor on which a high score indicates: that the subject prefers an art gallery to a game of cards on a fine afternoon; that he does not generally succeed in keeping his emotions under control; that he does not dislike being waited on in personal matters; and that he does not believe that racial characters have more real influence in shaping the individual and the nation than most people believe. Yet, at the same time, he does admit to fits of dread or anxiety for no apparent reason; he does try to bluff his way past a guard or doorman; and he has been known to be a sleepwalker and to talk a great deal in his sleep. Cattell has tentatively labelled this personality variable as 'Bohemian Unconcernedness'.

It is not that a factor analyst would necessarily start out with the notion of developing a scale designed to measure 'Bohemian Unconcernedness'. As a matter of fact, it is characteristic of the factor analytic procedure that not one but several scales result from the application of factor methodology – one for each of the factors obtained. It is also characteristic of the factor analyst that he has no necessary prior notion of what these factors may be, if found, nor what they may relate to. The name assigned a factor or scale is based upon an examination of the content of those items with high loadings on the factor and what these items will be is not necessarily known in advance. Furthermore, the number of factors obtained is limited only by the number of items initially used. And the initial number of items, in turn, is limited only by the capacity of the modern electronic computer.

The criterion group approach demands that we have two contrasting groups of subjects available. For example, one of these groups may consist of individuals labelled as schizophrenic by psychiatrists and the other of individuals not so labelled. These two groups are given a set of items and differences in the responses of the two groups to each item are examined. Tests of significance may be applied as a basis for selecting those items for which there is a statistically significant difference in response between the two criterion groups. Thus, it may be found that a significantly larger number of schizophrenics than normals answer True to the item: I frequently have pains in my feet. This item will then be selected for inclusion in a scale – along with any other additional items that differentiate between the two groups. Item selection is rigorously empirical, and the person who uses the criterion group approach is, in general, not at all concerned with item content. He asks only that the items included in the scale be those that have been found to differentiate between the two groups of interest. The name assigned to the variable supposedly measured by the scale is based on the nature of the criterion groups used in their selection. Thus, MMPI scales have been constructed to measure schizophrenia, delinquency, depression, hysteria, low back pain, and so forth. The number of scales which can be constructed following the criterion group approach is limited only by the number of contrasting groups that can be found.

If the goal of the criterion group approach is to develop a scale useful in the prediction of membership or lack of membership in groups comparable to the original criterion groups, the procedures followed seem highly appropriate. But if scores on the scale so developed are treated, as they so often are, as measuring variation along a single continuum or dimension of personality, that is another matter. No matter how rigorously the criterion groups are defined, it does not seem at all possible that they can ever be made comparable in all respects but one. It may be possible, of course, to equate them for such variables as age, sex, socioeconomic status, and so forth, but it is well known that as the number of variables on which two groups are matched is increased, there is a corresponding decrease in the number of cases that meet the requirements for membership in the criterion groups. If we retain substantial N's in both groups, then we may have groups differing with respect to the criterion, but this criterion will of necessity be complex – a multiplicity of many things.

Perhaps the reason so many scales have been developed to measure clinical rather than normal personality variables is because criterion groups for clinical variables are available in hospitals and institutions. We should keep in mind, however, that a scale developed in this manner can never be better than the criterion group which provided the basis for item selection. Thus, if a criterion group is established by psychiatric judgment and if psychiatric judgment is fallible, as it surely is, this may mean that if we use the judgments of other psychiatrists to establish the criterion group, it will not be the same as the original criterion group. This, in turn, may result in a different set of items being selected for inclusion in the scale than those selected on the basis of responses of the original group. Two scales so developed, although supposedly predicting the same criterion, may bear little relation to one another.

In using the construct approach to the development of a personality scale, the psychologist starts with at least a vague notion of a personality variable that is of interest to him. He may have noted, for example, that some people seem to desire to be the center of attention. They like to entertain others, to tell amusing stories, to make themselves conspicuous by wearing unusual clothing, and, in various ways, to draw attention to themselves. These isolated bits of behavior may be subsumed under a construct which is tentatively labelled exhibition. The objective of the construct approach is to develop a scale which, it is hoped, will measure the construct of interest. When this approach is used in the development of an inventory, one does not start with a heterogeneous collection of items. Rather the attempt in the initial stage of item formulation is to 'map the construct'. The kinds of items we seek are those which are believed to be relevant to the construct.

When a sufficient pool of items is available, the responses of an unselected group of subjects to the items are then analyzed. Correlational and factor analytic techniques may be used in the attempt to select homogeneous items for inclusion in the scale. Or total scores for the subjects may be obtained on the complete set of items and the individual items analyzed in terms of total scores. This, of course, is, in a sense, a criterion group approach, but with one important difference. The criterion groups, in this instance, are established on the basis of their behavior with respect to the items, rather than in terms of an external criterion.

A major limitation of the construct approach is that the items included in the scale are dependent upon the manner in which the investigator has mapped the construct initially. For example, one investigator's construct of exhibition may not be the same as another's. Thus, although they may use the same labels, the mapping of the construct may be quite different with the result that the items in the two scales may also be different. Further research with the scales, along the lines suggested by Peak (24) and by Cronbach and Meehl (7), with respect to construct validity may prove of value in clarifying the difference between the two constructs represented by the two scales.

Item Endorsement and Social Desirability Scale Value

Regardless of the approach used in the development of a personality scale, there are certain common problems relating to the finished product. One of these relates to what I have come to call the social desirability variable and it is this problem that I now wish to discuss.

You are all familiar with the methods devised by Thurstone for scaling attitude statements. A number of statements relevant to some issue or institution are collected and these are submitted to a judging group. The judging group is not asked to respond in terms of whether they agree or disagree with each statement, but only to judge the degree of favorableness of each statement on, say, a 9-point scale. On the basis of the distribution of judgments for each statement, scale values are obtained by either the method of equal-appearing intervals or the method of successive intervals.* The scale value of a given statement is taken as an indication of its location on a psychological continuum such that high values indicate very favorable statements and low values very unfavorable statements.

I have applied these methods in scaling statements of the kind that we ordinarily find in personality inventories. The instructions given to the judging group are such that they are not asked to respond in terms of whether they agree or disagree with each

* These and other methods of psychological scaling are described by Edwards (12) and Guilford (18).

statement, or in terms of whether they think it does or does not describe them, but rather they are asked to judge the degree of social desirability or undesirability of each statement. In other words, I ask them to rate how desirable or undesirable they would consider the behavior or characteristic in other individuals. On the basis of the distribution of judgments, a scale value is obtained for each statement by one of the psychological scaling methods. The scale value of a statement is taken as an indication of the location of the statement on a psychological continuum ranging from highly socially undesirable to highly socially desirable. High scale values indicate statements that are socially desirable and low scale values statements that are socially undesirable.

Suppose that we have obtained social desirability scale values for a large number of statements. The statements are then printed in the form of a personality inventory. A new group of subjects is given the inventory and they are asked to respond to each statement in the usual manner of obtaining self-descriptions. For each statement we find the proportion of those responding Yes or True and we then plot these proportions against the corresponding, but independently obtained, social desirability scale values. The first time that I did this I found a linear relationship between the two variables. The product-moment correlation between the proportion endorsing an item and the social desirability scale value of the item was ·87 (8).

Calvin Wright (27) repeated this study with a minor variation. He gave 140 items to 127 college students and asked them to rate the degree to which each statement characterized them on a 9-point scale. The mean rating assigned to the statements in self-description was then correlated with the social desirability scale values of the statements. The product-moment correlation between these two variables for this sample was ·88.

Using a Q-sort to obtain self-descriptions with the same statements and with still another sample, I found correlations of ·87 between mean Q-sort rating and social desirability scale value for 50 females and ·84 for the same variables for a group of 50 males (10).

I have also scaled the items in the *Interpersonal Check List* for social desirability. The ICL was then given to another group of subjects who were asked to describe themselves without signing their names to their test booklets. The product-moment correlation between probability of endorsement and social desirability scale values for the 128 items in the ICL was ·83 (11).

These findings have subsequently been confirmed by various investigators with still other samples of items. Kenny (21), for example, scaled twenty-five personality items, originally used in an investigation by Zimmer (28), for social desirability. The rank order correlation between the social desirability scale value and the proportion endorsing an item was ·82 for these 25 statements. Hanley (19), working with items from the MMPI, reports correlations of ·89 and ·92 between probability of endorsement and social desirability scale values for 32 items randomly selected from the Sc or Schizophrenia scale, and correlation of ·82 and ·86 between probability of endorsement and social desirability scale value for 25 items selected at random from the D or Depression scale.

I believe it is possible to generalize, on the basis of the studies described, and to state that, whenever we have a personality inventory in which the items in the inventory vary with respect to their social desirability scale values, we may expect to find a substantial positive correlation between probability of endorsement of an item and social desirability scale value of the item. Consider one possible implication of this finding. Although Hanley (19) established the relationship between probability of endorsement and items in the Sc scale of the MMPI using only 32 of the 79 items in this scale, his selection of items, he states, was random. Let us assume, therefore, that the relationship would hold for the complete set of 79 items. Now, recall how the Sc scale was developed. To be included in the Sc scale, an item had to differentiate significantly between a group of diagnosed schizophrenic patients and a group of normal controls. This means that either a significantly larger proportion or a significantly smaller proportion in the schizophrenic group had to endorse an item compared with the corresponding proportion in the normal-control group. But, on the basis of Hanley's findings, we have evidence that the relationship between the proportion in the normal group endorsing an item and social desirability scale value is linear with a product-moment correlation of ·92 expressing the degree of the relationship. In essence, then, if an item was to be included in the Sc scale, the proportion in the schizophrenic group endorsing the item would be likely to deviate significantly from the linear regression line relating probability of endorsement to social desirability scale value for the normal group.

Does this mean that the relationship between probability of endorsement and social desirability scale value is not linear for the schizophrenic group? That is one possibility. Another is that the relationship is linear for the schizophrenic group, but that for this group the regression line is parallel to that obtained for the normal group, differing from it only in terms of the Y intercept. Still another possibility is that both the Y intercepts and the slopes of the regression lines differ for the two groups. Or, perhaps the social desirability scale values of the items established by the judgments of the schizophrenic group would differ from those established by judgments of the normal group. I do not know the answers to these questions, but they could easily be obtained through research. We do have some evidence, from a study by Klett (22), indicating that social desirability scale values based upon the judgments of diagnosed psychotic patients are related to the social desirability scale values of the same items obtained from judgments of a non-psychotic group. Klett, for example, reports a correlation of ·88 between the social desirability scale values based upon the judgments of psychotic patients and scale values based upon the judgments of college students.

The Social Desirability Hypothesis

Some years ago, Cronbach (5, 6) called attention to the importance of response sets as factors influencing scores on psychological tests. It was his observation that individuals may show very stable response tendencies to items in tests such that these tendencies are relatively independent of item content. The number of True responses that a person gives to a set of items may possibly be a measure of a general tendency to agree, or, as Cronbach called it, acquiescence. Similarly, the number of False responses that a person gives to a set of items may be a measure of a general tendency to disagree or dissent, that is, to be negative. If an Undecided category is provided, the number of such responses may be a measure of a general tendency to avoid committing oneself or to be evasive.

If the majority of the items in an inventory are keyed True, then a high score on the inventory may measure not only the variable of interest but also the tendency of the subject to acquiesce. Similarly, a low score may not necessarily indicate a lack of the variable, but only the tendency of the subject to respond negatively. Comparable complexities may enter into the interpretation of a score when the majority of the items are keyed False.

I do not, however, consider the tendency to respond True or the tendency to respond False as of primary importance in personality inventories. My reason for this belief is that both of these response-set hypotheses, at least in personality inventories, have been shown to lead to predictions which are contrary to fact, whereas an alternative hypothesis leads to predictions that are in accord with fact. This alternative hypothesis, I have called the social desirability or SD hypothesis (13).

The SD hypothesis proposes that, just as individual differences have been found in the tendencies of subjects to respond True, Undecided, or False, regardless of item content, so also are there individual differences in the tendencies of subjects to give socially desirable responses to items in personality inventories, regardless of whether the socially desirable response is True or False. I have devised various scales to measure this tendency and these scales are referred to as Social Desirability scales or SD scales (9, 13).

An SD scale is relatively easy to develop. Suppose we take any heterogeneous set of personality statements and scale them for social desirability. We desire items heterogeneous with respect to content simply because we do not wish subjects who are to be given the developed SD scale to believe we are measuring some particular personality variable, such as, for example, dominance. On the basis of the evidence cited previously, we expect to find a linear relationship between probability of endorsement of these items and their social desirability scale values. To develop an SD scale we take those items with socially desirable scale values and key the True response. For those items with socially undesirable scale values, we key the False response. A person's score on the scale is simply the number of times he has given the keyed response in self-description, that is, the number of socially desirable responses he has given. As I have said earlier, I have developed a number of such SD scales, but most of the research that has been done to date is based upon a scale consisting of 39 items from the MMPI (13).

Now, let us suppose we take any existing personality inventory of interest and examine the scoring key for the items contained in the inventory. If the trait being measured by the inventory is itself a socially desirable trait, then we would expect to find a majority of the keyed responses to be socially desirable also. The scoring key for the trait, in essence, would be much the same as the scoring key we would obtain if we keyed the responses as we would in developing an SD scale. If the inventory were scored by each key, we would expect to find a high and positive correlation between the scores resulting from each key. This should, in general, be true for all personality inventories designed to measure traits which are themselves considered socially desirable. Similarly, if a high score on a given personality inventory indicates a trait that is itself considered socially undesirable, then the scoring key for this inventory should be just the reverse of the scoring key we would obtain if we keyed the same items as in an SD scale. Scoring the inventory by each key, we would expect to find a high negative correlation between the scores resulting from each key, that is, the trait key and the SD key.

In the cases described, it could be argued that the resulting correlations were artefacts of the scoring keys applied to the same items. By having available a separate and independently constructed SD scale, based upon a different set of items, and by correlating scores on this SD scale with those of a given personality inventory, we are no longer correlating two sets of scores necessarily dependent by virtue of scoring the same set of items by two keys which are not themselves independent.

Correlations Between the SD Scale and Other Scales

A person with a high score on the SD scale can be described as one who has given a large number of socially desirable responses in self-description, whereas a person with a low score can be described as one who has given relatively few socially desirable responses in self-description. If this is a stable and consistent personality characteristic, we should find it evidenced in performance on a variety of other personality inventories, regardless of the particular traits supposedly being measured by these inventories. For example, suppose we have an inventory on which a high score indicates a socially desirable trait. Then individuals who are likely to give socially desirable responses in self-description are also likely to obtain high scores on this inventory. We should expect, therefore, that individuals who score high on the SD scale will also score high on the trait, whereas individuals with low scores on the SD scale will score low on the trait. As a result, we should find a positive correlation between scores on the SD scale and on the trait inventory.

Consider, for example, the Guilford-Martin (15) scales designed to measure Cooperativeness, Agreeableness, and Objectivity. High scores on these three scales indicate traits which, I believe, would be considered favorable or socially desirable. The product-moment correlations between scores on these three scales and scores on the original 79-item SD scale for a sample of 106 college males and females are ·63, ·53, and ·71, respectively (9). There are three MMPI scales on which high scores would be considered as indications of socially desirable traits: The Dominance, Responsibility, and Status scales. The tetrachoric correlations between scores on these scales and scores on the 39-item SD scale, as reported by Merrill and Heathers (23) for a sample of 155 males, are: ·49, ·52, and ·61, respectively.

If we consider inventories on which high scores would be taken as indications of socially undesirable traits, then, following the same line of reasoning as we did earlier, we should expect to find negative correlations between scores on these inventories and scores on the SD scale.* Within the MMPI we can find a wide variety of scales for which high scores indicate socially undesirable traits. Tetrachoric correlations were obtained by Merrill and Heathers (23) between scores on these scales and scores on the 39-item SD scale for a sample of 155 males. The tetrachoric correlations are as follows:

MMPI Scales	Correlation with the 39-Item SD Scale
Neuroticism	— ·50
Dependency	— ·73
Hostility	— ·75
Manifest Anxiety	— ·84
Social Introversion	— ·90

For the various clinical scales of the MMPI, Merrill and Heathers (23) report the following tetrachoric correlations with the 39-item SD scale for the same sample:

MMPI Scales	Correlation with the 39-Item SD Scale
Hs Hypochondriasis	— ·52
Pt Psychasthenia	— ·85
Sc Schizophrenia	— ·77
D Depression	— ·61
Pd Psychopathic Deviate	— ·50
Hy Hysteria	·08
Pa Paranoia	— ·09
Ma Hypomania	— ·13

The three lowest correlations with SD are those of ·08, —·09, and —·13 with Hysteria, Paranoia, and Hypomania, respectively.

* According to Berg's (2) deviant set hypothesis, if a subject tends to make responses *avoided* by the majority of a group of subjects, this tendency may be related to other forms of deviancy from normative standards. On the SD scale, deviant responses would result in low scores. On the SD scale, then, deviancy would be more or less synonymous with 'social undesirability' which, in turn, has been shown to be related to 'abnormality', as measured by the clinical scales of the MMPI.

As a result of my work with the SD scale, I have become so accustomed to finding substantial correlations between SD and scores on other inventories that, when low correlations are obtained, I seek for an explanation in terms of the relationship between the social desirability scale values of the items and the manner in which the item responses are keyed.

Factors Influencing Correlations with SD

In general, a low correlation between scores on the SD scale and scores on another personality inventory could result from at least two conditions. We know, for example, that, if the trait being measured by an inventory is itself socially undesirable, then, in general, most of the keyed responses will, in turn, be socially undesirable. To obtain a high score on the inventory, the subject must, in fact, attribute to himself socially undesirable characteristics. Suppose, however, that it is possible to obtain at least some items such that the keyed response is a socially desirable response, yet the variable itself is socially undesirable. For example, it might happen that, using the method of criterion groups, some of the items included in the clinical scales of the MMPI are such that the keyed response is a socially desirable response. Then to these items, a socially desirable response would be keyed as indicating a socially undesirable variable. If a scale contains a number of such items, then this would tend to lower the correlation between scores on the scale and scores on the SD scale.

Some evidence on this point is available. A study by Hanley (19) indicates that approximately 75 per cent of the items in the Sc scale have socially undesirable scale values, with 25 per cent falling in the neutral and socially desirable categories. For the D scale, on the other hand, only approximately 52 per cent of the items have socially undesirable scale values, whereas 48 per cent have scale values falling in the neutral and socially desirable categories. Hanley classified the items in these two scales according to whether the True response was keyed or not keyed in determining scores on the scales. With the dichotomy, keyed and not keyed, point biserial correlations were obtained with the social desirability scale values of the items as the continuous variable. For the Sc items, the point biserial correlation was ·84 and for the D items it was ·58. These findings indicate that the keying of items in the D scale is somewhat less related to the social desirability scale values of the items than in the case of the Sc scale. We should, therefore, expect to find, as we have consistently found, that scores on the D scale correlate lower with scores on the SD scale than do those on the Sc scale.

There is another possible way in which we might obtain a low correlation between scores on the SD scale and scores on another personality inventory. We might, for example, have an inventory in which a substantial number of the items have social desirability scale values in the central section of the psychological continuum. That is, these items may be relatively neutral with respect to their social desirability scale values. If we have a number of items with neutral scale values, a subject whose responses are primarily influenced by social desirability considerations will be in a quandary as to how he should respond. If the scale value of an item is truly neutral, then there is no socially desirable or undesirable response that can be made by a subject in answering it. In this situation, we might argue, his responses are more likely to be influenced by the content of the item. The correlation between SD and scores on the inventory should thus decrease as the number of neutral items in the inventory is increased.

Subtle Items

Some years ago, Wiener (26) attempted to classify the items in the various MMPI scales into two groups, one of which he called subtle and the other obvious. For five of the MMPI scales he was able to find two such groups of items. The three scales, Hysteria, Paranoia, and Hypomania, for which low correlations with SD are reported by Merrill and Heathers (23), are among the five. The two additional scales are the D and Pd scales. Hanley (19) has suggested that subtle items are those with neutral social desirability scale values. I have expressed the opinion that not only may a neutral item be a subtle item, but that any item for which a socially desirable response is keyed as a sign of socially undesirable trait would be a subtle item (13). In the case of socially desirable traits, a subtle item would be one for which the socially undesirable response is keyed. Recall that I define socially desirable and undesirable responses on the basis of an item's social desirability scale value.

Let us accept this hypothesis concerning subtle items, for the moment, and see if we can predict what we should find when we correlate scores on the SD scale with those on the subtle and obvious scales of the MMPI. For the obvious scales, we should have more items for which the keyed response is a socially undesirable response than in the cases of the subtle scales. The subtle scales, on the other hand, should

399

contain more neutral items and/or more items for which the keyed response is a socially desirable response than in the case of the obvious scales. If this argument is sound, then we should find a substantial negative correlation between the SD scale and the obvious scales. For the subtle scales, the correlations with SD should definitely be lower, with the magnitude and sign of the correlation depending solely upon how many neutral items the scale contains and upon the number of items for which the socially desirable response is keyed. If we have many items for which the socially desirable response is keyed, the correlation with SD should be positive in sign.

At my suggestion, Fordyce and Rozynko (14) drew a sample of fifty MMPI records from the files of a VA hospital and obtained product-moment correlations between scores on the 39-item SD scale and total scores on the D, Pd, Pa, Ma, and Hy scales. They then calculated the correlations between the SD scale and the separate subtle and obvious scales. The results are as shown below:

MMPI Scale	Correlations with the 39-Item SD Scale		
	Total	Obvious	Subtle
D	−·69	−·78	·33
Pd	−·67	−·85	·27
Pa	−·52	−·72	·06
Ma	−·08	−·53	·40
Hy	−·28	−·71	·54

Note that in every instance the negative correlation of SD with the obvious scale is greater than it is with the total scale consisting of both subtle and obvious items. This is as it should be. The correlations between SD and the subtle scales, on the other hand, are all positive in sign. These findings support the contention that the subtle scales contain neutral items and/or items for which a socially desirable response is keyed to a greater extent than do the obvious scales. The fact that the positive correlations between SD and the subtle scales are not of the same magnitude as the negative correlations between SD and the obvious scales indicates that the subtle scales contain fewer keyed socially desirable responses than the obvious scales contain keyed socially un-desirable responses.

I have spent considerable time with the MMPI and social desirability. This is not because I believe the MMPI to be the only personality inventory in which the social desirability variable operates. It is rather because the MMPI is such a widely used personality inventory that the data in which I was interested were readily available. The points I have made would apply, I believe, equally well to any other inventory of the True-False kind.

Minimizing Social Desirability

If we do not desire scores on objective personality inventories to be influenced by the social desirability variable, what can we do about it? One suggestion is that we can attempt to correct for social desirability by means of such scales as the SD scale. For example, if we know the correlation between the SD scale and scores on another personality inventory, then we can predict the score that a person would receive on the inventory by means of a linear regression function of these scores on the SD score. If we then subtract the predicted score from the actual score, it can readily be shown that these deviation scores will be uncorrelated with the SD scores. Unfortunately, however, the correlations between SD and scores on various personality inventories are of such magnitude that the residuals or deviation scores may represent little more than error variance. It is well known that the reliability of difference scores is, in general, considerably lower than the separate measures involved in the difference scores.

Another possibility would be to search for items that are relatively neutral with respect to their social desirability scale values. I do not know whether this is a hopeless search or not. I can only say that, on the basis of my experience in scaling personality items, the number of items with relatively neutral scale values is much smaller than the number I find with socially desirable or socially undesirable scale values.

Along the same lines, we might seek items such that the socially desirable response is the keyed response in scales designed to measure socially undesirable variables. For scales designed to measure socially desirable variables, we would, of course, attempt to find items for which the socially undesirable response is keyed. The five subtle scales of the MMPI are perhaps the closest approximations we have, at the present time, to scales of this kind. Additional research directed towards the development of subtle scales designed to measure normal personality variables is needed.

A third approach to the minimization of social desirability in personality inventories is the one I have used in developing the Personal Preference Schedule. In this inventory, an attempt is made to minimize the operation of the social desirability variable by pairing statements representing different personality variables on the basis of their social desirability scale values in such a way that the social desirability scale values of the two statements are comparable. The subject is then asked to choose between the two statements. In this way, we hope to minimize the probability of the choice being determined by social desirability considerations alone.

References

1. Allport, G. W., Vernon, P. E., and Lindzey, G. *Study of values.* (Rev. ed.) Boston: Houghton Mifflin, 1951.
2. Berg, I. A. Response bias and personality: the deviation hypothesis. *J. Psychol.*, 1955, **40**, 61–72.
3. Cattell, R. B. *Personality.* New York: McGraw-Hill, 1950.
4. Cattell, R. B. *The Sixteen Personality Factor Questionnaire.* Champaign, Ill.: Institute for Personality and Ability Testing, 1950.
5. Cronbach, L. J. Response sets and test validity. *Educ. psychol. Measmt.*, 1946, 6, 475–94.
6. Cronbach, L. J. Further evidence on response sets and test design. *Educ. psychol. Measmt.*, 1950, **10**, 3–31.
7. Cronbach, L. J., and Meehl, P. E. Construct validity in psychological tests. *Psychol. Bull.*, 1955, **52**, 281–302.
8. Edwards, A. L. The relationship between the judged desirability of a trait and the probability that the trait will be endorsed. *J. appl. Psychol.*, 1953, **37**, 90–93.
9. Edwards, A. L. *Manual for the Personal Preference Schedule.* New York: Psychol. Corp., 1953.
10. Edwards, A. L. Social desirability and Q sorts. *J. consult. Psychol.* 1955, **19**, 462.
11. Edwards, A. L. Social desirability and probability of endorsement of items in the Interpersonal Check List. *J. abnorm. soc. Psychol.*, 1957, **55**, 394–6.
12. Edwards, A. L. *Techniques of attitude scale construction.* New York: Appleton-Century, 1957.
13. Edwards, A. L. *The social desirability variable in personality assessment and research.* New York: Dryden, 1957.
14. Fordyce, W. E. and Rozynko, V. The correlations between the SD scale and the subtle and obvious scales of the MMPI. Unpublished study. Cited by A. L. Edwards, (13, above, p. 47).
15. Guilford, J. P. *The Guilford-Martin Personnel Inventory.* Beverly Hills, Calif.: Sheridan Supply Co., 1943.
16. Guilford, J. P. *An Inventory of Factors* STDCR. Beverly Hills, Calif.: Sheridan Supply Co., 1940.
17. Guilford, J. P., and Martin, H. G. *The Guilford-Martin Inventory of Factors* GAMIN, Abridged Edition. Beverly Hills, Calif.: Sheridan Supply Co., 1943.
18. Guilford, J. P. *Psychometric methods.* (2nd ed.) New York: McGraw-Hill, 1954.
19. Hanley, C. Social desirability and responses to items from three MMPI scales: D. Sc. and K. *J. appl. Psychol.*, 1956, **40**, 324–8.
20. Hathaway, S. R. and McKinley, J. C. Manual for the Minnesota Multiphasic Personality Inventory. (Rev. ed.) New York: Psychol. Corp., 1951.

21. Kenny, D. T. The influence of social desirability on discrepancy measures between real self and ideal self. *J. consult. Psychol.*, 1956, **20**, 315–18.
22. Klett, C. J. The social desirability stereotype in a hospital population. *J. consult. Psychol.*, 1957, **21**, 419–21.
23. Merrill, R. M., and Heathers, Louise, B. The relation of the MMPI to the Edwards Personal Preference Schedule on a college counseling center sample. *J. consult. Psychol.*, 1956, **20**, 310–14.
24. Peak, Helen. Problems of objective observation. In: L. Festinger and D. Katz (Eds.), *Research methods in the behavioral sciences.* New York: Dryden, 1953, pp. 243–99.
25. Strong, E. K., Jr. *Vocational Interest Blank for Men.* Stanford University, Calif.: Stanford University Press, 1938.
26. Wiener, D. N. Subtle and obvious keys for the Minnesota Multiphasic Personality Inventory. *J. consult. Psychol.*, 1948, **12**, 164–70.
27. Wright, C. E. Relations between normative and ipsative measures of personality. Unpublished doctor's dissertation. University of Washington, 1957.
28. Zimmer, H. Self-acceptance and its relation to conflict. *J. consult. Psychol.*, 1954, **18**, 447–9.

THE CONCEPT OF VALIDITY
IN PERSONALITY STUDY

At a concert an unfamiliar work is sometimes played twice –
once at the beginning and once at the end. A case could be
made out for doing something similar with this article, since
it contains material which might well be considered both
before and after reading the other contents of this book.

Considerations of validity are, however, slightly different
if one asks 'validity for what purpose?' Controversy arising
from opposed views of the functions of personality assessment,
and even of clinical psychology in general, came to a head in
1954, with the publication of Meehl's *Clinical versus Statistical
Prediction* (2). A stimulating account of the issues at stake is
given by Miller (3), and an attempt at reconciliation, although
avowedly from the clinical standpoint, by Holt (1). Similarities
to the contrast between holistic and dimensional methods in
personality study are close, but by no means complete.

The text of this article is a slight abridgement of Chapter 13
of Professor Vernon's recent book *Personality Assessment* (5).
The whole book is essential reading for the serious student;
it contains much acute critical comment, not only on general
issues, but on many of the individual topics covered in these
Readings. It may also be said to supplement the author's own
earlier survey of testing techniques (4).

References
1. Holt, R. R., Clinical *and* Statistical Prediction. *J. abnorm. soc. Psych.*
   56, 1–12, 1958.
2. Meehl, P. E. *Clinical* versus *Statistical Prediction.* Minneapolis:
   Minnesota University Press, 1954.
3. Miller, G. A., *Psychology: the Science of Mental Life.* London:
   Hutchinson, 1964, Chapter 20.
4. Vernon, P. E. *Personality Tests and Assessments.* London: Methuen,
   1953.
5. Vernon, P. E., *Personality Assessment: a Critical Survey.* London:
   Methuen, 1964.

19 P. E. Vernon

The Concept of Validity in Personality Study

P. E. Vernon. *Personality Assessment;* Methuen, London; John Wiley, New York; 1964.

One frequently hears the complaint voiced that current personality tests are low in validity. Why is this so, and what, indeed, do we mean by validity? Various definitions have been proposed, but they mostly imply, in essence, that a test is valid in so far as it indicates or measures whatever it is supposed to. We intend to argue a somewhat more unorthodox view – that a test measures only itself, but that it is valid in so far as it can be shown to correlate with other observable behaviour. That is, its validity lies in the inferences we are entitled to make from it. Before this position is reached, it is necessary to discuss the several types of validation which are customarily distinguished.

Face and Content Validity

In some instances the content of the test is sufficient guarantee of what the test measures. Reaction time tests measure reaction time; spelling tests sample the child's spelling; similarly bar-pressing in rats, sociometric choices of children, and so on. While this is quite legitimate, the trouble is that testers are continually tempted to infer beyond the behaviour itself – to regard the spelling test as measuring spelling ability in general, not just ability at that kind of test item, reaction time as a measure of 'quickness of response', sociometric choices as showing popularity or other qualities. Content validity thus shades over easily into the 'face' validity which psychometrists unanimously condemn, that is judging what a test measures by what it 'looks like', or by analysing its content subjectively. This has been the bane of vocational aptitude testing, and it was widely accepted in the early days of personality testing. Thus personality questionnaires were made up of items believed to be characteristic of the neurotic, the extravert or introvert, the liberal or conservative, etc., and were straightaway assumed to measure neuroticism or other traits, or attitudes. Educational psychologists can reasonably argue for what they term *logical validation* – that an achievement test which systematically covers the desired information and skills requires no validation, since in itself it is a better criterion of achievement than, say, teacher's marks. The weakness in this argument is that different tests in the same school subject often correlate only to a moderate degree, showing that their authors were not justified in inferring from the items they selected to all-round achievement in the subject.

At the same time, as Mosier points out (1947), the apparent or face validity of a test is of considerable importance in winning acceptance from test-users and test-takers. Both employers and candidates for employment will complain if the latter are rejected by tests that don't 'look' relevant to the job.

External Validation (Concurrent or Predictive)

For many years, then, the orthodox view was that a test must be validated against an external criterion of what it is supposed to measure. Either it should correlate with present evidence, such as ratings of the trait or aptitude concerned, or it must predict future performance, e.g. in school or a job. Insufficient distinction was drawn between 'notional' and 'empirical' criteria, since admittedly they overlap. Empirical or objective criteria are hard to come by even in the occupational field (cf. Vernon and Parry, 1949), and it is often necessary to resort to employers', supervisors' or other assessments, which are obviously open to many kinds of bias. Nevertheless there is a clear difference between such real-life facts as receiving job promotion, committing legal offences, being diagnosed as schizophrenic, benefiting from shock therapy, choosing to enter a particular occupation, etc., and estimates of traits or 'constructs' such as neurotic, intelligent, ascendant, honest, etc. We will deal with empirical validation later. Notional criteria are extremely unsatisfactory because of their inevitable subjectivity, even when they take such forms as school grades, or where, say, a new group intelligence test is validated by correlating with Stanford–Binet. We can never tell how far weak validity is due to the defects of the criterion, or to those of the test.

In a critical discussion of validation, Ebel (1961) objects to 'notional' and 'construct' validation (see below), since both imply the philosophical fallacy that we are measuring some pre-existing trait or entity in the individual, i.e. an abstraction rather than an operationally definable concept such as physical scientists or engineers measure. It suggests too that each test has some single, fixed validity, instead of recognizing that it can be used for various purposes, and that its validity will vary with the circumstances and often with the population studied. For example a mechanical aptitude test would give different correlations with success at different mechanical jobs or training courses.

Factorial Validity

Even when we measure a fairly straightforward construct such as general intelligence, external validation is inapplicable. For though intelligence test items have often been selected on a basis of improvement with age, or correlations with teachers' ratings, the test is intended to replace these unsatisfactory criteria of ability. Hence, following Spearman, intelligence was thought of as the g factor that runs through any sub-tests or items with good content validity (i.e. any which appear to involve higher intellectual processes); and the best tests were those with the highest loadings. Similarly, many personality questionnaires, attitude scales and educational tests selected their items on a basis of internal consistency (correlations with total score).

Spearman's conception of factorial validity has been followed, in the personality field, by the present writer, by Cattell and others, as shown in the previous chapter, where its inadequacy was also pointed out. The common element running through a set of intercorrelated tests may be a response set, or halo or social desirability, rather than the presumed trait. In other words, factorial validation and internal consistency validation reduce to much the same thing as content or face validity. This is largely true also of ability factors such as Spearman's, Thurstone's or Guilford's. Factorists have presented impressive evidence for a large number of reasoning, creativity, evaluative, memory and other factor-constructs, but have seldom demonstrated that these represent anything more than factors running through particular kinds of psychological test; i.e. they are 'instrument factors' which may or may not be related to the constructs or thinking functions *with the same name* that we observe in everyday life.

Construct Validation

In 1954, however, a committee of the American Psychological Association pointed out that factorial evidence could make a valuable contribution to the broader conception of construct validity. The fundamental principles of this approach were formulated by Cronbach and Meehl in 1955. The psychologist is primarily interested in such constructs or 'intervening variables' as anxiety, authoritarianism, intelligence, extraversion-introversion, defence mechanisms, etc. which are not observable, and for which no satisfactory external criterion is conceivable. He cannot do without these theoretical abstractions but he can and should test out their implications in as many ways as possible if they are to retain their usefulness as explanatory principles. This is clearly true of clinical and experimental studies of personality where, for example, the investigator wishes to discover the effects of some method of upbringing, or therapeutic treatment, on the child's Super-ego structure. But it holds good also for a great deal of applied or decision-making psychology. The vocational counsellor is not much concerned with the validity of a test for predicting success in a particular occupation. If he applies a mechanical comprehension test he wants it to correlate consistently with a wide variety of indices of 'mechanical-mindedness'. And in the personality area, he requires information on such constructs as the counsellee's main interests and goals, his persistence in pursuing them, his adaptation to different social situations, etc. Even the personnel selector, who is more likely to adopt an empirical approach, tends to think of the job criteria and the selection procedure in terms of underlying personality dispositions and generalized rather than specific abilities.

Construct validation implies testing out the theory underlying the test, or determining the psychological meaning of the test score. For example, if 'sociability' is a measurable construct, there should be factorial consistency. Sociability should manifest itself in several types of test which intercorrelate positively, but which do not correlate with other factors or variables which are hypothesized as distinct. A valid test of sociability would be expected to show some, though not necessarily high, correlations with acquaintances' judgements, sociometric choices, etc. Experimental evidence that people tested as sociable react differently to certain situations from those tested as unsociable would also be of value. Group differences, introspective analysis and longitudinal data can also be incorporated: thus children brought up in one way should be more sociable than those with a different upbringing. Eysenck's work on extraversion–introversion conceived as excitation–inhibition is another good example of construct validation. If the predictions from the theory are not confirmed it must, of course, be abandoned or modified. But one would expect a whole network of relationships with the construct to be elaborated and verified; and it is in terms of these relationships that the construct, and the tests devised for it, are accepted as valid.

Limitations of Construct Validation

This approach has considerably clarified the work of the personality tester. It has been particularly useful in projective testing, where the classical approach to validation of, e.g., Rorschach scores, was most inadequate. Yet it is not without its dangers, since theoretical speculation is apt to get out of touch with experimental verification. Thus Adorno *et al.* (1950) presented a wide range of supporting evidence for the construct of authoritarianism, but failed to realize that much of what they were measuring with the F-scale was acquiescence. Similarly, Jesser and Hammond (1957) point out that a test such as the Taylor Manifest Anxiety scale, which is supposed to measure the Hullian construct of anxiety as a drive, is based more on convenience of administration than on the properties of the construct. The 'naming fallacy' or overgeneralization, so characteristic of content validation, is by no means eliminated. However, the construct validity approach provides a way out, since any psychologist is at liberty to propose an alternative theory, and to devise experiments which demonstrate its superior explanatory value, as Messick and Jackson (1961) did with the F-scale. The most valuable feature of this approach is that it calls for statements of explicit hypotheses: these can fairly readily be retested by other workers, or further corollaries can be tried out, so that the evidence is cumulative.

There is a very real difficulty, however, when the evidence is necessarily circumstantial or indirect, in deciding standards of acceptability. When validity was regarded simply as a correlation with a criterion we at least thought we knew how valid for practical predictions was a correlation of say 0·6. But how complete must the confirmation of a construct be? We have already criticized the subjectivity of Eysenck's and Cattell's standards of acceptance of factorial evidence. Many other authors are much less cautious. [. . . .]

Conclusion

While accepting the usefulness of the construct validity approach, we would prefer to formulate validity rather differently, along similar lines to Ebel (1961). We share his distrust of abstract constructs (except as useful guides to research), but would suggest that the difference between these and operational or concrete qualities is merely a matter of degree. Many of the psychologist's measurements, as we have seen, require no more validation than the physicist's – they are direct records of the behaviour in which he is interested. But when he measures, say, reaction time and calls it a test of 'quickness of reaction' he is in fact talking about a construct, albeit not a highly abstract one. It is just as necessary for him as it is for the tester of 'anxiety' and the like, to explore the correlates of his test, what conditions affect it, what other aspects of the generalized ability – quickness of reaction – it does not cover.

Fundamentally, then, a test measures itself, and its further vaildity rests entirely on its established relations to other behavenurs. It is the network of its relations to other variables and otoiral-life situations that gives its meaning. We can follow the co struct validity approach provided we realize the need always to return ultimately to external data of some kind. A valid test must give meaningful results; that is, it must link up with various kinds of observable behaviour which have been predicted from the construct. Thus intelligence tests are acceptable, not merely because they conform to a factorial model (useful as this is), but because they do correlate with educational and other kinds of achievement, and with observers' judgements, in a logical way. Many attitude and interest tests, despite their weaknesses such as fakability and prominent response sets, measure up well to similar real-life criteria, whereas personality inventories, performance and projective tests usually don't – however promising the underlying constructs or the factorial confirmation. Nevertheless the personality inventory is entirely valid if it is accepted as a sample of the person's Self-concept at the topmost or 'public' level. It is only when it is generalized beyond this to some much more abstract construct such as neuroticism that additional evidence is needed.

The value of a test rests not only on the richness of its correlates, but also on their stability. Thus although the construct of intelligence is open to various criticisms, the Terman–Merrill test not only correlates with many kinds of behaviour which we might expect to be affected by intelligence, but succeeds in doing so almost everywhere it is applied to almost any kind of English-speaking children. Mannheim and Wilkins (1955) point out similarly that the indices they find most useful in the actuarial prediction of recidivism are those that have proved predictive in many studies of delinquents in many parts of the world – previous offences, broken home background, unstable employment record, etc. This notion of the stability and range of predictions differs from the psychometrist's classical conceptions of reliability and validity, and there is as yet no accepted means of measuring it.

Cattell (1957) recognizes that, in personality testing, we need to take account not only of repeat reliability (freedom from short-term function fluctuation) and internal consistency or homo-geneity (all the component parts of the test measuring the same thing – which he considers often to be overstressed), but also of administrator and scorer reliability (stability with different testers). But even when these sources of error are controlled, instability may result from test-taking attitudes and sets, and there is no guarantee how far the test results are generalizable.

Actuarial or Empirical Validation

In view of the apparent vagueness of the construct approach to testing, there is considerable justification for those tough-minded psychometrists who distrust theorizing about the traits or mental processes of testees, and advocate going straight from their responses to an external objective criterion. It does not concern them whether subjects are 'telling the truth' or 'acting naturally', provided the responses can be shown to be predictive. Also, as mentioned earlier, the criterion is not some 'notional' quality, but an observable, objectively recorded, piece of behaviour. The empirical approach to test validation and test construction mani-fests itself in a number of guises.

1. *Actuarial selection or prediction procedures*. Several tests or indices that may be related to achievement, prognosis or some other outcome are followed up, and those with the highest validities are picked for future use. The efficiency of prediction can be maximized if the intercorrelations of the predictors are also known, since they can then be appropriately weighted. As in any multiple regression or discriminant function procedure, some variables may have very low validities by themselves and actually receive negative weights; and yet be useful as 'suppressors'. This can be illustrated by Figure 1, where the circle C represents the criterion, and the ellipses A and B are two tests. A overlaps the criterion considerably; it has good validity and is likely to receive a high weight or regression coefficient. B has little validity, but it correlates highly with the *invalid* component of A. Hence if some fraction of the B scores is *subtracted* from the A scores, the validity of A will be improved.

A simplified version of this occurs in the MMPI, where the scale scores may be corrected by subtracting some fraction of the K (defensiveness) score, with the object of reducing the tendencies to undue self-depreciation or undue negativism. There is considerable doubt, however, as to its effectiveness. Theoretically, we could similarly adjust any inventory or attitude scale for social desirability, acquiescence, etc., if we had a suitable external criterion.

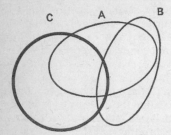

Figure 1 Hypothetical Test Correlations

2. *Criterion analysis.* Eysenck's procedure is essentially similar. A general factor is found running through a battery of tests which – with or without rotation – closely matches the correlations of the tests with the neurotic vs. normal dichotomy, or other criterion. A simple weighting of the tests based on their factor loadings is likely to be almost as effective a predictor as the full regression equation.

3. *Differential and prognostic tests.* A complex test such as the Rorschach yields numerous scores and indices, and those signs which best differentiate mental patients who benefit under shock therapy from those who do not benefit are picked out. The mere sum of these signs, or a simple weighting, is used for future prognosis. Similarly, a series of perceptual, motor or autonomic tests, which may or may not appear to have meaningful connexions with the criterion, may be combined empirically.

The same procedure, in effect, was used by Strong in developing scoring keys for his Vocational Interest Blank and by Hathaway and others in constructing MMPI scales. Here the main features are that multiple criteria are employed, and that the tests contain very large numbers of items. Full regression analysis would not be possible, but simple weightings are calculated for the positive, negative and doubtful responses to every item, based on the extent to which they differentiate any occupational-interest group (or pathological group). Thus some responses are keyed for several of the criteria, others for one or two, and some items are still retained though they have so far shown little or no differential value.

Another type of empirically scored test is the Biographical Inventory. This was almost the only motivational or personality test that was found to be of any use for selecting USAAF pilots in World War II (Guilford and Lacey, 1947). It consists of a large number of multiple-choice items dealing with the candidates' background, educational and vocational career, interests, etc., most of which are formulated initially on the basis of hunches that they might be relevant to the qualities which differentiate a good from a poor pilot. They need, however, to be validated in a very large group – preferably in several comparable groups – before a scoring key is established for the significant items. The technique has had considerable application in the American services, and in other situations involving large populations.

Berg (1959) makes the interesting suggestion that items for any of these differential tests should *not* be chosen for initial face validity. For example interest items might differentiate pathological groups, and pathological items differentiate occupational groups all the better than those where the Subject can see how his responses may be scored. This is much less illogical than it sounds, the point being that, if we want to differentiate one group of people from another, we are likely to do better with items where their responses tend to deviate from the norm than with those where everyone answers pretty much alike. Berg describes tests based on preferences and response sets in judging meaningless drawings, claiming that these differentiate successfully among nosological groups (cf. Barnes, 1955). However, we shall see shortly that there are strong grounds for doubting the effectiveness of this extreme empiricism.

4. *Paired item measures*. McQuitty (1953) has suggested that differences in response patterns to pairs of items within a single inventory would provide an objective approach to personality measurement. For example, pairs can be found which most Subjects answer alike (either Yes or No), but abnormal Subjects more frequently answer them differently (one Yes, the other No). He has proposed other techniques for empirical differentiation (1959), but seems to have had little following, presumably because of the tediousness of analysing response patterns.

5. *Forced-choice rating scales or inventories*. These consist of pairs (or blocks) of items, one member of each pair having been proved to have higher empirical validity than the other. The members are, however, equated on Social Desirability, or other variables which the tester desires to eliminate. Clearly this is an alternative to the suppressor procedure shown in Figure 1 for eliminating unwanted sources of variance. [. . . .]

6. *Moderating variables*. It has been suggested that the personality variables measured by inventories or other tests, although they fail to correlate consistently with some outcome such as educational or vocational achievement, may nevertheless indirectly affect or 'moderate' the operation of other predictors. In other words, different personality 'types' may apply or use their abilities differently.

For example, Furneaux (1962) has given the Maudsley Personality Inventory to successive batches of engineering students, and classified them into those above and below average on the neuroticism-stability and extraversion-introversion scales. He claims very different correlations between ability measures and subsequent achievement in these different personality groups. Among stable extraverts the predictive value of ability tests is quite high; they are uncomplicated people whose educational success depends mainly on their aptitudes. But among unstable introverts, correlations are around zero, and previous attainment provides a much better prediction. Stable introverts and unstable extraverts tend to be intermediate, and a combination of aptitude and attainment measures gives a better basis for prediction. Similarly, Frederiksen and Melville (1954) used reading speed and comprehension tests to classify students into 'compulsive' and 'non-compulsive' groups, and found higher correlations between interests (as measured by the Strong VIB) and achievement in the latter group. Obsessional students, it was suggested, will work hard at anything, whereas the others are more dependent on interest in a subject if they are to do well at it.

Neither of these claims has yet been confirmed by independent investigations. But clearly such an approach, through patterns of scores, could have important bearings in counselling.

Shrinkage and Instability in Empirical Validity

It has long been realized that the multiple correlation of a battery of tests with a criterion is lower in practice than when it is initially calculated. Both the validity coefficients of the separate tests and their intercorrelations are subject to chance errors, particularly when the group of Subjects is small, and regression analysis capitalizes on these errors. Thus, if test A has an unduly high validity in the initial group, and test B an unduly low coefficient, the former will be overweighted, the latter underweighted, in the regression equation. Applying these weights to a fresh group, the errors are likely to alter, hence the multiple correlation with the criterion drops. Wherry has proposed a formula for estimating the consequent shrinkage. But a better precaution, favoured by most psychometrists, is that of 'cross-validation': the effective validity of a battery of tests is assessed, not from the group on which the weights are calculated, but from a fresh group.

Just the same difficulty applies to all the procedures mentioned above. Indeed it is all the more serious when test items or Rorschach signs and the like are validated, since their reliabilities are lower than those of most sub-tests, the error component of their validity coefficients larger. In a test such as Strong's, this matters little, both because so many items are keyed and because Strong normally insists on very large groups (500 or so representatives of any occupation) in working out his weights. In many Rorschach sign studies it is fatal, since the number of patients representing any particular syndrome is likely to be small. This was true also for several of the original MMPI standardization groups, hence such keys have failed to stand up to cross-validation.

Unfortunately the stability of validity coefficients and regression weights is even poorer than would be expected from statistical consideration of chance errors. Even in personnel selection on a basis of ability tests, remarkable variations occur between apparently similar groups, presumably because of unanticipated and uncontrollable variations in the conditions of testing or in the criterion (e.g. the selected employees who are followed up may be assessed by different instructors and this alters the relative validities of the selection tests).* Variability is even more marked in the personality field, on account of variations in the Subjects' test-taking attitudes, and the unreliability of any criteria based on ratings, psychiatric diagnoses and the like.

Another aspect of this problem is that any difference or ratio scores (or the regression coefficients of suppressor variables) have lower reliabilities than those of the variables from which they are derived. This is simply demonstrated by the formula for the reliability of differences between scores in two tests, A and B, when the reliabilities of the initial tests are r_{AA} and r_{BB}.

* An example of this is described by Vernon (1958, p. 30).

$$r_{(A-B)(A-B)} = \frac{r_{AA} + r_{BB} - 2r_{AB}}{2(1 + r_{AB})}$$

Suppose A is an impure test of authoritarianism mixed with acquiescence, whose reliability is 0·85, B a pure measure of acquiescence with a reliability 0·65, and that the two inter-correlate 0·50. Then if we try to correct the A test by subtracting B, the reliability of the A — B score would be only 0·167. Perhaps a less extreme, yet similar, drop would occur if we held acquiescence constant by partial or multiple correlation or by the forced-choice item technique. Psychologically this shows itself in the reluctance of Subjects to answer forced-choice items (or raters to judge people on forced-choice scales); they feel that their choices are unreliable when they are prevented from discriminating in terms of their habitual response sets (social desirability, acquiescence, halo, etc.). In practice, tests of this type with 'built-in' corrections never do retain their purity. Although the Edwards PPS forced-choice items were chosen to be of equal social desirability, the scores still show some social desirability influence, though less than in ordinary inventories. The reason is, of course, that the correlations of each item with the desired trait and with social desirability, used in item selection, were unstable; chance errors were capitalized, and when the test is applied to a fresh group, trait-correlations tend to drop, social desirability ones to rise.

The US Army psychologists have unrivalled experience in the construction of forced-choice and other empirical inventories, e.g. for officer selection, though most of their work has not reached the standard journals. Osborn et al. (1954) suggest that forced-choice items should be as valid as, or more valid than, 'straight' items, particularly in a long test, because their inter-correlations are lower (their common social desirability variance having been removed). However, other reports suggest that they are dissatisfied with forced-choice or other types of corrected scores, because they do not retain their validities. 'Straight' inventories at least stand up fairly well to repeated use in fairly varied contexts, even if their scores are often distorted by social desirability.

Why do interests tests such as Strong's and even forced-choice ones like the Study of Values and the Kuder Preference Record retain more stable validities than tests of personality traits? The reason is surely that in these the tester wants to measure self-concepts – the Subject's underlying notions of his own business, artistic or other consistent interests and attitudes; whereas in the personality inventory such self-concepts and attitudes are treated as disturbing response sets; and for the statistical reasons we have outlined, any attempt to remove or control them is likely to be disappointing. Hence we cannot agree that Berg's approach (p. 415), which wilfully disregards self-concepts, is capable of yielding tests with satisfactory stability. It is noteworthy that in those instances cited by Meehl where actuarial prediction has worked well, the psychometrist's raw material has consisted of surface characteristics, having high face validity, not of indirect, and subtle tests. [. . . .]

A particularly good example of the failure of the empirical approach is supplied by Ryans' (1960) excellent investigation of teacher-success.

The concept of 'the good teacher' is, of course, complex and vague; and hundreds of studies of teacher-selection and teacher-competence have broken down through inadequacies in the criterion. However, Ryans arrived at well-defined and usable criteria by factorizing observations of their classroom behaviour. Three factors or dimensions of behaviour were obtained, which could be assessed with high reliability:
X. Understanding, friendly vs aloof, egocentric.
Y. Responsible, business-like, systematic vs evading, unplanned, slip-shod.
Z. Stimulating, imaginative, enthusiastic vs dull, routine.
He and his colleagues then set out to construct tests which would correlate with or give useful predictions of these criteria. Extremely varied techniques were exploited, including tests of attitudes, biographical inventory items, word association, sentence completion, pictorial situations, etc., the only restriction being that they should be readily applicable in group form, and objectively scorable. Each sub-test, and all the items within each sub-test, were given repeated trials. Yet the best validation for the combined battery obtained with fresh groups of teachers averaged around 0.37 at the elementary and 0.31 at the secondary levels. And when the tests were applied for predicting success 2 or 3 years ahead (e.g. in student selection), the mean correlations with X, Y and Z ratings dropped to around 0.12.

Maybe teacher-traits are particularly difficult to assess with printed group tests, or they are greatly affected by situational influences, or are very unstable over the years of teacher training. But similar difficulties are likely to arise in predicting personality characteristics in almost any occupation or educational context. And if Ryans, with considerable financial and staff backing, and with great ingenuity in test construction and psychometric sophistication, could do no better, then the prospects for empirical measurement of personality traits in general, along the lines envisaged by Berg, Guilford, or Eysenck, are not very bright.

Actuarial Prediction

The actuarial approach to prediction is limited to 'recurrent situations' where the type of population, the conditions of testing and the nature of the criterion all remain stable. The above discussion raises the question whether it is not indeed so inflexible that it can only exceptionally be applied in practice. Take the classical example of a weighted battery of aptitude tests for vocational selection purposes. It is no use calculating the weights by following up a group of one or two hundred candidates since, as we have seen, they vary much more from one group to another than would follow from ordinary statistical unreliability. Only occasionally, as in the war-time selection of USAAF pilots, in the selection of pupils for English secondary grammar schools, or of American college students, can large samples be obtained repeatedly, so as to iron out these irregularities. Once the procedure is put into effect, it cannot be altered since only those candidates who pass the tests are accepted; and though we can follow them up to try to ensure that the battery of predictors is still effective, the correlations within a selected group provide rather inaccurate estimates of the correlations among unselected candidates (on which the weightings must be based). If we wish to introduce a new test, or if the kind of candidate alters, or the job for which we are selecting changes, it is necessary to start again from scratch and to follow through hundreds of unselected candidates before fixing the revised weightings. Obviously the difficulties are enhanced when personality variables rather than aptitude test scores are involved, since these tend to be even more unstable.

Maybe this sounds unduly gloomy, and it is true that regression weights can alter over quite wide limits without markedly reducing the multiple correlation of the predictors with the criterion. But if we look at the instances from the literature where actuarial prediction or empirically constructed tests have worked, we will realize that they are decidedly limited.

Conventional tests of educational attainments and intelligence are more often constructed on a basis of face or content validity and internal consistency than by selecting items against an external criterion. However, such tests work well over a considerable range of contexts, with a wide variety of populations, because such abilities possess a relatively high degree of generality and stability. Almost any combination of school grades or attainment tests with almost any intelligence tests gives fairly efficient predictions of all-round educational capacity over the next few years. But educational psychologists have been notably less successful in devising tests or batteries for giving trustworthy predictions of more specific outcomes (e.g. grades in engineering courses), or for differential placement of students.

We have commented already on the good results consistently obtained with certain attitude and interest tests, attributing this to the fact that they measure rather stable and broad self-concepts. Moreover these contain large numbers of items, hence variations in their item validities in somewhat different populations or contexts do not matter much. A rather different principle enters in the actuarial prediction of delinquency and recidivism: relatively few symptoms or indices may be selected, but they tend to be highly objective (not, like test responses, dependent on the Subjects' attitudes). It is usually possible to investigate large numbers so as to stabilize the weights, and the criterion is a well-defined and stable one.

It seems unlikely that actuarialism will have many applications in abnormal psychology in view of the subjectivity of diagnosis and of criteria of 'improvement', and the paucity of stable symptoms and other predictors. Its limitations in vocational psychology, e.g. in making professional and managerial appointments, are no less obvious. Taft (1959) agrees that in most selection or other situations where decisions have to be reached about individuals, the information regarding each person may have to be synthesized by clinical, subjective methods, because no formula for empirical weighting exists. Empirical techniques are likely to find their main application in mass-screening procedures, though even here – Taft notes – validities show an unfortunate susceptibility to 'drift'.

None the less some progress has been made, for example, in isolating consistent patterns of MMPI scale scores (Hathaway and Meehl, 1951; Dahlstrom and Welsh, 1960) which are associated with psychopathological syndromes. But this is very different from purely empirical selection of items to yield a scale for mechanically diagnosing a syndrome: rather it is a type of construct validation. It may be that such patterns, combined with symptom ratings scales such as Wittenborn's (1955), background items, scores on the Wechsler intelligence scales, etc., will enable us to approximate to something like the actuarial tables or cookbooks which Meehl (1956) envisages using in clinical diagnosis. Certainly the search should be continued. Furthermore, almost any actuarial research contributes useful information regarding the correlates of personality tests which contribute to their construct validity. What we must insist, however, is that empirically constructed tests and actuarial procedures show little prospect of providing the answers to all problems of personality assessment, as many contemporary psychometrists would have us believe.

[. . . .]

References

Adorno, T. W., Frenkel-Brunswik, E., *et al.*, *The authoritarian Personality*, New York: Harper, 1950.

Barnes, E. H. 1955. The relation of biased test responses to psychopathology. *J. abnorm. soc. Psychol.*, **51**, 286–90.

Berg, I. A. 1959. The unimportance of test item content. In: Bass, B. M., and Berg, I. A., *Objective Approaches to Personality*. New York: Van Nostrand, pp. 83–99.

Cattell, R. B. 1957. *Personality and Motivation Structure and Measurement*. Yonkers, N.Y.: World Book Co.

Cronbach, L. J., and Meehl, P. E. 1955. Construct validity in psychological tests. *Psychol. Bull.*, **52**, 281–302.

Dahlstrom, W. G. and Welsh, G. S. 1960. *An MMPI Handbook*. University of Minnesota Press.

Ebel, R. L. 1961. Must all tests be valid? *Amer. Psychologist*, **16**, 640–7.

Frederiksen, N., and Melville, S. D. 1954. Differential predictability in the use of test scores. *Educ. Psychol. Measmt.*, **14**, 647–56.

Furneaux, W. D. 1962. The psychologist and the university. *Univ. Quart.*, **17**, 1, 33–47.

Guilford, J. P., and Lacey, J. I. (ed. 1947). *Printed Classification Tests*. Washington, D.C.: Government Printing Office.

Hathaway, S. R., and Meehl, P. E. 1951. *An Atlas for the Clinical Use of the MMPI*. University of Minnesota Press.

Jesser, R., and Hammond, K. R. 1957. Construct validity and the Taylor Anxiety scale. *Psychol. Bull.*, **54**, 161–70.

McQuitty, L. L. 1953. A statistical method for studying personality integration. In: Mowrer, O. H., *Psychotherapy Theory and Research*. New York: Ronald Press, pp. 414–62.

McQuitty, L. L. 1959. Differential validity in some pattern analytic methods. In: Bass, B. M. and Berg, I. A., *Objective Approaches to Personality*. New York: Van Nostrand, pp. 66–82.

Mannheim, H., and Wilkins, L. T. 1955. *Prediction Methods in Relation to Borstal Training*. London: H.M. Stationery Office.

Meehl, P. E. 1956. Wanted – a good cookbook. *Amer. Psychologist*, **11**, 263–72.

Messick, S., and Jackson, D. N. 1961. Acquiescence and the factorial interpretation of the MMPI. *Psychol. Bull.*, **58**, 299–304.

Mosier, C. I. 1947. A critical examination of the concepts of face validity. *Educ. Psychol. Measmt.*, **7**, 191–205.

Osburn, H. G., Lubin, A., *et al.* 1954. The relative validity of forced choice and single stimulus self description items. *Educ. Psychol. Measmt.*, **14**, 407–17.

Ryans, D. G. 1960. *Characteristics of Teachers*. Washington, D.C.: American Council on Education.

Taft, R. 1959. Multiple methods of personality assessment. *Psychol. Bull.*, 56, 333–52.

Vernon, P. E. 1958. Educational testing and test form factors. *Research Bulletin* 58-3. Princeton, N.J.: Educational Testing Service.

Vernon, P. E. and Parry, J. B. 1949. *Personnel Selection in the British Forces*. University of London Press.

Wittenborn, J. R. 1955. *Wittenborn Psychiatric Rating Scales*. New York: Psychological Corporation.

Further Reading

Since this book deals with assessment rather than personality in general, and since the introductions to the various articles, as well as the authors' own lists of references cover a very wide range of reading, there is little need for a still further list.

Gathered below are the titles of some useful compendia and other works of a general kind, together with some miscellaneous references to writings mentioned in the Introduction or elsewhere.

In so far as most assessment techniques are based on or involve 'Tests and Measurements' – to quote a term widely current in the United States – general books in the field of psychological testing become relevant. The best known are those of Anastasi (A.2) and Cronbach (A.7). Each contains a very full account of methods in personality assessment, and of the tests themselves, with much penetrating comment. Similar in scope, but different in approach and treatment, are the various *Mental Measurement Yearbooks* (A.5) of which six have now appeared, all under the editorship of O. K. Buros. These contain not only full particulars of all tests and relevant books, but also reviews, including all important reviews from the periodical literature, and others specially commissioned, and as complete citations as possible of published work dealing with the tests listed. Successive editions supplement what has gone before, and a separate book *Tests in Print* (A.6) acts as a cumulative index to the first five *Yearbooks*.

Several good surveys are available in the field of projective techniques. Bell's (A.4) is the most comprehensive: unfortunately it is now rather dated, but it gives an excellent survey of research findings up to the time of its publication (1948). The books listed by Abt and Bellak (A.1) and by Anderson and Anderson (A.3) are compilations of articles by groups of contributing authors; the latter has the wider coverage, going well beyond the range of projective methods proper. In both cases the approach is largely descriptive, and some of the contributions could almost serve the function of a manual for the technique described.

Less detailed in treatment, but wider in scope, is David and Brengelmann's *Perspectives in Personality Research* (A.8), a collection of eighteen articles by authors of many different nationalities. This international coverage is a feature shared with the book's predecessor *Perspectives in Personality Theory* (A.9), to which it was designed to be a sequel. Relevant to the present book, although not directly mentioned in any of the articles reprinted are such topics as 'person perception'; 'longitudinal' research; and assessment by means of 'experimental' methods, in the generally-accepted sense of that term.

A rather similar approach, with emphasis on empirical findings, is that of Eysenck in his *Structure of Human Personality* (A.10). This book is less well-known than Eysenck's other books with similar titles (see Reading 16, Eysenck 1947; 1952), with which it should not be confused. While the two earlier books deal mostly with the contribution of the Maudsley school, this one presents a highly critical account of the work of other writers, arranged according to methods employed.

References

A.1 Abt, L. E. and Bellak, L., *Projective Psychology: Clinical Approaches to the Total Personality*. New York: Knopf, 1952.

A.2 Anastasi, Anne, *Psychological Testing*. Second Edition. New York and London: The Macmillan Company, 1961.

A.3 Anderson, H. H. and Anderson, G. L., *An Introduction to Projective Techniques and other Devices for Understanding the Dynamics of Human Behavior*. New York: Prentice Hall, 1951.

A.4 Bell, J. E., *Projective Techniques*. New York and London: Longmans, Green, 1948.

A.5 O. K. Buros (Ed.). *The Third, Fourth, Fifth and Sixth Mental Measurement Yearbooks*. Highland Park, N.J.: The Gryphon Press. 1949, 1953, 1959, 1965.

A.6 O. K. Buros (Ed.), *Tests in Print: a Comprehensive Bibliography of Tests for use in Education, Psychology and Industry*. Highland Park, N.J.: The Gryphon Press, 1961.

A.7 Cronbach, L. J., *Essentials of Psychological Testing*. New York and London: Harper and Row, 1961.

A.8 David, H. P. and Brengelmann, J. C., (Eds.). *Perspectives in Personality Research*. New York: Springer; London: Crosby Lockwood, 1960.

A.9 David, H. P. and Von Bracken, H., *Perspectives in Personality Theory*. London: Tavistock, 1957.

A.10 Eysenck, H. J., *The Structure of Human Personality*. London: Methuen; New York: Wiley, 1953.

A.11 Hartshorne, H. and May, M. A., *Studies in Deceit; Studies in Service and Self Control*. New York: Macmillan, 1928, 1929.

A.12 Lowenfeld, Margaret, *The Lowenfield Mosaic Test*. London: Newman Neame, 1954.

A.13 Moreno, J. L., *Who Shall Survive?* New York: Beacon House, 1934

A.14 Mucchielli, R., *Le Jeu du Monde et le Test du Village*. Paris: Presses Universitaires de France, 1960.

Acknowledgements

Acknowledgements are due to the following for permission to publish extracts in this volume: American Medical Association, *Archives of Neurology and Psychiatry 34*, C. D. Morgan & H. A. Murray, 'A Method for Investigating', 1935; American Psychological Association, *American Psychologist*, D. W. McKinnon, 'The Nature and Nurture of Creative Talent', Vol. 17, 1962; Basic Books Inc., Hilgard, Kubic and Pumpian-Mindlin, *Psychoanalysis as Science*, E. R. Hilgard, 'Experimental Approaches to Psychoanalysis as Science', 1952; Bollingen Foundation, Routledge & Kegan Paul Ltd, *Contributions to Analytical Psychology*, C. G. Jung, 'Psychological Types', 1928; Columbia University Press, *Story Sequence Analysis*, M. B. Arnold, 'The TAT as a Projective Method', 1962; Harper and Row, Publishers Inc., *The Varieties of Temperament*, W. H. Sheldon & S. S. Stevens, copyright 1942, by Harper & Brothers; Holt, Rinehart & Winston Inc., *Pattern and Growth in Personality*, G. W. Allport, 'Expressive Behaviour', 1961, *The OSS Assessment Staff's Assessment of Men*, 'Pattern and Growth in Personality', 1948; J. M. Dent & Sons Limited, E. P. Dutton & Co., Inc., *Inquiries into Human Faculty*, F. Galton, 'Mental Imagery'; John Wiley & Sons Inc., *Rorschach Psychology*, M. A. Rickers-Ovsiankina, 'Synopsis of Psychological Premises Underlying the Rorschach', 1960; John Wiley & Sons Inc., Methuen & Co. Ltd., *Personality Assessment*, P. E. Vernon, 'The Concept of Validity', 1964; *Journal of Abnormal and Social Psychology*, C. E. Osgood and Z. Luria, 'A Blind Analysis of a Case of Multiple Personality using the Semantic Differential', Vol. 49, 1954; *Journal of Nervous and Mental Disease*, H. Rorschach, 'The Application of the Interpretation of Form to Psychoanalysis', published posthumously by E. Oberholzer, 1924, Vol. 60; New York Academy of Sciences, *Annals of the New York Academy of Sciences*, R. Schafer, 'The Expression of Personality and Maladjustments in Intelligence Test Results', Vol. 46, (Art 7) 1946; National Institute of Industrial Psychology, *Occupational Psychology*, B. S. Morris, 'Officer Selection of the British Army 1942–1945', Vol. 23, 1949; Psychological Corporation, *MMPI Manual*, S. R. Hathaway & J. C. McKinley, 'Manual for Administration and Scoring', copyright 1943, 1951 by the University of Minnesota, Reprinted by special permission; Robert R. Knapp, Routledge & Kegan Paul Ltd, *The Causes and Cures of Neurosis*, H. J. Eysenck and S. Rachman, 'Dimensions of Personality', 1965; Routledge & Kegan Paul Ltd, *Contributions to Analytical Psychology*, C. G. Jung, 'Psychological Types', 1928; Van Nostrand & Co. Inc., Bass and Berg, *Objective Approaches to Personality*, A. L. Edwards, 'Social Desirability and Personality Test Construction', 1959.

Author Index

Author Index

Abraham, K., 99, 104
Abt, L. E., 425, 426
Adorno, T. W., 120, 411, 422
Adkins, M. M., 296
Adler, A., 55, 58
Ahrenfeldt, R. H., 161, 162
Alcock, T., 219, 220
Alessi, S., 364, 365, 383
Allport, G. W., 9, 10, 13, 35, 36, 46, 57, 58, 59, 200, 324, 341, 388, 402
Anastasi, A., 360, 425, 426
Anderson, A. L., 382
Anderson, H. H., and G. L., 425, 426
Arenberg, D., 295
Aristotle, 50
Arnheim, R., 263, 274
Arnold, Magda B., 274, 285, 287
Atkinson, J. W., 288, 292, 295, 296
Augustine, St., 79, 80

Babcock, H., 218
Baldwin, M. V., 295
Bannister, D., 297, 298
Barker, R., 120
Barnes, E. H., 415, 422
Barron, F., 181, 190, 200
Bartlett, R. J., 179
Bass, B. M., 385, 386, 387, 422
Bash, K. W., 265, 274
Baynes, H. G., 73
Beck, S. J., 219, 220
Beethoven, 55
Behn-Eschenburg, H., 227
Bell, J. E., 275, 425, 426
Bellak, L., 285, 425, 426
Beloff, H., 339, 341
Berelson, B., 58
Berg, I. A., 386, 387, 397, 400, 415, 419, 420, 422
Bevertock, A. G., 179

Binder, H., 269, 274
Bingham, W. van D., 183
Blake, R. R., 274
Blake, William, 25
Bleuler, E., 332
Blum, G. S., 60, 101, 106, 120
Boisbaudran, Lecoq de, 28
Bogen, H., 60
Bracken, H. von, 426
Bravais, A., 325
Brengelmann, J. C., 425, 426
Bridger, H., 179
Brodeck, A. J., 120
Brosin, H. W., 274
Brozek, J., 288, 291, 295
Bruner, J. S., 199, 200, 274
Brunswik, E., 51, 58
Buros, O. K., 425, 426
Burt, C., 15
Byron, 281

Cantril, H., 57, 59
Cattell, R. B., 321, 322, 323, 336, 339, 341, 343, 349, 351, 357, 388, 402, 409, 413, 422
Chapple, E. D., 54, 59
Chein, I., 288, 295
Chotlos, J. W., 59
Claridge, G., 348, 353, 354, 357
Clark, J. H., 382
Clark, R. A., 291, 295
Cleckley, H. A., 301, 319, 382
Cobb, E. A., 296
Cohen, Jozef, 303
Cottle, W. C., 364, 365, 382
Couch, A. S., 357, 385, 386
Cowie, Valerie, 356, 357
Cox, C. M., 16
Craik, K., 197
Crites, J. O., 181, 182
Cronbach, L. J., 360, 391, 394, 402, 409, 422, 425, 426
Crusoe, Robinson, 282

431

Subject Index

Subject Index

Studies in Social Pathology
General Editor G. M. Carstairs

FREUD AND THE POST-FREUDIANS

J. A. C. Brown

Freud and the Post-Freudians explains the main concepts of Freudian psychology, and goes on to review the theories of Adler, Jung, Rank, and Stekel. Later developments in the orthodox Freudian school are also discussed, as are those of the American Neo-Freudians and the Post-Freudians in England.

This is the first book published in Britain to bring together all these psychological and sociological schools and criticize them, both from the Freudian standpoint and that of the scientific psychologists.

New Horizons in Psychology

Edited by Brian M. Foss

Psychology as a science of observation and experiment is 100 years old. In the last decade it has expanded greatly, exploring new fields of human behaviour and using new techniques.

New Horizons in Psychology is both a progress report and a guide to exciting developments in coming years. All of them will affect scientific thinking in many fields and some of them will influence the way we live.

Visual illusions, information theory, creativity – genetics, motivation, drugs, – operant conditioning, programmed learning, behaviour therapy – personal construct psychology, small groups, cross cultural studies – psychology is seething with new ideas and methods today. These and many others are explained here by a distinguished team of experimental psychologists. A linking commentary by the editor, Professor Foss, paints the conceptual background to each topic.